A DEBATE OVER

*To Veronica,
with best wishes*

Nigel Farmer

16.3.2000

A DEBATE OVER RIGHTS

Philosophical Enquiries

MATTHEW H. KRAMER
N.E. SIMMONDS
HILLEL STEINER

OXFORD
UNIVERSITY PRESS

OXFORD
UNIVERSITY PRESS

Great Clarendon Street, Oxford OX2 6DP

Oxford University Press is a department of the University of Oxford.
It furthers the University's objective of excellence in research, scholarship,
and education by publishing worldwide in
Oxford New York
Athens Auckland Bangkok Bogotá Buenos Aires Calcutta
Cape Town Chennai Dar es Salaam Delhi Florence Hong Kong Istanbul
Karachi Kuala Lumpur Madrid Melbourne Mexico City Mumbai
Nairobi Paris São Paulo Singapore Taipei Tokyo Toronto Warsaw
and associated companies in Berlin Ibadan

Oxford is a registered trade mark of Oxford University Press
in the UK and in certain other countries

Published in the United States
by Oxford University Press Inc., New York

© Kramer, Simmonds & Steiner 1998

The moral rights of the author have been asserted

Database right Oxford University Press (maker)

First published 1998

First published new as paperback 2000

All rights reserved. No part of this publication may be reproduced,
stored in a retrieval system, or transmitted, in any form or by any means,
without the prior permission in writing of Oxford University Press,
or as expressly permitted by law, or under terms agreed with the appropriate
reprographics rights organization. Enquiries concerning reproduction
outside the scope of the above should be sent to the Rights Department,
Oxford University Press, at the address above

You must not circulate this book in any other binding or cover
and you must impose this same condition on any acquirer

British Library Cataloguing in Publication Data
Data available

Library of Congress Cataloging in Publication Data
Kramer, Matthew H., 1959–
A debate over rights: philosophical enquiries/Matthew H.
Kramer, N. E. Simonds, Hillel Steiner.
p. cm.
Includes bibliographical references and index.
1. Human rights—Philosophy. 2. Civil Rights—Philosophy.
3. Law—Philosophy. I. Simmonds, N. E. (Nigel E.)
II. Steiner, Hillel. III. Title.
JC571.K65 1998 323'.01—dc21 98-18234
ISBN 0-19-826853-X
ISBN 0-19-829899-4 (Pbk)

1 3 5 7 9 10 8 6 4 2

Printed in Great Britain
on acid-free paper by
Biddles Ltd., Guildford and King's Lynn

Preface

I wrote my main contribution to this volume in the first two months of 1996. Nigel Simmonds finished his essay nearly a year later, and Hillel Steiner did not complete his contribution until the closing days of 1997. As my two co-authors are well aware, I became quite exasperated from time to time during the long period of waiting for them; I imagine that they became equally exasperated by my continual nagging. At any rate, the product of the waiting and the nagging is now before the reader.

Because of the order in which the essays were written, and because of the need to close off the debate at some point, Nigel and I have forborne from responding to Hillel's arguments—notwithstanding that we disagree strongly with some of them. My willingness to abstain from advancing any rejoinders is based partly on the fact that some suitable replies by me to Hillel can readily be inferred from a number of the lines of reasoning which I develop in my essay. Nigel is likewise content to let his current piece speak for itself, along with his earlier critique of Hillel's work ('The Analytical Foundations of Justice', 54 Cambridge Law Journal 306 [1995]).

I am very grateful to my two co-authors and to my father. I am similarly indebted to Churchill College and the Cambridge University Law Faculty for the excellent computing and other facilities which I have enjoyed throughout the period of my work on this book. I likewise wish to thank the British Academy for a Research Leave Award that assisted me in bringing this volume through the process of publication. I should also mention here Pavlos Eleftheriadis and Alon Harel, with whom I have had some valuable discussions about rights. My gratitude extends as well to John Louth and Myf Milton, who worked with remarkable alacrity in shepherding this book through the Oxford University Press. Finally, I thank all the Jurisprudence students at Cambridge who have asked discerning questions about the matters discussed herein.

Matthew H. Kramer
Cambridge, England

Contents

Introduction 1
Matthew H. Kramer

Rights Without Trimmings 7
Matthew H. Kramer

1 Setting the Hohfeldian Table 7
2 Rights Without Trimmings 60
   Appendix: Getting Hohfeld Right 101

Rights at the Cutting Edge 113
N. E. Simmonds

1 Background 115
2 The Fundamental Issues 134
3 Hohfeld and the Fragmentation of Rights 146
4 Hohfeld and the Kantians 176
5 The Interest Theory of Rights 195
6 The Modern Will Theory 211

Working Rights 233
Hillel Steiner

1 Preliminary Intuitions about Rights 235
2 From Hohfeld to Hart: The Modern Will Theory Explored 239
3 Some Apparent Problems with the Will Theory 248
4 From Hart to Kant: The Classical Will Theory (Partly) Redeemed 262
5 Some Real Problems with the Interest Theory 283

Index 303

Introduction

The three principal essays in this book debate a number of issues concerning the fundamental nature of legal and moral rights. Instead of seeking to prescribe which rights should be held by whom, the essays endeavour to ascertain what the holding of a right involves. While aiming to pin down what a thing must be if it is to count as a right, we abstain from lauding some specific varieties of rights in preference to other such varieties. None the less, the fact that our essays proceed at a philosophical level of abstraction does not mean that they are devoid of normative disputation. Indeed, a prominent theme of Nigel Simmonds's contribution is that philosophical controversies over the nature of rights cannot be resolved except on political/moral grounds. Even the austerely analytical piece by Matthew Kramer acknowledges that evaluative assumptions—that is, assumptions concerning what is generally good for human beings—must undergird any attributions of rights to individuals or groups.

Some of the central questions addressed by our essays are as follows. What are the necessary and sufficient conditions for the existence of a right? To what extent can the task of singling out those conditions be purely analytical rather than normative? What is the connection between the existence and the enforcement of a right (ie, between rights and remedies)? Can jurists ascertain the existence of a legal right without having to rely on evaluative assumptions? Should evaluative assumptions play a central role in one's theory of rights? What are the similarities and differences between rights and other sorts of entitlements? What are the basic values which rights protect? To what extent can rights be in conflict? In regard to the conferral of rights, is there any fundamental divide between the criminal law and the civil law?

Our disputes revolve around the long-standing division between the 'Interest Theory' and the 'Will Theory' of rights. Though full and precise accounts of those conflicting theories emerge in the essays below, a brief discussion is in order here. Roughly stated, the Interest Theory maintains that all rights consist in the protection of individual or corporate interests. To ascribe a right to someone is to say that some aspect of that person's well-being is legally or morally shielded against interference or non-assistance. By contrast, the Will Theory (roughly stated) maintains that all rights consist in the enjoyment of opportunities for individual or corporate choices. Rather than seeing rights as tied to sundry facets of the well-being of right-holders, the Will Theory submits that each right invests its holder with some degree of control over his or her situation. To ascribe a right to someone is to say that that person is empowered to make a choice about the fulfilment of someone else's duty; such an ascription does not perforce suggest that any other aspect of the right-holder's well-being is legally or morally protected.

Abstruse though the controversy between the Interest Theory and the Will Theory may appear, it raises most of the problems that have to be tackled by any philosophical investigation into the fundamental characteristics of rights. While taking positions within the Will/Interest controversy, the essays in this book address all the important questions that were recounted two paragraphs ago. In turn, the answers to those questions can shed helpful light on some of the liveliest present-day political debates, such as debates over abortion, euthanasia, and animal rights. Although neither the Interest Theory nor the Will Theory logically commits its proponents to any particular positions in those political disputes, someone with a clear understanding of the two rival theories will be able to detect how often the participants in the aforementioned disputes are guilty of confusion or unsupportable dogmas.

As will be quite plain to any attentive reader of this book, the positions taken by the authors do not come in packages that can be neatly contrasted with one another. In some respects Simmonds is aligned with Hillel Steiner against Kramer, whereas in certain other respects Kramer and Simmonds are at one in their opposition to Steiner; and in still other respects Kramer and Steiner agree in rejecting certain key elements of Simmonds's approach. At the same time, there are some methodological and substantive points that are common to the three essays—the most notable of which is an adherence to the framework of jural and deontic logic developed by Wesley Hohfeld.

Kramer is the only one of the three authors who upholds the Interest Theory of rights. His essay begins with a detailed exposition of Hohfeld's analytical scheme—an exposition that sets the stage not only for Kramer's own essay but also for each of the other contributions to the volume (notwithstanding that Steiner dissents from a few portions of the exposition). Though Hohfeldian categories are neutral between the Interest Theory and the Will Theory by and large, they enable the authors to formulate fresh versions of those theories with much greater exactitude than would otherwise be attainable. As a result, the points of contention which divide the authors are defined very sharply.

After elaborating Hohfeld's analytical framework and showing its versatility and fruitfulness, Kramer proceeds to criticize the Will Theory and to argue in favor of the Interest Theory. He highlights the awkwardness of the Will Theory's implications, and he rejects the view that the Will Theory is to be preferred on political grounds—as well as the view that the choice between the Will Theory and the Interest Theory should be primarily political rather than primarily analytical. Kramer then attempts to show that the Interest Theory can present a philosophical account of rights that avoids the pitfalls of the Will Theory (and other pitfalls). He concludes by acknowledging that evaluative assumptions are necessary for the identification of rights as such, but he maintains that those assumptions are needed under the Will Theory as much as under the Interest Theory; and he argues that the evaluative assumptions can and should be kept to a minimum, in any event.

Simmonds's essay explores in considerable depth the history of the debate over the Interest Theory and the Will Theory, in order to trace the connections between those theories and some broader developments in socio-economic conditions and in jural thought. Simmonds then goes on to take positions that differ strikingly from those adopted by Kramer. Espousing the Will Theory, Simmonds argues that that theory is preferable to the Interest Theory on political or moral grounds. Unlike Kramer, Simmonds believes that one's conception of the formal aspects of rights should hinge centrally on one's moral/political values; he perceives Kramer's austerely analytical approach as arid. Moreover, he contends that the Interest Theory leads to disconcerting snags that can be avoided by the Will Theory. At the same time, he looks askance at Steiner's efforts to challenge the Interest Theory on purely formal or analytical grounds. Though Simmonds and Steiner both belong to the Will Theory camp, they disagree about the reasons for being there.

Having joined Simmonds in supporting the Will Theory, Steiner joins Kramer in thinking that the evaluative assumptions underlying any theory of rights can and should be kept to a minimum. (Indeed, Steiner feels that evaluative assumptions can and should be eschewed altogether.) Steiner, however, sees a much closer relation between the formal aspects and the substantive tenor of rights than does Kramer. He regards a philosophical theory of rights as a prolegomenon to a theory of justice, a prolegomenon with definite substantive implications. Kramer, by contrast, regards such a theory principally as an exercise in clarification and precise understanding.

Steiner begins his essay with some general thoughts on the role or function of rights, and he then turns his attention specifically to the Will Theory—a theory which he perceives as singularly illuminating because it correctly captures the role or function which he attributes to rights. He attempts to shore up that theory by defending it against a number of possible criticisms. This defensive stance soon gives way to an aggressive posture, as Steiner endeavors to expose the shortcomings of the Interest Theory; he argues that the Interest Theory is neither formally nor descriptively adequate. As the target of some censorious comments in Simmonds's and Kramer's essays, Steiner seeks to reply at several junctures. Throughout, he advances some broad reflections on the general implications and associations of the Will Theory. His essay serves not only as a piquant contribution to a three-sided debate but also as a fitting *compte rendu*, for he ponders sustainedly on each of the other contributions and on the debate as a whole.

In sum, each of the authors is exploring basic questions of legal and moral philosophy by participating in the dispute over the Interest Theory and the Will Theory. In the course of addressing such questions, each of us takes positions that overlap and conflict with positions taken by one or both of the other authors. For instance, Kramer disagrees with his fellow authors by dint of his espousal of the Interest Theory, but largely agrees with Steiner against Simmonds in regard to the appropriate grounds for endorsing either of the rival theories of rights; contrariwise, he agrees with Simmonds against Steiner by highlighting the underivability of substantive conclusions from purely formal starting points, and by insisting on the potential separation between legal powers and legal liberties-to-exercise-those-powers. Likewise, although Simmonds and Steiner converge in their adherence to the Will Theory, the methodological dissimilarities between Simmonds's straightforwardly political argumentation and Steiner's formal analyses are considerable—far more considerable than the methodological dissimilarities between Steiner and Kramer.

Yet, divergent though the authors' approaches might be, they are united by common concerns and by some common assumptions. Each of us is keen to get rights right, in that each of us is seeking to provide a philosophical explication of the concept of 'rights'. To be sure, Simmonds's reasons for upholding a Will Theory explication are very different from Kramer's reasons for upholding an Interest Theory explication, and are markedly different from Steiner's reasons for favouring the Will Theory. But the authors share an ambition to come up with a comprehensive account that overarches the numerous possible instances and varieties of rights. In pursuit of that ambition, each of us has sought to expound and refine an Interest Theory position or a Will Theory position that can withstand the criticisms which are usually mounted by the opponents of the championed theory. Our numerous examples and discussions of details are all oriented toward the fulfilment of a philosophical aspiration.

Even more apparent than the uniformity of the general objectives pursued by the essays in this book is the uniformity of our general ways of understanding entitlements. As has already been remarked, the work of Hohfeld is a vital inspiration for each of the authors. As a consequence, the theories developed within this volume are in many ways more closely akin to one another than to any non-Hohfeldian accounts of rights. Kramer, for example, far more frequently quarrels with non-Hohfeldian exponents of the Interest Theory (such as Joseph Raz, Jeremy Waldron, and Neil MacCormick) than with Simmonds or Steiner. In short, our essays are united not only by a general aspiration but also by basic conceptual demarcations.

As should be apparent from the citations in the essays, the issues which we discuss are issues that cut across several disciplines: jurisprudence, political philosophy, political science, moral philosophy, and sociology. Both the affinities and the manifold points of contention among our essays can help to illuminate problems that are of concern to anyone interested in the general nature of rights and other entitlements.

Rights Without Trimmings

MATTHEW H. KRAMER

To participate in an intellectual dispute, one must explicitly or implicitly define its terms; and, by defining the terms of the dispute, one will already have begun one's participation therein. This essay, which joins the debate between the Will Theory (or 'Choice Theory') and the Interest Theory (or 'Benefit Theory') of rights, will seek to define the terms of that debate precisely and expressly. In doing so, the essay will prepare the way for its verdict that the Interest Theory—in a somewhat modified form—is superior to the Will Theory.

Before endeavouring to set forth directly the points of contention between the Interest Theory and the Will Theory, this essay discusses at length the analytical framework of jural relations that was devised by the American legal theorist Wesley Hohfeld. Hohfeld's work has received wide attention since the second decade of the twentieth century, but it has often met with misguided criticisms and incorrect applications. We are therefore well advised to take a careful look at his analytical scheme. Though Hohfeld's work is not entirely beyond reproach, it offers a matrix of conceptual distinctions that is elegant, rigorous, and subtle. His distinctions are invaluable for anyone trying to make an informed assessment of the Interest Theory/Will Theory debate. While Hohfeld's analytical framework is strictly neutral in that debate (for reasons which will later become apparent), it enables the contenders in the debate to achieve exactitude when stating their differences. It is a framework that significantly informs each of the essays in this book.

1 Setting the Hohfeldian Table

Hohfeld distinguished four sets of legal relations, comprising eight legal positions.[1] His basic table of relations, slightly modified, is as follows:

---

[1] The main essay by Hohfeld on which I am drawing is 'Some Fundamental Legal Conceptions as Applied in Judicial Reasoning,' in his *Fundamental Legal Conceptions*

| Right | Liberty | Power | Immunity |
| Duty | No-right | Liability | Disability |

Each of the columns in the table consists of a pair of 'jural correlatives': namely, two legal positions that entail each other. By contrast, the diagonal pairs in the first two columns ('right'/'no-right' and 'duty'/'liberty') and the diagonal pairs in the last two columns ('power'/'disability' and 'liability'/'immunity') each consist of 'jural contradictories': namely, two legal positions that negate each other.

Hohfeld wrote about legal relations, as opposed to strictly moral relations. Hence, my exposition below will concentrate chiefly on legal entitlements and will make few references to starkly moral entitlements. None the less, virtually every aspect of Hohfeld's analytical scheme applies as well, *mutatis mutandis*, to the structuring of moral relationships. (Only two differences are worth even a brief mention here. First, the distinction between genuine

---

as Applied in Judicial Reasoning (New Haven: Yale University Press, 1923) (W Cook, ed) [hereinafter cited as *FLC*], 23–64. Also important for my purposes is his 'Fundamental Legal Conceptions as Applied in Judicial Reasoning,' in *FLC*, 65–114. I have departed from Hohfeld on two points of terminology. First, I have substituted 'liberty' for 'privilege'. Notwithstanding Hohfeld's arguments to the contrary in *FLC*, 44–9, the latter term strikes me (and many other analysts) as highly misleading. Second, I have substituted 'contradiction' or 'negation' for 'opposite'. As has been recognized since the 1920s, Hohfeld's analyses define jural contradictories rather than jural opposites. (To avert misunderstandings, I should here include a few clarificatory words in anticipation of the subsequent junctures where I write of 'abstaining' or 'forbearing' or 'refraining' from particular actions. As construed in this essay, abstaining from ϕ is equivalent to not doing ϕ. That is, abstaining from ϕ is the negation or contradiction of doing ϕ. As glossed here, an abstention *can* of course involve a refusal to take an opportunity, but it does not *have* to involve such a refusal; it can arise as well from the absence of any opportunity. Even if one has not had any realistic chance to do ϕ, and therefore even if one has not consciously kept oneself from doing it, one has abstained or refrained or forborne from ϕ by simply not doing it.)

My resistance to Hohfeld's use of 'opposite' does not lead me to endorse the criticisms of his analytical scheme that are levelled in Andrew Halpin, 'Hohfeld's Conceptions: From Eight to Two', 44 Cambridge LJ 435 (1985). For some other highly unsatisfactory critiques of Hohfeld, see Roy Stone, 'An Analysis of Hohfeld', 48 Minnesota L Rev 313 (1963); and Arthur Jacobson, 'Hegel's Legal Plenum', 10 Cardozo L Rev 877 (1989). More sophisticated than these other critical articles, but just as unhelpfully confused, is Alan Anderson, 'Logic, Norms, and Roles', 4 *Ratio* 36 (1962). Anderson attributes to Hohfeld the indefensible thesis that 'x is privileged [ie, is at liberty] to do p if and only if x has no duty to do not-p' (ibid, 48). In fact, the perfectly sound thesis to which Hohfeld subscribed was that x has a liberty to do p if and only if x has no duty not to do p. Anderson's article is aptly criticized in Philip Mullock, 'The Hohfeldian Jural Opposite', 13 *Ratio* 158 (1971).

entitlements and nominal entitlements—a distinction that will surface at several junctures in this essay—is of uncertain application in the domain of morality. Second, the potential for conflicts between duties is not as uncontroversially demonstrable in the domain of morality as in the domain of law.)

An Exposition of the Jural Relations

Being endowed with a legal **right** (which Hohfeld also labelled as a **claim**) consists in being legally protected against someone else's interference or against someone else's withholding of assistance or remuneration, in regard to a certain action or a certain state of affairs. The person who is required to abstain from interference or to render assistance or remuneration is under a **duty** to behave so. A right or claim, then, is the legal position created through the imposing of a duty on someone else. If a person X has a right to be free from any interference by a person Y with X's project P, then Y has a duty to abstain from interfering with P; conversely, if Y has a duty to abstain from interfering with P, then X has a right to be free from any such interference by Y.

A genuine right or claim is enforceable. (Unlike a purely moral claim—which is also enforceable in certain ways—a genuine legal claim is enforceable through the mobilizing of governmental coercion, if necessary.) None the less, as will become clearer shortly, the power to seek enforcement does not necessarily lie within the discretion of the person who has the claim. So long as a claim is duly enforceable, its status as a genuine Hohfeldian claim is unaffected by the precise location of the power to seek enforcement; that power may be held by the claim-holder, or it may be held by someone acting as a fiduciary on behalf of the claim-holder, or it may be held by a governmental agency.

Each right or claim is held by a specific person or group of persons against another specific person or group of persons. However, each right can exactly parallel any number of other rights held by the same person in regard to the same activity or state of affairs.[2]

---

[2] Hohfeld insisted that a right held 'against the world' is really a set of indefinitely numerous rights, each of which is held against a particular person. See *FLC* (n 1 above), 91–6. For a colourful presentation of Hohfeld's position on this matter, see Karl Llewellyn, *The Bramble Bush* (New York: Oceana Publications, 1951), 98. For two recent endorsements of Hohfeld's position, see Pavlos Eleftheriadis, 'The Analysis

Suppose, for example, that X is a typical landowner. He will not only have a right to be free from any encroachments on his land by Y but will also have a right to be free from any encroachments by every other person to whose presence he has not consented. (In the arsenal of X's legal entitlements, some of his other rights might not be accompanied by indefinitely numerous parallel rights or indeed by any parallel rights. For instance, if X has formed a contract with Y and has not formed a similar contract with anyone else, then X's contractual right against Y is *sui generis* in the assemblage of his legal entitlements.)

To have a **liberty** to engage in a certain action is to be free from any duty to eschew the action; likewise, to have a liberty to abstain from a certain action is to be free from any duty to undertake the action. Like any right, each liberty is held by a specific person or group of persons against another specific person or group of persons. The person against whom the liberty is held has a **no-right** concerning the activity or state of affairs to which the liberty pertains. None the less, although that person has no *right* to the halting of the activity or state of affairs, he himself may well have a *liberty* to interfere. He cannot successfully have recourse to the mechanisms of public governance, but he can have recourse to his own devices (within the confines imposed by the liberty-holder's rights).

---

of Property Rights', 16 Oxford J of Legal Studies 31, 43–53 (1996); Christopher Wellman, 'On Conflicts Between Rights', 14 Law and Philosophy 271, 278 (1995). In the present essay, by and large, I do not challenge Hohfeld's view. (And I certainly disagree with Joseph Raz, who dismissively proclaims that 'Hohfeld's insistence that every right is a relation between no more than two persons is completely unfounded and makes the explanation of rights *in rem* impossible, as has often been noted.' Joseph Raz, *The Concept of a Legal System* (Oxford: Clarendon Press, 1980) (2nd edn), 180.) None the less, I see no harm whatsoever in the view which Hohfeld vigorously rejected—ie, the view that a right held 'against the world' is a single entitlement with indefinitely numerous applications, each of which brings a particular person within the sway of the duty that is correlative to the right. Though this latter view is not always superior to the view taken by Hohfeld, it often is indeed preferable. *Pace* Hohfeld, it is fully consistent with the defined correlativity of rights and duties; and, for some analytical purposes, a characterization of a right-in-rem as an abiding entitlement with continually shifting applications can be clearly more pertinent than a characterization of such a right as a bundle of continually shifting entitlements.

I should add that I agree with Max Radin's observation that the crucial feature of a right held 'against the world' is not the *numerousness* of the parallel rights, but the *indefiniteness* of their number. Hohfeld did not distinguish sufficiently between those two features. See Max Radin, 'A Restatement of Hohfeld', 51 Harvard L Rev 1141, 1155–6 (1938).

Consider an example. Suppose that Z enjoys a liberty, against Y, to express opinions about various public matters. Y therefore cannot correctly maintain that his rights are violated by Z's pronouncements on those matters. As a consequence, there will not warrantedly occur any governmental intervention for the purpose of upholding Y's rights by suppressing Z's speech. Yet, although Y cannot rely on the coercive mechanisms of government to stop Z from speaking, he can permissibly do his utmost himself to interfere with Z's voicing of opinions, so long as he does not violate any of Z's rights (such as the right to be free from physical assaults). Perhaps Y will contort his face in ways that cause Z to laugh helplessly and thus to stop speaking. Or perhaps Y will make so much noise that he drowns out Z's words and thereby causes the frustrated Z to desist from further pronouncements. Whatever be the exact methods of interference, Y himself enjoys a liberty—within the constraints imposed on Y by Z's rights—to impede the activity of speaking which Z is at liberty to undertake. (Of course, if Z has a right to be free from any such obstructive behavior by Y, then Y will owe Z a duty to refrain from that behavior and will accordingly not enjoy a liberty to engage in it.)

As the example in the last paragraph suggests, acts or omissions that are based on liberties can be protected quite extensively even though the liberties do not themselves place restrictions on anyone. Not only will a liberty-to-do-ϕ combine sometimes with a right-to-be-free-from-interference-with-the-doing-of-ϕ specifically, but it often combines with other rights—such as the right to be free from physical assaults—which effectively shield the doing of ϕ, albeit perhaps imperfectly. Though Z's liberty to consume her dinner does not itself require Y to abstain from impeding her consumption, her right to be free from bodily attacks and her right to be free from the theft of her belongings (and also her right to be free from severe emotional distress) will very likely make the impeding of her consumption quite difficult. Much the same can be said about Z's liberty to donate some of her money to a charity. Y is free to try to dissuade Z from handing over the money, but the laws against theft and assault and defamation confer rights on Z and on the charity which substantially limit Y's freedom to prevent the transfer of funds. In these examples and in countless other possible situations, one's actions or inactions grounded in liberties are effectively protected—to a considerable extent—by rights that do not pertain specifically to those actions or inactions. Indeed, in almost every situation outside the Hobbesian state of nature, conduct in accordance with a liberty will receive at least a modicum of protection through a person's basic rights.³

The shielding effect just mentioned is only one aspect of the relationship between the right/duty axis and the liberty/no-right axis; there are also some important formal or structural aspects. One such dimension that has already been indicated is the contradictoriness between the diagonal poles of the two axes. If Y has a right to be free from Z's interference with Y's project ϕ, then Y does

³ This point has been widely recognized in the literature on rights. For some important discussions, see John Finnis, 'Some Professional Fallacies About Rights', 4 Adelaide L Rev 377, 378–9 (1972); HLA Hart, 'Legal Rights', in *Essays on Bentham* (Oxford: Oxford University Press, 1982) [hereinafter cited as Hart, 'Legal Rights'], 162, 171–3; Alf Ross, *On Law and Justice* (London: Stevens & Sons, 1958) [hereinafter cited as Ross, *Justice*], 165–6; Alf Ross, *Directives and Norms* (London: Routledge & Kegan Paul, 1968) [hereinafter cited as Ross, *Directives*], 129–30; Nigel Simmonds, 'The Analytical Foundations of Justice', 54 Cambridge LJ 306, 322–31 (1995); and Hillel Steiner, *An Essay on Rights* (Oxford: Blackwell, 1994) [hereinafter cited as Steiner, *Rights*], 75–6, 86–101 *passim*. For an untenable view that liberties are reducible to the rights which protect the exercise of them, see Andrew Halpin (n 1 above). For an equally unsustainable view that liberties entail duties of non-interference, see Michael Freeden, *Rights* (Milton Keynes: Open University Press, 1991), 44, 77–8, 79. See also Richard Flathman, *The Practice of Rights* (Cambridge: Cambridge University Press, 1976) [hereinafter cited as Flathman, *Practice*], 89–90, 91. For some more accurate views of right/duty and liberty/no-right relationships, see R M Hare, *Moral Thinking* (Oxford: Clarendon Press, 1981), 149–50; and Jonathan Harrison, *Our Knowledge of Right and Wrong* (London: George Allen & Unwin, 1971), 363. An accurate view is also taken (albeit not for entirely correct reasons) in Theodore Benditt, *Law as Rule and Principle* (Hassocks: Harvester Press, 1978), 162–4.

Of course, if the exercise of a liberty-to-do-ϕ is protected by a perimeter of rights so sweepingly that all physically possible ways of interfering with the doing of ϕ are outlawed, then we can aptly say that a right-against-interference-with-the-doing-of-ϕ exists—just as much as it would exist if it had been created *directly* (or by logical implication) via one or more authoritative enactments or decisions. This sort of situation will not very often arise, since a perimeter of rights will usually fall short of debarring all physically possible ways of interfering with the exercise of some liberty. Nonetheless, when X's doing of ϕ does indeed enjoy comprehensive legal protection by virtue of the cumulative shielding effects of some of X's rights, we should agree that X holds a right-against-interference-with-the-doing-of-ϕ. My arguments throughout this essay do not need to distinguish between rights created in this indirect manner and rights created directly (or by logical implication) under the terms of enactments or judgments. (Incidentally, for an otherwise sophisticated analysis which gives insufficient attention to the fact that legal rights (as opposed to legal liberties) must be based directly or indirectly on a source or set of sources, see Stephen Hudson and Douglas Husak, 'Legal Rights: How Useful is Hohfeldian Analysis?' 37 *Philosophical Studies* 45 (1980). For an apt rejoinder, see Thomas Perry, 'Reply in Defense of Hohfeld', 37 *Philosophical Studies* 203 (1980).)

not have a no-right in regard to Z's interference. Likewise, if Y has no right to be free from Z's interference, then, obviously, he does not have a right of that sort against Z. More subtle is the contradictoriness between duties and liberties. As Hohfeld was fully aware, the contradiction lies not between a duty to do ϕ and a liberty to do ϕ but between a duty to do ϕ and a liberty to *abstain from* ϕ—or between a duty to abstain from ϕ and a liberty to do ϕ.[4] If Y has a duty to abstain from interfering with Z's project ϕ, then Y does not have a liberty to interfere. Similarly, if Y has a duty to render certain assistance to Z for the doing of ϕ, then Y does not have a liberty to refuse to give such assistance. Conversely, if Y does have a liberty to interfere with Z's doing of ϕ, then Y does not have a duty to refrain from interfering; and if Y does have a liberty to withhold assistance from Z, then Y does not have a duty to provide the assistance.

An important contrast between Hohfeldian rights and liberties, often overlooked because of everyday patterns of discourse, is that rights must be specified by reference to the actions of the people who bear the correlative duties—rather than to the actions of the people who hold the rights—whereas liberties must be specified by reference to the actions of the people who hold the liberties. Any right of Y against Z concerning ϕ will mean that Z has to forbear from interfering with ϕ or has to assist with ϕ in some way. In itself, the right does not directly specify how Y must or should behave; it specifies only the conduct which Z is duty-bound to undertake (or the conduct which Z is duty-bound to eschew). Hence, our ordinary

---

[4] See *FLC* (n 1 above), 39. In spite of having emphasized this point—as is recognized in Benditt (n 3 above), 160; Stig Kanger and Helle Kanger, 'Rights and Parliamentarism', 32 *Theoria* 85, 102–3 (1966); and Thomas Perry, 'A Paradigm of Philosophy: Hohfeld on Legal Rights', 14 *American Philosophical Quarterly* 41, 42 (1977)—Hohfeld has been reprimanded for failing to notice it. See, eg, RWM Dias, *Jurisprudence* (London: Butterworths, 1976) (4th edn), 40; Frederic Fitch, 'A Revision of Hohfeld's Theory of Legal Concepts', 10 *Logique et Analyse* 269, 270–1 (1967); J W Harris, *Legal Philosophies* (London: Butterworths, 1980), 81; Glanville Williams, 'The Concept of Legal Liberty', 56 Columbia L Rev 1129, 1135–9 (1956). (For an extreme version of this gratuitous reprimand, see Andrew Halpin (n 1 above).) Still, we are doubtless warranted in paying attention to the general point that lies behind the reprimands, since some analysts have neglected it. See, eg, Flathman, *Practice* (n 3 above), 38–9: 'Hohfeld's analysis of rights is cast largely in terms of what he called the *opposites* [ie, contradictions] and *correlates* of each of the main uses of the concept that he identified. The *opposite* [ie, the contradiction] of a right refers to that which is the opposite of what A has if he has a right in a particular sense. In the case of liberties the opposite is a duty; the opposite of A's having a liberty to do X is for him to have a duty to do X.' (Emphases in original.)

ways of speaking about rights as entitlements to do various things are loose and non-Hohfeldian. As Glanville Williams has remarked: 'No one ever has a right to do something; he only has a right that some one else shall do (or refrain from doing) something. In other words, every right in the strict sense relates to the conduct of another.'[5] Though the urge to talk about someone's right to do something is probably irrepressible even among analysts of Hohfeld, we should recognize that such talk is in fact referring to an entitlement which requires that a *duty-bearer* forgo interference or afford assistance or provide remuneration.

A liberty, by contrast, specifies some behavior in which the *liberty-holder* is free to engage (or behavior which the liberty-holder is free to avoid). From our knowledge that Y has a liberty against Z to do ϕ, we indeed know something about the conduct of Y himself; we know that, at least as far as Z is concerned, Y is legally or morally free—though perhaps not physically able—to do ϕ. At the same time, the liberty held by Y against Z does not in itself establish how Z ought to behave. Simply from our knowledge of such a liberty, we cannot yet know if Z is legally or morally free to interfere with Y's doing of ϕ. Nor, of course, do we yet know if Z is legally or morally required to assist Y in the doing of ϕ. The content of Y's liberty against Z stipulates what Y is allowed to do, not what Z is required or permitted to do.

One of the most important features of the relationship between rights and liberties is the absence of any entailment between them. A right to do ϕ—that is, a right to be free from interference with the doing of ϕ, or a right to be assisted in the doing of ϕ—will not entail a liberty to do ϕ and is not entailed by such a liberty. Someone can have a right to be free from interference with the carrying out of some act which she is not at liberty to perform, and someone can be at liberty to carry out some act even though she is not entitled to be free from manifold obstacles that prevent her from performing the act successfully. The latter of the two points just mentioned, the point that a liberty to do ϕ does not entail a right to be free from interference with the doing of ϕ, is quite straightforward and has

---

[5] Glanville Williams (n 4 above), 1145. For similar insights, see John Finnis (n 3 above), 380; LW Sumner, *The Moral Foundation of Rights* (Oxford: Clarendon Press, 1987) [hereinafter cited as *MFR*], 25. Such insights are unfortunately obscured in Rex Martin, *A System of Rights* (Oxford: Clarendon Press, 1993) [hereinafter cited as Martin, *System*], 40–50.

already been touched upon. In the Hobbesian state of nature, no one has any rights to non-interference even though everyone has a liberty to do all that is necessary for survival. In any less bizarre situation as well, we find that a liberty to do ϕ cannot per se entail a right which would demand that no interference with ϕ should occur. Think, for example, of a merchant who is free—within the confines of antitrust laws, anti-fraud laws, and the like—to outperform his competitors and thus to take business away from them. Although the competitors are not entitled to be shielded from the merchant's permissible striving, they very likely do not have any duties to refrain from selling their own wares expeditiously (within the confines of the aforementioned laws). If each merchant has a liberty to peddle his goods rapidly, then each has no entitlement to be insulated from the other merchants' similar practices which sap the efficacy of his own endeavors. Each has a liberty without having a cognate right.

Less easily grasped than the absence of entailment between liberties and rights is the absence of entailment between rights and liberties. Quite plainly, a legal or moral liberty to do ϕ does not entail a legal or moral right to be unimpeded in the doing of ϕ; equally surely, but less plainly, a legal or moral right to be unimpeded in the doing of ϕ does not entail a legal or moral liberty to do ϕ. Someone can have a right to be unobstructed in the performance of an activity which she is not allowed to perform. In order to see this point clearly, we should look at an example more elaborate than the ones offered so far.

Suppose that a huge factory begins to operate along the shore of a lake. Noxious discharges from the factory contaminate the lake's waters so badly that the fishermen who once earned their livelihood on the lake are forced out of business. As effluents continue to spew into the once vibrant body of water, the fishermen sue the factory's owner for his violation of their right to non-interference with the plying of their trade. The court holds that the fishermen should indeed be awarded damages for the fouling of the lake and for the consequent loss of their livelihood. (Most likely the damages are in the form of a lump-sum payment, but they can also be in the form of year-to-year payments. Note that the granting of an injunction against the factory would introduce certain complications into this example but would not alter its basic point at all.) None the less, despite the compensation to the fishermen for the factory owner's breach of his duty to abstain from spoiling the lake and their livelihood, they remain disgruntled. They make their way to the factory's outlet pipes, where they manage to occlude the pipes and thus force a temporary shut-down of the factory's operations. Once again the parties to the dispute appear in court, but now the factory owner sues the fishermen for their obstruction of his outlets which has caused extensive interference with the running of his business. The court now holds that the factory owner should be awarded damages for the fishermen's breach of their duty to abstain from interfering with the normal operations of his factory. Albeit the factory owner does not have a liberty to emit large quantities of toxic substances into the lake, he has a right to be unimpeded in the discharge of just such emissions. (Incidentally, nothing in this example hinges on the order in which the lawsuits are brought. Whether the fishermen are the first to sue or the first to be sued, the point of this example will stand.)

In the scenario just sketched, the factory owner has an obligation to abstain from polluting the lake but also has a right to be unhindered in his pollution. If we were to adopt the loose 'right to do' phrasing of which Glanville Williams disapproved, we could say that the factory owner has a right to commit a wrong—or a right to undertake what he is not permitted to undertake. If one opts instead for more accurate but less exciting terminology, one will say that the factory owner has a right to be free from interference with his perpetration of a wrong. His enjoyment of a right to be unobstructed in his processes of manufacturing does not entail his enjoyment of a liberty to carry on the processes that are protected against obstruction. (Note that the focus of my example—its focus on (1) a right to be free from interference with a certain activity and (2) a (non-existent) liberty to engage in the same activity—is quite different from the focus of the following remarks by Joseph Singer: '[R]ights do not imply privileges [ie, liberties]. A's right to keep trespassers off her land does not necessarily imply a privilege in A to use the land. Thus one might conceive of a remainderperson who has no liberty to enter the land but retains a right to keep trespassers off.'[6] We should hardly be surprised that the right and the liberty

---

[6] Joseph Singer, 'The Legal Rights Debate in Analytical Jurisprudence from Bentham to Hohfeld', (1982) Wisconsin L Rev 975, 988. For a fine critique of Ronald Dworkin that is broadly similar to my own analysis of the fishermen and the factory (though very different in its specifics), see Finnis (n 3 above), 382–4. See also Benditt

discussed by Singer are not connected in any relationship of entailment, since they have different contents. The right is a right to be free from the encroachments of interlopers, whereas the liberty is a liberty to enter the land from which the interlopers are barred. Even a *liberty* to keep trespassers out would not entail, or be entailed by, a liberty to enter the land oneself. Hence, the remarks by Singer are correct but glib. What he could and should have demonstrated—but what he clearly has not demonstrated—is that one's right to be free from interference with one's entry onto some land does not entail one's liberty to enter the land.)

Also in need of highlighting here is the absence of entailment between *duties* and liberties. In an extremely sophisticated discussion of Hohfeld, L. W. Sumner errs when he proclaims that

(n 3 above), 162–3; Theodore Benditt, *Rights* (Totowa: Rowman & Littlefield, 1982), 9, 24–5; Duncan Kennedy and Frank Michelman, 'Are Property and Contract Efficient?' 8 Hofstra L Rev 711, 752–3 (1980); Nigel Simmonds, 'Epstein's Theory of Strict Tort Liability', 51 Cambridge L J 113, 135 (1992); Jeremy Waldron, *Liberal Rights* (Cambridge: Cambridge University Press, 1993), 73–6. For an example of the position that is refuted by my analysis, see Joel Feinberg, *Social Philosophy* (Englewood Cliffs: Prentice-Hall, 1973) [hereinafter cited as Feinberg, *Social Philosophy*], 58: 'One can have a liberty which is not also a right, but one cannot have a right which is not also a liberty, for rights can be understood to contain liberties as components. If I have a right to do X, then I cannot also have a duty to refrain from doing X. ... Hence, if I have a right to do X, I must also be at liberty to do X'. See also Alan White, *Rights* (Oxford: Clarendon Press, 1984) [hereinafter cited as White, *Rights*], 59: '[T]he presence of a duty (or obligation) not to V implies the absence of a right to V'. For a subtle variant of the same error, see Wellman (n 2 above), 285. (Wellman wrongly maintains that the defendant in *Vincent v Lake Erie Transp Co*, 10 *Minn* 456, 124 *NW* 221 (1910), had a liberty to tie his boat to someone else's dock during a storm. In fact, the boat owner had a duty to abstain from using the dock and a right not to be prevented from using it.) For yet another variant of this *faux pas*, see Eleftheriadis (n 2 above), 40–1, where we are incorrectly told that one's retention of absolute rights against interference with one's use of some asset would preclude the retention of such rights by anyone else in any other asset.

I should observe, incidentally, that my example of the fishermen and the factory can be redescribed in ways that would remove the parallelism between the content of the factory owner's duty and the content of his right. I have presented the example in order to show that the factory owner holds a right-against-interference-with-his-polluting-of-the-lake and also bears a duty-not-to-pollute-the-lake. Either the right or the duty could be recharacterized so as to eliminate the precise homology between their contents. None the less, given that every set of circumstances can be accurately described in myriad ways, and given that any other appropriate ways of characterizing the situation of the fishermen and the factory would be consistent with my own characterization, the potential for redescriptions of that situation is utterly harmless. To make my point, I need maintain merely that my own formulations of the factory owner's legal positions are accurate; I need not maintain that they are *uniquely* accurate.

'an act is permitted if it is required' and that a 'liberty to do something is...entailed by, a duty to do it' (*MFR*, 23, 33). These statements affirm that a duty to undertake something must entail a liberty to undertake it. Yet a Hohfeldian duty to undertake ϕ does not perforce involve a liberty to undertake ϕ; it involves merely the absence of a liberty to abstain from ϕ. The absence of a liberty to abstain from something does not entail a liberty to undertake it, since a person can be under conflicting duties—that is, a duty to undertake ϕ *and* a duty to refrain from ϕ. Such a posture is somewhat strange but is far from inconceivable, as can be seen from the following example.

Suppose that a law places a non-waivable duty on the eldest son in each family to pay his mother £3,000 per year while she is still alive after he has reached the age of forty. Suppose further that the penalty for non-compliance with the duty is a fine of some specified amount. Now presume that Joe and his mother have formed a contract under which the mother (who treasures her sense of independence) has agreed to visit Joe weekly in return for his promise to refrain from paying her any money. And, finally, presume that the relevant body of contract law provides that the contract between Joe and his mother is valid even though the contract fails to relieve him of his duty to support her with the required payments. Hence, Joe is under a duty to pay £3,000 per year to his mother, and is also under a duty to forbear from making the payments (so long as she visits him weekly). His duty to do ϕ is accompanied by a duty to abstain from ϕ, and thus his duty to do ϕ is not accompanied by a liberty to do ϕ. (Sumner elsewhere appears to recognize this point, when he writes as follows: 'If we assume that a rule system will not both require and prohibit the same act then if I am required to attend [a] meeting I am also permitted to do so. It follows that I have a liberty to do whatever I have a duty to do' [*MFR*, 26]. In this passage, Sumner again adverts to the uncombinability of a duty-to-do-ϕ and a duty-to-abstain-from-doing-ϕ, but he presents that uncombinability as wholly contingent. No one should gainsay that a legal system *can* rule out any junctions of such duties;[7] the contention here is simply that a legal system or any other system of

---

[7] Indeed, as Glanville Williams points out, Anglo-American law has generally avoided the imposition of conflicting duties; see Williams (n 4 above), 1140–1. For a partly insightful but partly muddled discussion of such duties, see Lon Fuller, *The Morality of Law* (New Haven: Yale University Press, 1969) (rev edn), 65–70. For a

norms will not *necessarily* rule out such junctions. Unlike a duty to do ϕ and a liberty to abstain from doing ϕ, a duty to do ϕ and a duty to abstain from doing ϕ are not starkly contradictory. They are in conflict rather than in contradiction. Though the fulfilment of either one must rule out the fulfilment of the other, the existence of either one does not in any way preclude the existence of the other. This non-contradictoriness is one main feature of jural logic (with its categories of 'permissibility', 'impermissibility', and 'obligatoriness') that prevents it from being collapsed into modal logic (with its categories of 'possibility', 'impossibility', and 'necessity').)

Because conflicting duties are possible, conflicting rights—a right to X's performance of ϕ and a right to X's non-performance of ϕ— are possible as well, of course. Even more obviously possible are

much more perceptive discussion, see Simmonds (in 3 above), 334–40. (Simmonds, however, does not ponder any conflicting duties that are owed to one person rather than to separate people.) For several instances of the error which I am here confuting—the erroneous view that a duty to do ϕ entails a liberty to do ϕ—see Mullock (n 1 above, 159–60, 161–2. (Mullock's article is otherwise admirably rigorous.) For some further writings which commit the same error, see Anderson (n 1 above), 39, 45; Fitch (n 4 above), *passim*; Joseph Raz, *Practical Reason and Norms* (Princeton: Princeton University Press, 1990) (2nd edn), 89–90. Similarly mistaken is Andrei Marmor, 'On the Limits of Rights', 16 Law and Philosophy 1, 5 (1997): 'A duty to do wrong is surely an oxymoron'. See also Feinberg, *Social Philosophy* (n 6 above), 69, where we are told of 'the permission trivially entailed by duty'. (Later, however, Feinberg correctly observes that there 'is no contradiction in saying of a person that he *ought* not to perform one of his duties' (ibid, 75, emphasis in original).)

Through some straightforward formal notation, one can show the non-contradictoriness of conflicting duties. Let 'X' and 'Y' stand for any two persons. Let 'O' designate a relationship of obligation between one person and another, such that 'O($X d_1 Y$)' indicates that X owes a duty to Y with a content symbolized by 'd_1'. Now, suppose that a current jural relationship between two particular people can indeed be properly formulated as 'O($X d_1 Y$)', which means that X owes a duty of such and such a content to Y. What relationship between the two people would contradict the relationship just mentioned? Clearly, the contradiction of 'O($X d_1 Y$)' is '$\neg$O($X d_1 Y$)', where the symbol '$\neg$' indicates negation. The contradictory formula can be rendered as 'It is not the case that X owes a duty of such and such a content to Y', which in turn is equivalent to 'X has a liberty *vis-à-vis* Y to abstain from whatever d_1 would require, or to do whatever d_1 would prohibit'. A conflicting duty is different, both in formal notation and in English. Formally, a duty that conflicts with 'O($X d_1 Y$)' would be 'O($X \neg d_1 Y$)', which can be rendered as 'X owes Y a duty that conflicts with 'O($X d_1 Y$)' would be 'O($X \neg d_1 Y$)', which can be rendered as 'X owes Y a duty to abstain from whatever d_1 would require, or to do whatever d_1 would prohibit'. Hence, although conflicting duties certainly involve competing demands on the duty-bearer, and although the fulfilment of one such duty therefore precludes the fulfilment of the other, the duties themselves are not contradictory. They can coexist. A conflict between two duties (between a duty to ϕ and a duty not to ϕ) pertains solely to each duty's *content*, whereas a contradiction between a duty and a liberty (between a duty to ϕ and a liberty not to ϕ) pertains not only to the duty's content but also to its *existence*.

contrary rights, that is, rights to inconsistent states of affairs. Joel Feinberg commits an error when he declares that 'Grunt's right to the exclusive possession and control of ten acres at Blackacre is logically inconsistent with Groan's right to the exclusive possession and control of precisely the same ten acres' (Feinberg, *Social Philosophy*, 69). Logically inconsistent are Grunt's exclusive possession and Groan's exclusive possession; but the two men's *rights* to exclusive possession can perfectly well coexist. If those two rights do coexist, they can eventuate in one of the following three outcomes, among others: (1) Grunt and Groan both refrain from entering the ten acres at Blackacre, in which case neither man's right of exclusive possession has been violated by the other man; (2) one of the two men takes possession of the ten acres and is required to compensate the other man for the violation of the other's right of exclusive possession; (3) each man takes possession of part of the land, and each is required to compensate the other for the partial infringement of the other's right to exclusive possession.

Let us turn now to the third and fourth pairs of legal positions in Hohfeld's analytical table. Whereas the initial two pairs of legal positions are first-order relations, the subsequent two pairs are second-order relations. Some first-order relations apply directly to people's conduct and social intercourse, without the mediation of any second-order relations; by contrast, all second-order relations apply directly to people's entitlements and only indirectly (but crucially) to people's conduct and social intercourse.

Someone who holds a **power** can expand or reduce or otherwise modify, in particular ways, his own entitlements or the entitlements held by some other person(s). Someone who bears a **liability**, on the other hand, is exposed to the exercise of a power; the entitlements of the liability-bearer are open to being amplified or diminished or shifted in certain ways. In short, a power consists in one's ability to effect changes in legal or moral relations, while a liability consists in one's being unshielded from the bringing about of changes by the exertion of a power.

As Hohfeld was plainly aware (*FLC*, 60 n 90), a susceptibility to changes in one's entitlements is by no means always unpleasant. A promisee can benefit greatly from the entitlements vested in her by a promisor, and an heir can benefit greatly from the entitlements vested in him by a will. Of course, not all changes imposed on one's legal or moral standing by someone else are desirable from one's own perspective; but many such changes are indeed desirable, and thus an exposure to the imposition of such changes is not necessarily onerous at all. (As will become clear later, the chief reason for the possibility of advantageous exposures is that the distinctive functions of the third and fourth pairs of Hohfeldian legal positions are definable in a strictly non-evaluative manner.)

Like the other Hohfeldian legal positions, powers and liabilities are always held between particular persons in regard to specified actions or states of affairs. A power is always a moral or legal ability to change *someone's* entitlements (quite often the power-holder's own entitlements). In a corresponding fashion, a liability is always a susceptibility to *someone's* exercise of a power (quite often the liability-bearer's own exercise of a power). X may therefore hold a power to change Y's entitlements in a certain way, without holding a power to change anyone else's entitlements in a parallel fashion. Alternatively, of course, X's power over Y's entitlements may be paralleled by X's similar powers over the entitlements of any number of other people.

Likewise strictly relational between persons are **immunities** and **disabilities**. The holder of an immunity is not exposed to the exercise of a power by someone, with respect to any entitlements covered by the immunity. If X has an immunity from any efforts by Y to alter X's proprietary rights in a piece of land, for instance, then Y's efforts to modify those rights will come to nought. With regard to those proprietary rights, Y will have run afoul of a disability. Perhaps various other people can change X's proprietary rights—or perhaps not—but, in any event, Y will be unable to change them so long as X has an immunity that shields her from his attempts.

The connections between the two dyads of second-order legal positions (the immunity/disability axis and the power/liability axis) are precisely similar to the connections between the two first-order dyads (the right/duty axis and the liberty/no-right axis). Just as a liability is the absence of an immunity, so a no-right is the absence of a right; and just as a disability is the absence of a power, so a duty to abstain or to do is the absence of a liberty to do or to abstain. Note that immunities are the second-order counterparts of rights, while powers are the second-order counterparts of liberties. Just as a liberty has to be specified by reference to the liberty-holder's conduct and latitude, so a power has to be specified by reference to the power-holder's legal or moral ability. Likewise, just as a right has to be specified by reference to what the duty-bearer must do or not do, so an immunity has to be specified by reference to what the person disabled by the immunity cannot do.[8]

Clarifications and Elaborations

Having outlined Hohfeld's analytical scheme, this essay now seeks to clarify and extend some of the general features of that scheme. Through much of this discussion, we shall have to examine stumbles committed by other theorists. As an appendix to this chapter reveals, manifold writers have misunderstood specific elements of Hohfeld's table; as will become apparent here, a lot of them have likewise misunderstood the general cast of his approach.

A key to grasping Hohfeld's project is to recognize that it was purificatory (analytically purificatory) and definitional rather than empirical or substantive. Hohfeld put forth a framework of deontic logic, with positions connected by purely logical relations of entailment and negation; he did not attempt to prescribe or recount the substance and the distribution of actual entitlements. His framework is therefore not susceptible to moral objections or empirical refutation.

Hohfeld of course did make an effort to define his terms in ways that squared with the definitions attached to them (explicitly or implicitly) by many jurists. Indeed, his writings occasionally become

---

[8] For a very good discussion of the immunity–right and liberty–power homologies, see *MFR* (n 5 above), 29–31. Such homologies are logical homologies, in that they follow from the logical structures of entitlements. For any entitlement, the basic logical structure consists in three key terms: X (the entitlement-holder), Y (the person occupying the position correlative with the entitlement), and r (the jural relation between X and Y). The relationship r is determined by its mode and by its content or substance. Each relationship's mode consists in one of the four axes presented in Hohfeld's table—eg, the right/duty mode. Each relationship's substance consists in the actions or the state of affairs to which the relationship pertains. Now, for any liberty/no-right relationship or any power/liability relationship, the specification of the relationship's substance must perforce have reference to the actions or abilities of the entitlement-holder (X). For any right/duty relationship or any immunity/disability relationship, by contrast, the specification of the relationship's substance must perforce have reference to the actions or abilities of the person (Y) who occupies the position correlative with the entitlement. Thus, since the features here described are the only essential features of the logical structures of entitlements, and since they align powers with liberties and rights with immunities, the power–liberty alignment and the right–immunity alignment are logical parallels.

quite tiresome in their lengthy highlighting of the harmony between his own usages and the usages favoured by certain judges. Had he not sought to align his terminology at all with the terminology employed by judges—for example, had he used terms such as 'rice' and 'spaghetti' to denote his eight legal positions—his project would have been pretty strange. None the less, Hohfeld's frequent criticisms of judicial language and arguments are evidence that his analytical table was not designed principally to chart the patterns of judicial discourse. Instead, that table was chiefly meant to introduce some much more precise and rigorous patterns of discourse that could overcome the paralogisms and non sequiturs into which so many judges had been led. Hohfeld's analysis was corrective more than descriptive. Therefore, we should brand as misconceived the criticisms of Hohfeld which point out that his vocabulary does not exactly match the vocabulary of his fellow jurists.[9]

Hohfeld adopted a stipulative or definitional approach, in order to realize his objective of analytical purification. Although this aspect of his analysis is a central feature thereof, many critics have neglected it as they seek to offer empirical 'refutations' of Hohfeld's theses. Hohfeld's conception of a right, for example, is stipulative; yet critics have often countered it with alternative stipulations as if they were engaged in an empirical controversy. To be sure, there is room for someone to argue that Hohfeld's definition of a right is inadvisable because it suggests that only one class of entitlements is deserving of the label 'right'. However, such an objection—which implies that we should use only 'claim' to denote the entitlement which Hohfeld sometimes designated as a 'claim' but more frequently designated as a 'right'—has nothing to do with any empirical refutation of Hohfeld. Someone raising such an objection would forswear Hohfeld's definition, but only because the definition is (supposedly) not very useful rather than because it has (supposedly) been disproved.

Critics who do try to refute Hohfeld with empirical counterexamples are missing the point of his analytical scheme and are therefore shadow-boxing. Far from demonstrating the inadequacy of Hohfeld's definitions, such critics merely demonstrate that alternative definitions will yield alternative applications. Consider, for instance, Neil MacCormick's assertion that a labour-relations

---

[9] For one such criticism, see Harris (n 4 above), 82.

statute has belied Hohfeld's analysis by bestowing on every worker a right that is in fact composed of sundry Hohfeldian entitlements.[10] MacCormick's assertion is no more telling than the complaints about the inconsistency between Hohfeld's definition of 'right' and the meanings attached to that word by judges. If someone employs the term 'right' in a non-Hohfeldian manner, then, undoubtedly, he or she employs that term in a non-Hohfeldian manner. So what?

A supporter of Hohfeld can easily respond to MacCormick with the following two points: (1) as MacCormick himself concedes, the diverse entitlements that make up the labour statute's 'right' are all perfectly describable in a Hohfeldian vocabulary; and (2) the overall set of entitlements can be described along Hohfeldian lines through the substitution (within the statute) of 'every worker shall be entitled' for 'every worker shall have the right'. Were the appropriate substitution of phrases to be effected, the statute would not pose even a superficial difficulty for a Hohfeldian approach. In any event, it certainly does not establish any entitlements—be they specific or overarching—that cannot be handled by Hohfeld's categories.

By far the most frequent target for the critics who aim to refute Hohfeld with empirical counter-examples is his postulation of the correlativity or mutual entailment between rights and duties. Empirically oriented challenges to that postulation (a postulation which I shall designate as his 'Correlativity Axiom'), like the empirically oriented challenges to the various other aspects of his definitions, are based on a disregard of the stipulative nature of his enterprise. For Hohfeld, rights and duties—quite as much as the elements in each of the other three pairs of legal positions—were always correlative *by definition*. He did not draw his Correlativity Axiom as a contingent conclusion from empirical data. He posited the correlativity of rights and duties as a definitional fundament of his theory, by explicating the concepts of 'right' and 'duty' in such a way that each entails the other; each is the other from a different perspective, in much the same way that an upward slope viewed from below is a downward slope viewed from above. Hence, the adducing of empirical counter-examples is a task as pointless as the

---

[10] Neil MacCormick, 'Rights in Legislation', in PMS Hacker and J Raz (eds), *Law, Morality, and Society* (Oxford: Clarendon Press, 1977) [hereinafter cited as MacCormick, 'Legislation'], 189, 205–6.

adducing of empirical counter-examples to the proposition that all bachelors are unmarried.

Misdirected though the task of supplying empirical disproof may be, it has allured many critics of Hohfeld. Because the efforts to provide such disproof have extensively overlapped, we shall look at only two of them—one by Neil MacCormick, and one by Alan White. MacCormick's putative confutation of the Correlativity Axiom is sufficiently famous to deserve scrutiny, while White's animadversions on that axiom are the lengthiest attempt heretofore to furnish such a confutation.[11]

[11] Ibid, 200–2; White, *Rights* (n 6 above), 59–73. MacCormick repeats his argument in 'Children's Rights: A Test-Case', in *Legal Right and Social Democracy* (Oxford: Clarendon Press, 1982) [hereinafter cited as MacCormick, 'Children's Rights'], 154, 161–2. For some of the many other attempts to refute the thesis that rights and duties are always correlative, see Benditt (n 3 above), 164–73; Benditt (n 6 above), 6–7, 19, 23–4; Howard Davies and David Holdcroft (eds), *Jurisprudence* (London: Butterworths, 1991), 242–3; Dias (n 4 above) 37–9; Joel Feinberg, 'Duties, Rights, and Claims', 3 *American Philosophical Quarterly* 137, 140, 142–3 (1966); Feinberg, *Social Philosophy* (n 6 above), 62–4, 66–7; Flathman, *Practice* (n 3 above), 92–3; Harris (n 4 above), 81–5; HLA Hart, 'Are There Any Natural Rights?' in Jeremy Waldron (ed), *Theories of Rights* (Oxford: Oxford University Press, 1984) [hereinafter cited as Hart, 'Natural Rights'], 77, 80–3; Jacobson (n 1 above); Marmor (n 7 above), 3–4, 6, n 9; David Miller, *Social Justice* (Oxford: Clarendon Press, 1976), 60–2; Raz (n 2 above), 225–7; Joseph Raz, 'On the Nature of Rights', 93 *Mind* 194, 199–200 *et passim* (1984) [hereinafter cited as Raz, 'Nature']; Joseph Raz, 'Right-Based Moralities', in Jeremy Waldron (ed), *Theories of Rights* (Oxford: Oxford University Press, 1984), 182, 195–7; Steiner, *Rights* (n 3 above), 61–2; Jeremy Waldron, *The Right to Private Property* (Oxford: Clarendon Press, 1988) [hereinafter cited as *RPP*], 68–70, 83–5. Most of the works listed here are aimed directly against Hohfeld.

One of the most commonly invoked examples of duties that are supposedly uncorrelated with rights is each person's moral duty to exhibit charitableness. (For a largely representative presentation of this example, see Waldron (n 6 above), 14–16.) However, such a duty can be handled with ease by anyone who adheres to the Correlativity Axiom. We first may question whether there is a general duty of beneficence or charity at all, any more than there is a general duty to exhibit bravery. Virtues in the abstract are probably not best understood as obligatory, and general failures to show such virtues are probably not best understood as breaches of general duties. In any case, even if we suppose that there is indeed a general duty of charitableness, there are numerous candidates for the role of holding the correlative right. People who belong to the major faiths can attribute the right to God, whereas humanists can attribute it to our overall species. Someone less prone to flights of fancy can ascribe the right to each person's community, broadly or narrowly defined. No matter where exactly we locate the right, we certainly can locate it *somewhere* without strain. (Many analysts who presume otherwise have made a mistake that will be frowned upon later in this essay—the mistake of thinking that only individuals can hold rights.) Furthermore, while continuing to view charitability as duty-fulfilling, we can perhaps best understand its requisiteness as stemming from two sets of specific duties that are strictly correlated with rights. First, each reasonably well-off person W

Before looking at those attempted disconfirmations, however, this essay will briefly clarify (or reclarify) what the message of the Correlativity Axiom is. Notwithstanding the straightforwardness of that message, it has suffered misrepresentation at the hands of some critics. Neil MacCormick, for instance, has declared that '[t]o rest an account of claim rights *solely* on the notion that they exist whenever a legal duty is imposed by a law intended to benefit assignable individuals... is to treat rights as being simply the "reflex" of logically prior duties. Accordingly, for any statement about rights there could always be substituted a statement about duties which would be at a more fundamental level analytically' (MacCormick, 'Legislation', 199, emphasis in original). MacCormick continues: 'It is however no part of my intention here to advance a theory according to which even "claim rights" are conceived as being merely the reflex of duties, as though the latter must always be understood as being in every way prior to rights' (MacCormick, 'Legislation', 200, footnote deleted). Jeremy Waldron has echoed MacCormick by submitting that Hohfeld analysed 'rights-statements of all sorts in terms of what he appears to regard as the more primitive notion of a duty' (*RPP*, 68). Waldron offers no textual support for this reading of Hohfeld, and indeed there is none. For Hohfeld, correlativity or mutual entailment was indeed correlativity or mutual entailment, and was not the priority of one correlative element over the other. Just as a slope's downward direction is not logically or existentially prior to its upward direction, a duty is not logically or existentially prior to the right with which it is correlated. The existence of each is a necessary and sufficient condition for the existence of the other.

In the background of MacCormick's and Waldron's misrepresentations of correlativity is H. L. A. Hart's well-known insistence that 'if to say that an individual has... a right means no more than that he is the intended beneficiary of a duty, then "a right" in this sense may be an unnecessary, and perhaps confusing, term in

bears a duty to furnish aid to each needy person in his proximity who cannot obtain succour from any other source. Such a duty is of course conditional on W's retention of enough funds to meet the needs of himself and his dependents. Second, W owes a complex duty to each indigent person and charitable group, whereby W has to donate a certain portion of his income to each such person or group *unless* he elects to donate the relevant portion to some other such person or group. In sum, we can explicate the obligatory status of charitableness in ways that are perfectly consistent with the Correlativity Axiom.

the description of the law; since all that can be said in a terminology of such rights can be and indeed is best said in the indispensable terminology of duty' (Hart, 'Legal Rights', 181–2). What is objectionable about Hart's comment is its one-sidedness. To be sure, given the strict correlativity of rights and duties, Hart is correct in saying that every situation describable with reference to rights can be redescribed with reference to duties. But a corresponding point applies to situations describable with reference to duties, which can always be redescribed with reference to rights. When we probe Q's right to be free from any assaults by R, we can indeed recharacterize it as R's duty to forbear from assaulting Q; but, when we probe R's duty to forbear from assaulting Q, we can equally well recharacterize *it* as Q's right to be free from any assaults by R.[12]

With the message of the Correlativity Axiom firmly in mind, we should now ponder the arguments that have been mounted against it by MacCormick and White. MacCormick refers to a Scottish statute that includes the following provision: 'Where an intestate is survived by children, they shall have right to the whole of the intestate estate' (MacCormick 'Legislation', 200). MacCormick contends that this statutory provision bestows a right on each one of an intestate's children even before a correlative duty has been imposed on an executor of the estate. Each child gains a right to an equal share of the intestate's assets at the moment of death, even though there is not at that moment an executor to bear a correlative duty. MacCormick thus presumes that the statute belies in practice the strict right–duty correlation that has been expounded by certain theorists. 'Vesting of the right is temporally prior to the vesting in any other individual of the correlative duty, which can occur only when an executor has in due course been judicially confirmed or appointed' (MacCormick, 'Legislation', 200).

MacCormick is wrong in thinking that the entitlements brought about by the Scottish statute cannot be accommodated by Hohfeld's analytical scheme. We should take our cue from a statement in a case—*West, Saint Louis, & Pacific Railway Company v Shacklet*— cited by Hohfeld himself: 'So in the present case, appellee's intestate had *a right in rem, or a general right*, which entitled him, if free from fault himself, to be protected and indemnified against injuries

---

[12] I have made this same point more tersely in my *Legal Theory, Political Theory, and Deconstruction: Against Rhadamanthus* (Bloomington: Indiana University Press, 1991), 286–7, n 15.

resulting from the negligence of all persons whomsoever, including the appellant.'[13] Under the statute which MacCormick discusses, each child of an intestate acquires certain Hohfeldian rights at two separate stages. *At the moment of the intestate's death*, each child gains a right held 'against the world' (ie, against everyone) to be free from interference with the proper distribution of the estate. *From the moment at which an executor is appointed*, each child also holds a right specifically against the executor requiring a proper performance of the executorial functions. Other entitlements are doubtless involved as well, but my singling out of these two rights or sets of rights is sufficient to show that Hohfeld's Correlativity Axiom is scarcely belied by the Scottish law governing the disposition of intestates' assets. (How *could* that axiom be belied, given that it is true by definition?) At each relevant stage—the moment of the intestate's death, and the moment at which an executor is appointed—every child of an intestate holds rights that are strictly coeval with the pertinent duties borne by others. Only by mistakenly identifying the right that exists from the moment of the death can MacCormick maintain that a right against the executor mysteriously antecedes its correlative duty.

MacCormick also emphasizes that, under the Scottish law, a child of an intestate is entitled to be preferred to other parties when a court appoints an executor for the estate. MacCormick declares: 'In this case, therefore, it is not only the case that the vesting of a given right is temporally prior to the vesting of the correlative duty, but it is also the case that the vesting of the right in a given individual is a ground for confirming him in that office to which is attached the duty correlative to the like rights of his brothers and sisters; so that in this context right is logically prior to duty as well' (MacCormick, 'Legislation', 201). To the extent that MacCormick's analysis is tenable, it does no damage to Hohfeld's Correlativity Axiom. The right that accrues to each child of an intestate at the moment of the intestate's death—the right, held 'against the world', to be free from interference with the proper winding up of the estate—is a factor that apparently entitles a child (the eldest child?) to be appointed as

---

[13] 105 *Illinois* 364, 379 (1883), quoted in *FLC*, 83 (emphasis in original). For a discussion of MacCormick's example that is partly parallel to my own analysis, see NE Simmonds, *Central Issues in Jurisprudence* (London: Sweet & Maxwell, 1986), 134–5. Simmonds's approach is followed in JE Penner, 'The Analysis of Rights', 10 *Ratio Juris* 300, 309–10 (1997).

the estate's executor, in preference to other people. On being appointed as executor, the scion owes duties to his siblings. Those duties are indeed logically and temporally posterior to the right that triggers the appointment of the scion to the office which carries the duties. But so what? Plainly, the scion's initial right concerning non-interference is not correlative with his subsequent duties concerning his executorial functions; the initial right is *held by* the scion *against* all other people, whereas the subsequent duties are *owed by* the scion *to* some other people (his siblings). As the Correlativity Axiom pertains only to rights that are held by the same person to whom the correlative duties are owed, it clearly does not bear on the scion's initial right *vis-à-vis* his subsequent duties. And so a highlighting of the initial right's logical and temporal priority over the subsequent duties is simply beside the point, in so far as MacCormick is aiming to oppugn the Correlativity Axiom.

White's attack on that axiom is much more diffuse than MacCormick's tightly focused approach. Many of the comments by White do not warrant extensive investigation—since he repeatedly refers to various liberties as 'rights', and then trumpets the fact that those 'rights' are not correlated with any duties. Let us look at only one of the many passages in which he resorts to this manoeuvre:

[C]learly, one person's right to something does not logically give rise to any duty (or obligation) in another person. Thus, my right to treat people in certain ways, such as to teach them, heal them, protect or punish them, does not impose on them a duty (or obligation) to be treated or to allow themselves to be treated in these ways by me. Still less does my right to treat animals or inanimate things in certain ways lay on them any duty to allow themselves to be so treated, for the idea of their having a duty is absurd. No one has a duty (or obligation) corresponding to my right to assume, expect, hope for, or resent something, or to complain, suggest, or query, or to condemn, sneer at, or despise someone. (White, *Rights*, 64.)

White is wrong in thinking that schoolchildren are not duty-bound to undergo lessons and that prisoners are not duty-bound to undergo appropriate punishments; but his chief error in this passage and in manifold other passages is his persistent classifying of liberties as 'rights'. One's entitlement to behave in a certain way or to adopt a certain attitude is always a liberty rather than a right (albeit, of course, one's actions in accordance with the liberty might be protected by a right or a set of rights). Now, given that liberties are correlated with no-rights and not with duties, we should hardly be surprised when White does not find any duties that would correlate with the liberties to which he wrongly refers as 'rights'.

Some of the other arguments propounded by White are worthy of more sustained consideration. Two of his most important points, which have previously been raised by other analysts, will soon be examined in depth and will therefore only be mentioned now. First, White maintains that many duties in criminal law—and other public duties—are not correlated with any rights. Second, he (correctly) observes that a duty to confine or otherwise harm some person X is importantly different from a duty to advance X's interests in this or that way, and he (incorrectly) asserts that the difference is somehow damaging to the Correlativity Axiom. We shall explore each of these two lines of reasoning presently.

In the meantime, we ought to peruse some of White's specific examples that supposedly are at odds with the correlativity of rights and duties. His basic misstep consists in his belief that Hohfeld drew an 'inference that a right implies a duty' (White, *Rights*, 69). As has been emphasized herein, the Hohfeldian doctrine of correlativity is a definitional stipulation rather than an inference. Though Hohfeld did select terms (for legal positions) by reference to ordinary patterns of discourse among jurists, he did not present his categories as empirical generalizations. On the contrary, he submitted his scheme of jural categories as a framework of logical relations that could be employed to classify and clarify *all* empirical phenomena that might be found. For anyone who accepts Hohfeld's definitions, the correlativity of rights and duties is a matter of logical necessity and is not something that can be confirmed or confuted through experience. Far from being an inference, the principle of correlativity is a bedrock axiom.

Offering specific examples to disprove the Correlativity Axiom, White maintains that '[a] doctor has certain duties to his patients, a teacher to his pupils, and a sovereign to his subjects which do not give them any rights, however "extra-regarding" these duties may be, as when the doctor dutifully does not indulge the patient's desire for drugs, the teacher keeps his pupil's nose to the grindstone, and the sovereign sees that his subjects are always militarily prepared' (White, *Rights*, 62). If we correctly understand the duties owed by the doctor, the teacher, and the sovereign, then—*pace* White—there are indeed correlations with rights. The doctor has a duty to care for his patient as skilfully as he can in accordance with professional standards; the teacher has a duty to educate his pupils as capably as he can in accordance with professional standards; and the sovereign has a duty to further the long-term welfare of his subjects. Straightforwardly correlating with each of those duties is a right. The patient has a right to be treated as skilfully as her doctor can manage, in accordance with professional standards; each pupil has a right to be educated as well as is reasonably possible, in accordance with professional standards; and the subjects collectively have a right to be governed in a manner that promotes their well-being as far as is reasonably possible. To be sure, the patient does not have a right to be indulged whenever she makes a request. Nor does the student have a right to be indulged if he wants to shun intellectual work. (Indeed, the student does not even have a liberty to pursue such a desire.) Nor do the subjects have a right to be indulged if they wish to see long-term security sacrificed for short-term expediency. But these non-existent rights to indulgence are not the correlatives of the duties that are actually owed. The fact that the rights to indulgence are non-existent is hence not at all surprising or troubling for anyone who espouses the Correlativity Axiom.

White proclaims that '[e]ven if we have duties to animals and to infants, it is debatable whether they can have rights'. He adds that '[i]f we have duties to the dead, for example to tend their graves or not to slander their memory, it does not follow that they have a corresponding right' (White, *Rights*, 62). Whether animals and infants and dead people have rights (or can have rights) is a major topic of controversy in the Interest Theory/Will Theory debate, and is therefore a topic to which we shall return. What can be parried straightaway, however, is the suggestion that the fate of the Correlativity Axiom hinges on the outcome of the controversy just mentioned. Once again we ought to recall that that axiom is a tautology for anyone who adheres to Hohfeld's definitions of his terms. When those definitions are operative, an assertion that we have duties to animals and infants *must* entail an assertion that animals and infants have rights against us. If White thinks that he can make the former assertion without being committed to the latter assertion, then he is clearly not abiding by the definitions of 'duty' and 'right' that Hohfeld laid down. Far from refuting Hohfeld's Correlativity Axiom, White has changed the subject of discussion.

Much the same can be said about White's remark concerning dead people. In so far as we adhere to Hohfeld's definitions of 'duty' and 'right', our acknowledging that we have duties to dead people is tantamount to acknowledging that they have rights against us. Either acknowledgment entails the other. Therefore, since White believes that he can acknowledge the existence of the duties without being committed to an acknowledgment of the existence of the rights, he is manifestly construing 'right' and 'duty' along non-Hohfeldian lines; and so his example is beside the point, as a riposte to Hohfeld. (In any event, we scarcely need to shrink from ascribing rights to dead people. Within Hohfeld's analytical scheme, a right is an entitlement to the state of affairs (ie, the required non-interference or assistance or remuneration) that is specified in the imposition of a duty on someone else. To say that dead people have rights, then, is simply to say that they are entitled to the states of affairs which our duties to them require. Even on the plane of everyday discourse, the attribution of rights to the dead is not peculiar. After all, 'claim' is a synonym for 'right' in Hohfeld's vocabulary; and, in ordinary discourse, we do not hesitate to speak of the 'claims' which the dead have on the living.)

White offers a somewhat more interesting argument when he draws an analogy between contractual relations and familial relations:

[B]oth B's right to repayment and A's duty to repay him arise from A's debt to B. A contract between A and B will give rise to various rights and duties in A and B. But the existence of A's duty is no part of the notion of B's right. The various rights and duties of husband and wife, child and parent, employer and employee, different ranks in an institution, etc arise not mutually from each other, but jointly from the common system in which all participate. By analogy, it is no part of the notion of A's having a father that there should be a B who has an uncle, though if A and B are first cousins, then when A has a father B will necessarily have an uncle. (White, *Rights*, 70, footnotes deleted.)

Some assertions in this passage are as manifestly question-begging and subject-changing as the arguments by White that we have already probed. For example, if he is maintaining that the duty of a wife to her husband concerning ϕ and the right of a husband against his wife concerning ϕ are not mutually entailing, then he is adhering to strange non-Hohfeldian definitions of 'right' and 'duty' and is thus once again engaging in futile shadow-boxing. However, the final sentence of the passage introduces a more impressive argument, albeit an unsuccessful argument. White's comments on

A's father and B's uncle are accurate; hence, if the analogy between the A–B relationship and the right–duty relationship were sound, then White would indeed have managed to show that rights and duties are not inevitably connected. Yet, unsurprisingly, the analogy is not sound.

Unlike A's having a father and B's having an uncle—where the connection between B's having an uncle and A's having a father is not knowable until we learn that A and B are first cousins—a right held by X against Y concerning ϕ and a duty owed by Y to X concerning ϕ cannot occur apart from each other in any possible world. A's having a father can be fully specified without any reference to B, and thus A could have had a father even if B had not existed or had not been A's first cousin. (White himself stresses that 'it is not part of the notion of A's having a father that there should be a B who has an uncle'.) Likewise, B's having an uncle can be fully specified without any reference to A, and thus B could have had an uncle even if A had not existed or had not been B's first cousin. By contrast, X's Hohfeldian right against Y concerning ϕ cannot be specified without a specification of the Hohfeldian duty owed by Y to X concerning ϕ, and so the right cannot obtain if the duty is non-existent. Equally, Y's Hohfeldian duty to X concerning ϕ cannot be specified without a specification of the Hohfeldian right held by X against Y concerning ϕ, and so the duty cannot obtain if the right is non-existent. Whereas A can have a father even if A has no first cousin B (who will have an uncle by dint of A's having a father), a slope cannot have an upward direction without having a downward direction as well. While A's having a father and B's having an uncle are conceptually connected only because of the contingent fact of the kinship between A and B, a slope's having an upward direction and the same slope's having a downward direction are conceptually connected *tout court*. Since Hohfeldian rights and duties are correlated in the same way as a slope's upward and downward directions, White's example serves merely to highlight the gap between Hohfeldian correlations and the conditional correlations which the example of A and B describes.

Another argument marshalled by White against the Correlativity Axiom focuses on the possibility of an ineffectual statute: '[O]ne person's breach of a statutory duty will usually give another person a right of action unless there is a remedy or penalty laid down; otherwise the statute would be ineffectual. But ... this is not a logical implication of a right' (White, *Rights*, 72, footnote deleted). White's statement of the law is not entirely inaccurate here,[14] yet his observation does nothing to undermine the Correlativity Axiom. If we abide by Hohfeld's definitions of 'right' and 'duty', then an assertion that a statute imposes duties which are not backed up with effective remedies is equivalent to an assertion that the statute confers rights which are not effectively enforced. Such rights are merely nominal rights rather than genuine rights, but, equally, the duties are merely nominal duties rather than genuine duties. Though an absence of enforcement deprives rights of their genuineness, it has exactly the same effect on the rights' correlative obligations. Hence, an unenforced statute maintains a strict correlativity of duties and rights; just as genuine duties must correlate with genuine rights, nominal duties must correlate with nominal rights.

Let us close our perusal of White's analyses by pondering another scenario that has figured saliently in the dispute between proponents of the Interest Theory and proponents of the Will Theory. (We shall explore the relevant scenario in greater depth later.) White argues that 'someone can have a legal duty to do so and so without owing this duty to anyone, who might, thus, have gained a right. If A contracts with B to do something for B and C, then A has a duty to do it for B and C. He may even have a duty to B. But he has none to C and C has not thereby been given any right, even though in some kinds of contracts third parties can have rights' (White, *Rights*, 63). Now, if we agree with White's dubious pronouncement that *A* does not owe any duty to *C* (as opposed to *B*), then we hardly should be baffled when we are informed that *C* does not have any right against *A*; given the absence of a duty, the absence of a right is precisely what the Correlativity Axiom ordains. White apparently supposes that that axiom is belied by the fact that *C* could have been given a right. If White is saying that *C* could have had a right without being owed a duty, then he once again is construing 'right' and 'duty' in a non-Hohfeldian fashion and is thereby once again presenting his own unclear stipulations in the guise of empirical findings.

---

[14] However, White is guilty of considerable oversimplification. For an introduction to some of the complexities in this area of law, see RFV Heuston and RA Buckley, *Salmond & Heuston on the Law of Torts* (London: Sweet & Maxwell, 1996) (21st edn), ch 10. We should also notice here that the so-called right of action to which White refers is in fact a Hohfeldian power—a power of gaining a remedy for a violation of the particular right that is correlative to the statutory duty.

Plainly, Hohfeld's doctrine of correlativity can withstand all assaults mounted by scholars who mistakenly believe that that doctrine can undergo empirical refutation. However, notwithstanding that the Correlativity Axiom is insusceptible to being disproved (or, rather, *because* it is insusceptible to being disproved), we have to ask how useful and powerful that axiom really is. If Hohfeld's analytical scheme in a slightly modified form is to function well as a crucial element in a theory of rights, it had better be highly illuminating and serviceable. Though the tenets of Hohfeld's scheme are neither true nor false empirically—since they are true by definition—they can certainly be assessed for their heuristic strength and their adaptability. To be sure, very few commentators have doubted the rigour of Hohfeld's analysis; but some have felt that the rigorousness involves an undue rigidity. My essay, which draws on a number of the major strands of Hohfeld's analysis, must therefore seek to reveal that his analysis is not troublesomely confining and that it in fact is marvellously capacious and flexible. At a minimum, what needs to be shown is that Hohfeld's Correlativity Axiom tallies unstrainedly with some basic features of law and legal theory—and morality and moral theory—that are sometimes seen as not easily reconcilable with it.

A prominent characteristic of certain political and moral theories is that they focus either on rights or on duties but not on both alike, when they variously expound the norms that should govern human interaction. (Of course, some theories do focus on rights and duties alike.) Some theorists may justify norm N because they view it as offering protection for the freedom or other vital interests of the individuals who hold rights under the norm. For such theorists, the duties that correlate with the rights which N confers are not especially significant or commendable in themselves; the duties imposed by N are significant and desirable only because they are necessary for the protection of the vital interests that are of real concern. Constraints on people's behaviour—constraints imposed as duties—are thus perceived as valuable only instrumentally, and not intrinsically. In other words, the focus lies on each individual *qua* someone whose freedom or well-being is safeguarded by the constraints, rather than on each individual *qua* someone whose latitude to harm his fellows has been limited.

Certain other theorists may view duties rather than rights as the legal positions that are of paramount significance for the justification of any norms that should govern human intercourse. Under this approach, the justificational focus lies on each individual *qua* someone whose leeway to hurt his fellows has been cabined, rather than on each individual *qua* someone whose well-being has been fortified by the restrictions imposed on others. Theorists who adopt this duty-based approach to justification can invoke various reasons for attributing primary importance to duties; for example, perhaps they regard the duties as essential for maintaining the decency of the duty-bearers, or perhaps they view the duties as the means by which each person's higher autonomy (ie, autonomy from base desires) can be realized. Whatever be the exact reasons that inspire someone's focus on duties, that justificational focus consists in the advocacy of norms on the basis of their ability to serve the higher interests of duty-bearers (by restricting the duty-bearers' freedom in appropriate ways).

Two examples, very tersely recounted, may help to clarify the distinction between right-based justifications and duty-based justifications of norms. Think of a norm that proscribes mendacity in most circumstances. A right-based justification of such a norm will focus on each person's interest in not being deceived. A duty-based justification, by contrast, will focus on the integrity and self-respect which each person gains by forbearing from telling lies to her fellows. Much the same duality can occur in respect to a norm that proscribes torture. A right-based justification will concentrate on the obvious interest of each person in not being subjected to brutal treatment. A duty-based justification, on the other hand, will concentrate on the need to prohibit the would-be torturers from degrading themselves.[15]

Oddly enough, this split between right-based and duty-based modes of justification has seemed to some analysts to be inconsistent with Hohfeld's Correlativity Axiom. Ronald Dworkin, for instance, appears to posit such an inconsistency in the following passage:

[G]oals can be justified by other goals or by rights or duties, and rights or duties can be justified by goals. Rights and duties can also be justified, of course, by other, more fundamental duties or rights. Your duty to respect

---

[15] For a much longer treatment of the example of mendacity, see *RPP* (n 11 above), 70–3; for a longer treatment of the example of torture, see Jeremy Waldron, 'Introduction', in Jeremy Waldron (ed), *Theories of Rights* (Oxford: Oxford University Press, 1984) [hereinafter cited as Waldron, 'Introduction'], 1, 13.

my privacy, for example, may be justified by my right to privacy. I do not mean merely that rights and duties may be correlated, as opposite sides of the same coin. That may be so when, for example, a right and the corresponding duty are justified as serving a more fundamental goal, as when your right to property and my corresponding duty not to trespass are together justified by the more fundamental goal of socially efficient land use. In many cases, however, corresponding rights and duties are not correlative, but one is derivative from the other, and it makes a difference which is derivative from which. There is a difference between the idea that you have a duty not to lie to me because I have a right not to be lied to, and the idea that I have a right that you not lie to me because you have a duty not to tell lies. In the first case I justify a duty by calling attention to a right; if I intend any further justification it is the right that I must justify, and I cannot do so by calling attention to the duty. In the second case it is the other way around.[16]

To be sure, the language in this extract is somewhat ambiguous. Having not mentioned Hohfeld at all, Dworkin *might* be referring only to justificational correlativity (and derivativeness) rather than to analytical or existential correlativity (and derivativeness). That is, he *might* be referring to levels of priority within a justificatory argument only—and not to levels of priority within an analytical exposition or within a legal system. If so, then Dworkin is not proclaiming that Hohfeld's Correlativity Axiom somehow fails to apply to the legal positions commended by duty-based and right-based theories. None the less, the quoted remarks at best are misleading.

Much less ambiguous are some comments of a broadly similar tenor by Neil MacCormick, who has sought to highlight 'the possibility that rights are or could be *logically* prior to duties', and who has quipped that 'Austin and Hohfeld might be scandalized' (MacCormick, 'Children's Rights', 161, emphasis added). MacCormick feels a need to emphasize the potential for the logical priority of rights because he wishes to support his pronouncement that 'it is *because* children have a right to care and nurture that parents have

---

[16] Ronald Dworkin, *Taking Rights Seriously* (Cambridge: Harvard University Press, 1978), 171. For a particularly subtle and complicated expression of the view that the existence of duty-based and right-based theories is incompatible with the Correlativity Axiom, see *MFR* (n 5 above), 106. For another version of the same view, with reference specifically to a right-based theory, see Marmor (n 7 above), 3. See also MJ Detmold, *Courts and Administrators* (London: Weidenfeld and Nicolson, 1989), 112, 113–14.

the duty to care for them' (MacCormick, 'Children's Rights', 162, emphasis in original). Such a pronouncement, however, is manifestly justificatory rather than analytical; hence, MacCormick must believe that the existence of justificational priorities is somehow incompatible with the logical correlativity of rights and duties.

Such a belief about justificational foci and logical correlativity is even more explicitly and directly stated by Jeremy Waldron, who declares that 'the possibility that rights and duties may stand in generational or justificatory relationships to each other, *rather than relationships of logical equivalence*, provides an opening for the distinction between right-based and duty-based theories' (*RPP*, 69–70, emphasis added). Waldron goes on to affirm that 'the justificatory role of rights means that they cannot be regarded as strictly correlative to duties, and therefore that statements about rights are not strictly equivalent to statements about duties. The last point is crucial if rights are to be seen as justifications: one statement cannot justify another if the two are equivalent' (*RPP*, 84). Here again we discover the perception of a conflict between the possibility of a right-based or duty-based political theory and the universal sway of right/duty correlativity. According to Waldron, one's ability to adopt a justificatory focus that prioritizes a right over a duty (or a duty over a right) must rule out the doctrine of strict mutual entailment between the prioritized element and the subordinated element. '[T]his distinction [between right-based and duty-based theories] is bound to seem mysterious if we simply postulate a *logical* relationship between rights and duties. If P's having a right is *defined* in terms of Q's having a duty, how can some theories be right-based while others are duty-based?' (Waldron, 'Introduction', 12, emphasis in original.)

Must anyone drawing on Hohfeld's analytical framework renounce the idea of right-based and duty-based political theories? Fortunately, the answer is a resounding 'no', since a justificational focus does not commit anyone to the notion of an existential or analytical hierarchy. Suppose that a political theory exalts a right as a key desideratum and that it views the trammels of the right's correlative duty as valuable only because they enable the protection of the interest to which the right is attached. Such a theory can and should recognize that the right's protections and the duty's restrictions are perforce correlative (as the mutually constituting sides of a single relationship), even though the protections are valued for their own sake while the restrictions are valued only because they form the protections. Indeed, it is precisely because the right and the duty are logically correlative that a theory which prizes the right must have a place also for the duty; the right cannot be presented in a justificationally exalted role unless the duty is simultaneously taken aboard in a justificationally subordinate role.

If a person X very much desires a slope in his yard so that he can enjoy the downward perspective from the top, he can and should recognize that his having the slope will also provide the yard with an upward perspective from the bottom. Perhaps X will attach little or no independent value to the upwardness of the slope, and will accept it only because it is an ineluctable correlate of the slope's downwardness, which he keenly wants. In that event, his justification for introducing the slope into the yard is focused solely or principally on its top-down inclination, to the exclusion of its bottom-up inclination. Yet, if X is sensible, his advancing of such a justification will not lead him to maintain that the top-down direction of the slope is logically or existentially prior to its bottom-up direction. Thorough simultaneity, as opposed to anteriority and posteriority, is what marks the logical and temporal relationship between the downwardness and the upwardness of the slope. That relationship of strict simultaneity between the upwardness and the downwardness is scarcely undone by a justificatory concentration on one or the other of those two simultaneous aspects.

When a political theorist takes a right-based or duty-based approach to the justification of various norms, she thereby focuses her attention on some of the roles or statuses that people occupy, and she de-emphasizes other such roles or statuses. In the course of furnishing moral and political justifications of norms, a right-based theory concentrates on each person *qua* potential beneficiary of normative protection for certain freedoms or other interests, whereas a duty-based theory concentrates on each person *qua* responsible agent whose integrity can be realized or furthered through his heeding of appropriate limits on his conduct. To concentrate on one or the other role (or set of roles) for justificational purposes, however, is not to commit oneself to the notion that a right can exist without the simultaneous imposition of a duty or that a duty can exist without the simultaneous conferral of a right. Just as someone who relishes the downward inclination of a slope in his yard should recognize that the yard must also contain the slope's upward inclination (by dint of containing its downward inclination), so a person who advocates the imposition of certain duties should recognize that she is thereby calling implicitly or explicitly for the creation of certain rights; and a person who advocates the creation of certain rights should recognize that she is thereby calling implicitly or explicitly for the imposition of certain duties. Her moral/political focus may lie on only the right-holding role or only the duty-bearing role that each person can occupy—but her analytical scrutiny should reveal to her that, in calling for the bestowal of a right (or the imposition of a duty) on *X vis-à-vis Y*, she is calling for the imposition of a duty (or the bestowal of a right) on *Y vis-à-vis X*.

In short, Hohfeld's Correlativity Axiom is entirely consistent with a justificational focus that attaches primary importance to rights (or duties) and secondary importance to duties (or rights); the Correlativity Axiom stipulates a *logical* and *existential* nexus of mutual entailment between rights and duties, in distinction from a nexus of *justificative* parity. Moreover, the Correlativity Axiom can facilitate the reaching of wise decisions about the rights (or duties) that should receive justification, since it helps to make clear the full implications of the establishment of any such rights (or duties). Consider, for example, the endowing of everyone with a right not to be made miserable by anyone else. Someone inattentive to the duty imposed on everyone by such a right may substantially overestimate the right's attractiveness. After all, the benefits accruing to each person *qua* right-holder through such a right would not be inconsiderable. Yet, if any sensible theorist might be inclined to plump for the anti-misery right with a justificatory argument that would highlight the role of each person *qua* holder of such a right, the theorist will almost certainly lose his inclination as soon as he takes account of the repressive duty that would have to be borne by everyone.

Were the anti-misery right to be established along with its correlative duty, then Mary who is deeply beloved by John would have a duty to accede to his solicitations even if she feels no love for him at all. (Of course, if the overtures by John render Mary profoundly despondent, then he would have a duty to forbear from them—quite as much as she would have a duty to yield to them, in order to avoid making *him* despondent.) A world in which Mary would have to give herself to the unloved John, and in which countless equally bizarre requirements would arise, is hardly a world that should win the favour of any sensible theorist. And so the conferral of an anti-misery right on everyone should not win the favour of such a theorist. However appealing that right may seem when we concentrate only on the role of each person *qua* right-holder, it shows itself to be dreadful when we realize what it logically entails. Thus, here and elsewhere, the Correlativity Axiom's emphasis on the mutual entailment between rights and duties can enhance the sophistication of a right-based or duty-based approach to the selection of patterns of entitlements.

If Hohfeld's doctrine of correlativity is consistent with right-focused and duty-focused modes of justification, it likewise is perfectly compatible with the distinction between general (or abstract) entitlements and specific (or concrete) entitlements. A general entitlement comprises an indefinite number of specific entitlements that instantiate it or develop it. A right against being assaulted, for example, encompasses any number of rights against being assaulted in specific ways. Of course, since generality and concreteness are matters of degree, an entitlement E can be general in relation to an entitlement F and concrete in relation to an entitlement G. For example, while the right against being assaulted is abstract *vis-à-vis* the rights against being assaulted in specific ways, it is specific *vis-à-vis* the abstract right to security.

An important aspect of the relationship between general and specific entitlements is that a general entitlement can lead to new specific entitlements, as circumstances evolve. Consider the following remarks by Joseph Raz:

> The existence of a right often leads to holding another to have a duty because of the existence of certain facts peculiar to the parties or general to the society in which they live. A change of circumstances may lead to the creation of new duties based on the old right. The right to political participation is not new, but only in modern states with their enormously complex bureaucracies does this right justify, as I think it does, a duty on the government to make public its plans and proposals before a decision on them is reached. ... This dynamic aspect of rights, their ability to create new duties, is fundamental to any understanding of their nature and function in practical thought. (Raz, 'Nature', 199–200.)

This 'dynamic aspect' of rights and other entitlements is surely an aspect that ought not to be overlooked or elided by any theory of such entitlements. If we are to believe Raz, however, the notion of a strict correlativity between rights and duties does indeed obscure the dynamic aspect of rights: 'Unfortunately, most if not all formulations of the correlativity thesis disregard the dynamic aspects of rights. They all assume that a right can be exhaustively stated by stating those duties which it has already established' (Raz, 'Nature', 200).[17] Raz offers no citations or arguments to support this assertion, and in fact it is unsupportable.

To see that Raz has gone astray, we must keep in view the distinction between abstract entitlements and concrete entitlements (a distinction emphasized in Raz, 'Nature', 210–12). The Correlativity Axiom points to one-to-one correlations between rights and duties of the *same* degree of specificity. It does not point to such correlations between rights and duties of *differing* degrees of specificity, and indeed it rules such alignments out—because it insists that a right must have the same content and hence the same degree of specificity as the duty with which the right is correlated. Thus, for instance, X's general right to be free from invasions of his privacy by Y will correlate only with Y's general duty to abstain from invading X's privacy; it will not correlate with the specific duties that are imposed on Y as a consequence of the general duty. Accordingly, X's general right is not tied to any specific duty or to any set of specific duties. It can generate as many specific duties as the specific rights to which it leads (each of which will be correlated with a specific duty). Whenever circumstances such as new inventions require the elaboration of further concrete norms to effectuate the abstract right concerning privacy, X will gain new concrete rights and Y will incur new concrete duties. A strict one-to-one correlation obtains throughout, as X's abstract right correlates with Y's abstract duty, and as each concrete right held by X is correlated with a concrete duty borne by Y.

We therefore should take issue with Raz when he looks askance at the Correlativity Axiom for 'misleadingly suggest[ing] that to every right there corresponds one duty[.] ... Many rights ... may ground many duties not one. A right to personal security does not require others to protect a person from all accidents or injury. The right is, however, the foundation of several duties, such as the duty not to assault, rape or imprison the right-holder' (Raz, 'Nature', 199). As has here been explained, any proponent of the Correlativity Axiom should readily agree that a general right can 'ground many

---

[17] For a similar view, see Joseph Raz, 'Legal Rights', 4 Oxford J of Legal Studies 1, 14–15 (1984) [hereinafter cited as Raz, 'Legal Rights']. See also Waldron, 'Introduction' (n 15 above), 10; Marmor (n 7 above), 3–4.

[specific] duties' and can serve as 'the foundation of several [specific] duties'. After all, the grounding relationship between the abstract right and the concrete duties is not a *correlation* between them. The abstract right correlates only with an abstract duty, while each concrete duty correlates only with a matching concrete right—a concrete right that has been generated by the abstract right. At least as construed by Hohfeld, a correlation is a logical tie of mutual entailment rather than a generality/specificity relationship (which may be logical but may instead be merely justificative, and which in any event does not involve *mutual* entailment).

An acceptance of the Correlativity Axiom, then, does not at all impede anyone from taking account of the 'dynamic aspect' of rights. Once we distinguish carefully between the dynamic generality/specificity relationship and the one-to-one correlativity of rights and duties, we can see that neither excludes the other. An abstract right that is strictly correlated with an abstract duty can comprise or undergird any number of concrete rights, each of which will of course be strictly correlated with a concrete duty. This point has been aptly acknowledged by Jeremy Waldron, who on the whole is very sympathetic to Raz: '[T]he "dynamic aspect" could equally be captured by making the [abstract] right correlative to a rather abstract duty and saying that changing circumstances etc might lead to the derivation of different concrete duties from that' (*RPP*, 85). With the generality/specificity distinction in hand, we can retain the rigour of Hohfeld's approach while also fathoming the ability of rights to justify the creation of further rights.

This discussion of the abstract/concrete distinction and of rights' dynamic aspect has affirmed that an abstract right can serve as a ground for the establishment of various concrete rights (and their correlative duties, of course). The only thing thereby indicated is that the existence of the abstract right can yield the concrete rights in two basic ways. First, a general right can encompass certain concrete rights as its logical consequences; for example, the right to be free at all times from unprovoked assaults will logically entail the right to be free on Tuesdays from unprovoked assaults. Second, and more important, a general right can warrant the creation of specific rights that are deemed to be crucial for the fulfilment of the general right. For instance, the broad right of each person to be free from intrusions into his privacy by governmental officials can underpin the conferral upon him of a more specific right to be free from the wire-tapping of his telephone by such officials. In this situation, the ties between the abstract right and the concrete right are not logical but are instead partly instrumental and partly explicative or interpretative. Precisely such ties account for the fact that rights (relatively general rights) are often invoked as justifying reasons for the establishment or recognition of rights (relatively specific rights).

What has *not* been indicated here by the references to a general right's 'grounding' of specific rights and duties is what Raz sometimes means when he describes a right as a 'ground' of duties. At times Raz uses such a description in much the same way in which it has been employed here, but at other times he uses it in a way directly opposed to the Correlativity Axiom. He declares, for example, that 'the right is the ground of the duty. It is wrong to translate statements of rights into statements of "the corresponding" duties. A right of one person is not a duty on another. It is the ground of a duty, a ground which, if not counteracted by conflicting considerations, justifies holding that other person to have the duty' (Raz, 'Nature', 199). To be sure, Raz is at liberty to define the term 'right' in a non-Hohfeldian manner, and thus the statements just quoted (along with his many other similar statements) are not erroneous when construed on their own terms. (They *would* be flatly erroneous if they were supposed to be abiding by the definitions which Hohfeld attached to his lexicon; but Raz clearly is making no effort to follow Hohfeld's patterns of usage.) Nonetheless, although Raz has not committed an outright error when adopting his own definitions, his peculiar argot can at any rate give rise to confusion. Specifically, it can easily induce readers to confuse interests with the moral or legal protection of interests.

Although definitions are not true or false, they are more useful or less useful; and Raz's definitions are not especially useful, because they lead too readily to the aforementioned confusion (between interests and the protection of interests). Albeit Raz himself has not muddled the distinction between interests and entitlements, his terminology tends to engender such a muddle and should consequently be eschewed. Given how frequently theorists have run afoul of that muddle,[18] we ought sedulously to avoid any language that smacks of it.

[18] Hohfeld strove to combat the running together of interests and entitlements. See, eg, *FLC* (n 1 above), 79, n 34 (emphasis in original): '[T]here is a very obvious difference—and one vitally important for the solution of problems in the conflict of

However, Raz and MacCormick and their followers would doubtless object that the replacement of Raz's patterns of usage with Hohfeldian patterns will leave us unable to account for some basic features of rights. Both Raz and MacCormick have maintained, for example, that we can attribute a right to someone even if we cannot yet specify how the right should be fleshed out—and therefore even if we cannot yet specify the person against whom the right will be held.[19] How can we explain this phenomenon unless we acknowledge that rights are the logically and temporally antecedent grounds of duties?

To meet the query just posed, this essay must show that a theory based on the Correlativity Axiom can readily take account of the phenomenon to which Raz and MacCormick have pointed. Can we suitably re-characterize that phenomenon if we employ Hohfeldian definitions of entitlements instead of Raz's definitions, and if we therefore take rights and duties to be strictly correlative? The answer, of course, is 'yes'; moreover, the re-characterization will help to avert any running together of interests and entitlements.

laws—between a mere *factual interest* and its *legal recognition* (legal claims, privileges, etc.).' Cf Penner (n 13 above), 306–14. None the less, the interest/entitlement conflation has continued to surface frequently. See, eg, Benditt (n 3 above), 170 ('It seems to me to be more perspicuous... to identify the right with the interest straightaway, for this seems to be the only way... of preserving the notion that people's rights can sometimes constitute the legal reasons for certain decisions'); Davies and Holdcroft (n 11 above), 243 ('So, in so far as a theory is right-based, it will argue that correlative duties are required to protect the rights [*sic*] of individuals, which are things of value in their own right; whereas the rationale of the correlative duties is such that they are of value not in their own right but simply because of their function of protecting things of value, viz individual rights [*sic*]'); Dworkin (n 16 above), 172 ('Right-based theories, however, treat codes of conduct as instrumental, perhaps necessary to protect the rights [*sic*] of others, but having no essential value in themselves'); Richard Posner, *The Problems of Jurisprudence* (Cambridge, MA: Harvard University Press, 1990), 331 ('[A] right is an important interest presumptively protected against interference by others'); Waldron, 'Introduction' (n 15 above), 15 ('On the most straightforward model, a right is nothing but a particularly important interest'); Jeremy Waldron, *The Law* (London: Routledge, 1990), 105 ('We call *rights* those interests which should not simply be thrown into the social calculus along with everything else'); *RPP* (n 11 above), 83–4. The running together of interests and entitlements is one form of the broader confusion between non-legal (or non-moral) facts and legal (or moral) facts. For an attack on that broader confusion, see *FLC* (n 1 above), 27–31. For a recent work that is marred by such confusion, see Martin, *System* (n 5 above).

[19] See, eg, Raz, 'Nature' (n 11 above), 211–12; MacCormick, 'Children's Rights' (n 11 above), 163. See also Feinberg (n 11 above), 142–3.

This re-characterization must demarcate at least three stages in the setting of entitlements—though these stages could easily be divided further, if we so wished. First are people's interests of various sorts, including their interests in being unrestricted. Second are inchoate entitlements. Any ascriptions of such entitlements consist in judgments that certain interests deserve moral or legal protection as yet unspecified. Third are defined entitlements (be they genuine or nominal, general or concrete), which consist in the forms of moral or legal protection that are eventually bestowed. For our present purpose, what needs most attention is the second of these stages and the transition from it to the third. When Raz and MacCormick and their followers refer to situations 'in which we are much more certain that children [or others] have a right to something than we are certain about what is the right or the best way of giving effect to it' (MacCormick, 'Children's Rights', 163), they are in fact referring to inchoate entitlements rather than to any defined rights. In other words, to say that someone holds a right even though nobody yet knows what it involves is to say merely that a certain interest has been deemed worthy of moral or legal protection; to say that every child holds an unspecified 'right' to an education, for example, is to say merely that every child's interest in receiving an education ought to enjoy moral or legal protection.[20]

Two connected but distinguishable conditions have to be established before an inchoate entitlement can become a defined entitlement or a set of defined entitlements. Both the *kind* of moral or legal protection and the *bearing* of that protection must be settled. Determining the kind of protection involves a decision about the moral or

---

[20] This discussion may seem to take for granted the veracity of the Interest Theory of rights. Two caveats, then, should be entered. First, because Raz and MacCormick are both proponents of the Interest Theory, a retort to them on the present point is likely to be framed in language which is redolent of that theory (especially when the retort comes from someone who is also a proponent of that theory). Second, my analysis here does not in fact beg the question in favour of the Interest Theory against the Will Theory, because it leaves room for occasions on which the best way of protecting someone's interests is to confer a set of entitlements upon someone else. Many proponents of the Will Theory have perceived such occasions as indicative of an interest/entitlement gap that tells in favour of their own view. (As will be argued later, however, any tenable version of the Interest Theory can handily take note of such occasions.)

I should also mention that I am not attempting to reproduce the distinction that WD Ross drew between prima-facie obligations and all-things-considered obligations in his *The Right and the Good* (Oxford: Clarendon Press, 1930), ch 2. Still, my categories do bear *some* resemblance to those laid out by Ross.

legal relation(s) that will appropriately safeguard an interest which has been deemed to deserve support. For any given interest, the support can range from a bald liberty (ie, a simple lack of restrictions) to a panoply of liberties, rights, powers, and immunities. A child's unspecified 'right' to an education, for example, might eventuate in some of the following components, among others: a right not to be excluded or greatly hindered from obtaining an education, a right to be furnished with adequate pedagogical services and materials, a liberty to attend school and engage in lessons regularly, an immunity from being divested of these educational rights and liberties, and a power to seek enforcement of these educational rights. (This first phase of specification which has to be undergone by inchoate entitlements in the course of becoming defined entitlements is obviously akin to the elaboration of general entitlements through their justifying of concrete entitlements. But general entitlements such as general rights are defined rather than unspecified, notwithstanding their generality. A general right is indeed a general right and is not a general entitlement of some other sort; by contrast, an unspecified 'right' is insufficiently defined to be distinguished from other sorts of unspecified entitlements such as unspecified 'liberties'. Perhaps the most obvious manifestation of this difference between general entitlements and unspecified entitlements is that general entitlements can entail certain concrete entitlements—a general right to be free at all times from unprovoked assaults will have entailed a concrete right to be free from unprovoked assaults on Tuesdays, for example—whereas unspecified entitlements can never strictly entail other entitlements.)

As important as specifying each moral or legal relation's type is the task of specifying its bearing, that is, its particular direction or application. Not only do we have to fix upon the sorts of defined entitlements that ought to be held by someone with an inchoate entitlement, but we also have to decide who should hold the position (duty, no-right, disability, or liability) that correlates with each entitlement. Consider again the child who holds an inchoate 'right' to an education. We not only have to determine whether the child should have a right to be supplied with adequate pedagogical services and materials, for example, but we also have to determine who should bear the duty to provide such services and materials. Much the same is true, *mutatis mutandis*, of each defined entitlement that ensues from the unspecified 'right'. (This need to define the bearing of an initially unspecified entitlement is what most clearly distinguishes the present discussion from my earlier discussion of general and concrete entitlements. Even a general entitlement, if defined, must obtain against some particular person or group of persons. In this respect, most plainly, general entitlements are specified despite being non-specific. When we say that someone has such an entitlement, we are saying more than that the person has an interest which is worthy of being protected; we are also able to indicate the person or persons against whom the protection is aimed.)

Note that, although we can theoretically separate the two factors which must be specified before an inchoate entitlement can become a defined entitlement or a set of defined entitlements, those factors will very often be fixed upon simultaneously. The proper determination of each factor will almost always significantly affect the proper determination of the other, and thus in practice the choosing of one cannot usually be disentangled from the choosing of the other. Certainly, neither factor necessarily takes precedence over the other; if the type and the bearing of some entitlement are not selected simultaneously, then either can be selected first.

How, then, does this tripartite framework of 'interests', 'inchoate (or incipient) entitlements', and 'defined entitlements' compare with Raz's framework of 'interests', 'rights', and 'duties'? With the categories outlined and recommended herein, we can fully take account of the various functions of entitlements which Raz describes; yet we can also stay away from his language and its tendency to blur the distinction between interests and the moral or legal relations which protect interests. By emphasizing that the 'grounds' of duties are not defined rights but are inchoate entitlements which eventuate in defined rights (with their correlative duties, of course), and by emphasizing that any imputation of an inchoate entitlement is merely a judgment that some interest of someone deserves protection in a way not yet specified, we can keep a distance from the confusion which Raz's argot may breed. Moreover, apart from being able to accommodate Raz's analytical points without his somewhat misleading terminology, the framework commended here retains the Correlativity Axiom. It therefore enables us to draw on the rigour and subtlety of Hohfeld's jurisprudential scheme. Contrary to what Raz and MacCormick and others have supposed, the Correlativity Axiom is flexible and adaptable as well as highly precise. We need not sacrifice that axiom in the course of recognizing the sundry functions of entitlements; we saw as much when looking at the 'dynamic aspect' of rights, and we have seen as much here.

Having been largely (though not unfailingly) supportive of Hohfeld hitherto, this essay concludes its discussion of his work by criticizing him for his stance on a topic that pertains in quite an important way to the Correlativity Axiom: the topic of collectivities and their legal positions. Hohfeld stated his views on this topic most extensively in one of his less renowned essays, dealing with the responsibility of stockholders for corporate debts. He began the relevant portion of his analysis quite unexceptionably by asserting that 'it has not always been perceived with perfect clearness that transacting business under the forms, methods, and procedure pertaining to so-called corporations is simply another mode by which *individuals* or *natural persons* can enjoy their property and engage in business' (*FLC*, 197, emphasis in original). More dubiously, however, he wrote of the 'necessity of emphasizing... the realities of corporate forms, methods, and procedure and of looking beneath the fictional language tending to obscure those realities' (*FLC*, 197 n 9). In an equally questionable vein he declared that '[w]hen all is said and done, a corporation is just an association of natural persons conducting business under legal forms, methods, and procedure that are *sui generis*. The only conduct of which the state can take notice by its laws *must* spring from natural persons—it cannot be derived from any abstraction called the "corporate entity"' (*FLC*, 198, emphasis in original, footnote deleted). He then delivered himself of some starkly nominalist pronouncements, of which only two representative portions will be quoted here. Consider first the statement that '[w]hen, therefore, in accordance with the customary terminology, we speak of the corporation, as such, as contracting in the corporate name, as acquiring, holding, and transferring property, and as suing and being sued, and when we speak of stockholders as mere claimants against the corporation, holding stock, which is a species of personal property—and so on indefinitely—we are merely employing a short and convenient mode of describing the complex and peculiar process by which the benefits and burdens of the corporate members are worked out' (*FLC*, 199–200). Equally heavy-handed is the following contention:

> In reality when we say that the so-called legal or juristic person [such as a corporation] has rights or that it has contracted, we mean nothing more

than what must ultimately be explained by describing the capacities, powers, rights, privileges (or liberties), disabilities, duties and liabilities, etc, of the natural persons concerned or of some of such persons. ...

Doesn't this roundabout process of explanation necessitated by calling the association a juristic person suggest the same objection that has been made concerning a certain other legal fiction? Is it not like looking at things through smoked glass and then holding a candle on the other side in order to see them? If this be so, it appears even more objectionable to speak of a corporation as an abstract entity or personality distinct from the sum of the stockholders. Is it not better, then, as a matter of words and definitions, to say with emphasis that, as applied to associations of natural persons considered as units, the terms, *right, duty, contract, etc*, should never be used except in a figurative sense—that is, as a sort of legal shorthand? (*FLC*, 199–200 n 14.)

These lengthy extracts from Hohfeld's arguments reveal his belief that statements about any jural relation involving any collective person can be reduced to statements about certain jural relations involving some or all of the individuals who make up that collective person.[21] A statement of the former sort is at best an instance of figural shorthand; the relation to which it seemingly refers is fictive. Only a statement of the latter sort, a statement about the connections between individuals, directly refers to anything real.

To be sure, we should not lose sight of the sophistication of Hohfeld's perspective on this matter. His arguments clearly do not

---

[21] I therefore regard as unduly generous the assessment of Hohfeld in HLA Hart, 'Definition and Theory in Jurisprudence', in *Essays in Jurisprudence and Philosophy* (Oxford: Clarendon Press, 1983), 21, 42, n 22: 'I think [Hohfeld] also saw that statements concerning companies cannot be "reduced" to statements concerning individuals, but are as he says "sui generis".' (However, I do not agree with the criticism of Hohfeld in ibid, at 40–2—criticism resting on a general position that was later repudiated by Hart.) More accurate, in my view, is Perry (n 3 above), 208, n 1: '[Hohfeld] hoped that . . . complex relationships could be analyzed without remainder into his two-term relations [between individuals].' See also Dias (n 4 above), 360–1. For an analysis even more pugnaciously nominalist than Hohfeld's, see Radin (n 2 above), 1147, 1153–4, 1160–2. Cf Joseph Jaconelli, 'Rights Theories and Public Trial', 14 *Journal of Applied Philosophy* 169, 173 (1997). For some analyses opposed to the nominalist stance on this point (without expressly mentioning Hohfeld), see AH Campbell, 'Some Footnotes to Salmond's Jurisprudence', 7 Cambridge L J 206, 210–11 (1940); Freeden (n 3 above), 80–1, 87–8; Geoffrey Marshall, 'Rights, Options, and Entitlements', in AWB Simpson (ed), *Oxford Essays in Jurisprudence (Second Series)* (Oxford: Clarendon Press, 1973) [hereinafter cited as Marshall, 'Rights'], 228, 237, 238; Raz, 'Nature' (n 11 above), 204, 208; Joseph Raz, *The Morality of Freedom* (Oxford: Clarendon Press, 1986), 207–9; Joseph Raz, 'Intention in Interpretation', in Robert George (ed), *The Autonomy of Law* (Oxford: Clarendon Press, 1996), 249, 263, 264; Sumner, *MFR* (n 5 above), 209–10, 211; Waldron (n 6 above), 361–7.

assert that theses about a corporation's entitlement-concerning-ϕ (for instance, about its right-concerning-ϕ) are perforce reducible to theses purely about the same sort of entitlement-concerning-ϕ held by some individual—or to theses purely about multiple instances of the same sort of entitlement-concerning-ϕ attached to various individuals. Hohfeld far more subtly maintained instead that theses about a corporation's entitlement-concerning-ϕ are perforce reducible to theses about some set of entitlements (perhaps, in very rare circumstances, only one entitlement) held by one or more individuals. He saw, in other words, that reducibility does not amount to straightforward homologousness. His aim was to highlight the unreality of corporate entitlements while recognizing that the task of translating propositions about such entitlements into propositions about real individual entitlements is an enterprise that differs from case to case.

Even when discussing the entitlements of collectivities, then, Hohfeld displayed admirable astuteness. None the less, he clearly went astray when he embraced an outright nominalism, for he thereby confused *explicability* with *reducibility* and *fictitiousness*. On the one hand, we indeed have to expound the implications of any corporate entitlement by tracing the individual entitlements through which it operates. To specify what the workings of the corporate entitlement are, we have to specify the congeries of individual entitlements in which those workings consist. On the other hand, we do not thereby exhaust the meaning or strip away the reality of the corporate entitlement. A group's legal positions are not reducible to any set of individuals' legal positions; the individuals' legal positions can all exist even if the group's positions do not, and the group's basic positions can abide even if the individuals' positions have all changed. Anyone adhering to a doctrine of reducibility must contend that there is no real difference between individuals' having certain entitlements on their own and individuals' having those same entitlements as the components of a group entitlement. The believer in reducibility must likewise contend that the protections offered by rights and immunities (and the constraints imposed by obligations and disabilities) cannot produce impacts on groups that would occur as anything more than the particular impacts on the groups' members. In these respects, Hohfeld espoused an untenable view.

Let us first examine the difference between individual entitlements on their own and individual entitlements as the ingredients of a collective entitlement. Suppose that a certain association's right concerning ϕ involves the conferral of some rights and liberties and immunities and powers on some of the people who belong to the association. Now, there is nothing in principle that would prevent the conferral of exactly the same entitlements on exactly the same people even if those people did not belong to an organization with a right concerning ϕ. Although such a matrix of entitlements would comprise legal positions on their own rather than as the elements of a collective right concerning ϕ, it would comprise the very same legal positions that are classified as all the elements of the collective right if that right does obtain. Accordingly, statements about the network of those positions do not exhaust the meaning of statements about the collective right concerning ϕ. Because the network of the relevant legal positions can exist even when there is no organization to which a right-concerning-ϕ can be attributed, we cannot collapse statements about a collective right-concerning-ϕ into statements about the individual legal positions which operationalize that collective right. The need for the existence of a group intervenes between the two sorts of statements, preventing the reduction of statements on the former level (which, if true, require the existence of a group) to statements on the latter level (which can be true irrespective of the existence of a group). Something more than an explication in terms of individual entitlements is necessary for a full understanding of any ascription of some right to a collectivity; because the individual entitlements can obtain even if the collectivity does not, and therefore because the individual entitlements in themselves can never account for their own standing as the elements of a collective right when indeed they are such elements, any statements about the collective right refer to something beyond the individual entitlements which form the collective right's workings. Those statements refer as well to a collectivity, to which the individual entitlement-holders are deemed to belong as members.

Not only does Hohfeld's doctrine of reducibility blur the gap that has just been described—the gap between statements about collective entitlements and statements about the individual entitlements which form the workings of the collective entitlements—but it also neglects the difference between the impact of a corporate entitlement on the group which holds it and the impacts of that entitlement on the individuals whose legal positions operationalize it. Let us approach this point by focusing briefly on a puzzling aspect of the current discussion. Hohfeld's insistence on reducibility is somewhat baffling, given that his analytical scheme of jural relations can handle corporate rights and other corporate entitlements with ease. Within that scheme, rights supply various forms of protection (pertaining to non-interference or assistance or remuneration) while the correlates of rights impose various limitations. Hence, to declare that a group holds a certain right is merely to say that it enjoys moral or legal protection against someone else in a certain specified manner; likewise, to declare that a group bears a duty which correlates with someone else's right is merely to say that someone enjoys moral or legal protection against the group in a certain specified way. Far from being mystificatory or fanciful, these ascriptions of legal rights and duties are straightforward Hohfeldian ascriptions. Why was Hohfeld so uneasy about them, then?

Undoubtedly, Hohfeld's concern stemmed from his belief that statements about the characteristics of groups are simply shorthand for more complex statements about the people (or the characteristics of the people) who compose the groups. Time and again he ridiculed the notion that a corporation can in any way be distinct from its stockholders and other members. Now, to be sure, such scorn is apposite when it is construed rather generously as a reminder that every corporate action must be an action or a set of actions taken by some individual(s). But when Hohfeld proceeded to deride as fictional the imputation of any entitlements to groups, he confused explicability with reducibility. A group's characteristics can be fully explicated by reference to its members and their characteristics, without being reducible thereto.

Before looking at the explicability/reducibility distinction specifically in regard to the imputation of entitlements, we should ponder it in regard to an easily grasped example. Suppose that somebody declares that a certain group of people is large. Obviously, such a declaration does not maintain that the group's members are large; they might be midgets. But the declaration does describe a characteristic of the group that can be fully explicated by reference to individual members. More precisely, the largeness of the group can be explicated by reference to the multiplicity of its members. Once the number of members has passed a certain level—a level that will be defined variously by different observers—the group will come to be classified as large. Nothing other than the members' numerousness accounts for the group's largeness. To seek to expound that largeness by reference to anything else would be asinine. However, the fact that the group's largeness can be fully explicated through our highlighting of the manifoldness of its members does not imply that a description of the group as large is fictional or misleading. Our explication does not undermine such a description or render it superfluous. On the contrary, the largeness so expounded is a characteristic of the members *in their collective status as a group*. With respect to collectivities, the word 'large' means 'consisting of many members'; such a meaning, which defines largeness by pointing solely to individuals, cannot apply to individuals except in so far as they are *constitutive of a group*. Far from showing the falseness or dispensableness of references to associations of individuals, the individual-focused exposition of an association's largeness reveals that such references are essential. Explicability does not amount to reducibility.

Much the same can be said when we turn our attention to the matter of collective entitlements. Just as the largeness of a collectivity can be fully expounded by reference to individuals without being reducible thereto, so the legal positions of a collectivity can be fully expounded by reference to individuals' legal positions without being reducible thereto. When we attribute an entitlement to a corporate body, we do more than attribute (implicitly) to individuals the entitlements that operationalize the corporate entitlement.

As has been mentioned, Hohfeld's jurisprudential framework is well suited to convey the nature of collective entitlements. When we impute to some group a right, for example, we thereby affirm that that group is entitled to non-interference or assistance or remuneration on the part of the person (individual or corporate) who bears the correlative duty. Such a situation can be explicated through descriptions of moral or legal relations between individuals, but cannot be reduced to such relations. To apprehend why there is no reducibility here, let us suppose that the group's right protects one or more of the group's interests. (The Interest Theory of rights entails this supposition, of course, while the Will Theory of rights allows it.) Let us suppose further that one of the protected interests is the group's interest in cohesion, a basic interest of just about any association. Now, this interest can be explicated by reference to individuals' interests. Each member of the group may well have an interest in continuing to interact with other members of the group along lines that would very likely be unavailable if the group were to dissolve. Each member may also have an interest in enjoying certain benefits that come from the interaction of other members—interaction that would be highly unlikely if the interacting parties were not members of the same association. Or, at any rate, *many* of the group's members may have these interests. Whatever be the exact nature of the benefits that flow to some or all of the relevant individuals from the continuation of their group, those benefits can be invoked to explicate the collective interest in the group's cohesion. None the less, although the collectivity's interest in its own cohesion is indeed susceptible to being expounded in this manner, it is not *equatable* with any set of individuals' interests. Once again, explicability is not collapsibility or reducibility.

We must distinguish here between an interest in a group's cohesion and an interest in certain benefits that result from a group's cohesion. Some or all of a group's members may each have a direct interest of the latter sort—in which case they each have an indirect or mediated interest of the former sort, an indirect or mediated interest in the cohesion of the group. Only in so far as the members are *constitutive of a group*, however, do they have a *direct* interest in the group's cohesion. *Qua* association, the members collectively have a direct interest in staying together (as an association); unless they stay together, after all, they will lose their very standing as an association. This direct interest of the members *qua* collectivity cannot be reduced to a welter of indirect interests, in part because no congeries of indirect interests can in themselves add up to a direct interest, and in part because the direct interest can abide even while the indirect interests shift or partly disappear.

On the one hand, to be sure, if *no* individuals are any longer benefiting at all from their participation as the members of some group, and therefore if none of them has any indirect interest in the continuation of the group, then their collective enterprise itself will be better off dissolved than sustained. Much the same will usually be true of a group that confers benefits on only a very small proportion of its members. In such circumstances, the members collectively in their status as an overarching body have no direct interest in the body's survival. On the other hand, when the continuation of a group does benefit a large proportion of its members, the group itself (from the perspective of its members as a collectivity) is better off sustained than dissolved; it has a direct interest in its own continued existence. That interest can abide even if the particular advantages conferred by the group on its members are continually shifting, and even if some members cease to derive advantages from the group altogether. To some extent, indeed, an association's interest in its own robustness can conflict with the interests of all or most of its members. So long as measures which reinforce the durability of an association do not reduce individual members' benefits too sharply, such measures can advance the interests of the association (specifically, its interests in its own continuation) at the expense of the individual members' interests. Subject only to the proviso that a group is not better off by enduring unless a large proportion of the people who belong to it will gain more than they lose therefrom, the needs and interests of the group relating to its own continuation will have transcended the individual needs and interests of the people who belong to it. Thus, although each member's indirect interest in a collectivity's existence must be invoked for a full explication of the collectivity's direct interest in its own survival—an explication which must elaborate all the manifold consequences of that survival—the direct interest is not equivalent or reducible to the indirect interests.

This point about an association's interest in its own cohesion will apply, *mutatis mutandis*, to the other interests of an association as well. Because a group is an overarching structure, it can never be reduced to the individual interactions that are its components—notwithstanding that it can be thoroughly explicated by reference to those components. Its interests do not amount to a sum or welter of individual interests, since its interests are those which characterize its members *qua* collectivity rather than those which characterize its members *qua* individuals. Therefore, given that at least some of the rights which are ascribed to corporate bodies will protect corporate interests such as the interest in cohesion, and given that corporate interests are irreducible to the interests of the corporate body's members, the functions of collective entitlements are irreducible to the functions of any set of individual entitlements.

Hohfeld himself unwittingly revealed the inadvisability of his views on collective entitlements, when he sought to explain why the 'only conduct of which the state can take notice by its laws *must* spring from natural persons' (*FLC*, 198, emphasis in original). In a footnote he quoted the following passage from a Harvard Law Review article by E. H. Warren: 'A human being is, in the nature of things, a unit. A philosopher might entertain a doubt upon this—*homo* might seem to him merely a convenient word by which to designate a large number of molecules [or body parts or behavioral roles or bits of experience]. But the common law judges seem never to have doubted'.[22] What Warren has indicated *malgré lui* is that the capacity of a being as an entitlement-holder will hinge not on the unproblematic unity of the being, but on the status bestowed by the relevant legal system. Like a group, a human being is in some respects a multiplicity and in some respects a unity (even if the group's multiplicity and the individual's unity are more obvious than the group's unity and the individual's multiplicity); yet the respects in which a human being is a multiplicity do not negate the respects in which he or she is a unity, and do not prevent him or her from holding entitlements which protect interests that are not reducible to the interests of his or her parts. Much the same can be said about groups, which—like individual human beings—are capable of holding entitlements that protect interests which are not reducible to the interests of the members. Hence, if a human being with multifarious components can hold entitlements because of his overall unity as a person which makes him more than a bald collection of parts, we ought not to be surprised that a collectivity with multifarious members can hold entitlements by dint of its overall unity as an organization (or corporate person) which makes it more than a simple medley of individuals.

Of course, the members of a group are different from the components of a human being in that they are themselves entitlement-holders. Accordingly, the temptation to be reductionist when we are analysing the entitlements of a corporate body is present in a way that does not apply when we are analysing the entitlements of an individual. None the less, for reasons that have been explored, an effort to equate collective entitlements with sets of individual entitlements cannot withstand scrutiny. Such an effort overlooks the fact that an individual-focused explication of how corporate entitlements *work*—which may be a scrupulously thorough explication—cannot exhaustively recount what such entitlements *do*. Only when the members of a collectivity are seen not only as individuals but also as a collectivity, can we exhaustively recount the *effects* of collective entitlements.

[22] EH Warren, 'Collateral Attack on Incorporation', 21 Harvard L Rev 305 (1908), quoted in *FLC* (n 1 above), 198, n 12. Cf Paul's First Letter to the Corinthians 12:12–26.

How, then, does this long discussion of collective legal or moral positions impinge on the Correlativity Axiom? Unless we recognize the reality of collective entitlements, we shall have to conclude that numerous duties are uncorrelated with any rights (for reasons which are presented below). And thus we shall have to concede that the Correlativity Axiom falls far short of a universal reign. However, given that that axiom has been presented herein as true by definition, we can scarcely accept that its reign is less than universal. Therefore, with the backing of the discussion that has just been offered, we are driven to reject Hohfeld's nominalism and to recognize the reality of collective entitlements.

Myriad analysts of the formal aspects of rights have observed that certain duties are not correlated with any rights held by individuals. Most notable among these duties are the so-called public duties such as the duty to pay taxes or the duty to engage in military service when required. A typical proponent of the Will Theory of rights would mention here also most of the duties established by the criminal law, which cannot be waived by the individuals whom they protect. Before we look more searchingly at these duties that are not correlated with individual rights, we ought to observe that Hohfeld never wrote about them in connection with his scheme of jural relationships. As this essay seeks to extend the Correlativity Axiom into the domains of public duties and the criminal law, it moves into territories which Hohfeld left largely unexamined. Hence, we cannot know whether he himself would have sought to bring his analytical scheme to bear on public duties and the criminal law, or whether he would have confined that scheme to private law and some kindred areas (such as the law of corporations). In any case, regardless of how Hohfeld might have reacted to this essay's extension of his Correlativity Axiom, we shall see that such an extension must forswear his stance on the reality of corporate entitlements.

Advocates of the Interest Theory of rights and advocates of the Will Theory agree that public duties are not correlated with individual rights. If a proponent of the Correlativity Axiom were to argue that public duties are owed to the officials who enforce them, then he or she would simply be misunderstanding the nature of such duties. My duty to pay my irksomely heavy taxes is not owed to the inspector who will investigate my failure to abide by that duty. Nor is that duty owed to any particular member of the general public.

(We shall later plumb the exact reasons for affirming that public duties are not correlated with individual rights. At present, an appeal to common sense will suffice.) As has been remarked, many proponents of the Will Theory of rights would add that most of the duties imposed by the criminal law are likewise uncorrelated with any individual rights.

Now, when confronted with duties that actually or supposedly do not correlate with individual rights, most analysts have inferred that the Correlativity Axiom does not apply to such duties. A far more advisable inference, however, is that the Correlativity Axiom encompasses collective legal positions—including collective rights, of course—as well as individual legal positions. Once we have grasped that a collectivity's legal positions are quite as real as an individual's legal positions, we can submit that any public duty is owed to a collectivity (the state, the nation, the community) which holds the correlative right. A strict right–duty correlation does indeed characterize every public duty along with every private duty; the only difference is that each public duty correlates with a collective right only, whereas each private duty correlates with an individual right. The party wronged by a breach of a public duty is the political grouping that holds the correlative right. (For scholars who perceive all or most criminal-law duties as uncorrelated with individual rights, we can of course extend the verdict of this paragraph. From the supposed fact that criminal-law duties are uncorrelated with individual rights, no one should infer that they are uncorrelated with rights *tout court*. Any criminal-law obligation is owed to the political unit which holds the right to compliance therewith. A strict right–duty correlation obtains here as much as everywhere else.)

Like other duty–right pairings, public duties and their correlative rights can be justified in a right-focused manner or in a duty-focused manner or in a manner that ascribes equal importance to rights and duties. Think, for example, of each individual's public obligation to serve in the armed forces. Duty-based justifications of such an obligation and its correlative right could stress the importance of military service in promoting the strength and hardihood and maturity of the men and women who undergo the discipline of such service. Additionally, the duty-based justifications might point to the salutary effect on the character of a person who must expect to make sacrifices in return for the benefits gained from living in his or her society; and, of course, the fairness of the demand for such sacrifices in return for such benefits would also probably be stressed. Right-based justifications, on the other hand, could emphasize the armed forces' need for reliable and large flows of entrants into their ranks. Such justifications might also join the duty-based justifications in stressing the fairness of conscription. Here, however, the focus would lie on the warrantedness of programmes which furnish vital support to public institutions that greatly benefit the people who are called upon for support—whereas the focus in a duty-based appeal to fairness would lie on the warrantedness of programmes which require people to give as well as receive.

It should go without saying that neither a right-based mode nor a duty-based mode of justification will belie the Correlativity Axiom. Quite the contrary. A right-based approach justifies various duties by dint of having justified their correlative rights, while a duty-based approach justifies various rights by dint of having justified their correlative duties. As was argued earlier, a justificational focus does not imply an analytical or existential priority. The justificational focus arises with respect to norms which come under the universal sway of the Correlativity Axiom. No matter whether rights belong to collectivities or to individuals, they must always correlate with duties.

2 Rights Without Trimmings

Having set the Hohfeldian table of legal positions, this essay will rely on that table while entering the debate between the Interest Theory and the Will Theory of rights. No trimmings will adorn the table as we proceed, for this essay will value analytical clarity and rigour more than any political considerations. To be sure, as will be demonstrated hereafter, no theory of rights can avoid drawing on evaluative assumptions. Still, those assumptions can be uncontroversial (albeit not incontrovertible, of course), and here they are indeed as pleasingly thin as possible. This essay aspires to present a framework wherein disputes about the proper substance and distribution of rights can occur; it does not itself attempt to prescribe which rights should be bestowed or how they should be allotted.

The second half of this essay begins by laying out the points of contention between the Interest Theory and the Will Theory. My conspectus will reveal that Hohfeld's analytical scheme is wholly neutral between the opposing theories. Although Hohfeld himself probably adhered to the Interest Theory,[23] he never declared his allegiance; in any event, his table of jural relationships can redound to the profit of the advocates of the Will Theory as much as to the profit of the champions of the Interest Theory. After having outlined the debate between the two broad accounts of rights, this essay examines some of the many shortcomings in the Will Theory. It then provides a detailed exposition of the Interest Theory. That exposition will defend the Interest Theory against certain charges that are often levelled at it, and will clarify some important problems that are usually not tackled by the proponents of the Interest Theory. Plainly, the version of the Interest Theory espoused here will depart in certain respects from other versions of that theory which have been propounded in recent years. Readers could infer as much from the fact that some prominent spokesmen for the Interest Theory (such as MacCormick and Raz) have sharply distanced themselves from Hohfeld. No such distancing will occur here. This essay continues largely in the spirit of Hohfeld even while it addresses itself to problems which he did not ponder.

An Overview of the Debate

The basic idea underlying the Interest Theory is that every right protects some aspect of a person's welfare, which may or may not include some aspect of the person's freedom. Many variants of such

---

[23] I admire John Finnis's analyses of Hohfeld, but I see little evidence for the assertion that '[i]t seems that Hohfeld himself would have favoured the [Will Theory] had he squarely faced the [debate between the Interest Theory and the Will Theory].' John Finnis, *Natural Law and Natural Rights* (Oxford: Clarendon Press, 1980), 202. Militating against Finnis's conjecture—albeit far from conclusively—is the language in *FLC* (n 1 above), 79, n 34 (emphases in original): 'Professor Beale ... defines "a right" as an "*interest*", not as some *legal relation* protecting the interest: there is a very obvious difference—and one vitally important for the solution of problems in the conflict of laws—between a mere *factual interest* and its *legal recognition* (legal claims, privileges, etc.).' What tells more potently against Finnis's view is that Hohfeld very frequently used the term 'rights' to refer to mere claims (which may or may not be coupled with powers of enforcement/waiver in the hands of the claim-holders). An advocate of the Will Theory would want to preserve a clear distinction between rights and claims.

a theory are possible (as has just been remarked), but virtually any doctrine classifiable as an Interest Theory of rights would subscribe to the following two theses:

(1) Necessary but insufficient for the actual holding of a right by a person X is that the right, when actual, preserves one or more of X's interests.
(2) X's being competent and authorized to demand or waive the enforcement of a right is neither sufficient nor necessary for X to be endowed with that right.

Much remains to be said about these two tenets, and indeed a large portion of this essay will seek to elaborate and defend them. Before we probe them further, however, we should juxtapose them with the main tenets of the Will Theory.

The basic idea underlying the Will Theory is that every right is a vehicle for some aspect of an individual's self-determination or initiative. The variants of such a theory are numerous, but all or most of them subscribe to the following three principles:

(1a) Sufficient and necessary for X's holding of a right is that X is competent and authorized to demand or waive the enforcement of the right.
(2a) X's holding of a right does not necessarily involve the protection of one or more of X's interests.
(3a) A right's potential to protect one or more of X's interests is not sufficient per se for X's actual possession of that right.

Note that the third of these tenets is characteristic not only of the Will Theory but also of the Interest Theory. Both theories insist that a right's mere potential to protect an interest is *not* a sufficient condition for the actuality of the right. In every other chief respect, however, the principles of the theories clash directly.

Certain aspects of the two theories need to be clarified, before we can see why Hohfeld's scheme of jural relations does not in itself favour one or the other side in this debate. For instance, we need to apprehend what counts as the enforcement or waiver of rights, to which the second principle of the Interest Theory and the first principle of the Will Theory refer. Enforcement or waiver is not a single event but is a process with stages, as H. L. A. Hart pointed out (Hart, 'Legal Rights', 183–4). Prior to any breach of a duty owed by X to Y, Y may have a power to waive the duty and thus to extinguish or suspend her own right. Once an unwaived duty has been breached, *Y* may have a power to decide whether or not a remedy should be sought through legal proceedings. Finally, if a judgment has been rendered in *Y*'s favour against *X*, *Y* may have a power to decide whether or not the terms of the judgment should be implemented. At these three main stages in the process of enforcement—each of which can be analysed into subdivisions—the holding of the relevant powers by *Y* will endow her with control over *X*'s duty. Versions of the Will Theory differ in regard to the number of enforcement/waiver powers that must be held by *Y* before we can classify her as a right-holder in her relation with *X*. The boldest versions of the theory insist that *Y* must hold an enforcement/waiver power at each of the three main junctures that have been described here.[24] In any case, whatever be the number of enforcing/waiving powers that will be deemed sufficient to get *Y*'s claim designated as a right, the fundamental idea is that such a designation implies that *Y* enjoys decisive control over the effectuation of her claim.

Another point that deserves some brief amplification is the notion of being 'competent and authorized' to demand or waive the enforcement of a claim. Being 'authorized' (by legal or moral norms) to demand or waive the enforcement of a claim is formally equivalent to holding a power (conferred by legal or moral norms) which enables one to choose between the demand and the waiver. A liberty to make such a choice usually accompanies the power to make the choice, but the latter does not *have* to be combined with the former. Someone can exercise decisive control over the effectuation of his own claim, while being under a duty not to do so; the breach of duty can incur a penalty without nullifying the exercise of the power.

To a large extent, the reference to competence in 'competent and authorized' is pleonastic, since one's legal or moral competence to do ϕ is a prerequisite of one's being legally or morally authorized to do ϕ. Legal or moral authorization entails legal or moral competence. (Hence, where there is no recognized competence, there is no authorization. For example, the reason that children are not authorized to determine the enforcement or waiver of their claims is that their youthfulness is deemed to render them incompetent to reach clear-sighted determinations.) None the less, the requirement of competence merits special emphasis—because formal authorization is not in itself sufficient for the holding of a genuine power, as

[24] For an example of this view, marred by missteps in the application of Hohfeld's framework, see Steiner, *Rights* (n 3 above), 68–73.

opposed to a nominal power. In addition to being formally authorized to make a choice, a person with a genuine power must be factually *capable* of making the choice. If X is authorized to select between the options of initiating legal proceedings and abstaining from such proceedings, and if X is none the less mentally incapacitated from choosing at all, then he does not hold a genuine Hohfeldian power. And, in such a situation, X certainly does not hold a power which the proponents of the Will Theory would acknowledge as meeting the standards of their doctrine.

A brief example can highlight the importance of factual competence. Suppose that Y has assaulted Z and has left him comatose and has thus left him unable to choose whether or not to initiate civil proceedings against Y. Suppose further that the law of the land does not make any arrangement for civil proceedings to be brought by someone else on Z's behalf in such circumstances; instead, the failure by Z himself to initiate the proceedings is deemed to be a straightforward eschewal of such proceedings. In this situation, Z's inaction has resulted in the extinguishing of his power to obtain a remedy against Y. Yet Z has exercised a power-extinguishing power in only a formal or nominal sense. His 'choice' to forbear from legal action has emerged purely by default, rather than as a consequence of any decision which he has made. Such a 'choice' is not sufficient to count as the exercise of a genuine Hohfeldian power and is plainly not sufficient to count as an instance of the sort of control (over one's rights) which the Will Theory's devotees have in mind.

Let us proceed, then, to consider the broader relationship between Hohfeld's jurisprudence and the Interest Theory/Will Theory controversy. In effect, the advocates of the Will Theory contend that rights and claims are not equivalent. Unlike Hohfeld, they apply the label of 'rights' only to claims that are coupled with genuine powers of enforcement/waiver on the part of the claim-holders; they do not attach the label of 'rights' to claims that are unaccompanied by genuine powers of enforcement/waiver on the part of the claim-holders. Not only does the adherent of the Will Theory submit that claims must be enforceable if they are to qualify as genuine claims—a proposition with which any adherent of the Interest Theory would firmly agree—but he also insists that the claims must be enforceable and waivable *by the claim-holders* if the claims are to qualify as *rights*. A champion of the Interest Theory (or, at any rate, a champion of the version of the Interest Theory propounded here), by contrast, is happy to join Hohfeld in using 'claim' and 'right' interchangeably.

We are now in a position to see why Hohfeld's account of jural relations is strictly neutral between the Interest Theory and the Will Theory, notwithstanding that the Interest Theory's application of the term 'right' is more in keeping with Hohfeld's patterns of usage. The key point here is that a Hohfeldian claim *can* be combined in a single person with a Hohfeldian power of enforcement/waiver but does not *have* to be so combined. Nothing prevents such a conjunction, and nothing necessitates it. As far as Hohfeld's analytical scheme is concerned, then, the difference between the Interest Theory and the Will Theory is simply a matter of labelling. If the exponents of the Will Theory want to use only the label 'claim' for the entitlement which Hohfeld styled as either a 'claim' or a 'right', and if they want to reserve the word 'right' for a claim accompanied by a power of enforcement/waiver in the hands of the claim-holder, then their departure from Hohfeld's scheme is merely terminological. They are not proposing any combinations or correlations which Hohfeld revealed to be untenable. So long as the Will Theorists recognize that rights as they define them are correlative with duties-plus-liabilities rather than simply with duties, they will have adhered faithfully to the matrix of correlations and negations which Hohfeld set forth.

Thus, no one can clinch the quarrel between the Interest Theorists and the Will Theorists simply by appealing to Hohfeld's insights. Sophisticated versions of the Will Theory can give heed to the logical structure of Hohfeld's analysis quite as much as can sophisticated versions of the Interest Theory, even if the latter theory presents a vocabulary closer to Hohfeld's own roster of terms. (I am loath to upbraid the Will Theorists merely because they have departed terminologically from Hohfeld's writings. After all, the theory presented here has substituted the term 'liberty' for 'privilege', which Hohfeld preferred. If the Will Theorists deserve rebukes, the justification therefor does not lie in the general fact that those theorists have declined to adhere sedulously to Hohfeld's set of labels; as we shall observe, the justification lies instead in the specific rearrangement of labels which those theorists have proposed.) Because the possession of a Hohfeldian power-of-enforcing-or-waiving-a-Hohfeldian-claim by the same person who holds the claim is neither impossible nor inevitable, the Will Theory cannot be conclusively disproved *or* conclusively supported on the basis of Hohfeld's analytical matrix. That matrix *allows* the Will Theory's definitional stipulations without *requiring* them in any way. Hence, an essay proclaiming the superiority of the Interest Theory over the Will Theory has to do much more than simply extol the virtues of Hohfeld's work. Although his work helps the three authors of the present book to state and pursue their disagreements rigorously, it does not obviate their disagreements.

On the Shortcomings of the Will Theory

One of the most striking features of the Will Theory is the tendency of its spokesmen to beg questions by taking its theses for granted. While professing to demonstrate the shortcomings of the Interest Theory and the merits of the Will Theory, the advocates of the latter theory tend to judge the former theory by measuring it against the distinctive criteria of their own stance. We should hardly be surprised that the Interest Theory falls short when the Will Theory is dogmatically presupposed as a touchstone; moreover, we ought not to be very troubled by the resulting verdict.

For an example of the Will Theorists' tendency to beg questions, let us look at Hillel Steiner's treatment of a problem that has received extensive scrutiny in the literature on rights: the problem of third-party-beneficiary contracts.[25] (We shall return to this general problem later, but for now we shall merely investigate Steiner's approach to it.) Steiner posits a situation in which he as a florist takes an order from someone for the delivery of flowers to someone else's wedding. He declares that the 'order you place with me makes you, and not the bride and groom, the holder of the right correlative to my duty to deliver flowers to their wedding' (Steiner, *Rights*, 61). He continues:

[25] For the two best analyses of this problem with which I am familiar, see Finnis (n 23 above), 203; Simmonds (n 3 above), 315–17. Also good is David Lyons, *Rights, Welfare, and Mill's Moral Theory* (New York: Oxford University Press, 1994) [hereinafter cited as *RWMMT*], 36–44. See also Benditt (n 6 above), 18–19. Much less commendable is MacCormick, 'Legislation' (n 10 above), 208–9—an analysis that is tellingly criticized in Steiner, *Rights* (n 3 above), 63–4. Some analyses that largely oppose the Interest Theory on the topic of third-party-beneficiary contracts are Benditt (n 3 above), 165; Dias (n 4 above), 37, n 1; Feinberg (n 11 above), 137–8; Hart, 'Natural Rights' (n 11 above), 81–2; Hart, 'Legal Rights' (n 3 above), 187; Miller (n 11 above), 62, 64–5; Ross, *Justice* (n 3 above), 163, 176; Ross, *Directives* (n 3 above), 127–8; White, *Rights* (n 6 above), 63. Cf Flathman, *Practice* (n 3 above), 72.

Here then is a significant feature of *correlative* duties... It is that their existence is controllable and that our non-compliance with them is rendered permissible—they are extinguished or waived—by virtue of a choice to that effect by the persons who control them but not by the persons whose interests are served by their being performed (where the two are different parties). If your flower order stands, I have a correlative duty to deliver. And if you cancel, I no longer have that duty: not even if my not delivering would seriously disserve the marrying couple's interests. With respect to my delivering the flowers, they are the beneficiaries but they are not the right-holders.

This fact, that the beneficiaries of a claim/duty relation can be rightless third parties, poses a considerable difficulty for [the Interest Theory]. ... For these are cases where right-holders not only lack the essential characteristic required by that theory, but also they possess the essential characteristic required by [the Will Theory]. It is the controllers of the duty, and not its beneficiaries, who are the right-holders. ... Contrary to [what the Interest Theory asserts], there is no one-to-one correspondence between being a right-holder and being the beneficiary of a correlative duty. (Steiner, *Rights*, 62.)

In light of the final sentence from this long quotation, we should note—in a very brief digression which will be amplified later—that no version of the Interest Theory postulates a one-to-one correspondence between being a right-holder and being a beneficiary of a correlative duty. Proponents of the Interest Theory maintain that every right-holder is a beneficiary of a duty, but they do not maintain that every beneficiary of a duty is a right-holder.

More relevant here, however, is Steiner's begging of the question. Not only has Steiner unwisely taken for granted that the person ordering the flowers is not a beneficiary of the florist's duty to deliver the flowers,[26] but he also has overconfidently presupposed the Will Theory's conception of rights when he declares that the marrying couple have no right to the delivery of the flowers by the florist. To be sure, the couple have no Will Theory right to the delivery of the flowers—because such a right consists in the combination of a claim and a power of enforcing/waiving the claim, and because the couple clearly have no power to enforce a claim to the florist's delivery. But the couple clearly *do* have an Interest Theory right to the delivery, because such a right is a claim that may or may not be conjoined with a power of enforcement/waiver in the hands

---

[26] This point is made very forcefully against Steiner in Simmonds (n 3 above), 316–17.

of the claim-holder. The fact that the couple have no power to enforce or waive their claim does not mean that they have no Hohfeldian claim. Indeed, they surely *do* have such a claim, quite as much as the person who ordered the flowers. For the Will Theory, of course, a claim unconjoined with a power of enforcement/waiver in the hands of the claim-holder is a mere claim rather than a right; only for the Interest Theory (and for Hohfeld) is a mere claim a right. Thus, Steiner would be correct to deny that the marrying couple have a right to delivery, *if* he were addressing himself solely to his fellow Will Theorists. However, since he purports to be doing battle with the Interest Theory through his example of the flowers, his insistence that the couple have no right is a patent begging of the question. Steiner should not expect Interest Theorists to be impressed by an example which works in his favour only when it is described in terms which the Interest Theorists reject. According to the definitions that are operative in the Interest Theory, the couple do indeed have a right to the delivery. Hence, far from 'pos[ing] a considerable difficulty' for the Interest Theory, Steiner's example poses no difficulty whatsoever when it is presented in the only guise which the Interest Theorists accept. Instead of needing to explain away the absence of a right in the hands of the marrying couple, an Interest Theorist can point out that a right (an Interest Theory right, of course) is there to be found.

Steiner's begging of the question is by no means atypical. Many of the analyses of third-party-beneficiary contracts that were cited above have likewise dogmatically presupposed the Will Theory's definition of 'right'. In any case, the lesson to be drawn here is that neither the Interest Theory nor the Will Theory should be evaluated by reference to the standards that are peculiar to the other theory. Interest Theorists who wish to attack the Will Theory and to defend their own stance should not make their attacks hinge on the definitions and criteria that distinguish their own stance from the Will Theory. In the present part of this essay, then, where we shall explore the weaknesses of the Will Theory, the force of the criticisms does not depend on an acceptance of the Interest Theory. Instead, the criticisms—which will continue to emerge in the next main part of this essay, where the chief purpose will be to elaborate and defend the Interest Theory—are aimed at showing how many bizarrely counter-intuitive implications the Will Theory involves.

One of the most arresting theses to which the Will Theory commits its upholders is the verdict that children and mentally incapacitated people have no rights. Because infants and mentally infirm people are both factually and legally incompetent to choose between enforcing and waiving their claims against others, and because children older than infants are legally incompetent and sometimes factually incompetent to engage in enforcement/waiver decisions, they hold no powers to make such decisions. Now, given that the Will Theory insists that claims must be enforceable and waivable by claim-holders if the claims are to count as rights, it leads to the conclusion that the young and the mad do not have any rights. In a famous 1955 essay, H. L. A. Hart grasped this nettle boldly:

These considerations should incline us not to extend to animals and babies whom it is wrong to ill-treat the notion of a right to proper treatment, for the moral situation can be simply and adequately described here by saying that it is wrong or that we ought not to ill-treat them or, in the philosopher's generalized sense of 'duty', that we have a duty not to ill-treat them. If common usage sanctions talk of the rights of animals or babies it makes an idle use of the expression 'a right', which will confuse the situation with other different moral situations where the expression 'a right' has a specific force and cannot be replaced by the other moral expressions which I have mentioned. (Hart, 'Natural Rights', 82, footnote deleted.)

Many people would shrink from a theory which defines 'right' in a way that commits the proponents of the theory to the view that children and mentally infirm people have no rights at all. Even when stripped of its ghastliness by being carefully explained, such a view tends to sound outlandish when stated.

Indeed, Hart himself eventually retreated from the firm confidence of his early pronouncements on children's rights. In an essay originally published almost two decades after his essay on natural rights, he delivered a much more qualified verdict:

Where infants or other persons not *sui juris* have rights, such powers [ie, powers of enforcement/waiver]... are exercised on their behalf by appointed representatives and their exercise may be subject to approval by a court. But since (a) what such representatives can and cannot do by way of exercise of such power is determined by what those whom they represent could have done if *sui juris* and (b) when the latter become *sui juris* they can exercise those powers without any transfer or fresh assignment; the powers are regarded as belonging throughout to them and not to their representatives, though they are only exercisable by the latter during the period of disability. (Hart, 'Legal Rights', 184, n 86.)

To be sure, this passage does not mark a thoroughgoing abandonment of the Will Theory. Hart was still not willing to allow that the unwaivable duties established by the criminal law are correlative with any individual rights (Hart, 'Legal Rights', 185, n 88), and the reasoning in the passage on infants would manifestly not cover the unwaivable entitlements that are ordained by minimum-wage laws, for example. (Although the unwaivability of the entitlements in a minimum-wage scheme can be introduced because such entitlements are perceived as serving the long-term interests of every worker, a more common reason for the unwaivability is that it helps to prevent the overall scheme from collapsing and that it thus serves the long-term interests of most workers (and the long-term interests of workers as a group).) None the less, the partial retraction of the Will Theory by Hart is clear enough. However grudgingly, he was prepared to acknowledge that infants have rights even though they cannot exercise the powers of enforcing/waiving those rights. If one of the leading spokesmen for the Will Theory was daunted by some of its implications, then the opponents of that theory need feel no qualms about finding fault with it.[27]

Apart from the oddness of the Will Theory's stance on the rights of children and imbeciles, the more general failing of the theory lies in the fact that many entitlements which have usually been designated as rights are enforceable and waivable by corporate persons or individual persons other than the right-holders (and not by the right-holders themselves). Not only does the control over children's claims lie in the hands of parties other than the children, but the control over myriad claims that are held by adults is similarly dissevered from the claims themselves. Yet such claims continue to be widely denominated as 'rights'.

Let us take an example. In the United Kingdom and the United States (as well as in numerous other countries), every person has

---

[27] For some of the analyses that take exception to the Will Theory's position on children, see Benditt (n 6 above), 14, 15; MacCormick, 'Children's Rights' (n 11 above); Marshall, 'Rights' (n 21 above), 234–6. For positions similar to Hart's, see Flathman, *Practice* (n 3 above), 72, 87; Ross, *Justice* (n 3 above), 180. I should note, incidentally, that Andrei Marmor errs when he asserts that the Will Theory is a position which Hart 'at some point maintained and later discarded' (Marmor (n 7 above), 6, n 8). Hart modified his position; he did not abandon it.

both an entitlement under civil law and an entitlement under criminal law to be free from unprovoked assaults. Without a doubt, the control exercisable by each person over his own entitlements is considerably greater in regard to the civil law than in regard to the criminal law; indeed, some elements of control that exist in the civil context are altogether removed from the hands of each private individual in the criminal context. Will Theorists hence must maintain, and do quite readily maintain, that the criminal-law entitlement against assaults is not a right or that it does not exist at all. Under the criminal law, according to the Will Theorists, no one has any right to be free from unprovoked assaults. Everyone has only a claim or has no individual entitlement whatsoever. To somebody not enamoured of the Will Theory, however, this notion—the notion that each individual under the civil law has a right to be free from assaults whereas each individual under the criminal law has at most only a claim to be free from assaults—is bound to appear strained. Given that the actual or potential penalties for breaches of duty under the criminal law are very often more severe than under the civil law, one can scarcely help being puzzled by the application of the label of 'right' to each person's civil-law entitlement while that label is withheld from each person's criminal-law entitlement. Even more is one likely to feel puzzled by the assertion that no individual entitlements of any sort exist under the criminal law. After all, each person under the criminal law receives protection against assaults as surely as under the civil law, and indeed the criminal-law protection is often more imposing. Why, then, should we say that the criminal-law protection (unlike the civil-law protection) constitutes no entitlements against one's fellows?

Now, of course, the Will Theorists can warrantedly object if someone goes beyond mere puzzlement and proceeds to make allegations of outright analytical solecisms. As has been acknowledged and indeed emphasized herein, the Will Theory when properly formulated can be impeccable by Hohfeldian standards. Will Theorists' descriptions of the criminal law plainly do not require any departures from the Correlativity Axiom. So long as the Will Theorists recognize that all the duties created under the criminal law must be correlative with claims held by individuals, by private corporations, by the public, or by the state, they commit no analytical blunders when they assert that that law confers no rights and perhaps even no claims on individuals or private corporations.

(If the criminal law gives rise to no claims for individuals or private corporations, then all duties under it are none the less correlated with claims—with claims held by the public or the state only.) The complaint here is not that the Will Theorists' accounts of the criminal law are starkly erroneous, but that they are needlessly odd. Analytically acceptable though those accounts may be, they flout too many entrenched linguistic intuitions to be very powerful.

In posing these objections to the Will Theorists' portrayal of the criminal law, one hardly should disagree with those theorists about the importance of duties that are not correlated with individual claims. That is, one scarcely should lose sight of the fact that every precept in the criminal law does indeed establish a duty owed directly by each individual to the public or the state. While declaring that many such precepts also establish duties which are owed to individuals, one does not have to go as far as Lon Fuller's contention that '[t]hough we sometimes think of the criminal law as defining the citizen's duties toward his government, its primary function is to provide a sound and stable framework for the interactions of citizens with one another'.[28] Such a contention unduly slights the significance of the obligations that are owed under the criminal law to the public or the state. An opponent of the Will Theory's conception of criminal law can and should accept that criminal offences are violations of public order at least as much as they are encroachments on individual rights. To stress the latter aspect of such offences when doing battle with the Will Theory is not to deny or overlook the former aspect.

The Will Theorists' approaches to the criminal law, with their bizarre stipulations about individuals' legal positions, are plagued by the general problem that was mentioned four paragraphs ago: the Will Theory cannot do justice to the fact that many claims normally classified as rights are enforceable and waivable only by persons other than the claim-holders. Neil MacCormick has dealt at some length with the strangeness of the Will Theory's insistence that claims must be enforceable and waivable by the claim-holders

---

[28] Fuller (n 7 above), 208. For an analysis of criminal-law duties that is much closer to my analysis, see Marshall, 'Rights' (n 21 above), 234–9. For some Will Theorists' accounts of the criminal law, see Hart, 'Legal Rights' (n 3 above), 182–6; Hart, 'Natural Rights' (n 11 above), 83; White, *Rights* (n 6 above), 60–1. Hart to some extent qualifies his account by taking note of a 'wider perspective' from which the criminal law can be deemed to confer rights on individuals. See Hart, 'Legal Rights' (n 3 above), 192–3.

themselves if the claims are to qualify as rights (MacCormick, 'Legislation', 195–9). MacCormick points out that extremely important interests such as one's interest in remaining alive are typically protected by inalienable claims, whereas a variety of less important interests such as one's interest in retaining one's possession of certain books are typically protected by alienable claims, that is, by claims coupled with powers of alienation. According to the Will Theory, then, only the latter set of claims will count as rights. Yet we thus are forced to conclude that—according to the Will Theory—the firmest protections of our truly vital interests do not amount to rights, whereas the less formidable protections of relatively inconsequential interests do amount to rights. MacCormick appositely inquires whether we really should think 'that the language of the practical lawyer does such violence to common understanding as to extrude...protections of [basic] human interests, when arguably at their most efficacious, from the category which it is interesting or useful to describe as "rights"?' (MacCormick, 'Legislation', 196.)

MacCormick furnishes other telling examples as well, in which he highlights the bizarreness of the Will Theory's classifications. For instance, he observes that—according to the Will Theory—each of us has a right to be free from minor assaults but no right to be free from truly grievous assaults. Perhaps the most incisive contribution of MacCormick's discussion, however, is his awareness that his attack on the Will Theory does not expose analytical errors but instead exposes some gratuitous contraventions of ordinary patterns of usage:

Admittedly, we are to some extent in the realms of stipulative definition when we enter into contention over the essential characteristics of the concept 'right'. Yet we are entitled to ask somebody who stipulates that there shall be held to be 'rights' only where there are choices, whether that stipulation does not go wholly against common understanding, and whether there is any profit derived from it. (MacCormick, 'Legislation', 196–7).

To be sure, the 'common understanding' to which MacCormick appeals should not always be determinative of our classificatory decisions. After all, as Hohfeld amply demonstrated, ordinary patterns of usage tend to categorize a number of liberties and powers and immunities as 'rights'. When those distinct entitlements are lumped together as 'rights', the 'common understanding' is to be resisted. However, unlike the distinctions on which the Will Theory insists, the Hohfeldian distinctions among entitlements are neither strange nor gratuitous; and the considerations underlying them are analytical rather than political.

When we distinguish rights from liberties and powers and immunities, and when we therefore say (for example) that each person has a liberty rather than a right to speak her mind on various issues, we are not introducing a risibly jarring pattern of usage. Even less does the right/liberty distinction create a jarring effect when we add that each person's liberty of speech is accompanied by a perimeter of rights such as rights to bodily and reputational integrity. Though the Hohfeldian terms do not get employed very precisely during most instances of everyday discourse, they do often get employed in largely the ways in which Hohfeld used them. Within the domain of common discourse, there is plainly nothing ludicrous about saying (for example) that each person has a power rather than a right to form contracts—a power that is almost certainly supplemented by rights to be free from certain kinds of interference with the making of contracts. When judged by the everyday ear, Hohfeldian terms fill their assigned roles smoothly and naturally. We do not find here anything counter-intuitive which might be comparable to the Will Theory's insistence that rights are no longer rights when they protect crucial interests unyieldingly.

While the terminological distinctions favoured by this essay are more acceptable to the common understanding than is the Will Theory's 'right'/'claim' distinction, they are also more clearly warranted. In the course of elaborating the basic structure of deontic logic, Hohfeld needed distinct tags for the two first-order entitlements and the two second-order entitlements. Although he could have selected only 'claim' instead of both 'claim' and 'right' in order to designate the correlative of a duty, he would thereby have omitted a key deontic term from his lexicon. And, indeed, given that the word 'right' so strongly suggests the imposition of a requirement, an omission of that term would have pointlessly kept it from filling a role for which it is eminently suitable. Considerably less impressive is the basis for the Will Theorists' use of 'right' to distinguish claims-with-powers-of-enforcement-or-waiver from mere claims. Such a distinction lends itself to being marked with phrases such as 'waivable right' versus 'unwaivable right', and 'alienable right' versus 'inalienable right'. Not only can these and other pairs of contrasting phrases do the work of the 'right'/'claim' pair, but they offer two advantages. First, they allow the expression of subtleties and variations; the waivable/unwaivable distinction is not exactly the same as the alienable/inalienable distinction, for example. Second, they highlight the fact that the Will Theorists' right/claim distinction is not between one basic Hohfeldian position and another, but between a compound position (composed of a claim plus a power) and a basic position. In sum, the Will Theorists' terminological dichotomy is redundant—for the particular use to which the Will Theorists put it—and is not as illuminating as some readily available alternatives. Moreover, it yields some results that tend to strike the ordinary observer as ridiculous.

As has been remarked, Hohfeld had to flag the distinctions between rights (or claims) and other entitlements in order to differentiate the positions that make up a structure of deontic logic. In other words, the considerations underlying his distinctions were fundamentally analytical. We encounter quite a different situation when we turn our attention to the Will Theory's right/claim dichotomy. Although there is of course an analytical distinction between a claim that is combined with a power of enforcement/waiver (in the hands of the claim-holder) and a claim that is not so combined, the principal motive for the Will Theorists' emphasis on the right/claim dichotomy is political. When Will Theorists reserve the term 'rights' for claims that are combined with enforcement/waiver powers and liberties in the hands of the claim-holders, they do so primarily because they want to stress the importance of individual discretion and self-determination. They are less concerned to highlight logical differences and logical relations than they are to pay homage to the value of individual choice, a value which they present as integrally connected with rights. Because the term 'right' is a highly respectful and respected label in the modern West, the Will Theorists wish to confine it to situations that are characterized by the ideal (namely, the ideal of individual self-determination) which they themselves respect most.[29]

[29] For some discussions of the political vision animating the Will Theory—some discussions by Will Theorists and by their critics—see MacCormick, 'Children's Rights' (n 11 above), 164–6; MacCormick, 'Legislation' (n 10 above), 207–8; Ross, *Justice* (n 3 above), 177–8; Ross, *Directives* (n 3 above), 127–8; Simmonds (n 3 above), 315, 316, n 23; Sumner, *MFR* (n 5 above), 96–101; Waldron, *RPP* (n 11 above), 98–9.

Now, of course, a fundamentally political basis for one's choice of a deontic vocabulary is not necessarily illegitimate, especially when one's political values are as attractive as those to which the Will Theorists pay tribute. But the Will Theorists often muddy the relevant political issues by propounding their value-laden stance in such a way that they appear to be making a fundamentally conceptual point. Even when such misleading appearances are kept to a minimum, the Will Theorists' pursuit of their political concerns is inadvisable—partly because that pursuit is not adequately straightforward, and partly because it is not adequately restrictive. Their tack is inadequately straightforward because it focuses not on the pertinent political questions directly, but on the proper use of the term 'right' and on the proper application of the concept of 'right'. Even when the Will Theorists make clear that their terminological preferences stem from their political preferences, they are engaging in a debate that is usually taken to be a conceptual controversy over the nature of rights. While seeking to influence our political predilections, the Will Theorists are embroiled in highly subtle and abstract disputes about the conditions that are necessary or sufficient for the holding of a right. Such disputes are of great interest to philosophers who wish to bring clarity and rigour into theoretical discussions of rights; somewhat doubtful is whether such disputes are of interest to more than a handful of the participants in politically charged exchanges about the desirability of individual self-determination.

In addition to being strangely remote as a means of shoring up the dignity of the individual, the Will Theory lends itself to a variety of notions about the factors that can and should result in the vesting of most claim-holders with powers of enforcing/waiving most of their claims. When the opportunity for individual self-determination is presented as a quasi-conceptual precondition for the existence of rights, other reasons for coupling claims with powers of enforcement/waiver can easily get overlooked. To be sure, one chief reason for favouring the endowment of most claim-holders with control over most of their claims is that an ability to exert such control will help each person to shape the course of her own life. But other reasons can also loom large. For instance, the advisability of vesting most people with control over their claims can lie in the consequent assurance that those with the greatest incentives to see the claims properly enforced will be able to direct the enforcement.

Alternatively, the granting of such control may spring from a recognition that modes of protection which are generally beneficial can be detrimental in specific applications; to avert or minimize the harm of such applications, a legal system may authorize each protected party to suspend his or her enjoyment of a mode of protection whenever prudence so dictates.

Of course, these alternative grounds for advocating the conferral of enforcement/waiver powers on claim-holders are not incompatible with the Will Theory. On the contrary, they provide further political support for the Will Theorists' terminological preferences. What should be noticed, however, is that the two alternative grounds just mentioned are both often associated with moral stances that attach little or no intrinsic importance to individual self-determination. The first of those grounds, relating to the incentives for enforcement, can easily form part of a doctrine which proposes that a legal system should set entitlements in a way that maximizes aggregate wealth; such a wealth-maximizing doctrine treats individuals' incentives as tools to be used in the service of the collective goal. Similarly, the objective of reducing the onerous effects of general norms can easily find a place within some versions of utilitarianism, in furtherance of the aspiration of maximizing overall happiness and minimizing overall displeasure.

Obviously, the two alternative rationales for claim–power combinations are not *ineluctably* associated with credos oriented toward the realization of aggregate maxima. But the rationales undoubtedly *can* be associated therewith—which means that the Will Theory can come to be embraced by the proponents of certain doctrines which many Will Theorists deplore. Such doctrines treat individuals' decision-making faculties as instruments rather than as intrinsically valuable features; those doctrines can align themselves with the Will Theory's emphasis on individual discretion while doing so merely because of the serviceability of such discretion for the promotion of the collective weal. In short, not only is the Will Theory too rarefied to be a highly effective political intervention, but it is also too protean in its politics. Someone who opts for the Will Theory on primarily political grounds will have thereby failed to commend his or her political values with sufficient specificity. The Will Theorists who wish to take stands in political controversies should participate in those controversies more directly and with a tighter focus. Until they do, they leave themselves in the position of a man pursuing a game of cards with opponents who are in another room and who are able to determine how his hand will be played.

In Praise of the Interest Theory

Thus far, we have looked at some of the weaknesses in the Will Theory. We have not explored *all* the weaknesses in that theory by any means, and we have not yet studied the advantages of the Interest Theory in any detail. This final main portion of my essay will highlight some further shortcomings in the Will Theory while undertaking a sustained exposition of a tenable Interest Theory.

Some of the notable strengths of the Interest Theory are simply the reversals of some inadequacies of the Will Theory. Unlike the latter theory, the Interest Theory can readily ascribe rights to children and to mentally incapacitated people (and indeed to animals, if a theorist wishes); it can acknowledge that the criminal law bestows individual rights on the people who are protected by the various statutes and other mandates that impose criminal duties; and it maintains that any genuine right does not have to be waivable and enforceable by the right-holder but can be waivable and enforceable by someone else instead. The last of the points just mentioned—the recognition of the possible unwaivability of a right by a right-holder—will have meant, for example, that the Interest Theory can attribute rights to workers under a minimum-wage law even though the workers cannot themselves waive or enforce their entitlements to be paid at a certain level.

In probing the defects of the Will Theory, then, we have already ferreted out some virtues of the Interest Theory. Moreover, some alleged difficulties for the latter theory have already been countered in this essay, at least *en passant*. One such putative difficulty is not peculiar to the Interest Theory but is something that must also be tackled by versions of the Will Theory which accept the Correlativity Axiom: namely, the absence of correlations between certain duties and any individual rights. As has been submitted, collectivities as well as individuals can hold rights. Hence, public duties do indeed correlate with rights—with collective rights rather than with the rights of any individuals. Once we recognize that groups can be endowed with rights which are not reducible to individual rights, we shall not presume that a Hohfeldian version of the Interest Theory must postulate a constant connection between duties and the safeguarding of *individuals'* interests.

Some other alleged shortcomings of the Interest Theory, which are seen as characteristic only of it and not of the Will Theory, have likewise been discounted here—albeit more obliquely. For instance, we are now in a position to respond to critics who condemn the Interest Theory for its failure to specify why some interests receive legal protection while others do not.[30] Contrary to what such strictures suggest, the Interest Theory (the Interest Theory expounded here, at any rate) is not a political theory; like Hohfeld's analytical jurisprudence, it does *not* attempt to prescribe the appropriate distribution of entitlements. Questions concerning who should hold which entitlements are questions not for analytical jurisprudence but for political philosophy and for ordinary political discourse. When the Interest Theory contends that rights are modes of protection for interests that are treated as worthy of such protection, it is setting forward a thesis about the general nature or structure of rights. It is not advancing any criterion or set of criteria for what should count as the 'worthiness' of an interest. Instead of flowing from the Interest Theory and instead of serving as essential aspects of it, any criteria for worthiness would supplement it.

Complaints about another supposed defect of the Interest Theory—its supposed inability to expound the jural relations involved in third-party-beneficiary contracts—have likewise surfaced herein and have been dismissed. When this topic arose earlier, we looked principally at the Will Theorists' question-begging assertion that a contract does not confer any right on a third-party beneficiary who lacks a power of enforcement/waiver. My discussion much more briefly indicated that the Will Theorists are also wrong in maintaining that the contractual party who elicits a promise for the benefit of a third person does not have an interest in the performance of the contract. Let us now give a bit more attention to this second point, since the Will Theorists' view of this matter is exceedingly dubious. A typical promisee who procures an undertaking for the good of a third party has at least two interests in the fulfilment of the undertaking by the promisor. One main reason for his generally wishing to see the fulfilment of the undertaking is that it constitutes the

---

[30] For an example of such criticism, see Steiner, *Rights* (n 3 above), 62–3. For a closely related (and equally misdirected) criticism, see Dias (n 4 above), 37, n 1.

fulfilment of an undertaking *to him*. A person generally has an interest in not being deceived. A second interest of the typical promisee lies in knowing that a gain of some sort will accrue to the person whom the promisee has sought to help. A typical human being X does not usually make arrangements to benefit Y unless X feels some concern for Y's well-being or unless he wants to ingratiate himself with Y or unless he aims to meet the terms of an independent commitment to Y. When X sets in motion a chain of events that will tend to satisfy his concern for the good of Y or his wish to endear himself to Y or his need to abide by an independent duty which he owes to Y, he has an interest in the completion of that chain. Only by disregarding the ways in which human agents sometimes harbour fellow feeling for one another and sometimes curry favour with one another and sometimes fulfil commitments by arranging goods or services for one another, can the Will Theorists declare flatly that a promisee does not have any interest in the execution of a contract which he or she has made for the furtherance of someone else's projects.

Hence, when we attribute a right to the promisee in a third-party-beneficiary contract, we should do so not because of his power to enforce or waive his claim against the promisor, but because of the interest-protecting claim itself. Such a claim or right is no exception to the Interest Theory's cardinal thesis that rights always safeguard interests (either genuinely or nominally). The promisee who holds such a claim or right does indeed have an interest that stands in need of protection.

We now have to face a query which this essay has not yet posed. If we shift our attention back to the status of the beneficiary under a third-party-beneficiary contract, we find that we have to distinguish the relevant beneficiary from other people whose well-being may be advanced by the execution of the contract. Suppose that X has contracted with Y for the payment of several thousand dollars by Y to Z. Suppose further that Z plans to spend all of her newly obtained money on some furniture from W's shop. In this scenario, W of course will have profited from Y's fulfilment of the contractual obligation. Now, given that the Interest Theory ascribes a right to Z—a right that is probably not enforceable and perhaps not waivable by Z—must it also ascribe a right to W? More generally, must it ascribe a right to anyone who might benefit from the carrying out of the contract?

Rights Without Trimmings 81

If the answer here were 'yes', then the Interest Theory would merit no further consideration as a serious theory of rights. Fortunately, however, Jeremy Bentham devised a satisfactory way of dealing with this problem; his solution, in a form that needs to be modified, has become widely known as a result of the exegetical labours of H. L. A. Hart (Hart, 'Legal Rights', 178–81). To decide whether someone holds a right under any contract or norm, we must ask what findings are sufficient to establish that a breach of the contract or norm has occurred. If at least one way of proving the breach will involve nothing more than a demonstration that a certain person has undergone some detriment (some unreceived benefit or some inflicted loss) at the hands of the duty-bearer(s), then that person holds a right under the relevant contract or norm. More precisely, any person Z holds a right under a contract or norm if and only if a violation of a duty under the contract or norm can be established by simply showing that the duty-bearer has withheld a benefit from Z or has imposed some harm upon him. Proof of the duty-bearer's withholding of a desirable thing from Z, or proof of the duty-bearer's infliction of an undesirable state of affairs on Z, must in itself be a sufficient demonstration that the duty-bearer has not lived up to the demands of some requirement. Otherwise, Z does not hold a right correlative to the obligation imposed by that requirement. (Note that Z's undergoing of some detriment at the hands of a duty-bearer does not necessarily amount to Z's actual suffering of an untoward result. Consider again the example of the third-party-beneficiary contract. If Y fails to abide by his duty to make a payment to Z, then Z has clearly undergone a detriment at the hands of Y. None the less, either openly or furtively, X might well step in and render the payment to Z himself. Or perhaps somebody else might intervene to render the payment. In such circumstances, Y's non-compliance with his duty to Z has not done any undeflected damage to Z—apart from the resentment that might be felt by the benefactor who has had to undertake the deflection.)

Let us briefly notice the difference between the version of Bentham's test just outlined and the version delineated by Hart. Hart erroneously presumed that the relevant question to be asked is whether proof of Z's undergoing a detriment at the hands of Y will be *necessary* in order to establish that Y has violated a certain norm or contract. In fact, the relevant question is whether such proof will be *sufficient* to establish a violation. To see why the pertinent question concerns sufficiency rather than necessity, we should consider a norm N that calls for two instances of legal protection, S and T. To show that N has been fulfilled, we have to show that S and T both obtain (ie, 'S & T'). To prove that N has been breached, conversely, we have to prove that 'S & T' is false—which amounts to proving that S does not obtain or that T does not obtain or that both of them do not obtain (ie, '$\neg S \vee \neg T$'). Sufficient but not necessary for proof of a violation, then, is a demonstration of $\neg S$; and likewise sufficient but not necessary for such proof is a demonstration of $\neg T$. The sufficiency of a demonstration of $\neg S$ indicates that the negation of $\neg S$ (ie, S) is a necessary condition for the satisfaction of N. Exactly the same applies to $\neg T$ and its negation (ie, T), of course. Conversely, the unnecessariness of a demonstration of $\neg S$ indicates merely that the negation of $\neg S$ is per se insufficient for the satisfaction of N. Again, exactly the same applies to $\neg T$ and its negation. Now, in inquiring whether a person Z holds a right under N, we want to know whether the generally beneficial state of affairs secured by N for Z—and for anyone similarly situated—is a necessary rather than contingent aspect of N. Ergo, we are interested in knowing whether a proof of the absence of that state of affairs is sufficient to establish a violation of N. If we let the generally beneficial state of affairs be symbolized by 'S' (or by 'T'), we thus must ask whether a demonstration of $\neg S$ (or of $\neg T$) is sufficient to prove that N has been breached. In short, to employ Bentham's test for the identification of right-holders, we shall be asking the query that was posed in my last paragraph, rather than the query which Hart suggested.

Bentham's test will work very smoothly when applied to the scenario of the third-party-beneficiary contract. To prove that Y has breached his contractual duty to X, one need only show that Y has inexcusably failed to make the required payment to Z. In other words, one need only show that Z has undergone an unexcused detriment at the hands of Y. Establishing that fact is sufficient for a successful demonstration of Y's breach of duty. Hence, Y's duty to X under the contract is conjoined with a duty owed by Y to Z; Z, in turn, holds a right to be paid by Y. Of course, in England and in most American jurisdictions, X would have a power to enforce his right whereas Z would not have any such power. For the Interest Theory, however, the unenforceability of Z's right by Z himself does not belie or preclude his holding of the right. Ascriptions of rights are distinguishable from ascriptions of the powers-to-enforce-those-rights.

Just as important as the ability of Bentham's test to place Z in the category of right-holders is its ability to keep W out of that category. While a demonstration of Y's inexcusable withholding of the requisite payment from Z is sufficient to prove Y's breach of contract, the same cannot be said about a demonstration of Z's failure to buy furniture from W's shop. Z's abstention from any purchases cannot by itself be adduced as sufficient grounds for concluding that Y has declined to fulfil his contract with X. Any number of other explanations for Z's decision not to patronize W's shop are possible, and hence we cannot validly infer from the absence of patronage that there has occurred a breach of contract by Y. Thus, since proof of a lack of sales by W to Z does not suffice to establish that Y has reneged on his duty to X and his duty to Z, W does not hold a right against Y under the contract that bestows rights on X and Z.

Bentham's criterion for the identification of right-holders will indeed yield the appropriate answers when applied to any number of situations. That criterion can shed crucial light, for example, on a point that was stated earlier without much explanation: namely, the point about the absence of correlations between public duties and individual rights. For ease of exposition, let us focus on a particular public duty—the duty to pay one's taxes. Sufficient to prove a breach of that public duty is a showing that a person has withheld some money which should have gone into the public coffers for the discharge of levies. Such a showing will have demonstrated that someone has committed harm against the regnant political-legal system or the public as a whole, because the withholding of the tax payments has reduced the overall revenues that should have been available for the funding of public institutions and programmes. (Moreover, if a prominent and influential person is guilty of flagrant tax-evasion, then such misconduct may tend to foster a disrespect for legal obligations generally.) Though the damage to the political-legal system or the general public from a particular individual's non-feasance may be exceedingly slight, it is damage all the same. In sum, because solid evidence of a person's unexcused holding back of some tax payments from the public treasury would suffice to establish her non-compliance with the duty to pay the relevant taxes, and because any such demonstration of a person's unlawful withholding of money would amount to proof of an injury committed against the interests of the prevailing political-legal regime or the public as a whole, we are quite correct in attributing to the public or its political/legal regime the right that correlates with each person's duty to pay taxes. The undergoing of a detriment by the public or its political-legal regime is precisely what we show when we come up with sufficient proof of a tax-law violation—that is, when we reveal that a person has declined to contribute duly to the public revenues.

By contrast, a demonstration of some loss suffered by any particular person does not suffice to indicate the non-payment or underpayment of taxes by someone else. Solid evidence showing that a person P has had to pay high taxes or has received meagre public benefits is not enough to indicate somebody else's delinquency in complying with levies. Such evidence about P is by itself insufficient to establish the non-compliance of some other person(s), because P's high taxes or low benefits can be due to any number of causes other than a fellow taxpayer's non-feasance. (Indeed, the highness of the taxes or the lowness of the benefits will almost never derive specifically from a single taxpayer's non-feasance.) Whereas a demonstration of a shortfall in the revenue payments that are due from a person Q to the public treasury will indeed suffice to prove that Q is in arrears on his taxes, a demonstration that other people are paying high taxes will not serve to establish anything about Q. Hence, by resorting to Bentham's test for specifying who is a rightholder under any contract or norm, we can know that each person's public duties correlate not with any individual rights but with rights held by the public or its political-legal regime.

A reliance on Bentham's test obliges us to consider two major problems: the problem of interpretation and the problem of evaluation, which we shall examine in turn. In order to know what constitutes a violation of a norm (whether the norm be a statutory precept, a judicial ruling, a contractual term, or some other mandate), and therefore in order to know what proofs are sufficient to establish a violation, we have to know what the norm means. Bentham's test thus requires us to engage in interpretation. Until we interpret a norm, we are not able to apprehend what it requires of whom, and so we are not able to say whether it bestows a right on this or that particular person—a right which, if it exists, will of course be correlative with a duty laid on someone else.

Now, one scarcely should be surprised by the general fact that we have to interpret each norm before we can decide who (if anyone) holds rights under it. But the problem of interpretation becomes more complicated as soon as we ask about the extent to which our interpretations should be focused on the intentions that underlie norms. Some versions of the Interest Theory have appealed to intentions as the vehicles for identifying the people who hold rights under various norms. Given that no sensible Interest Theorist wants to maintain that *every*one who benefits from the fulfilment of a duty has a right to be so benefited, the Interest Theory needs a criterion for deciding when the beneficiary of a duty does indeed have a right to the fulfilment of the duty; and some Interest Theorists have felt that the appropriate criterion must have reference to the intentions which animate norms. Under such a criterion, the task of deciding whether a beneficiary *B* counts as a right-holder will consist in determining whether *B* is the sort of person whom a norm is 'intended' or 'designed' or 'supposed' or 'meant' to protect against someone else.[31] Does that intention-focused approach amount to a useful elaboration of Bentham's test for defining the class of right-holders?

The answer to this query is 'no', at least at an abstract level. We should view Bentham's test as a way of avoiding an undue focus on intentions. On the one hand, to be sure, any process of interpretation that is necessitated by Bentham's test can undoubtedly raise questions about the aims of the people who have laid down a particular norm or set of norms. Grasping what a norm requires can involve our seeking to grasp the intentions of the people who devised the norm. On the other hand, however, the appeals to intentions are forgeable and problematic and often inapposite. Such appeals are forgeable because the authoritative canons of interpretation (and one's own canons of interpretation) can attach meanings to various forms of words irrespective of the meanings attached thereto by the people who have employed the words. Although an interpreter of a norm has to ascribe some purpose to it in order to figure out the norm's precise significance within various contexts, the ascription of a purpose does not have to

---

[31] This approach is conspicuous in David Lyons, 'Rights, Claimants, and Beneficiaries', in *RWMMT* (n 25 above), 23–46. See also Raz, 'Legal Rights' (n 17 above), 13–14. Closer to my own view is the account in Waldron, *RPP* (n 11 above), 81–3. For a position even closer to my own, see Hart, 'Legal Rights' (n 3 above), 180–1.

present itself as the ferreting out of the aims of the norm's formulator(s). Instead of striving to unearth the intentions of the people who have forged a norm, an interpreter can approach as a constructive endeavour the task of positing an objective or a purpose which the norm advances.

Not only are the appeals to intentions forgoable, but, when seen as *un*forgoable, they are decidedly problematic. For one thing, unless we are simply indulging in guesses, we have to infer the intentions behind the words of a norm by looking at other words or signs (for example, the words of legislative deliberations). If appeals to intentions are held to be unavoidable for proper interpretation, then the new words on which we rely will have to be construed by reference to the intentions which have undergirded them—which will force us to probe still further words or signs, and so on. A zealous attachment to intention-focused modes of interpretation will have launched us into an infinite regress, from which we can emerge only by severing the attachment.

Moreover, even if we accept *arguendo* that appeals to intentions are essential and groundable, we have to ask which aspects of the relevant intentions should make themselves felt in our interpretations. For example, legislators may intend to further the realization of the ideal of human equality by devising programmes which many interpreters would view as clashing with that ideal. When we have to construe the norms that set up the programmes, should we concentrate on the abstract intention to promote equality or on the specific intention to take certain anti-egalitarian measures?[32] This question does not lend itself to being resolved by way of any general focus on intentions, since each of the two main answers can rightly profess to square with such a focus.

In regard to the different levels of people's intentions, we can see that an interpretive stance which tries to follow the aims underlying a norm can often be markedly inapposite. Suppose, for instance, that a law regulating the competitive practices of clothing manufacturers has been passed with the primary aim of benefiting a particular clothing maker M. If we insist on elaborating Bentham's test (namely, his test for the identification of right-holders) in an intention-focused way, we shall have to decide between the specific

---

[32] This problem and other problems for intention-focused methods of interpretation are discussed in Ronald Dworkin, *Law's Empire* (London: Fontana, 1986), 50–65, 313–37.

intention and the general intention underlying the clothing law. Should we concentrate on the legislators' aim of laying down requirements and prohibitions that are formulated in general terms? Or should we concentrate on their more concrete design of supporting the enterprise of a particular manufacturer M? If we opt for the concrete aim, then we shall have to conclude that proof of any competitive practices which adversely affect the interests of M is sufficient to demonstrate violations of the clothing law, whereas proof of such practices that fairly or unfairly promote the interests of M is insufficient to demonstrate any violations of the law. We shall therefore have to conclude further that only M and anyone whose interests are necessarily tied to those of M will hold rights under the clothing law. (After all, evidence of the harming of other manufacturers' interests by unfair competitive practices will not be sufficient to constitute evidence of an infraction of the law. We shall need further evidence that can tell us whether or not the practices disserve M's interests.) Such a conclusion is perverse, however, since the law in its actual application will very likely benefit one or more manufacturers at the expense of M on certain occasions—ie, on occasions when M runs afoul of the law's requirements or prohibitions. If we look only at the legislators' concrete intention regarding M when we bring to bear Bentham's test on the clothing law, then we shall blind ourselves to the ways in which the law will almost certainly be applied. We shall thus fail to grasp that that law endows every clothing manufacturer with a right against every other such manufacturer. Only if we acknowledge that the concrete aims underlying certain laws are often properly disregarded during the actual application of those laws, will we characterize correctly in Hohfeldian terms the situations which those laws bring about.

What, then, should we conclude about modes of interpretation that do indeed search for the intentions of the people who have formulated the norms in a legal system? Should we dismiss such interpretive stances altogether? An outright dismissal would bespeak a misunderstanding of the arguments just presented. Although an insistence on intention-focused paths of interpretation as the only legitimate paths is highly problematic indeed, a much more modest commendation of such paths is perfectly reasonable. In so far as a focus on intentions presents itself as one powerful method of interpretation among others, it scarcely deserves our scorn.

Instead of rejecting the intention-highlighting method wholesale, we should recognize that it ought not to be enshrined at too high a level of one's analysis. My philosophical theory of rights, which incorporates Bentham's test for identifying right-holders, should forbear from suggesting that that test necessarily favours one interpretive method over others. While that crucial test *leaves room* for a focus on intentions, it does not *necessitate* such a focus and does not confine itself thereto. Bentham's standard for the identification of right-holders is an integral component of my theory of rights, and a process of interpretation is inevitable in anybody's use of that standard; but *no particular style* of interpretation is an integral component of Bentham's standard or of my theory. Rather than cramping a philosophical theory of rights by tying it to one interpretive method in contrast with others, we should equip it with Bentham's criterion for the identification of right-holders—the criterion that asks which facts are sufficient to constitute a breach of the law—and we should then leave open the question of the interpretive stance that ought to be adopted for the elaboration or implementation of that criterion. (The advisability of adopting some specified stance in preference to other stances will of course vary in relation to the specific legal materials with which we are dealing.) To avoid a conflation of philosophical and methodological issues, one ought to refrain from introducing an intention-focused position into one's analysis too early.

One should also abstain from trying to resolve at too high a level of one's analysis the interpretive difficulties that are posed by the instrumental and epiphenomenal status of certain rights. Consider a situation in which a right-constitutive mode of legal protection R is bestowed because of its serviceability in advancing a goal G. If R is granted expressly by a norm which explicitly or implicitly pursues G, then there are no difficulties about our maintaining that R is a full-fledged right conferred by the norm. Likewise, there are no difficulties about our maintaining that everyone vested by the norm with R is thereby a right-holder. Much the same can be said if R is a logical implication of the pursuit of G. But suppose that R is not expressly conferred by the G-promoting law and is not a logical implication thereof; instead, it exists—if it does exist—because it is a virtually indispensable means for realizing G. Should we say in such circumstances that R is a right bestowed by the G-ordaining law? Bentham's test might appear to call for a negative answer to this question, since any proof of acts that affect someone in a way inconsistent with R is apparently not by itself sufficient proof of an infraction of the G-focused law. Because the conferral of R on every relevant person is virtually indispensable *but not absolutely indispensable* for the achievement of G, any evidence of conduct at odds with R will have left open the possibility that G is being pursued by means other than by the granting of R. It thus leaves open the possibility that the G-promoting law has not been violated. With regard to any particular norm, then, Bentham's test seems to lead to a firm distinction between legal protection that is only instrumentally warranted and legal protection that is directly furnished.

Two points should be noted in response to the problems surrounding the instrumental status of certain rights. First, even if we accept that instrumentally justified rights are not bestowed as rights by the goal-oriented laws for which they are serviceable, they are indeed bestowed as rights through the judicial or executive decisions which implement those laws by granting those rights. Modes of protection not specifically conferred at one level of a legal system can be conferred at another level; a right not directly granted by a general norm can be granted by a more specific norm that puts the general norm into effect. That a right is justified instrumentally does not make it any less a right in its functioning.

Second, and somewhat more germane to the present discussion of interpretation, is the fact that the distinction between rights which are merely instrumental and rights which are directly ordained is largely a matter of interpretation. It is thus a matter that should not be settled at the philosophical level of my theory of rights. When asking which facts are sufficient to constitute a violation of a norm N—so that we can ascertain who holds rights under N—we must decide how strict our notion of 'sufficiency' is. If we confine ourselves to facts that run athwart N's express formulation and its logical implications, then we shall maintain that N itself does not confer any rights which are warranted only because of their serviceability (in promoting N's goal) rather than because of their having been strictly necessitated. If on the other hand we adopt a somewhat looser conception of 'sufficiency' to cover facts which are at odds with rights that are *virtually indispensable* for the attainment of N's objective, we shall contend that N itself has conferred such rights. If this looser approach is taken, we shall have to draw a line or a set of lines somewhere to stake off a realm of virtual indispensability between what is strictly necessary and what is merely useful. Where we should draw the lines, and whether we should draw them at all beyond the realm of strict necessity, are interpretive questions that ought not to be answered at a high level of abstraction.

Let us ponder a brief example to clarify the observations made in the last paragraph. If a norm N lays down the goal of a universally well-educated populace, and if such a goal cannot be legitimately pursued through the killing off of people who are not well educated, then N effectively bestows a right-to-be-educated on everyone. Does it more specifically bestow on everyone a right to be taught how to read? A right of the latter sort is not strictly entailed by the goal of a universally well-educated populace, since some people could conceivably become well educated without having learned how to read. None the less, the ability to read is virtually indispensable as a means for becoming and remaining well educated in the modern West, and hence we shall probably be inclined to say that N implicitly bestows on everyone a right to be taught how to read. That is, we shall probably be inclined to say that proof of someone's not having been taught how to read is sufficient proof of the non-fulfilment of N.

Whichever way we decide within the situation just sketched, we shall have reached an interpretive verdict that is best left to the stage at which we are dealing with particular norms. If we insist *in abstracto* on defining 'sufficiency' solely by reference to each norm's explicit wording plus the purely logical implications thereof, then we might be ruling out certain concrete applications of Bentham's test that are highly appealing. At any rate, even if we decide eventually to opt for a stricter definition of 'sufficiency', we should make that decision at the point when we are construing various norms—rather than at the philosophical level occupied by this essay. A philosophical framework should not attempt to eliminate or hamstring the interpretative discretion through which it becomes fleshed out. Such discretion is both inevitable and desirable. (Such discretion is inevitable not only because we always have to opt for stricter or looser conceptions of sufficiency, but also because the stricter conceptions themselves must fall short of *logical* sufficiency. Given that every norm is defeasible under certain conditions that are not all specified beforehand, no proof of a breach of any particular norm can be logically sufficient in the sense that the veracity of the proof would render necessarily false the thesis that no breach had occurred. Hence, even when we adopt a strict conception of sufficiency, we shall have watered it down from logical sufficiency by declining to insist that a demonstration of a breach must be indefeasible in order to be sufficient.)

Having investigated the problem of interpretation which a reliance on Bentham's test raises, we now should turn to the most complicated aspect of that test and of my whole theory: the problem of evaluation. Notwithstanding that this essay aspires to present a version of the Interest Theory without political trimmings, it cannot completely eschew evaluative assumptions. Any theory of rights, be it a version of the Interest Theory or a version of the Will Theory, must adopt at least a thin evaluative stance—'thin' in the sense that its assumptions are largely uncontroversial and indeed commonplace, notwithstanding their plainly evaluative tenor. To see why such a stance is unavoidable, we should ponder the contrast between two superficially similar duties.[33]

Suppose first that, as a result of a statute or a judicial ruling or some other mandate, X has a duty to provide his parents with a certain level of financial support after they reach the age of sixty-five. Suppose next that, as a result of some mandate, X has a duty to inform on his parents whenever they utter seditious sentiments. Now, in each of these situations, X bears a duty with a content that pertains to his parents. But in the first scenario the duty of X is owed to his parents, whereas in the second situation the duty is owed to the state; by the same token, the parents hold a right against X in the first situation, whereas they do not hold a right in the second scenario. Why do we ascribe to the parents a right-to-be-furnished-with-financial-support in the first setting, and deny that they have a right-to-be-informed-upon in the second setting?

---

[33] The examples in the following paragraph come from Lyons, *RWMMT* (n 25 above), 27. See also ibid, 39; White, *Rights* (n 6 above), 60–1, 63. Connections between rights and the good have of course been emphasized by Interest Theorists such as Raz, MacCormick, and Waldron. However, such connections have also been asserted by writers whose allegiance to the Interest Theory is at best qualified. See, eg, Flathman, *Practice* (n 3 above), 79–80; Sumner, *MFR* (n 5 above), 32; Ross, *Justice* (n 3 above), 175. I should note that my invocation of a 'thin' evaluative standpoint is a deliberate echo of John Rawls's 'thin theory of the good'; see John Rawls, *A Theory of Justice* (Cambridge: Harvard University Press, 1971), 60. I believe, however, that my thin evaluative stance is less problematic for my conception of rights than is the thin theory of the good for Rawls's conception of justice.

Interest Theorists—and Will Theorists, as will soon be argued—have to point out that a duty to provide Y with financial support is a duty to act in ways that are generally beneficial to Y's interests, while a duty to inform the police about Y's treasonous utterances is a duty to act in ways that are generally detrimental to Y's interests. Only when a duty concerning a person Y is a duty to engage in acts or omissions that are generally supportive of Y's interests, can we say that Y is the holder of the right which correlates with the duty. Unless we draw this distinction between the beneficial and the detrimental, we shall be unable to account for the ridiculousness of a right-to-be-betrayed (or a right to be subjected to any other grievously injurious treatment). In sum, given that we must draw the aforementioned distinction in order to know whether someone has a right, we cannot manage to do without evaluative assumptions in our analysis of rights. After all, decisions about what counts as a benefit and what counts as a detriment must stem from assumptions concerning what is generally good for human beings. We cannot forgo such assumptions when we construct a theory of rights; one's finely analytical exposition of rights must rest in part on an account of the good, an account that is probably taken largely for granted.

Now, since every right/duty axis can be reformulated (with suitable transpositions and signs of negation) as a liberty/no-right axis—because a right is the correlate of a duty, the negation of a no-right, and the correlate of the negation of a liberty—our need to rely on evaluative assumptions for the basic definition of rights will extend to every other first-order legal position as well. Second-order legal positions are somewhat more complicated.[34] Given that every second-order position has either a direct bearing or an indirect (mediated) bearing on some first-order positions, every second-order position must indeed be defined in part by reference to evaluative assumptions. However, as this essay has pointed out more than once, the distinctive functions of the second-order positions are defined in purely descriptive terms. Those distinctive functions consist in abilities, inabilities, susceptibilities, and insusceptibilities, all of which are detectable without any reliance on further evaluative notions. Although every second-order position must ultimately work its effects on first-order positions (perhaps through numerous

---

[34] For an odd failure to take account of the difference between first-order and second-order positions, see Anderson (n 1 above), 43–4. For a more alert view, see Dias (n 4 above), 47–8.

layers of other second-order positions), and although a full account of each second-order position must therefore incorporate the evaluative assumptions that are needed to define first-order positions, the account does not have to bring aboard any additional evaluative judgments. As a result, an ascription of a second-order entitlement to X does not necessarily mean that X's interests are generally served by his being endowed with such an entitlement; much less does it mean that his interests are *invariably* served thereby. As has been suggested herein, many second-order entitlements can be disadvantageous to their holders not only in some specific applications but also in general.

A right, by contrast, is normally advantageous. From the fact that a right is *normally* beneficial, however, we should not conclude that it is *invariably* so. On the one hand, each right protects some aspect of welfare or freedom that is usually desirable. On the other hand, some instances of the protection which a right provides can redound to the detriment of this or that particular right-holder. Among the many theorists who have well recognized this point is Neil MacCormick:

> It is not necessarily the case that each individual acquiring a right under the law should experience it as a benefit, an advantage, an advancement or protection of his interests. Perhaps there are some people who have been more harmed than benefited by an inheritance. Perhaps in some cases property inherited—eg slum properties subject to statutory tenancies at controlled rents—are literally more trouble than they are worth, and, besides, something of an embarrassment to their proprietor. None of that is in any way inconsistent with the proposition that the function of the law is to confer what is considered to be normally an advantage on a certain class by granting to each of its members a certain legal right.[35]

To elaborate this point, let us briefly focus on a situation that has already been depicted here in its broad outlines (with slight variations). Suppose that X is obligated to make monthly payments to support his mother financially after she has reached the age of seventy-five. In general, plainly, financial security during one's years of retirement is a major desideratum; and so the obligation on X to assist his mother does indeed correlate with a right held by

---

[35] MacCormick, 'Legislation' (n 10 above), 202. For similar observations, see Lyons, *RWMMT* (n 25 above), 10; Raz, 'Nature' (n 11 above), 208; Waldron, *RPP* (n 11 above), 89–90. For some partly captious but partly perceptive reflections on this aspect of the Interest Theory, see Jaconelli (n 21 above), 171–3.

her. All the same, regardless of how obviously desirable the financial security would be for most elderly people in most circumstances, it can quite conceivably harm certain people. Let us presume that X's mother has been admirably self-reliant and vigorous until she begins to receive the monthly payments from her son. Before too long, she loses her sense of independence and her desire for independence, and she becomes woefully languid. Her lassitude eventuates in alcoholism, which enfeebles her spirit still more. For her, then, the monthly payments from X have proved to be disastrous. Of course, most people on whom such payments have a detrimental impact will not experience calamities of the extent that X's mother has undergone. None the less, in numerous ways not quite so dramatic, mothers can lose more than they gain as a consequence of receiving monthly payments from their children. (Think, for example, of the mother who uses her monthly payments to triple her daily intake of cigarettes and who quickly dies of a heart attack as a result. Or consider the mother whose formerly affectionate son becomes embittered when he has to shoulder the burden of sustaining her with his funds.) The desirability of adequate support during one's senescence is a typical feature of that support, to which a number of exceptions are possible. Here, as in other circumstances where we have to determine whether the fulfilling of a requirement will tend to benefit the person(s) on whom it will have a direct impact, we have to reach a judgment that will be *generally* accurate rather than *unqualifiedly* accurate.

To notice one more of the many situations in which this distinction between generally advantageous positions and universally advantageous positions is manifest, we should glance at the effects of minimum-wage laws. If the rights conferred by such laws are not waivable by their holders, then the laws undoubtedly will have an adverse impact on some workers—most notably the workers whose skills do not warrant their being employed at the level of remuneration set by the laws. None the less, according to the Interest Theory, such rights are indeed rights. Although they redound to the disadvantage of some labourers who hold them, they serve the interests of most labourers because most gain higher wages or become assured of not falling below certain levels in their wages. Unfailingly beneficial the rights bestowed by the minimum-wage laws are not; but generally beneficial they doubtless are. (Of course, one can imagine far-fetched situations in which minimum-wage laws set their remunerational floors so high that they are detrimental to the interests of most workers, whose skills are simply not worth what employers are bound to pay for them. In such situations, we may be well advised to reconstrue the purpose or function of the minimum-wage laws. Instead of perceiving those laws primarily as devices for raising or solidifying the incomes of individual workers, we might come to perceive them primarily as devices for excluding people from the work force—particularly if the effect of such laws is to exclude altogether from the work force the members of some despised and unskilled minority groups. Once we reinterpret the minimum-wage laws in this fashion, we shall have to conclude that the duties imposed by those laws affect most labourers in roughly the way in which the duty-to-inform-on-one's-father affects one's father. That is, in the posited circumstances, the duties imposed on employers are correlative only with rights held by the state and not with rights held by all or most workers. When putative rights are generally detrimental to the people who hold them, they ought not to be classified as rights at all. In any event, the need for a reconstrual of the purpose of certain minimum-wage laws along these lines is very much an expository matter that will hinge on various details of the laws' likely and actual effects. Whether any particular set of laws should be so reconstrued is a concrete question of interpretation that is not to be answered at the abstract level of a philosophical theory.)

We have to rely on generalizations not only when we contemplate the beneficial effects of duties, but also when we contemplate their injurious effects. For example, when we presume that one's fulfilment of the duty-to-inform-on-one's-father will have a detrimental effect on one's father, we do not thereby disallow the possibility of a gratifying effect. If one's father believes zealously in the worthiness of the regime that seeks to crack down on dissidence, he may well be pleased by his own arrest whenever he has inadvertently given voice to sentiments that can plausibly be construed as treasonous. Such eager prostration is undoubtedly rare in liberal democracies, but has not been entirely unknown in some lands governed by tyrannies; at any rate, we certainly cannot rule it out on logical grounds as a possibility. Hence, when we ponder the impact of anti-sedition laws and when we characterize such laws as harmful for anyone who is informed upon, we are stating a proposition that is generally accurate rather than universally accurate. Much the same will be true of any other judgments we reach about the detrimental consequences of various norms.

Though our assumptions about the favourable or unfavourable effects of duties are generalizations and are not statements of universal laws, our attributions of rights to persons do indeed presuppose that those persons (be they individual or corporate) generally benefit from the fulfilment of the duties which are correlative with the rights. Unless our ascriptions of rights are based on notions of the generally favourable effects of duty-fulfilment, we shall be unable to distinguish between the duty to support one's parents and the duty to inform on one's parents. To see how abiding is this need for a thin evaluative stance whenever we ascribe rights to persons, we should ponder a scenario which might at first seem to tell against the view that rights are generally advantageous for their holders.

Suppose that the Nazis pass a law declaring that every Jew has a right to be free from unprovoked physical attacks while cleaning latrines. If Jews along with other people are already covered by a general prohibition on unprovoked physical attacks, then the new law adds nothing to the legally protected security of any Jew. Not merely at the level of particular applications, but also at the level of original formulation, the new law does not advance the interests of the Jews at all. Its only salutary effect is wholly redundant. Its prime purpose lies not in offering the Jews a needed shield, but in ridiculing them by associating them with filth and with menial tasks. In sum, in so far as the latrine-cleaning law has any bearing on the lot of the Jews, it works against their interests by holding them up to scorn; and its disadvantageousness for them is its *raison d'être* rather than a product of anomalous applications. Yet we still are probably inclined to say that the law confers a right on each Jew. Hence, do we not here encounter a right that is generally deleterious to the interests of each person who holds it?

We should answer this question in the negative by assailing the double standard that guides the reasoning in the last paragraph. On the one hand, because the security enjoyed under the latrine-cleaning law is entirely redundant, it has been deemed to serve no interests of the Jews whatsoever. On the other hand, notwithstanding that the right assigned to each Jew under the law is entirely redundant, it has been deemed to be a right after all—which means that it ought to carry general advantages for its holder. Yet what is sauce for the goose must be sauce for the gander. If reduplication renders non-existent each new instance of security, then it will have done the same to each new right; alternatively, if the reduplication does not prevent us from attributing a new right to each Jew, then it likewise does not prevent us from attributing a new element of protectedness to each holder of that new right. Because *ex hypothesi* both the novel right and the novel element of protectedness are wholly redundant, the reality-dissipating force of redundancy must affect the one as much or as little as the other. Indeed, given that rights are protections, their existence manifestly stands or falls with the existence of the protectedness which people enjoy by dint of being vested with the rights.

Thus, because the line of reasoning sketched in my penultimate paragraph has relied on a flagrant and utterly unsupportable double standard, it offers not the slightest ground for thinking that rights can exist as such without being generally advantageous to their holders. If nothing that would standardly count as a person's interest has been furthered in any way by a particular law, then no right has been added to that person, either. Although rights can work to the detriment of their holders in particular contexts, the rights as they are explicitly or implicitly established by norms must be generally beneficial—beneficial to typical human beings in most circumstances—if they are to qualify as rights at all. When a norm imposes (on a person Y) some duties concerning a person X that carry virtually no potential for advancing X's interests, it *pro tanto* does not endow X with any rights.

A resolute Will Theorist will very likely object, however, to my whole discussion of the difference between a duty to support one's parents and a duty to inform on them. For the Will Theorist, the distinction between the two sorts of duties does not hinge on the tendency of each duty to promote or damage the interests of one's parents; it hinges instead on the ability of one's parents to waive/enforce each duty. If X has a duty to furnish his mother with financial support, she very likely has a power to waive his fulfilment of that obligation. By contrast, if X has a duty to inform on his mother whenever she expresses seditious feelings, she almost certainly does not have a power to waive his compliance with that odious obligation. To ascertain whether the mother has a right and thus whether a duty incumbent on X is owed to her rather than just to the state, we need only to ascertain whether she enjoys a power to waive/enforce the duty. We do not need to ask about benefits and detriments. Such, at least, is the view taken by Will Theorists.

If the Will Theorists could sustain their view of this matter, then their doctrine in that respect would be superior to the Interest Theory. After all, in inquiring whether someone holds a power of waiver and enforcement, we do not have to rely perforce on any evaluative assumptions. Instead, we merely have to interpret any relevant norms and monitor any relevant patterns of conduct. Hence, if we could locate each right by simply finding out who holds the power to enforce or waive the duty that is correlative with the right, we could avoid the fuzziness introduced by any reliance on evaluative presuppositions. We could distinguish in a rigorously non-evaluative manner between a duty to support one's parents and a duty to inform on one's parents, for example. A purely descriptive account of the formal aspects of rights would be highly desirable indeed, and so the Will Theory's ability to yield such an account would tell strongly in favour of that theory and against the Interest Theory.

Fortunately for Interest Theorists, however, the Will Theory cannot eschew evaluative assumptions while retaining a minimal degree of plausibility as a theory of rights. For two main reasons, a thin evaluative stance is indispensable in the Will Theory as it is in the Interest Theory. First, and less important, is the waivability of certain obligations that are injurious to the interests of the persons who can waive them. Consider the situation in which X is duty-bound to inform on his mother whenever she utters any statements that can be construed as treasonous. Now, although the vesting of the mother with a power to waive X's fulfilment of his duty would indeed be very odd, it would not be flatly inconceivable by any means. Perhaps a regime takes an intensely scornful attitude toward the perceived cowardice of its citizens who are not willing to be informed upon, and it therefore deems punishment of them to be inessential (because they are viewed as insufficiently threatening). Or perhaps, in a zany extension of current Anglo-American doctrines pertaining to the culpability of insane people, a regime concludes that its citizens should not be informed upon and punished unless they recognize that they ought to be. Whatever are the grounds for a regime's decision to enable X's mother to waive X's compliance with his duty as an informant, that admittedly outlandish decision is clearly possible. In principle, that is, any duty which is generally harmful to the interests of a person Y can be waivable by Y. Hence, the Will Theorists find themselves in a predicament. If they maintain that Y in such circumstances holds a right to be harmed, they are offering a wildly implausible conception of rights. An ascription to X's mother of a right-to-be-betrayed, for instance, is bizarrely counter-intuitive. Yet, if the Will Theorists seek to avoid such a conclusion, they cannot forgo a thin evaluative stance.

A second and more important reason for the inescapableness of a thin evaluative stance is that the Will Theorists have to be able to specify the location of each duty's correlative claim. Recall that, for the Will Theorists, a right consists of a claim plus a power of enforcing or waiving the claim (plus a liberty to exercise the power and a liberty to forbear from exercising it). Thus, the Will Theorists must at a minimum be able to say whether or not someone holds a claim in any particular circumstances. Let us, then, consider the situation of X and his mother. If X has a duty to support his mother financially, and if the power of enforcing or waiving that duty lies with the state, then the mother does not have a Will Theory right to be provided with support by X. She does, however, have a *claim* to be provided with support by him—a claim that is not enforceable or waivable by her. Suppose now that X has a duty to inform the state of his mother's seditious utterances. If the mother has no power to enforce or waive X's duty, then she has no Will Theory right to be informed upon. Does she have a claim to be informed upon? Should the Will Theorists answer 'yes' to this question, they will have saddled themselves anew with essentially the same implausibility that attends any talk of the mother's *right-to-be-informed-upon*. Should the Will Theorists answer 'no', on the other hand, they will have had to rely on some evaluative assumptions in order to distinguish between the duty of informing and the duty of support. They have to explain why the latter duty is correlated with a claim on the part of the mother, while the former duty is not connected with such a claim. In sum, if the Will Theorists want to present their doctrine as a minimally credible account of rights, they will not be able to keep themselves aloof from a thin evaluative stance.

A Will Theorist might respond by seeking to reduce claims into empty positions that are invariably conjoined with the powers by which they are enforced or waived. This decidedly non-Hohfeldian move would effectively correlate duties with powers (which are invariably conjoined with the correlatives of duties, *ex hypothesi*), though, in order to circumvent the fallacy of suggesting a straightforward correlation between a first-order position and a second-order position, it would retain the category of 'claims' as an empty mediating device through which the duty/power axis can run. To know whether someone such as X's mother has a claim or not, we should merely ascertain whether or not the person has a power of enforcing and waiving the claim. The answer to the latter inquiry would settle the answer to the former inquiry. Hence, unless X's mother has a power of enforcing/waiving X's duty to provide her with sustenance, she has no claim to his provision of the sustenance—not even a claim which she is unable to enforce or waive. More generally, *any* particular claim must be absent from the normative arsenal of everyone who lacks a power to enforce or waive the claim's correlative duty (such as X's duty to inform on his mother). According to this latest manoeuvre by the Will Theorists, there is simply no such thing as a claim that is unenforceable or unwaivable by its holder; and there is likewise no such thing as a power of enforcement/waiver that is held by someone other than the person whose claim is to be enforced or waived.

Such a manoeuvre, though ingenious, will pose two major problems for the Will Theory. First, it obliges the Will Theorists to maintain that X's mother has a right-to-be-betrayed whenever she has the power to waive X's duty of informing. The positing of any number of general rights-to-be-badly-harmed—the ludicrous outcome which any acceptable theory of rights must avoid by distinguishing (for example) between a duty to support one's parents and a duty to inform upon them—is an outcome which the Will Theory appears unable to avert.

Second, the latest twist in the Will Theory bars that theory from acknowledging the existence of any nominal claims, which would correlate with nominal duties. If no claim can ever exist unaccompanied by a power of enforcement/waiver in the hands of the claim-holder, then unenforceable duties (that is, nominal duties) must not be correlated with any claims whatsoever. Thus, for instance, if Y's duty to reimburse Z for some goods or services is unenforceable—perhaps because of the passage of time—then Z has no claim at all against Y, not even a nominal claim. Ergo, Y's nominal duty to reimburse Z for the goods or services is not owed to Z! Nor, indeed, is the nominal duty owed to anyone else; after all, nobody has a power to enforce it, and thus nobody has a claim that correlates with it.

Confronted with these bizarre implications of a Will Theory that tries to do without evaluative assumptions, we should recognize that such assumptions must inform the Will Theory as much as the Interest Theory. Neither account of rights can transcend the need for a set of basic presuppositions that distinguish what is generally desirable from what is generally undesirable for normal human beings. In so far as a reliance on such presuppositions is a shortcoming—because it lessens the analytical rigour of one's overall account of rights—it is a shortcoming that mars the Will Theory along with the Interest Theory. (At any rate, one's dependence on evaluative presuppositions is not a cause for great distress. All or most of the requisite presuppositions can be pitched at a high level of abstraction and can therefore remain gratifyingly uncontroversial.)

In exploring the problem of evaluation, then, we have discovered anew one of the features that have marked this essay's encounter between the Interest Theory and the Will Theory: specifically, we have found again that the Interest Theory's imperfections are not satisfactorily overcome by the Will Theory. Moreover, we have previously found that many of the alleged imperfections in the Interest Theory are not imperfections at all. And we likewise have seen that the Interest Theory avoids the least palatable aspects of the Will Theory. In short, someone contemplating a shift of allegiance from the Will Theory to the Interest Theory has much to gain and very little to lose.

Appendix: Getting Hohfeld Right

This appendix to my main essay is not an integral part of my overall argument in favour of the Interest Theory. Instead, it deals with some specific mistakes by commentators in their discussions of Hohfeld's jurisprudence. Because of the importance of the Hohfeldian analytical framework for all three of the essays in this book, a clear and precise understanding of that framework is essential for anyone who wishes to grasp the exact points of contention among our essays. This appendix tries to promote such an understanding by correcting a number of errors that have appeared in the large secondary literature on Hohfeld's work. I shall seek to parry certain ill-advised criticisms by opponents of Hohfeld, and to counter certain misapplications of his insights by his supporters. The missteps singled out here are quite representative of those which have hindered a proper reception of Hohfeld's analyses; moreover, they have occurred at the hands of scholars who (for the most part) are far from unsophisticated. A look at those missteps will therefore serve as a salutary reminder of the intricacies and subtleties of Hohfeldian jurisprudence.

Let us begin with J. W. Harris, who maintains that—*pace* Hohfeld—not all liabilities correlate with powers. Harris argues as follows: 'As to "liabilities", my legal relations may change because of some occurrence which is not another's voluntary act—for instance, if a tree set on fire by lightning brings about a new duty to take care. Before the lightning struck, was I not subject to a "liability" which did not correlate with a "power"?'[36] Now, on the one hand, Harris is correct to suggest that his scenario does not portray the exercise of a Hohfeldian power. We can see as much from Hohfeld's own statement of what counts as a 'power':

A change in a given legal relation may result (1) from some superadded fact or group of facts not under the volitional control of a human being (or human beings); or (2) from some superadded fact or group of facts which are under the volitional control of one or more human beings. As regards the second class of cases, the person (or persons) whose volitional control is paramount may be said to have the (legal) power to effect the particular change of legal relations that is involved in the problem. (*FLC*, 50–1.)

On the other hand, within Hohfeld's matrix, a liability is a susceptibility to changes (in legal positions) *that are brought about by the exercise of a power*. It is not a more expansive susceptibility to changes (in legal positions) that are brought about by any means whatsoever. Hence, even if we accept that Harris's example of a burning tree does deal with a change of legal relations—rather than with the activating of duties that were existent but latent—we should recognize that the absence of any exercise of a power in that example is matched by the absence of any involvement of a liability. Only by using the term 'liability' with a non-Hohfeldian breadth, has Harris appeared to ferret out a liability that is

---

[36] Harris (n 4 above), 81. For a basically similar argument, see Campbell (n 21 above), 208–9. For a corrective, see Dias (n 4 above), 48, 51–2.

uncorrelated with a power. Once we take due account of Hohfeld's own use of the aforementioned term, we can recognize that Harris is talking past Hohfeld rather than landing any pertinent blows against him.

From the passage on powers that has just been quoted, we can tell that L. W. Sumner goes astray when he asserts that powers are entitlements to alter *or preserve* normative relations. He contends that 'I have the power to affect (that is, to alter *or sustain*) some normative relation just in case the rules of the system make it possible for me to do so' (*MFR*, 28, emphasis added). This view emerges at several junctures in Sumner's exposition. For example, he declares that 'I have a necessary power whenever some particular alteration of a relation is impossible for me. I then lack the power to alter it, but (trivially) have the power not to alter it' (*MFR*, 35, n 25). Sumner here mistakenly suggests that the absence of a power-to-alter is a power-not-to-alter. In fact, as the last quotation from Hohfeld makes clear, one's lack of any power to modify a particular entitlement is precisely the same as one's having no power at all with respect to that entitlement. Hohfeld described a power as the legal ability to effect a *change* in legal positions; he said nothing about a power to *preserve* legal positions. He aptly regarded the preserving of entitlements as the distinctive function of immunities and disabilities.

We encounter another error about powers in an essay by C. F. H. Tapper, who maintains that 'if *A* contemplates striking *B*, he might be thought to have a power since by striking he would probably alter their legal relationship to the extent of investing *B* with a right to damages, and himself with a duty to pay them. Yet it seems odd to say that *A* has a legal power to strike *B*.'[37] Not only is it odd to say that *A* has a power to strike *B*; it is incorrect. The power held by *A* is a power *to change certain entitlements* by striking *B*. Like other powers, *A*'s power bears directly on legal positions and only indirectly on human conduct. *A*'s power to change certain entitlements by striking *B* is a corollary of his genuine duty to forbear from striking *B*—which is why *A*'s exercise of his power will lead to his being susceptible to legal proceedings pursued by *B*. Given

---

[37] CFH Tapper, 'Powers and Secondary Rules of Change', in AWB Simpson, *Oxford Essays in Jurisprudence (Second Series)* (Oxford: Clarendon Press, 1973), 242, 245. For a more accurate treatment of the same basic problem, see Llewellyn (n 2 above), 99.

Hohfeld's definition of a power as a person's ability to change legal relations through a specified act or set of acts, there is nothing odd whatsoever in saying that *A* has a power to change the legal relationship between himself and *B* by striking *B*.

Joseph Raz has stumbled in much the same way as Tapper. In the course of arguing for a focus on legislative intentions, Raz writes:

[O]ne cannot identify a legal power with the ability to perform an act which has legal consequences. This would yield the paradoxical consequence that people have legal power to break the law. (Do we need legal powers for *that*?) A legal power can only be identified by the reasons which led the law... to attach those legal consequences to the act. The act is an exercise of a legal power only if the reason for attributing to it the legal consequences it has, is that it is held desirable to enable people to perform that act as a means to achieve those consequences, if they so wish.[38]

In so far as Raz has Hohfeld in mind here, he commits an *ignoratio elenchi*. From a Hohfeldian point of view, the entitlement at issue in this extract is not a power to break the law; rather, it is a power to change certain entitlements by breaking the law. Each person is indeed able to change certain entitlements by breaking the law, and therefore each person has (by definition) a Hohfeldian power in that respect. Nothing in Hohfeld's definition of 'power' presumes that a power or the exercise of a power must be desirable either from the perspective of the power-holder or from the perspective of legal officials. (Equally, nothing in Hohfeld's definition presumes that a power cannot exist unless it has been explicitly established as such.) Once the power described by Raz is correctly recounted in Hohfeldian terms, it can be taken on board unproblematically by a Hohfeldian analysis. Only someone adhering to a non-Hohfeldian use of the word 'power' could be troubled by the Hohfeldian characterization of potential law-breaking—which means that Raz's objection with its focus on that characterization has not unearthed any feature of Hohfeld's work that should be recognized as a flaw by people who accept Hohfeld's terminology. Instead of pointing to a real

---

[38] Raz, 'Legal Rights' (n 17 above), 13. (For similar statements of Raz's conception of legal powers, see Joseph Raz, *The Authority of Law* (Oxford: Clarendon Press, 1979), 18; Raz (n 2 above), 228; Raz (n 7 above), 102–3.) For an ingenious but unpersuasive attempt to deal with the sort of objection posed by Raz, see Tapper (n 37 above), 245–6. For a very cautious discussion of Raz's objection, see Richard Bronaugh, 'A Secret Paradox of the Common Law', 2 Law and Philosophy 193, 217, n 55 (1983).

difficulty, Raz is simply commending his own set of stipulative definitions as an alternative to Hohfeld's set.

For another dubious argument concerning powers, we can turn to an essay on Hohfeld by Walter Kamba, who writes that '[t]he mere making of an offer [by person *A* to person *B*] does not affect the legal relations of "A" and "B". The effect of an offer is to create a power in "B".'[39] The second of these quoted statements is at odds with the first. By making a full-fledged offer, *A* changes one of *B*'s disabilities into a power, and correlatively changes one of his own immunities into a liability. Hence, the mere making of the offer does indeed change the legal relations of the offeror and the offeree. Hohfeld certainly did not contend that a change in second-order entitlements is any less a change in legal relations than is a change in first-order entitlements.

An equally unfortunate misconception of powers is apparent in some remarks by Richard Flathman, who maintains that a person *A*, by dint of holding a power *vis-à-vis B*, 'is authorized to act in ways that might have far-reaching and seriously adverse consequences for *B* without *B*'s agreement or assent. And if *B* attempts to prevent or hamper *A*'s use of his powers, the state will come to *A*'s assistance against *B*' (Flathman, *Practice*, 54). The second sentence of this quotation conflates liabilities and duties. Contrary to what Flathman assumes, *A*'s liability does not necessarily involve a duty on *A* to abstain from interference with *B*'s power. If a thief has the power to extinguish my ownership of certain assets by transferring them to a bona fide purchaser, I am scarcely under a duty to allow the thief to dispose of my things as he pleases. Indeed—as this example of the dishonest transferor illustrates—not only can a liability be unaccompanied by a cognate duty, but it can even be unaccompanied by a cognate no-right. *Vis-à-vis* the thief, I have a right to be free from a non-consensual transfer of my assets. His power to extinguish my ownership of the assets is conjoined with his duty not to exercise that power. Flathman is therefore too sweeping when he later asserts:

A's persistent use of his powers in ways that harm or disadvantage others [is not] a ground for punishing him or for depriving him of those powers. So long as the powers remain established by law, *A* has use of them 'as a matter

---

[39] Walter Kamba, 'Legal Theory and Hohfeld's Analysis of a Legal Right', 19 Juridical Review 249, 261 (1974).

of right'—that is, according to his discretion. He may choose to use them in a manner that respects the desires, objectives, and so on, of *B*, but it is part of the definition of a power that he is not required to do so. (Flathman, *Practice*, 56–7.)

This passage wrongly presupposes that a power to effect a certain change must be accompanied by a liberty to engage in the actions which effect that change. Although a power to achieve a certain result *can* be conjoined with a liberty to engage in the actions which achieve that result, it certainly does not *have* to be conjoined therewith.

We can find yet another mistake about powers in a recent book by David Lyons, who declares that 'the rights [ie, entitlements] collected in Hohfeldian categories are not equally simple and equally elemental. One with a claim-right is empowered to enforce or waive another's correlative obligation, but this means that a claim-right includes a power as a proper constituent part.'[40] This essay has already touched upon the general nature of the misstep committed here by Lyons. The fact that a Hohfeldian claim must be enforceable in order to be a genuine claim (as opposed to a nominal claim) does not necessitate the vesting of the power-of-enforcement in the holder of the claim; the power can lie with someone else. So long as a claim is appropriately enforceable, it is a genuine claim even if its enforcer is not its holder.

Lyons has also stumbled in a manner partly reminiscent of Raz. He writes that 'it seems implausible to regard all Hohfeldian immunities as rights. According to Hohfeld's definitions, one has an immunity if one is prevented by law from inheriting property. But being legally barred from inheriting property hardly seems to qualify as a right.'[41] Hohfeld, of course, would scarcely be worried about the inapplicability of the term 'right'. One of the chief purposes of his most famous essays was to show that the term 'right' had been sloppily applied to entitlements that should have received

---

[40] *RWMMT* (n 25 above), 11–12. For a similar error, see Flathman, *Practice* (n 3 above), 49. Cf Ross, *Directives* (n 3 above), 127–8.

[41] *RWMMT* (n 25 above), 11. See also Hart, 'Legal Rights' (n 3 above), 191: '[E]ven in the loosest usage, the expression "a right" is not used to refer to the fact that a man is thus immune from an *advantageous* change. ... An individual's immunity from legal change at the hands of others is spoken and thought of as a right only when the change in question is *adverse*.' (Emphases in original.) For a comparable point about certain types of powers, expressed from a Hohfeldian perspective, see Dias (n 4 above), 56–7, 61.

different labels. He observed that 'the word "right" is overworked in the field of immunities as elsewhere' (*FLC*, 62), and he proposed the term 'immunities' to denote exemptions from undesirable changes in one's entitlements *and* exemptions from desirable changes in one's entitlements. As was discussed earlier in some detail, the distinctive functions of Hohfeld's second-order entitlements are defined in a non-evaluative fashion—without direct reference to advantages (or interests) and disadvantages (or burdens). In that respect, those entitlements diverge from the first-order rights and liberties. We therefore should hardly be surprised that there are many instances of second-order entitlements to which no one will feel inclined to extend the label 'right', a label that is inapposite in any event.

Richard Flathman commits a largely similar error in his account of Hohfeldian immunities, when he writes that '[i]mmunities are like liberties in that they leave A at liberty to do the X the immunity grants and they deprive B of any ground on which to claim that A's doing X is other than innocent' (Flathman, *Practice*, 58). Flathman's remark reaches far too broadly. Although some immunities do render their holders invulnerable to the stripping away of liberties, other immunities render their holders impervious to the extinguishing of duties. Immunities of the latter sort will yield results just the opposite of those mentioned by Flathman. Consider again, for instance, Joe's non-waivable duty to make an annual payment of £3,000 to his mother. If Joe's mother seeks to waive his duty, her efforts will come to nought because of his immunity from the exercise of a power that would eliminate his duty. Far from leaving Joe at liberty to refrain from paying the money, his immunity leaves him duty-bound to go ahead with the payment. Far from depriving his mother of any ground on which to claim that his non-payment is wrongful, his immunity will have had precisely the opposite effect.

Somewhat akin to Flathman's error is the misstep that was made by Alf Ross when he contended that the second-order legal positions established by 'norms of competence' are reducible to the first-order legal positions established by 'norms of conduct.' He wrote:

Norms of competence are logically reducible to norms of conduct in this way: norms of competence make it obligatory to act according to the norms of conduct which have been created according to the procedure laid down in them. Like obligation, 'competence' is a relationship between two persons, between, namely, the person who is endowed with competence and the person who is subject to his power, who is, that is to say, under an obligation to obey the norms created by him in the correct manner. (Ross, *Directives*, 118.)

Let us not dwell here on the unacceptable notion that the dynamic second-order functions of powers and liabilities can be reduced to the static first-order functions of rights and duties. Let us concentrate instead on Ross's mistaken belief that all exercises of powers result in impositions of duties. Such a belief is indeed mistaken, since powers can remove duties (along with their correlative rights) as well as engender them. If Y exercises his power to relieve Z of some duties that have been owed by Z to Y, then Y has scarcely thereby traded on Z's 'obligation to obey the norms created by him'. On the contrary, Z now enjoys latitude in areas—that is, the areas covered by the scope of his erstwhile duties—where he previously had none. He *may* act in compliance with his bygone duties (unless he bears other duties that cut against them), but he no longer is *required* to act in compliance therewith. Instead of being left to obey, Z has now been left to do as he pleases within the limits of his new liberties. In short, only by failing to keep in mind some major ways in which a power can bring about changes which are desirable from the perspective of a liability-bearer, could Ross wrongly assume that every exercise of a power eventuates in new duties. Though he later pointed out the advantageousness of certain liabilities (Ross, *Directives*, 132), he here did not show any awareness that one sort of advantageous liability is a liability leading to the removal of one's duties.

Rex Martin runs aground when discussing the various Hohfeldian entitlements involved in the act of voting. He declares that 'the act of voting creates a liability on the part of others (vote registrars, incumbent officials) to count the vote and give it effect' (Martin, *System*, 47). Far from *creating* a liability, the act of voting *trades on* a liability—that is, it exercises a power—in order to create a *duty*. It imposes a duty on the relevant officials to count the vote and give it effect. Unlike a duty, a liability does not require its bearer to take certain actions (or to forgo certain actions); instead, it consists in a vulnerability to the power-exerting actions of someone else.

Geoffrey Marshall—in an essay that is generally very impressive—has misunderstood the distinction between rights and liberties, which he construes as a distinction between unqualified and qualified entitlements:

[T]he sort of right that is often exemplified when juristic rights are contrasted with 'liberties' or 'privileges' ... tends to be illustrated by such examples as a debt or engagement between two parties. The obligation to pay has as its direct correlative the right to payment. The right here is simply defined and unqualified and the suggested need to distinguish it from other forms of entitlement by dubbing them 'liberties' is illuminating. What characterizes these other forms of entitlement is that they have no such exact correlative obligation as has the 'claim-right'. The use of the term 'liberty' seems in part a way of acknowledging that rights are frequently only qualified rights. The 'right' for example to carry on a trade is clearly not an unqualified one. It has to be adjusted to, and balanced against, the right to be protected from unfair competition. A's 'right' or 'liberty' to park on an unrestricted highway is obviously a shared right. It is not (unlike a right to payment [from a debtor]) an unqualified right. It is a right to park in a place of his choice provided that B or C or D do [*sic*] not park there first; and the rights of B, C, and D are similarly qualified. But since most rights are of this kind it is perhaps odd to choose the rather special case of an unqualified right to set the pattern for rights properly so called. A debt and a right to payment constitute one of the few unqualified right situations. (Marshall, 'Rights', 240–1).

Alas, the errors in this long passage are legion. Let us recall the chief differences between rights and liberties. A right consists in the protection bestowed on a person Y by dint of the establishment of a duty that is owed to Y by someone else. A right is therefore specified by reference to what the duty-bearer is required to do or forgo. A liberty, on the other hand, consists in the latitude enjoyed by Z as a result of her not owing a duty to Y concerning some matter. A liberty is therefore specified by reference to what the liberty-holder is permitted to do or forgo. Now, this straightforward distinction between rights and liberties has nothing to do with the distinction between unqualified and qualified entitlements. Few if any Hohfeldian rights in actual legal or moral systems are unqualified; for instance, *pace* Marshall, the right of a creditor against a debtor is defeasible through a number of contingencies in actual legal systems and in countless possible legal systems.[42] By contrast, all liberties in situations akin to the Hobbesian state of nature are unqualified. We scarcely should be surprised, then, to find that the

---

[42] For a brief discussion of this point (in the midst of a more doubtful discussion about the reducibility of collective persons to individual persons), see Radin (n 2 above), 1161–2. See also HLA Hart, *The Concept of Law* (Oxford: Clarendon Press, 1961), 135–6.

'qualified rights' singled out by Marshall do not correspond uniformly to Hohfeldian categories. For instance, the qualified 'right' to carry on a trade is in fact a liberty to carry on a trade, whereas the qualified right to be free from unfair competition is indeed a Hohfeldian right. Even more complicatedly, the qualified 'right' to park is in fact a liberty accompanied by a power to gird oneself with a temporary right to be free from encroachments on one's parking space. Notice how much more precise and nuanced the Hohfeldian distinctions are than the qualified/unqualified distinction. We have no reason to prefer fuzziness to Hohfeld's exactitude.

Immediately after the comments quoted in my last paragraph, Marshall argues as follows:

Trade unionists and employers for example have rights that impinge on each other. But only if all rights were unqualified would it be the case that the employer's right to carry on his business would imply that his employees had no right to strike. Since, however, 'right' does not mean 'unqualified right', and since even English judges in the nineteenth century cannot have imagined that it did, it may have been unnecessary to cavil at their usage; or to suppose that any faults in their decisions stemmed from it. It may be that the substitution of the term 'liberty' for right is not the best way of making the point that the competing 'rights' of trade unionists and employers react upon and modify each other. (Marshall, 'Rights', 240–1.)

Marshall has plainly gone astray in suggesting that a right to non-interference with one's business must be unqualified if it is to imply protection against the interference caused by strikes. An employer can have a right to be free from the disruptions of strikes without having a right to be free from numerous other types of interference. Marshall's defence of nineteenth-century English judges is equally ill-advised. Hohfeld never accused those judges of thinking that all rights were unqualified rights; the qualified/unqualified distinction was not something to which Hohfeld devoted much attention. What Hohfeld *did* contend was that the judges often mistakenly believed that mere liberties imposed duties in much the same way as veritable rights. He was amply justified in advancing such a contention—as his numerous quotations and examples confirm.

Let us finish this listing of specific errors by returning to the work of David Lyons. Consider the following passage from a 1970 essay:

Suppose that Alvin is atop a soap box speaking to a crowd against United States military involvement in Vietnam. His act is perfectly lawful, but he is assaulted by some private citizens, driven from the box and silenced. Their behavior is unlawful and constitutes unwarranted and prohibited interference with the exercise of his legal rights. In saying this we may refer to his general right of free speech or to a specific right to stand there addressing the crowd. In either case the right might be construed as a right *to do* something.[43]

Viewed from a Hohfeldian perspective, Lyons's comments are flawed. Alvin has a liberty to speak, rather than a right; the right that is violated by the citizens is his right to be free from assaults. Had the citizens been able to silence Alvin without assaulting him or violating any of his other rights, they could have done so. The fact that his speech is 'perfectly lawful' simply means that the government is not entitled to interfere with his discourse. Unless Alvin breaks the law, he (very likely) has a right against governmental interference and an immunity against being stripped of that right. However, such entitlements scarcely mean that private citizens must abstain from interfering with his discourse.

Lyons, however, has not blundered so much as he has reinvented the wheel. He goes on to stipulate that Alvin has a 'right' which consists of a pair of entitlements: an entitlement to speak before the crowd, and an entitlement to be free from interference with the speech. Viewed from a Hohfeldian perspective, this 'right' is a combination of a liberty and a claim. Without using Hohfeld's terminology, Lyons then observes that the 'right' which he has described is quite different from a claim that is not combined with a cognate liberty (Lyons, 'Correlativity', 49–50, 52–3). Had Lyons availed himself of Hohfeld's terms instead of employing the word 'right' as loosely as the jurists whom Hohfeld condemned, he would have been less inclined to dwell on an insight that was emphasized by Hohfeld and his defenders many decades ago.

---

[43] David Lyons, 'The Correlativity of Rights and Duties', 4 *Noûs* 45, 49 (1970) [hereinafter cited as Lyons, 'Correlativity'].

Rights at the Cutting Edge

N.E. SIMMONDS

Introduction

This essay concerns the analytical jurisprudence of legal rights.[1] It is both a reflection upon that subject and a contribution to it. Since the structure of the essay is somewhat complicated, it is best to begin with a brief outline of what follows.

Part 1 reflects upon some of the philosophical issues that form the background to the debate concerning legal rights. One object of the discussion is to challenge conventional conceptions of the division between analytical jurisprudence on the one hand and normative jurisprudence on the other. Analyses of legal rights have always, I suggest, been bound up with broader interpretations of the form of moral association that finds expression in our laws. Jurisprudential discussion has tended to focus upon the *form* of rights rather than upon their *content*, but this focus is misunderstood if it is taken to reflect a division between conceptual analyses and substantive moral or political theories. Complex separations and dependencies between form and content themselves point to significant features of the modern political community, and have given rise to paradoxical tensions that become manifest within the debate concerning rights.

Part 2 offers a preliminary account of the classical 'Interest' and 'Will' Theories of rights. These theories were in essence and in origin theories of the grounds of legitimacy rather than austerely analytical clarifications of a concept. They sought to exhibit the role of law in reconciling the subjectivity of interests and projects with the demands of collective governance. The Will Theory emphasised the systematic character of law and the boundary between private and public law. Rights were identified pre-eminently with private law, and were understood in terms of a Kantian theory of justice

---

[1] I am indebted to David Johnston for his comments on an earlier draft, and to Matthew Kramer for his comments on successive drafts. I am also indebted to RWM Dias, whose lucid expositions of Hohfeld first introduced me to the subject.

that separated the form of the will from its particular content. The Interest Theory, by contrast, emphasised the posited nature of law as a basis for the artificial demarcation of boundaries between conflicting interests. Both the Will Theory and the Interest Theory (in their classical versions) encountered severe problems. The Will Theory ran aground upon the emptiness and sterility of the Kantian theory of justice. The Interest Theory, on the other hand, found itself faced by unacceptable alternatives: either a collapse into naked instrumentalism, or a reduction of rights to the mere reflex of posited rules.

Parts 3 and 4 then turn to the Hohfeldian analysis of rights, an analysis which is fundamental to the whole essay. Part 3 aims to elucidate and defend certain features of that analysis, especially the separation between permissibility and inviolability, and to demonstrate the importance of that distinction in undermining the pretensions of Kantian jurisprudence, and thus of the classical Will Theory. Part 4 then pursues this theme further, mainly by reference to the Kantian theory of Hillel Steiner.

Part 5 addresses the classical and modern versions of the Interest Theory. In particular, I seek to demonstrate that the most influential modern versions of the Interest Theory present rights as playing a central part in the dynamic aspect of legal reasoning: that is, they treat rights as pivotal features of legal doctrine, providing reasons for the recognition of new remedies, duties, liabilities, and so forth. In making this move, however, they encounter a variety of difficult problems. They are, for example, forced into an unacknowledged abandonment of the idea that rights have peremptory force. Furthermore, they find it impossible coherently to elucidate the notion of the special 'weight' that is said (by such Interest Theorists) to attach to those interests that are accorded the status of a right. Consequently, the theory tends to collapse legal rights into markers of interests within a general process of balancing interests one against another. This erodes the integrity of legal doctrine and, with it, of the domains of liberty protected by such doctrine.

In Part 1 of this essay I point to the paradoxical tensions characterizing a modern political community and finding expression in the debate about the nature of rights. The very pluralism and diversity that leads us to emphasise the importance of rights also renders their existence problematic. In Part 6 we encounter a further twist to the problem, for Part 6 advocates, as the most satisfactory analysis of the concept of 'a right', a modest version of Will Theory in something like the form proposed by H.L.A. Hart. This theory does not treat rights as central to legal reasoning or to the dynamic development of law (as did both the classical Will Theory and influential versions of the modern Interest Theory). For consideration of those alternative theories shows us that to place rights at the centre of legal reasoning is to threaten the determinacy of doctrinal argument and so the integrity of rights themselves. The modest version of the Will Theory treats rights as powers of waiver or enforcement over legal duties. In this way it reflects two features that might be considered important constituents of the integrity of rights: the separation of private from public law, and the centrality to private law of private rights of enforcement. One does not protect the integrity of rights by placing them at the centre of our legal thinking, for down that broad and obvious path lies the indeterminacy of the classical Will Theory and the naked balancing of interests that constitutes the modern Interest Theory. Protecting rights effectively is not the same thing as talking or thinking about rights, and the most effective protections may well involve reliance upon criteria that do not employ the concept of a right at all. Possessing a right should involve, however, having some real element of control or choice such as is provided by the option of enforcement: rights need not and should not be at the centre of our legal thinking, but they should be and can be at the cutting edge.

1 Background

Analysis and Interpretation.

On 10 November 1837 the 19-year-old Karl Marx wrote a letter to his father. Marx had completed one year as a student in the Law Faculty at Berlin, and he gave his father an account of his legal and philosophical studies during the year. In the course of this account he speaks of having written a treatise on the philosophy of law, discussing 'the development of the ideas in positive Roman law' and analysing 'the necessary structure' of those ideas. Marx goes on to explain how he came to regard this enterprise as absurdly misguided, in so far as it assumed that the form of a legal concept could be separated from its positive content:

The mistake lay in my belief that matter and form can and must develop separately from each other, and so I obtained not a real form, but something like a desk with drawers into which I then poured sand.[2]

The topic of the present essay might raise in the minds of many lawyers a reaction resembling that of the young Marx: for the analytical jurisprudence of rights seems, like Marx's juvenile treatise on the philosophy of law, to detach the form of rights from their content. We are invited to address the question of the general nature of rights without saying anything of substance about what our rights may authorize or require. We may plausibly be assured that the analytical question of what it is to possess a right must be logically prior to the question of what rights we possess; that the concept of a right must first be clarified before decisions can be made about its applicability. Yet we may be forgiven for suspecting that this exercise will result only in the construction of drawers into which we will later 'pour sand'.

Indeed, few debates in modern jurisprudence seem so arid as that concerning the formal analysis of legal rights. Even amongst those who have actively battled in the tournament, there is little agreement about the prizes that may be at stake, or about the wider issues that may turn upon the outcome. Anyone acquainted with the analytical jurisprudence of rights at a tolerably sophisticated level is likely to conclude that our more 'conceptual' intuitions about rights can be regimented in a great diversity of ways. Each regimentation comes, of course, at a price, and protagonists in the controversy sustain a sense of intellectual progress by drawing attention to the price that others must pay, while making light of the entry fee to their own system. Human ingenuity guarantees that the repertoire of available intellectual positions is never exhausted, and the kaleidoscopic turns of the discussion can certainly exert their fascination; but, in the absence of some more convincing account of what is at stake, many will turn their attention elsewhere.

Too casual a dismissal of such controversies can, however, be a mistake. Even if we were to regard their existence as but a curious fact in the anthropology of developed legal systems, it would nevertheless be a fact that demands explanation and which may point us

---

[2] Extracts from the letter are printed in Maureen Cain and Alan Hunt, *Marx and Engels on Law* (London: Academic Press, 1979), 16, and David McLellan, *Karl Marx: Selected Writings* (Oxford: Oxford University Press, 1977), 7.

towards significant insights. Seemingly abstruse debates can sometimes be the expression of surprisingly deep tensions within the legal order. Thurman Arnold once defined jurisprudence as 'the shining but unfulfilled dream of a world governed by reason'.[3] Pursuing that thought, we may expect to discover within such dreams much that is of significance for our collective self-understanding.

One does not know one's own character by introspection. One must first act, in the world of things and persons. By retrospective reflection upon the character of our actions, we may come to know ourselves. Similarly, the political and legal institutions and practices of modern communities did not spring into being as a simple expression of newly formed political ideals arrived at in abstraction from the flood of historical events. Rather, we may hypothesize that those institutions and practices became manifest before they were identified as distinctive; only then were they reflected upon as sources of insight into our own nature and values; only then did those values begin to take shape upon the intellectual landscape. Interpretations of the modern political community which emphasize the autonomous character of its citizens and the individualistic nature of their values are therefore of one piece with interpretations of the character of law that make such autonomy and individualism seem possible. The practices of modern law and legal argument admit of diverse interpretations, and these interpretations carry with them significant implications for the self-understanding of the liberal political community and for the role of law within that community. The reflective conclusion that our polity expresses values giving a central priority to law is often of a piece with a view as to how law can be possible within such a community. Consequently, varying understandings of the problem of law's status suggest distinctly different solutions to that problem.

It is at this point that two classical theories of rights come clearly into view: the 'Will' and 'Interest' Theories. For these two theories are best understood as proposing rival interpretations of the nature of modern law and of the relationship between the individual and the collectivity.

Such a characterization of a seemingly esoteric jurisprudential debate will strike many as surprising and implausible. They may

---

[3] Thurman W Arnold, *The Symbols of Government*. Relevant extracts are collected in V Aubert (ed) *Sociology of Law* (London: Penguin, 1969), 46–51.

see little in the modern literature on the analytical jurisprudence of rights that suggests a concern with such fundamental issues. Contemporary forms of the contest between the Will and Interest Theories prove, however, to be but a pale and impoverished representation of the problems that originally gave shape to the rival positions. Those problems concerned the reconciliation of individual projects and entitlements with collective governance of the political community: the subjectivity of rights and the objectivity of law. Versions of the Will and Interest Theories can be reconstructed in a form that makes the centrality of such questions clear: I will describe such reconstructions as the 'classical' versions of the two theories, and will then seek to cast light upon the route whereby the classical versions metamorphosed into their more insipid contemporary descendants. This metamorphosis did not come about as a result of the common human tendency to continue seeking answers to a question long after we have forgotten our reasons for asking it. Rather, significance has appeared to seep away from this debate as a consequence of the intellectual and historical pressures to which the proposed solutions have been subject.

The factors which have led to this perceived loss of significance are no doubt quite varied; but one feature that calls for special attention is a subtle change in our conceptions of the proper task of philosophy, which seems to preclude philosophical reflection upon the established forms of legal and political community. For the very conception of our enterprise as an interpretation of contingent arrangements is obstructed by modern assumptions concerning the character of jurisprudence. It is frequently assumed that jurisprudence must *either* proffer analytic truths by way of conceptual clarification *or* must endeavour to ground categorical moral principles. Jurisprudence must (in short) be *either* analytical, *or* normative and foundational. Within the context of the first enterprise, we may seek a systematic description of practices and institutions. Within the context of the second enterprise we may *evaluate* those practices by reference to unconditioned moral principles. The stark terms of this dichotomy have tended to survive in spite of the doubts which have been cast upon the very notion of analytic truth[4] and the ever-repeated failure to discover

---

[4] WVO Quine, 'Two Dogmas of Empiricism' in *From a Logical Point of View* (Cambridge, Mass: Harvard, 1964). For criticism of Quine's position, and comparison with Wittgenstein's views, see Hans-Johan Glock, 'Necessity and Normativity' in

philosophically grounded moral principles. The survival is in large part explained by the belief that if philosophy cannot lay claim to a distinct field of inquiry (such as the analytically true, or the unconditioned foundation) it ceases to be an autonomous discipline.

Such stark alternatives were alien to older forms of legal philosophical thought. The major positions within the historic tradition of jurisprudence might well be thought of as reflections upon the form of moral association represented by law. Whether that association was understood in terms of Reason, of Will and Artifice, or of History,[5] law was its visible expression and was important for that reason. When our common human nature was seen as God's handiwork, and as a source of fundamental value for us, it was inevitable that a key to that nature would be sought in the practices and institutions in which it found expression. Law was not simply a sphere for the application of moral insights derived from elsewhere, but a significant focus for philosophical reflection and a source of self-understanding. Indeed, since jurisprudential reflection *upon* law has never been clearly separable from the intelligent development of doctrinal ideas, we may go further. Borrowing the words of Alasdair Macintyre, we may say that the 'living tradition' of jurisprudence 'is an historically extended, socially embodied argument, and an argument precisely in part about the goods which constitute that tradition.'[6]

Consideration of the values internal to political communities and juridical practices has become harder to comprehend, partly as a result of Kant's moral philosophy. In presenting a view of morality as conditioned neither by practice nor by desire, Kant's philosophy seemed to have the effect of reducing human practices and forms of association to brute facts without intrinsic moral status.[7] No longer seen as the expression of a normative human nature, nor as the outcome of a Divine Providence manifesting God's will, the observable features of human society were to be judged from the viewpoint of the categorical imperative. The idea that a form of human association

Hans Sluga and David Stern (eds) *The Cambridge Companion to Wittgenstein* (Cambridge: Cambridge University Press, 1996)

[5] Michael Oakeshott, *Hobbes on Civil Association* (Oxford: Blackwell, 1975).
[6] Alasdair Macintyre, *After Virtue* (London: Duckworth, 1981), 207.
[7] This has been the historical influence of Kant's emphasis upon the categorical nature of moral demands, but Kant's own position was more complex. The older approach received a muted echo in Kant's philosophy of history, and a late flowering in the thought of Hegel.

might serve as a source of moral insight is rendered problematic on this view, wherein moral examples are presented as secondary to, and wholly dependent upon, articulable moral principles.[8]

However, the older view has some surprisingly modern resonances. For, if we are not to fall into the errors of an extreme moral Protestantism which makes morality solely a matter of the private and individual will, we should acknowledge that morality embodies interests that can only be fulfilled in the context of shared social practices; and if we are to avoid a crude Hobbesianism that makes such practices a mere means to the satisfaction of one's private preferences, we must acknowledge that the interests so realized are our interests as moral beings, and not simply as seekers of private gratification. Our moral identities, therefore, must be bound up with constitutive forms of association, and reflection upon such forms of association must be an integral part of moral philosophy. If our interests as moral beings can be realised only in the practices of a political community, then the actual historical practices of such communities must contain at least *intimations* of moral reason, which the philosopher can seek to comprehend and elucidate.

Somewhat ironically, the detached deontology of Kantianism is itself occasionally presented as a response to the particular features of modern political communities. Thus, we find it argued that the notion of categorical obligation arose as an attempt to deal with the problem of pluralism in modern society: conditionality upon particular desires or forms of life will be inadequate in communities which exhibit diverse commitments and cultural practices.[9] Whether or not such explanations are plausible, they do not enable us to overcome our sense that moral requirements cannot be grounded simply in 'the way we do things around here'. For we are heirs to a sense of detachment from all such contingent and local practices: a detachment which fuels the demand for categorical moral foundations.

The idea of morality as autonomous and empirically unconditioned suggests the need for foundations that are abstract and monistic, forming a unified and all-encompassing perspective upon the world. The varying features of our moral and juridical practices

---

[8] See Kant, *Groundwork of the Metaphysics of Morals,* 2nd edn, (trans) HJ Paton, *The Moral Law* (London: Hutchinson, 1958), 73.
[9] Charles Larmore, *The Morals of Modernity*, (Cambridge: Cambridge University Press, 1996), 12. See also Alasdair Macintyre, *A Short History of Ethics* (London: MacMillan, 1967), ch 14.

are comprehended from such a viewpoint only by a process of subsumption and flattening out. The philosophical debate becomes a search for the aggregative or distributive goal which can most effectively subsume and explain the seemingly recalcitrant facts of practical history and experience.

Such tendencies towards monism and abstraction within political philosophy are, within jurisprudence, reinforced by more specific features of legal doctrinal analysis. For the model of doctrinal analysis which shaped the emergence of the legal treatise was one which emphasized the internal coherence of the law, coherence being understood as the capacity for subsumption under a limited range of highly general principles and categories. Pressures towards legal recognition of the diversity of human interests, however, forced the law to pursue an ever more complex agenda of goals and policies, many of which were mutually competitive. Consequently, it became difficult to view the legal order as the coherent expression of a single conception of justice structured by a set of ordered doctrinal principles. One response to this problem was, not to abandon the search for monistic systematization, but to seek for it at ever more abstract levels, thus encouraging the unhelpful perspectives adopted within philosophy.

I have elsewhere suggested that a model of doctrinal integrity founded on the idea of a domain's internal simplicity should be replaced by a model founded on the relative impermeability of the domain's boundary.[10] This perspective proves to be an important one for our understanding of the debate on rights. For, while contemporary theories of rights may appear to lack any obvious depth of significance (thereby differing from their classical ancestors) the appearance is in some respects misleading. The question which lay at the heart of the classical debate was one concerning the integrity of rights, and this question continues to press upon us. What we find here is not a loss of significance but a loss of confidence in the availability of sweeping and unqualified solutions. Classical versions of the Will and Interest Theories were the expression of a robust confidence that the problem of reconciling private entitlements with collective governance could be solved in a fully satisfactory manner at a level of considerable generality. There are now

---

[10] See Nigel Simmonds, 'The Possibility of Private Law', in John Tasioulas (ed), *Law, Values and Social Practices* (Aldershot: Dartmouth, 1997).

good reasons for doubting that confidence. Consequently, sweeping solutions are less likely to be successful than modest and piecemeal stratagems; categorical principles are less likely to be available than suggestive interpretations of actual, albeit contingent, arrangements; we will be unwise to claim that our account of rights is straightforwardly 'true', and better advised to suggest that it represents a way of understanding our practices that fosters those objectives that we take the practices to serve.

Form and Content

Marx's initial belief that the form of law might be studied independently of its content gave expression to some striking features of the post-feudal legal order (as we will see, the same might be said of his subsequent *rejection* of that idea). Indeed, the very notion that the law may be represented as a body of systematic principles independently of a description of the social relations to which the law applies is itself a manifestation of the dichotomies between form and content. If one were to open up a medieval law book such as Bracton, for example, one would find that an account of the law was bound up with an account of the political, social and economic relations of the polity. A modern law book dealing with a central area of private law (such as contract or tort) would by contrast reveal very little about the society to which the law applied. Such differences in the character of legal exposition reflect differing moral or political assumptions. For medieval legal thought, the institutions of law and government were established in hierarchical form as a source of discipline for sinful men and women. The political hierarchy was in continuum with a hierarchy stretching throughout God's creation. An exposition of the assemblage of rights, franchises, lordships and servitudes composing the social and political hierarchy was in itself an exposition of the law. For modern legal thought, by contrast, rights are not inherently or naturally hierarchical in character: rather, the assumption is that the diverse concrete rights of individuals may be derived from juridical principles which in some sense apply equally to everyone, defining a level of entitlement at which all rights are equal.

The emergence of systematic structures of legal rights, grounded in juridical equality, marked the separation between the modern liberal polity and the old society of feudalism. In shaking itself free from immersion in the hierarchies of the social structure, and presenting itself as a body of principles defining equal rights, the legal order generated systematic bodies of doctrine of a type which had not previously existed. Every social relation, when presented in legal doctrinal terms, needed to be analysed in terms of highly general principles and relations. The *form* of law came to be an important focus for attention. Indeed, the priority given to form over content within the scheme of doctrinal legal thought led Lukacs to claim that 'the whole revolutionary period of the bourgeoisie was based on the assumption that the formal equality and universality of the law (and hence its rationality) was able at the same time to determine its content'.[11]

In grounding itself on this assumption, modern legal thought gave rise to a body of juristic *theory*. The simple exposition of posited rules and decisions was subsumed under an enterprise of systematic integration whereby concrete provisions were treated, not as discrete, but as reflective of some central constellation of principles. At the same time, it was hoped that the determinacy of the law's content could be sustained without being infected by aggregative or distributive questions characteristic of the political realm. It might well be thought that the attempt to separate a body of relatively abstract legal concepts and distinctions from all questions about the purpose or justification of those concepts and distinctions would make the law seem 'like a mysterious language with a formal grammar but no real meaning of its own'.[12] Classically, however, the aspiration was to create a systematic body of doctrine structured by a handful of general concepts (such as the notions of property, fault, and the will) bearing its reasonableness and its groundedness in principle open upon its face. The most influential theory for the period when legal doctrinal systems were being systematized and consolidated was a theory of Kantian provenance. For it was believed that reason could determine a set of principles which represents the mutual compatibility of individual wills: in this way, each person's freedom might be reconciled with the freedom of everyone else, and the content of the necessary system of rules could be determined without privileging the will and preferences of any individual. It is on this plane of

---

[11] G Lukacs, *History and Class Consciousness*, (trans) Rodney Livingstone, (London: Merlin Press, 1971), 107.
[12] Jeremy Waldron in Dennis Patterson (ed), *A Companion to Philosophy of Law and Legal Theory* (Oxford: Blackwell, 1996), 10.

juristic theory that the debate concerning the nature of rights emerges into prominence, giving rise to just such discussions of the 'form' or 'necessary structure' of legal ideas as those which had been embarked upon by the youthful Marx.

The abstraction of juridical principles from the complex social relations to which they applied gave law an appearance of austerity and rigour. Yet at the same time, the emergence of such a distinct juridical realm ultimately involved a recognition that the social structure was not a natural landscape forming the unalterable horizon for human affairs, but was itself subject to the choices of the collectivity. In his essay 'On the Jewish Question',[13] Marx was to highlight the connection between (on the one hand) the emergence of a public political state distinct from the proprietary and familial realms of civil society, and (on the other hand) the conceptualization of that civil society as a region of competition between independent actors, rather than as an organically united or divinely ordered sphere. The dissolution of civil society into independent actors was a recognition of an individual identity distinguishable from inherited social roles; while the emergence of the political state fostered recognition of the collective choices that sustained the framework of civil society. States may have evolved out of complex patterns of behaviour independently of any collective choice, but once they are in existence they transform the moral situation of their members by making possible collective choices which can alter the inherited outcomes of a customary order.[14] This was to pose problems for theories that interpreted juridical thought in terms of a formalistic Kantian theory of justice, for such theories tended to founder upon the emptiness of their own formalism once the presupposition of some given social background was removed or called into question.

I have elsewhere described the problem to which this gave rise as involving two competing values, which I dub 'private project pursuit', and 'collective project pursuit'.[15] On the one hand we value the capacity of individuals to formulate and pursue their own plans and

---

[13] Karl Marx, 'On the Jewish Question', in *Karl Marx: Early Writings* (London: Penguin, 1975).

[14] I am here seeking to describe the assumptions that structure our political values. The substantial reality of collective choice may be a different matter. See, for example, Claus Offe, *Modernity and the State* (Cambridge: Polity, 1996), who speaks of a 'widely shared sense that sovereignties have become nominal, power anonymous, and its locus empty' (p. ix).

[15] Simmonds (n 10 above).

projects; but, on the other hand, we value our ability collectively, through the organs of our political community, to exercise control over the character of our social life. The value that we place on these capacities does not, of course, imply that we believe that there are no truths about how such capacities should be exercised, or about which choices should be made in the course of their exercise. The point is simply that we value the capacity to choose quite independently of the value we put upon the content of such choices. We do not regard the general character and profile of our society as a natural landscape over which we have no control; nor do we regard the course of our individual lives as being inflexibly determined by inherited social roles. Knowing that these things are alterable, we believe that it is our responsibility as moral agents to exercise choice about whether and how they might be altered.

Collective and private project pursuit conflict. A society which gave full scope to private project pursuit would abdicate collective control by allowing its overall character to be determined by the unpredictable outcome of millions of unco-ordinated individual choices; while a society which gave full scope to collective control would obliterate any room for private projects.[16]

It is through the institution of the rule of law that the political community seeks to achieve a stable way of recognizing and respecting the competition between values which is inherent in this situation. The notion of the rule of law, however, is far from transparent, and rival accounts of its requirements mirror in significant ways the dichotomies of the rights debate. On the one hand is a theory which emphasizes the separation between public and private law: public law is viewed as the instrument of collective choice, while private law is portrayed as an autonomous realm of reasoning which is independent of political deliberation. On the other hand is a theory which emphasizes a contrast between the legislative decision to enact rules and adjudicative judgments concerning the applicability of such rules once enacted: collective project pursuit is respected in our capacity to choose which general laws and systems of rights we will enact; while private project pursuit is respected by protecting

---

[16] This is argued at greater length in 'The Possibility of Private Law' (n 10 above). Attempts to deny the reality of the competition between these values are legion. Most recently, Ronald Dworkin has argued that the distributive goal of 'equality of resources' represents a collective project that is fully compatible with private project pursuit. See Ronald Dworkin, *Law's Empire* (London: Fontana, 1986), ch 8.

actions performed within the scope of such rights, even when those actions impede attainment of the collective goals. Advocates of the first view have tended to favour the classical Will Theory, with its emphasis upon the principled and systematic character of law, and have felt at ease with the gradual development of legal principles by judges and jurists; advocates of the latter theory have preferred the emphasis placed by the Interest Theory upon posited rules, and they have frequently favoured codification.

The general issue underlying a concern for the integrity of private rights, and the problematic relationship between 'rights' and 'law', tends to be nearer to the surface of debate in those countries that distinguish 'law' from 'rights' by the distinction between 'objective' and 'subjective' right: for this way of expressing the distinction makes it abundantly clear that we have here a question of the relationship between the projects or preferences of the individual and the impersonal demands of the collectivity.

Kantian conceptions of the rule of law represent law not as a simple aggregation of posited rules, but as a system guided by immanent values based on the autonomy of the will. Where law is developed by judges and jurists in the context of litigated disputes, and where systematic consistency in the doctrinal resolution of such disputes is a highly prized virtue, it is easy to assume that juridical evolution is guided by the ideal of a realm of jointly possible domains of autonomy. Moreover, while the German terminology of 'subjective' and 'objective' right may alert us to the competing values which underlie the debate about rights, that terminology is also inclined to suggest too facile a resolution of the conflict; for it is too easy to conclude that the concepts of 'subjective' and 'objective' right somehow refer to the same system of jointly possible liberties, but from different perspectives. Thus, in nineteenth-century German jurisprudence:

> Law is... compared to an invisible line of demarcation between the provinces of the wills of different individuals. The domain appertaining to each represents the collection of his Rights, and in this way the German distinguishes between the two meanings of the word *Recht*. This province in which the will of the individual reigns represents *Recht* in the subjective sense; the line which surrounds the province, and erects a barrier against the intrusion of other wills, is *Recht* in the objective sense.[17]

---

[17] John M Lightwood, *The Nature of Positive Law*, (London: Macmillan, 1883), 264 (summarizing the position of Savigny).

An exclusive focus upon the form of relationships, conceived in terms of the actors as bearers of *will*, was central to this theoretical resolution. Consider, for example, the following passage from the writings of the German jurist Puchta:

> The Relationships of Right are thus relations of men to one another, and they may be appropriately called juridical or jural relations. But as man stands in the sphere of Right as a person, we may at once determine the conception of these relations more definitely: they are *Relations of Persons as such to one another*. Hence it is immediately apparent that the human relationships do not enter in their full extent into the sphere of Right, nor into the series of relations of Right. For the notion 'Person', rests upon an abstraction, and thus it does not embrace the whole being of man, but only includes directly the fact that he is a subject of will, while his other qualities are only indirectly taken into account, according to their nearer or more distant connection with it.[18]

Puchta here combines an assertion of the distinctiveness of law with a particular interpretation of that distinctiveness. The distinctiveness of law consists in its tendency to abstract from many of those circumstances of human situations that we would ordinarily consider relevant to their ethical evaluation. Thus, as Puchta goes on to explain, a sick man who borrows money to provide for his family is legally in the same position as a rich man who borrows in order to speculate. An 'effort of abstraction is required to view as equal and the same in right' these two different situations. The interpretation proposed is one based on what I shall call the 'classical' Will Theory: jural relations are relationships between persons conceived of as bearers of *will*. The act of abstraction involved in this focus upon the 'will' gives rise to a realm of 'jural relations' which are the jurist's special concern.

The Return of the Repressed

Radical critics of law have always exhibited hostility towards the abstraction and blinkered vision of legal categories, and have longed for a realm of direct and 'unmediated' social relations. Thus, the early Marx viewed communism as a realm free from the

---

[18] *Outlines of the Science of Jurisprudence: translated and edited from the Juristic Encyclopaedias of Puchta, Friedlander, Falck and Ahrens* by W Hastie (Edinburgh: T and T Clark, 1887), 64 (emphasis in original).

rigidity of social roles and categorisations;[19] and the mature Marx was to observe that 'a right can by its nature only consist in the application of an equal standard, but unequal individuals (and they would not be different individuals if they were not unequal) can only be measured by the same standard if they are looked at from the same aspect, if they are grasped from one *particular* side'.[20] Such dreams of immediacy and transparency have spawned a whole genre of political rhetoric that turns upon the contrast between 'abstract' rules and concrete particulars.

Those of a more reformist tendency have rejected as illusory the contrasts between abstraction and immediacy upon which the revolutionary critics rely, and have preferred to redress the one-sidedness of classical juridical thought by other measures: not by an abandonment of rules, but by an abandonment of the exclusive focus upon the 'will'. The general endeavour has been to incorporate into the content of the law some concern for material interests and for the contexts within which choices must be made. Thus it has been said that 'the overriding theme of contemporary law and legal thought ... is the commitment to shape a free political and economic order by combining rights of choice with rules designed to ensure the effective enjoyment of these rights'.[21] Sometimes by the introduction of new doctrines into established areas of law, and sometimes by the development of wholly new bodies of law, the legal order has been re-organized as 'a binary system of rights of choice and of arrangements withdrawn from the scope of choice the better to make the exercise of choice real and effective'.[22]

Such doctrines and bodies of law departed from an austere focus upon the juridical person as a bearer of 'will', and endeavoured to accommodate a greater concern for the variable circumstances and interests of the citizen. At the same time, the experience of lawyers was beginning to demonstrate the truth of what the philosophers had realized much earlier: that the unadorned notion of the autonomous will offered no guidance in the construction, analysis, or application of legal doctrines, so that (behind the cover of an

---

[19] See Marx and Engels, *The German Ideology*, CJ Arthur (ed) (London: Lawrence and Wishart, 1970), 54.

[20] Karl Marx, 'The Critique of the Gotha Programme' in *The First International and After*, David Fernbach (ed) (London: Penguin, 1974), 347.

[21] Roberto Unger, *What Should Legal Analysis Become?* (London: Verso, 1996), 26.

[22] ibid, 27.

outwardly formal system) reference must constantly be made to circumstances that were officially excluded by the system of Right.

These developments, together with some others to be studied later in this essay, forced the abandonment of the classical Will Theory and its associated forms of juristic scholarship. In response to this situation, various versions of 'Interest Theory' gained in influence. According to these theories, legal rights were not protected spheres of freedom, but protected interests; and the system of legal doctrine was not an austere expression of the formal relations between mutually consistent wills, but a complex engagement with the material circumstances of life. The defeat of the classical Will Theory did not, however, entail straightforward triumph for its rival: for the Interest Theory itself had a tendency to split into distinct alternatives, each of which faced serious problems. Perhaps by virtue of its close historical connection with an emergent regulatory state, the Interest Theory tended to collapse the determination of existing legal rights into open-ended policy discussions concerning the purpose of this or that law, or the 'weight' to be attached to this or that interest. This clearly threatened the integrity of legal rights and their independence from the calculus of collective policy objectives. At the same time, the very notion of rights as protected forms of 'interest' appeared to make legal reasoning dependent upon an inquiry into contentious conceptions of well-being, in a manner seemingly inconsistent with the notion of a pluralistic liberal community. Meanwhile, fresh interpretations of the Will Theory were developed, abandoning the theory's commitment to a Kantian account of justice. At this stage, the debate as we are familiar with it was joined.

By now we should be in a position to see that this seemingly esoteric debate was and is generated by quite fundamental tensions within our form of political community. Autonomy and the good; political purposes and the integrity of laws; abstract freedoms and the material circumstances of choice: such dichotomies provide the basic dynamic of the analytical debate on rights. Once we appreciate that fact, we are in a position to attach new significance to Marx's youthful excursion into jurisprudence.

Having identified, as the mistake underlying his legal treatise, the 'belief that matter and form can and must develop separately from each other', Marx proposes an alternative approach deriving very directly from his fascination with Hegel. The law must be regarded as 'the concrete expression of a living world of ideas', and 'the object itself must be studied in its development; arbitrary divisions must not be introduced, the rational character of the object itself must develop as something imbued with contradictions in itself and find its unity in itself.'[23]

These remarks may perhaps seem to be more evocative than informative. They might well be equated with a familiar rhetorical contrast between the 'grey' of philosophical analysis on the one hand, and the living 'green' of richly articulated social practices on the other. The philosopher's love for arid deserts of the mind has long been an important feature of intellectual life, in jurisprudence no less than in other fields. The philosopher may be tempted to seek in abstract forms a deep metaphysical foundation for the juridical ordering of human conduct. Philosophers of law have frequently sought to honour law by grounding it in such foundations, free from historical contingency; yet what they treat as a foundation may in fact be (in Nietzsche's words) but 'the last smoke of evaporating reality'.[24]

While it is no doubt correct to see the young Marx as concerned with the problematic relationship between form and content, it would be a mistake to construe the sudden reversal in his thinking (and consequent dismissal of his juvenile excursion into the philosophy of law) as a simple shift from one side to the other of a set of dichotomies. Such an interpretation would overlook something to which our reflections thus far should have alerted us: the way in which the separation of form from content might itself express both the 'rational character' of the juridical community, and its character as something 'imbued with contradictions in itself'. True to his newfound Hegelian enthusiasms without entirely realizing it, Marx had stumbled upon a complex dialectic between the self-understanding of a concrete historical community, and the concern for abstract form to which that understanding gave rise. His juvenile efforts in the philosophy of law, in focusing upon 'necessary structure' at the expense of positive content, were themselves unconsciously reflecting significant historical contingencies. His evolving thought was not concerned to reverse this order of priorities so much as to

---

[23] n 2 above.
[24] Nietzsche, 'Reason in Philosophy', ss 1 and 4, *Twilight of the Idols* (various editions).

exhibit the dichotomy's groundedness in a particular political understanding and form of social life.

For it is only in so far as the practices of a community are bearers of meaning that they can exhibit 'contradictions', rather than simply conflicts. The juridical community that was constituted by law's detachment from the hierarchies of the social structure was in part constituted by a set of theoretical conceptions, separating form from content; yet it had in turn to undertake the systematization of that content within the formal categories of doctrinal thought. In this way a basic tension was established between two theoretical approaches (of which the Will and Interest Theories are manifestations). One approach sought to maintain the rigour of the formal system as a basis for the integrity and peremptory force of rights; but it encountered severe difficulties in accommodating the law's necessary engagement with the complex and conflictual world of human interests. The other approach sought fully to engage with the reality of conflicting interests and the dependence of legal thought upon such unsystematized considerations; but it thereby sacrificed the special force of rights and threatened to collapse their integrity into the general calculus of interests.

Marx and Savigny

Marx had available to him a tradition of legal study that claimed to reflect upon the development of law as 'a living world of ideas': the Historical School of Jurisprudence, inspired by Savigny and sustained by Savigny's disciples. By considering that tradition, he could have been led to discern some of the complex relationships that obtain between formal abstraction in law and the varied particularities of historical formations. He might then have discovered that his juvenile attempt at juristic analysis could provide important clues to the political puzzles that were to occupy his attention for the rest of his life.

On one level, Marx was vigorously to reject the claims of the Historical School, saying that it merely 'legitimizes the infamy of today with the infamy of yesterday'.[25] Yet it is possible to argue that Marx's own tendency to immerse law in a background of relations

---

[25] Karl Marx, 'Contribution to the Critique of Hegel's Philosophy of Right' in *Karl Marx: Early Writings*, translated by Rodney Livingstone and Gregor Benton (London: Penguin, 1975) 245.

of production was itself an extension of one aspect of the Historical School's thought, namely that school's emphasis upon law as an expression of actual practice and observance, grounded in the spontaneous growth of custom.[26] Similarly, Marx's interest in the distinctive *form* of modern bourgeois law mirrored the Historical School's sense that the spontaneous evolution of law had reached a culmination in the systematic studies of the scholarly jurist. Both Marx and the Historical School found themselves wrestling with the problem of a seemingly autonomous body of law that nevertheless reflected, in that very appearance of autonomy, the existing social formation.

Savigny endeavoured to marry his historical concerns to an essentially formalistic Kantian jurisprudence which abstracted the form of the will from its content, and the form of social relations from their historical particularities. He thus sought to combine his claims about the historical and customary rootedness of law with a seemingly conflicting set of beliefs about the need for a professional cadre of scholarly jurists remote from everyday practice and politics; and entrusted with responsibility for the law's preservation as a living and evolving inheritance. Deep immersion in the history of law led Savigny to the conclusion that the classical Roman Law represented an ideal fulfilment of legal evolution, even for Germany. The German reception of Roman Law at the end of the Middle Ages represented, in his view, a rational necessity, as did the separation of technical juristic doctrines from the moral understandings and political aspirations of the populace generally. Law fulfilled its nature and destiny by becoming a system of doctrinal principles and categories the intellectual coherence of which reflected the abstract requirements of a realm within which a multiplicity of diverse individual freedoms were conjointly exercisable.[27]

The complex relationships between formal abstraction and historical particularity that we find in the thought of Savigny are echoed within the thought of Marx. Thus, although Blandine Kriegel is in one sense right to see Marx as submerging the autonomy of

---

[26] See Blandine Kriegel, *The State and the Rule of Law*, translated by Marc A LePain and Jeffrey C Cohen (Princeton, New Jersey: Princeton University Press, 1995); James Q Whitman, *The Legacy of Roman Law in the German Romantic Era* (Princeton, New Jersey: Princeton University Press, 1990), 207–8.

[27] For an insightful discussion, see Peter Stein, *Legal Evolution* (Cambridge: Cambridge University Press, 1980), 56–65.

law in the complex practices of civil society,[28] it is important to remember that Marx would see a very significant difference in this regard between modern bourgeois law, on the one hand, and the feudal legal order on the other. Whereas the body of feudal law directly reflected the hierarchical character of the social and economic structure, modern law takes on the more detached character of juridical equality. The development of law as a body of abstract principles in the hands of scholarly jurists reflects this new impression of the law's autonomy; but this very appearance is (according to Marx) itself but an expression of the relations of production under capitalism. Since capitalism extracts surplus value under the form of equality, capitalist law mirrors that general form. The workings of abstract equality within the details of legal thought propel doctrinal analysis onto a level of abstraction and of apparent autonomy from social and economic life.

Marx was quick to perceive and comprehend the historical watershed whereby juridical thinking appeared to shake itself free from the hierarchical complexities of the social structure.[29] In his view, the public, political realm of law and rights had emerged to present itself as an illusory heaven standing above and beyond the particular oppressions of production, distribution, and the family. Ultimately, Marx was to portray this development as driven by the internal logic of the capitalist mode of production, in particular the latter's 'mode of extraction of surplus value' under the form of equality. Thus, having first perceived the formalistic abstractions of juridical science as merely pointless and misconceived, Marx was later to see them as profoundly significant expressions in the development of 'the rational character of the object itself . . . as something imbued with contradictions'.

The works of both Savigny and Marx may, in their very different ways, serve to remind us that a concern for abstract form may itself be grounded in a desire to understand the significance of certain concrete historical formations. If we seek to grasp the peculiar character of modern political communities, and to elucidate the distinct problems of law within those communities, we must inevitably investigate the law's appearance of system and autonomy; and, from that point of view, we might well do worse than to focus upon

[28] n 26 above.
[29] See Karl Marx, 'On the Jewish Question' in *Karl Marx: Early Writings* (n 25 above).

questions of the form of law and of rights. Likewise, critics of formalism in law (from Ihering to the realists and beyond) need to reflect upon the extent to which the promotion of content at the expense of law's formal character may undermine necessary features of a liberal polity. Separations and dependencies between form and content may themselves be a clue to the political character of modernity.

It is in something like this spirit that the present essay seeks to reconstruct the debate concerning legal rights. For, rather than seeing this controversy as one concerning the setting forth of a concept's contours by means of careful excavation, we should think of it as an attempt to construct a coherent concept from the ragged materials of gradually evolving doctrinal forms. Reflection upon the debate is fruitful primarily in so far as it alerts us to the political tensions of which the debate is but an expression. At the same time, such reflection should make us sceptical of the possibility of any final resolution at the level of theory, and should incline us towards responses which are modest, makeshift, and accepting of the permanent dependence of legal doctrine upon the wider context of a political community articulated into distinct realms of practice and value.

2 The Fundamental Issues

The Classical Will and Interest Theories of Rights

We may reconstruct the Will and Interest Theories, in their most substantial and interesting forms, as interpretations of the moral significance of systems of legal rights. As we have already observed, the emergence of systematic structures of legal rights, grounded in juridical equality, marked the separation between the modern liberal polity and the old society of feudalism. In shaking itself free from immersion in the hierarchies of the social structure, and presenting itself as a body of principles defining equal rights, the legal order took on the appearance of an autonomous realm of concepts abstracted from the texture of everyday social life. The *form* of law thus came to be an important focus for attention.

Reflection upon the form of law was likely to highlight two aspects: law's positive character, and its systematic character.

These two aspects were accommodated in different ways by the Will and Interest Theories.

The Will Theory of rights was to place its primary emphasis upon law's systematic character, for this theory (finding its most powerful expression in Kant's *Metaphysics of Morals*) derived the legitimacy of law from a system of rights grounded in the form of the will. Kant equated the normativity of law with moral bindingness, and therefore argued that, even in a system of wholly posited laws one would still require a basic natural law that established the moral authority of the law-giver.[30] The possible scope of positive law was consequently determined by the extent of such moral authority; and, since law is enforced coercively, the extent of legitimate authority could be determined by reference to the conditions in which coercion might rightly be employed. In Kant's view, rights were the basis of any authorization to use coercion, and an adequate theory of the scope and content of rights would therefore trace the conditions for any possible system of positive laws.[31]

Coercion is in general wrong because it interferes with the individual's freedom to choose; but if freedom is used to hinder the freedom of others, one may coercively restrain that exercise of freedom and thereby act consistently with equal freedom. The system of rights therefore describes the possibility of universal reciprocal freedom. Rights concern the external relationship between actions (the extent to which my action may impede yours) and are therefore concerned with the *form* of the relationship between wills: rights do not concern the virtue or desirability of my objectives, but the extent to which my pursuit of those objectives may impede your pursuit of your objectives. Kant believed that it was possible to delineate principles which would flesh out this notion of equal freedom: 'Right is therefore the sum of the conditions under which the choice of one can be united with the choice of another in accordance with a universal law of freedom.'[32]

There were considerable resonances between this model of a system of rights founded upon equal freedom, and the post-feudal legal order (unsurprisingly, given the extent to which philosophical theories tend to arise from interpretations of the political community's

---

[30] Immanuel Kant, *The Metaphysics of Morals*, translated by Mary Gregor (Cambridge: Cambridge University Press, 1991), 51.
[31] ibid, 55.
[32] ibid, 56.

history and institutions). The tendency of the modern law to analyse every relation on a level of principle that abstracts from the social identities of the parties naturally suggested that the concrete rights of parties might be derivable from a realm of equal freedoms which provided the ultimate source of legitimacy; and the growing pervasiveness of contract as a basis for the analysis of such relations suggested that inequalities in concrete rights might well be explicable as resulting from the free exercise of the parties' will. Lawyerly concerns with the internal coherence of the system of legal rights implied the possibility of some ideal model of pure coherence immanent within the practices of doctrinal legal reasoning, and such a model seemed to be aptly provided by the Kantian system of rights reflecting the joint possibility of equal freedoms.

The Kantian Will Theory was to find its nemesis in a set of related intellectual discoveries. Within political philosophy, an increasing number of scholars were led to conclude that the Kantian theory of justice was empty: it was simply impossible to derive any real content from the bare idea of the joint possibility of free wills, or the notion of equal freedom. In order to give content to the system one must make further assumptions: one must assume the existence of a particular context of moral and political institutions, thereby making justice dependent upon contingent empirical facts and variable human arrangements; or one must measure the extent of freedom by reference to the value and importance of the particular freedoms involved, thereby making perfectionist ideals of 'the good' prior to questions of justice and right. The emptiness of the Kantian theory was most famously pointed out by Hegel,[33] but was recognized by others too. Thus Schopenhauer regarded the Kantian notion of '*Recht*' as trying to occupy a no-man's-land that excluded both ethical conceptions of the good and posited rules. Kant's theory 'tries to make jurisprudence separate from ethics, yet not to make the former dependent on positive legislation, i.e. on arbitrary obligation, but to allow the concept of right to exist by itself pure and *a priori*. ... With Kant, therefore, the concept of law or right hovers between heaven and earth, and has no ground on which it can set its foot.'[34]

---

[33] GWF Hegel, *The Philosophy of Right*, s 135; translated by TM Knox (Oxford: Oxford University Press, 1952) and HB Nisbet (Cambridge: Cambridge University Press, 1991).

[34] Arthur Schopenhauer, *The World as Will and Representation* (3rd edn, 1859), Vol 1, translated by EF Payne (New York: Dover, 1966), 528. See also Schopenhauer,

Within jurisprudence, the discovery of emptiness at the heart of Kant's theory of justice was reinforced by more technical developments in the analytical representation of rights. For it was found that, when held up for close analysis, the seemingly unified notion of 'a right' simply fell apart into a series of distinct concepts. This discovery exposed logical equivocations in passages of argument that might previously have seemed to be deductive in character, and thereby revealed that the classical view was sustained more by naïve assumptions about the compatibility of freedoms than by any inherent logic of the system of rights. Not only was the Kantian theory undermined within philosophy, but legal reasoning now lost the appearance of exemplifying the working out of a Kantian system of jointly possible freedoms.

The Will Theory of rights has come to be associated with much more limited and seemingly analytical theses than the claims put forward in the Kantian theory. Yet even those more limited theses may to some extent be founded on a desire to preserve an association between rights and the values of autonomy or liberty.[35] It is because the Kantian theory represents this association in the

---

On the Basis of Morality (1841), translated by EF Payne, (Oxford: Berghahn Books, 1995). This lack of content in the Kantian jurisprudence impels some towards a republican interpretation of Kant that emphasizes the autonomous *collective* choices of citizens, rather than the system of their individual wills. For Kant is not invariably understood as a theorist of natural rights grounded in reason: he is also construed as a theorist of collective self-determination. This expedient, however, simply reproduces the tension between collective and private project pursuit (and the consequent threat to the integrity of private rights) that the Kantian theory was thought to overcome. Thus Habermas, in his recent work on legal theory, expresses enthusiasm for the Kantian system of rights, while rejecting as empty the idea of a system based on the pure form of the will in priority to consensus reached through actual public discourse. He is, however, careful to note the tensions to which this gives rise. Republican readings of Kant have to face up to the fact that (in both Kant and Rousseau) 'there still is an unacknowledged *competition* between morally grounded *human rights* and the *principle of popular sovereignty*'. Habermas takes much trouble to demonstrate the way in which Kant subordinates the theme of popular sovereignty to a scheme of natural (or human) rights derived from his fundamental conception of justice, and suggests that 'Kant did not interpret the binding of popular sovereignty by human rights as a constraint, because he assumed that no one exercising her autonomy as a citizen *could* agree to laws infringing on her private autonomy as warranted by natural law'. Jurgen Habermas, *Between Facts and Norms*, translated by Williem Rehg (Cambridge: Polity, 1996), 94 and 101.

[35] Hart's version of the Will Theory is of a modest, analytical form. Yet Hart had earlier developed his analysis as one aspect of a broader Kantian theory of rights: see Hart 'Are There Any Natural Rights?' 64 *Philosophical Review* 175 (1955), reprinted in A Quinton, *Political Philosophy* (Oxford: Oxford University Press, 1967).

clearest and most ambitious way (and also because the Kantian theory exerted a profound influence upon legal thinking, particularly in continental Europe)[36] that I describe it as the 'classical form' of the Will Theory. Later, more modest versions will be presented as responses to the failures of the classical view.

Just as we may construct a classical version of the Will Theory, where that theory is not a matter of analytical explication so much as the basis for a theory of legitimacy, so we may do the same for the Interest Theory; and just as the classical Will Theory is both a political theory of legitimacy and an interpretation of the character of legal institutions, so the same may be said of this version of the Interest Theory. Where the Will Theory saw the key to law's character and legitimacy in its abstraction from the content of social relations, and its striving for system and coherence, so the Interest Theory focused upon a different aspect of law's form: its posited, source-based character.

The Will Theory emphasizes the mutual consistency of rights and the absence of conflict between them, since the rights are derived from the notion of a 'universal law of freedom' describing the conditions under which the autonomous choices of a multiplicity of individuals may be jointly possible. Positive law-making will be necessary to the realization of the conditions of freedom, for a variety of reasons (for example, to give specificity to the universal law of freedom, to establish conventions which may be prerequisites for its realization, and to ensure compliance); but such law-making is always guided by, and derives its legitimacy from, the underlying principles of reason that constitute the realm of freedom. Legal rules in general are regarded by the theory as only superficial manifestations of a system of rights which underlies and orders such rules.

The classical Interest Theory, by grounding rights in interests, emphasizes the absence of any set of ideal conditions under which all interests may be reconciled and rendered mutually consistent. Consequently, the theory urges the need for positive law-making if a reasonable ordering of interests is to be achieved. Here, a realm of mutually consistent interests is the product of artifice, not a dictate of reason. Lawyerly concerns with principle and with the

---

[36] 'By 1800 influential legal thinkers such as Hugo, Feuerbach, and Savigny had confessed their debt to Kant in one way or another.' Franz Wieacker, *A History of Private Law in Europe*, translated by Tony Weir, (Oxford: Clarendon Press, 1995), 282.

systematicity of the legal order are explained either as aspects of the consistent application of posited rules, or as aspects of the enterprise of incrementally adding to the system of rules to improve the demarcation and protection of otherwise clashing interests.[37]

One might at first be tempted to say that the classical Interest Theory requires a rather strict and narrow account of law as a body of source-based posited rules. On such a view, the law's content can be ascertained by reference to a discrete body of posited rules, without any need to rely upon more open-ended inquiries into the appropriate justifications for the rules so enacted, or the proper extent of the interests so protected. For it is reasonable to assume that only laws possessed of a content identifiable independently of such open-ended questions will be capable of policing the bounds between interests that naturally conflict and compete. The reality is in fact somewhat less simple, and the Interest Theory's dependence upon such a form of legal positivism[38] is only one part of the whole picture. We will discover in due course that the classical Interest Theory is in general torn between two alternative lines of thought. On the one hand, the theory could emphasise the integrity and determinacy of posited rules as instruments for the regulation of conflicting interests. To adopt this line, however, is to problematize the sense that rights are important constituents of juridical thought: assertions about rights become merely peripheral observations about the point of the posited rules, playing no real part in adjudicative reasoning. On the other hand, one can emphasize the centrality of the right (or interest) in informing interpretations and applications of the rules. One then makes 'rights' very central to legal reasoning, but at the price of eroding the integrity of the posited rules. This erosion of posited rules leads in turn to a treatment of rights as interests that must be balanced against each other. The law ceases to provide clearly demarcated boundaries between conflicting interests, and legal reasoning becomes a more fluid medium within which interests are weighed and traded off against each other.

---

[37] Jeremy Bentham, *Theory of Legislation*, edited by CM Atkinson (Oxford: Oxford University Press, 1914), Vol 1, 198–9.

[38] The term 'legal positivism' is so riddled with ambiguities that it is perhaps best avoided altogether. Here and throughout this essay, however, the term is used to refer to a thesis about the criteria whereby the content of law may be ascertained. I (stipulatively) take 'legal positivism' to claim that the law's content can be inferred from a corpus of posited rules without reliance upon information extraneous to the

One characteristic trajectory for the Interest Theory is exemplified by the development of Ihering's thought. Ihering began his career as an orthodox follower of Savigny and the Will Theory. His great study *Geist des Romischen Rechts* was intended to be a work within this tradition, and he anticipated that it would be his life work. In the course of writing it, however, he hit upon the idea that rights might fruitfully be thought of as representing interests rather than (as the orthodox view then held) being grounded in the will. He proposed to develop this view further in the succeeding volume of the treatise. It is worth quoting his own reflections upon this critical stage in his career:

The concept of Interest made it necessary for me to consider Purpose, and 'right in the subjective sense' led me to 'right in the objective sense'. Thus the original object of my investigation was transformed into one of much greater extent, into the object of the present book, *viz.*, Law as a means to an end. Once this question came before me, I was no longer able to avoid it; it always emerged again in one form or another. It was the sphinx which imposed its question upon me, and I must solve its riddle if I would regain my scientific peace of mind.[39]

The classical Interest Theory necessarily emphasizes positive law as a means of defining and policing the bounds between otherwise conflicting interests; this can in turn lead to a removal of the notion of 'rights' from the centre of legal thinking, in favour of a focus upon 'laws'. Rather than deriving its legitimacy from some rationally grounded scheme of rights, law now derives its legitimacy from its posited character, and from its consequent ability to surmount the problem of conflicts between interests. Law becomes, on this view, essentially instrumental; and when doctrinal thinking concerns itself with the coherent and systematic character of law, it cannot occupy an abstract realm of ideas concerned solely with the

body of rules, and not in the possession of all competent speakers of the relevant language. 'Positivism' in my sense is therefore undercut as much by dependence upon diffuse factual information (such as information about the attitudes or understandings of legislators or citizens) as by dependence upon evaluative judgment.

As a number of scholars have pointed out, such theses concerning the mode of ascertainment of law's content are quite distinct from other claims often thought to be the essential hallmark of 'legal positivism'. Thus, such theses are consistent with the claims that there are necessary connections between law and morality, that legal obligations are a species of moral obligation, and so forth.

[39] Rudolf von Ihering, *Law as a Means to an End*, translated by Isaac Husik, (Boston: Boston Book Company, 1913).

form of the will, but must reflect upon the complex world of real human objectives and concerns.[40]

Private Law and the Integrity of Rights

I observed earlier that the modern analytical debate about rights strikes many scholars as inevitably inconclusive: our 'conceptual' intuitions about rights can be regimented in a variety of ways, and the (modern) Will and Interest Theories are but two ways of achieving such regimentation. Given the inconclusive nature of purely analytical considerations, the motivating factors behind the choice of one or other theory frequently lie elsewhere: in a sense that the preferred theory sits more comfortably with some favoured evaluative stance; or a belief that the distinctions highlighted by that theory are (from a moral, political, or juridical point of view) more important than those highlighted by its rival.

One issue which has struck many jurists as important, and which has been thought to favour the analysis offered by the Will Theory, concerns the distinctiveness of private law. Even when jurists have abandoned the prospect of reconstructing private law as an expression of the Kantian system of right, they have still tended to hope that private law can be preserved as a body of reasoning distinct from the collective goals pursued within public law. In some such preservation of doctrinal boundaries may lie the best chance of protecting the integrity of private rights. Modern versions of the Will Theory equate a right with the power of control (the power of enforcement or waiver) over a duty incumbent upon some other person. Where the operative force of a duty, or its enforcement, is made conditional upon an exercise of will by some person, the duty may be said to be correlative to a right possessed by the person whose will is thereby made decisive. In other cases, where the duty is not in any way conditional upon another's will, the duty has no correlative right. This seems to suggest that rights are primarily

---

[40] We might also consider the example of Roscoe Pound, whose notion of law as 'social engineering' is closely linked to his thesis that the notion of 'an interest' is logically prior to that of 'a right'. See Roscoe Pound, *Jurisprudence* (St Paul: West, 1959), Vol IV, 50 *et seq*. Morton Horwitz sees Pound's views as expressive of American law's abandonment of categorical principles in favour of looser tests involving the balancing of interests: see Morton Horwitz, *The Transformation of American Law, 1870–1960* (Oxford: Oxford University Press, 1992), 18.

characteristic of private law: they exist within public law only in those special contexts (such as the conferment of welfare benefits) where public law is employed to secure particular benefits for individuals. The concept of a 'right', on this account, is strongly linked to the value of individual choice, and to the primacy of private law in protecting such choices.

Advocates of the Will Theory are consequently inclined to regard Hohfeld's analysis of 'jural relations' (to which we shall turn in due course) as an analysis of the structure of private law. There are a number of reasons for taking this view. For example, it is interesting to note that one of the most striking features of Hohfeld's approach (his treatment of jural relations as obtaining between pairs of individuals) may well have been drawn from Savigny's own analyses of private law,[41] and Savigny's jurisprudence (as Habermas has recently emphasized) ascribes an intrinsic value to private law as an expression of individual autonomy.[42] The Hohfeldian analysis of legal concepts explicates those concepts in terms of bilateral relations between pairs of individuals, and private law is frequently regarded as structured by the bilateral form of private law adjudication. Private law deals not simply with 'wrongs', but with people who have been 'wronged'; the duties of private law are duties *owed to* specific individuals. When the same act constitutes both a civil and a criminal wrong, the civil (or private) aspect of the act is precisely its breach of a duty owed to a specific person; the criminal (or public) aspect of the act is its deviation from standards of conduct that are placed upon all persons as a general demand. Crimes constitute breaches of the general peace, or departures from general standards of propriety.

Hohfeld depicts claim-rights and duties (powers and liabilities, etc) as correlative, but this correlativity could be construed in a number of different ways. We might take Hohfeld to be proposing perfectly general definitions of 'duty' and 'claim-right' (etc) wherein the definition of each term entails its correlative. Or, alternatively, we might take him to be offering an analytical representation of some bounded sphere (such as private law) and claiming that the

---

[41] Savigny, *System of Modern Roman Law*, Vol 2, translated by WH Rattigan (under the title *Jural Relations*) (London: Wildy and Sons, 1884), s 60: 'Every Jural Relation consists in the relation of one person to another person.'

[42] Jurgen Habermas, *Between Facts and Norms*, translated by William Rehg, (Cambridge: Polity, 1996), 85.

correlativity obtains within that sphere. On this latter view, duties would entail claim-rights *within private law*, and Hohfeld's theory would not be proposing a general definition of duty so much as explicating a structure in virtue of which such entailments will obtain.

To construe the Hohfeldian analysis as applicable only within the limited sphere of private law may be thought to be a significant concession, and the necessity of making some such concession may therefore be considered an important weakness in the Will Theory. For, if the analysis applies only to private law, the entailments traced by Hohfeld can be regarded as flowing from the meaning of the Hohfeldian concepts only if those concepts are taken to be definitions of 'private claim-right', 'private duty', 'private power', and so forth. This impression will be reinforced if one reflects upon the way in which some of the other Hohfeldian correlatives do indeed seem to involve perfectly general relationships of mutual entailment, without any need to confine the concepts to a limited sphere of private law. Thus it is hard to imagine *any* plausible account of legal powers that would not portray them as correlative to liabilities; similarly, immunity seems to entail disability (and vice versa) not simply within some limited context, but without qualification and in virtue of the meaning of the words. When complex qualifications and epicycles are forced upon us by the Will Theory, is it not sensible to abandon that theory in favour of a simpler alternative?

The idea that a simpler alternative is available, however, may be a mistake. For the seemingly tight and general connections between power and liability (and between immunity and disability) cannot obtain between duty and claim-right, even for the Interest Theory. The Interest Theorist may well claim that all actual legal or moral duties concern acts that in some way affect the interests of others: but, even if this is true, it is not true in virtue of the meaning of the word 'duty'. There is nothing incoherent about the idea that we have certain duties that depend upon the intrinsic propriety of the act, rather than upon the way in which the act serves someone's interest. We may, for example, have duties to act with reverence for the 'sacred', and this may be so even if God is unconcerned with our acts of reverence (indeed, even if God, as a being possessing interests, does not exist). The Interest Theorist may well deny that there are any such duties; but, the idea of such a duty nevertheless appears to be a perfectly coherent one. The connection between duty and interest is established either as a purely contingent feature concerning the content of legal or moral duties, or perhaps as a necessary truth flowing from some conception of 'law' or of 'morality'. Thus the Interest Theory, like the Will Theory, is unable to treat the correlativity of rights and duties as a simple consequence of the meaning of those words (except by stipulation in clear departure from ordinary meanings: and two can play at this game). Each theory must therefore treat Hohfeld's scheme as an analysis of the relationships obtaining within some bounded sphere: private law, in the case of the Will Theory; a legal or moral system that is grounded in interests, in the case of the Interest Theory. While the Interest Theory is able to ascribe far greater generality to the Hohfeldian scheme, the issue of principle remains the same for both theories. Naturally, the Will Theorist will not see the ascription of greater generality to Hohfeld's analysis as an asset, because the Will Theorist sees that analysis as important precisely in so far as it elucidates the distinctive conceptual structure flowing from the bilateral bonds of private law.

Positivist solutions to the problem of the integrity of rights attach no great significance to the boundary between public and private law. Instead, they rely upon a distinction between the legislative enactment of rules and the adjudicative application of rules. Such a distinction seems at first both sound and obvious. Yet it does not require a high degree of legal experience or jurisprudential sophistication to see that a reconciliation of the competing values which is based on this distinction alone may well be flawed. For the theory assumes some way of subsuming actions under rules without reopening the question of the (collective) purposes that the rules were meant to serve. Such a mode of adjudicative subsumption may or may not be available. When laws are enacted in a canonical verbal formulation, their possible meanings will be constrained by formal semantic rules which are independent of the legislative purpose; but formal semantic rules are rarely sufficient to determine univocal meanings in the absence of detailed contextual understandings; and such contextual understandings (in the case of law) will frequently be bound up with interpretations of the rule's purpose. The dependence of interpretation upon an appeal to purpose does not, of course, rob the rule (and rights conferred by it) of all integrity: the wording of a rule may be construed by reference to its purpose without becoming equivalent to a simple injunction to pursue that purpose. Nevertheless, purposes are not discrete entities, but are capable of description at varying levels of abstraction. Such variability tends to open up considerable scope for dispute about the true significance of the posited rule. (In any case, it is questionable how far legal doctrine can plausibly be viewed as a set of canonically formulated rules.)

Even if each discrete rule can be given a precise meaning without reference to the rule's purpose, we will still have to face the problem of how to adjudicate upon conflicts between rights. In the absence of some doctrinal features or theoretical stratagems which might limit the frequency of such conflicts,[43] there is no reason why the conflicts should not be all-pervading. Within a Kantian theory, any such apparent conflicts would be handled by reference to the overall system of rights: the conflict would be shown to be apparent *only*. Within an interest-based theory, however, the resolution of such conflicts will necessitate recourse to the general balancing of interests that underlay the enactment of rules in the first place. It seems hard to avoid the conclusion that the decision will have to be shaped by considerations drawn from the collective project.

These worries take a more concrete, albeit contingent, form when we reflect that positive laws confer rights within the context of existing legal doctrines, and some familiar legal doctrines appear to introduce distributive or aggregative considerations (typical of collective projects) into the heart of adjudicative decisions upon the scope of private rights. Thus, the negligence test has been variously analysed as a cost/benefit test concerned with aggregate wealth, and an egalitarian test concerned with distributive equality.

The cumulative effect of all these arguments is to raise the following doubt: perhaps the scope of our rights can only be determined in adjudication by considering the impact of our action upon the distributive or aggregative goals of the collectivity. In that case, our rights would extend only up to the point where our actions ceased to make a net contribution to the collective project: our rights, when conceived as a safeguard for private project pursuit, would in fact be illusory.

---

[43] See Simmonds (n 10 above).

3 Hohfeld and the Fragmentation of Rights

Hohfeld's Intentions

Hohfeld is sometimes regarded as a forerunner of the American realist movement, and there are certainly features of his work that tend to support this view. His analysis had the effect of exposing equivocations in what might otherwise have seemed to be deductive passages of legal reasoning, and in this way he contributed to the realist's exposure of indeterminacies in legal doctrine. Moreover, his focus upon jural relations as obtaining between pairs of individuals sat very comfortably with the characteristic realist focus upon the cutting edge of the law in litigated disputes. Most important of all, Hohfeld's analysis had the effect of shattering the law's appearance of system and integration by fragmenting into a diversity of different jural relations the 'rights' which might otherwise have been proffered as focal points for the systematic reconstruction and presentation of the law.

This radical achievement, however, may conceivably have been quite contrary to Hohfeld's own intentions. For in many respects, his work seems to proceed from assumptions which are characteristic of somewhat traditional forms of legal scholarship rather than the realist assault upon those forms. We have grown accustomed to a style of legal writing that focuses on practical questions of application; we doubt the value of debates about the classification or analysis of this or that concept or doctrine when those debates are not immediately related to practical distinctions. From the belief that the intelligent interpretation and application of law can never be wholly separated from questions about the purpose of the law, we have inferred (perhaps erroneously) that general definitions and analyses of technical concepts are valueless if they are not located within some specific context of purposes and disputed applications. In this sense, and to that extent, we are heirs to the realist revolution. When we turn to Hohfeld's work, however, we seem to confront a style of legal scholarship that is now virtually extinct. Throughout his two most famous essays (published in 1913 and 1917)[44] Hohfeld discusses such doctrines and institutions as the

---

[44] Reprinted in book form as WN Hohfeld, *Fundamental Legal Conceptions*, edited by WW Cook, and with introductions by WW Cook and AL Corbin, (Westport, Connecticut: Greenwood Press, 1978).

trust, the escrow, or the sheriff's powers under a writ of execution, and subjects them to minute analysis. The assumption seems to be one that Hohfeld might comfortably have shared with Savigny's formalist heirs: legal concepts have an intellectual existence, and they may be held up for analysis in isolation from any questions about the purposes or policies served by such concepts. To the imaginary objection that such discussions are without practical value, Hohfeld insists that proper analysis is the prerequisite of correct application, and 'the deeper the analysis, the greater becomes one's perception of the unity and harmony in the law'.[45]

One seemingly radical move that Hohfeld made was to focus debate upon the cutting edge of law where it is invoked in a dispute between two parties. As we will discover in due course, this led him to analyse the concept of 'jural relations' as obtaining between pairs of individuals, and to treat the concept of a legal right as operating on the level of specific legal remedies, acts, and causes of action. Modern critics of Hohfeld not infrequently criticize this aspect of his thinking, and propose a deeper level of rights from the perspective of which Hohfeld's claim-rights, powers, privileges, and immunities are merely protective instrumentalities rather than the fundamental anchor points for legal reasoning. In this way they seek to restore the sense that rights form a systematic and integrated structure, a sense that Hohfeld's analysis fundamentally undercuts. Yet even here, in this potentially radical move, Hohfeld may have been following an older tradition of formalistic legal scholarship. We noted above that, like Hohfeld, Savigny too analysed jural relations as obtaining between pairs of individuals, and asserted that 'a Right is never manifested more clearly than when, being denied or attacked, the judicial authority intervenes to recognise its existence and its extent.'[46]

Indeed, such a focus upon disputes between pairs of individuals might well be seen as a consequence of the formalistic Kantian view that a right is an authorization to use coercion, and that the system of rights demarcates the legitimate bounds between potentially conflicting wills. It is interesting to observe, for example, that the present day Kantian formalist Ernest Weinrib places a heavy emphasis upon the bilateral relationship between wrong-doer and victim, or defendant and plaintiff, as the key to the nature of private

---

[45] ibid, 64.   [46] Quoted in Lightwood (n 17 above), 265.

law.[47] If such an equation between Kantian formalism and the bilateral relationship is justified, the result is richly ironic: for it is precisely the centrality given by Hohfeld to the bilateral character of jural relations that leads to his dramatic (and perhaps unintentional) destruction of the Kantian notion of a right.

Hohfeld did not see his analysis of rights as in itself *resolving* any of the disputed classificatory questions which might interest the formalist scholar, but as providing the analytical tools which would (he thought) be an essential prerequisite of such resolution. The analysis presented in his two most famous essays is aimed at reducing 'jural relations' to the 'most basic conceptions' out of which all other legal concepts are constructed. Later essays were to deal with 'typical and important interests of a complex character'.[48] In fact, however, his analysis was to shatter the assumptions and aspirations of much traditional legal scholarship by exposing in legal reasoning gaps of a kind which could be bridged, not by analytical reflection, but only by political choice.

The Hohfeldian Analysis

Hohfeld tells us that it is an error to assume that all legal relations can be analysed in terms of rights and duties. The attempt so to analyse them leads to a 'chameleon-hued' use of the words 'right' and 'duty' whereby a single word is being employed to cover several distinct concepts. Hohfeld aims to isolate these distinct concepts, which he describes as 'the lowest common denominators of the law'.[49]

Hohfeld regards these 'lowest common denominators' as *sui generis* and as therefore not susceptible to definition *per genus et differentiam*. Rather, their meaning is to be elucidated by exhibiting their place within a scheme of relationships, the significance of which lies in its connection with adjudication between disputing parties. Consequently, he regards the clarification of the concept of 'a right' as best achieved by careful distinctions between different 'jural relations', the latter being conceived as relationships obtaining between pairs of individuals.

---

[47] Ernest Weinrib, *The Idea of Private Law* (Cambridge, Mass: Harvard University Press, 1995).
[48] Hohfeld (n 44 above), 27.
[49] ibid, 64.

Rights at the Cutting Edge 149

This focus upon jural relations between pairs of individuals gave Hohfeld's work a hard-nosed style and a focus on the remedial cutting edge of law that greatly appealed to the American realists who drew upon his work. For our purposes, however, its importance lay in the way that it exposed the diverse implications that were regularly drawn from assertions concerning the existence of legal rights. Sometimes, for example, the existence of a right was treated as entailing the existence of a duty incumbent upon some other party; on other occasions the existence of a right was treated as entailing the permissibility of an action performed by the right-holder; on yet other occasions a right might be thought to validate the purported exercise (by the right-holder) of a legal power, or to demonstrate the invalidity of some such purported exercise by someone other than the right-holder. It was not clear, however, how a single concept might have all of these very diverse entailments. Indeed, even quite a modest knowledge of the actual contents of existing legal doctrines was sufficient to demonstrate that the concept of 'a right' could not have all of these consequences. For examples abounded of situations where one might be committing no wrong in performing an act and yet others might be free to interfere (in certain ways) with one's performance; or one might be under a duty not to exercise a power, and yet the power if exercised (in breach of duty) would nevertheless be effective in altering legal rights; and so on. Since it was clear that the various supposed logical consequences of a right could come apart in this way, it was clear that they were not genuine logical consequences of a single concept of 'right'.

Two responses to this discovery were possible. One was that adopted by Hohfeld, and it consisted in the disaggregation of the general concept of 'a right' and its replacement by a set of distinct concepts, characterized by distinct entailments. The other was the response adopted by certain modern exponents of the Interest Theory of rights (notably Raz and MacCormick). Here the general concept of a right is retained, and the Hohfeldian disaggregation is resisted; but an attempt is made to accommodate the devastating effects of Hohfeld's main insight by weakening the connection between the concept of a right and the implications that possession of a right has for conduct (both the conduct of the right-holder and of other persons). Thus, on this view, possession of a right in one person does not *entail* the existence of any particular duties, powers, permissions, or the like. Rather, a right is a very important interest which gives us a reason for imposing or recognizing such duties, permissions and powers where they are desirable to protect the relevant interest. The reason is said to be 'sufficient' for holding other persons to be subject to a duty, but only 'other things being equal': the interest will justify the duty only 'if not counteracted by conflicting considerations'.[50]

There are various substantial objections to this version of the Interest Theory. For example, it renders the existence and content of legal rights quite uncertain,[51] and (as we will see in due course) it robs rights of their peremptory character. What is important for present purposes, however, is to note the relatively *obvious* nature of the move made by the analysis,[52] and the extent to which it misses the real force of Hohfeld's theory. Hohfeld's attempt to reduce jural relations to their 'lowest common denominators' seeks to disaggregate complex associations of ideas by showing that they are linked by pragmatic implication rather than by strict entailment. There is surely nothing very remarkable in the discovery that what has been thus carefully separated by analytical reflection can be recombined on the basis of looser forms of association.

These modern exponents of the Interest Theory have revealed no real flaws in the Hohfeldian analysis: they merely propose that a useful general concept of 'right' can be constructed above the cutting edge of remedial provision on which Hohfeld focuses. That suggestion is, as we shall see, questionable. It is worth reiterating

[50] See Joseph Raz, *The Morality of Freedom* (Oxford: Clarendon Press, 1986), 166 and 171.

[51] If we find these uncertainties troubling, our fears will not be allayed when we learn that one major exponent of this anti-Hohfeldian view of legal rights is able to conclude that 'The right to political participation is a legal right in English law.' (Raz (n 50 above), 172) But fear not: all is not what it seems! The legal right to political participation does not mean that anyone can seek a remedy insisting upon political participation (unless 'political participation' simply means casting one's vote). All that the right means is that the interest in political participation is recognized in law as a sufficient reason for imposing an appropriate duty on someone if there are no countervailing considerations of greater weight. What exactly this conception of rights is thought to have added to our understanding, beyond considerable potential for obfuscation, remains unclear.

[52] Thus, Roscoe Pound observed that '(I)t has long been understood that "a right"... is a composite idea. It may mean the legally recognized and delimited human want or demand, or some one of the conceptions by which that recognized interest is given form in order to be secured by the legal order, or the complex of these conceptions plus the recognized and secured interest.' Roscoe Pound, *Jurisprudence* (St Paul: West, 1959), Vol IV, 53.

that, in spite of its generally anti-Hohfeldian posture, the Raz/ MacCormick theory in effect concedes the impossibility of deducing specific duties (or permissions, powers, immunities, etc) from the general rights that the theory favours. For, on the Raz/MacCormick view, the interests that constitute such general rights are only non-conclusive reasons for imposing duties: they do not *entail* duties. Therefore, we can pass from the asserted right to the consequential duty only via a complex process of balancing various interests and considerations. It is difficult to see, on this analysis, how the assertion of a general right differs from the assertion of an important interest. At any rate, the analysis concedes the Hohfeldian point that such general rights cannot *entail* specific duties.

Critics of the Hohfeldian analysis have frequently objected to what they see as the cumbersome and artificial consequences of an analysis focused upon jural relations obtaining between pairs of individuals. For example, it seems that in Hohfeld's framework it would be incorrect to speak of me as having a right not to be assaulted: what I possess is a series of distinct rights against distinct individuals. Thus I have a right against you that you should not assault me; a right against your mother that she should not assault me; a similar right against the Bishop of Ely, and so on. This strikes many critics as introducing an unacceptable degree of complexity into the concept of a right. What is wrong with the idea that I have a general right not to be assaulted, and that the various duties are consequences of that right?

Criticisms such as this can have the unfortunate effect of lending undue credibility to the anti-Hohfeldian position of Interest Theorists such as Raz and MacCormick. For the general right not to be assaulted seems to be an instance of a fundamental interest (in not being assaulted) which provides the ground for duties borne by various individuals; and if this is so, why may we not go further and view this general interest as the basis for various legal consequences other than such duties (permissions, powers, immunities, and the like, aiming at protection of the fundamental interest)? We seem to be faced with a stark choice between accepting the cumbersome approach of Hohfeldian analysis, which excludes talk of general rights that are independent of any particular jural relation, and accepting the Raz/MacCormick Interest Theory.

The dilemma presented in such an argument is false. There is nothing in Hohfeld's analysis that would prevent us from talking about a general right not to be assaulted, *provided* that such claims are understood only as summary statements about the existence of various more specific rights obtaining against particular individuals. What Hohfeld wishes to resist is the belief that such a claimed general right can entail conclusions about the duties incumbent upon all other individuals; and he is right to resist such a belief. From the fact that I have a right against you not to be assaulted, and a similar right against your mother (and a similar one against your brother, and so on) it does *not* follow that I have such a right against the Bishop of Ely (for example, the Bishop and I may have entered into a boxing match within which we consent to the possibility of blows which would otherwise count as an assault). Provided that the impossibility of any such direct inference is understood, there is no harm and no difficulty in referring to general rights (such as the right not to be assaulted) as a shorthand way of summarizing the content of a multiplicity of particular jural relations.[53]

Other critics of Hohfeld have pointed to his departures from ordinary usage as a ground for rejecting or amending his analysis. In a sense, there is little point in seeking to defend Hohfeld from the accusation that he departs from ordinary usage: the same must be true of any conceptual regimentation of the discourse of legal rights. Departures from the Hohfeldian scheme that are aimed at securing closer conformity with ordinary usage not infrequently purchase such conformity at the price of increased complexity, thereby sacrificing one of the principal virtues of the analysis. Indeed, for some of Hohfeld's critics, increased complexity is the aim, rather than an unfortunate consequence, of their criticisms: for the general impetus behind many of the familiar criticisms is to suggest that 'rights' cannot be identified with the simple Hohfeldian elements of claim, power, liberty, or immunity, but must be analysed as complex assemblages of those elements, or as protected choices or interests

---

[53] It must be admitted, however, that Hohfeld is mistaken in his unqualified claim that all jural relations obtain between pairs of individuals. Since legal powers involve the ability to alter the legal position of some person X, each power must also entail the ability to alter the position of some person Y (X's legal position cannot be altered without Y's also being altered). In most private-law contexts, either X or Y will be the relevant power-holder, and it will consequently be correct to say that the relation obtains between a pair of individuals; but this will not be invariably so. See Carl Wellman, *A Theory of Rights* (Totowa, New Jersey: Rowman and Allanheld, 1985), 43.

providing the rationale for such assemblages. Many of these criticisms seem to be unsoundly based, in so far as they neglect the resources that Hohfeld's analysis offers for accommodating seemingly difficult counter-examples.

David Lyons, for example, has suggested that not all Hohfeldian immunities should be regarded as 'rights', his example being the inability to inherit property.[54] Lyons is surely correct that it would be anomalous to regard the inability to inherit as a 'right'. What he fails to see, however, is that such an inability cannot be straightforwardly identified with a Hohfeldian immunity. Since the ownership of property can be onerous, an immunity from inheriting *without one's consent* would indeed be an advantageous protection of one's interests or autonomy such that we might well describe it as a right. On being informed that, independently of my consent, I have become the owner of a massive Scottish estate and am now faced with responsibilities for its management and upkeep, I might well object that I had a right to refuse the property, such an assertion being a reference to an immunity. An immunity of this kind might be combined with a power to waive the immunity. An inability to inherit regardless of consent would then be an immunity combined with a disability (the absence of a power of waiver). Since the immunity in itself is advantageous, it is the presence of the disability that makes us (in some contexts) hesitate to describe the inability to inherit as a right.

What needs to be kept in mind here is the fact that an immunity accords *negative* recognition to the right-holder's choices, by ensuring that (in some relevant respect) the right-holder's jural relations cannot be changed merely by the say-so of some other person. Such negative recognition may or may not be conjoined with *positive* recognition in the form of a power of waiver. Where the immunity is not so linked to a power of waiver, it is combined with a disability. When we speak loosely of 'the inability to inherit', we may be focusing our attention upon *either* the immunity *or* the disability: indeed the formulation strongly suggests a focus upon the disability.

---

[54] David Lyons, *Rights, Welfare and Mill's Moral Theory* (New York: Oxford University Press, 1994), 25n. Hohfeld was inclined to regard only claim-rights as rights in a strict sense; but he also accepted a wider 'generic' sense of 'right' as applicable to liberties, powers, and immunities. We will see later that the modern Will Theory claims that the various Hohfeldian advantages are united by their (positive or negative) recognition of the right-holder's choices.

Since disabilities are not Hohfeldian entitlements, there is nothing in Hohfeld to conflict with our disinclination to describe that inability as a 'right'. It is always conceivable, however, that some appropriate set of circumstances might render a focus upon the immunity more pertinent than a focus upon the disability, and in such circumstances we will certainly find it appropriate to speak of 'a right'.

It is possible to defend Hohfeld's treatment of immunities as rights even in instances devoid of the obviously onerous implications of inheriting a Scottish estate. Hart suggests that 'even in the loosest usage, the expression "a right" is not used to refer to the fact that a man is thus immune from an *advantageous* change', and he cites as an example the City Council's inability to award me a pension.[55] Yet it is conceivable that one might wish to assert the existence of a right in such circumstances, and there would be no impropriety in doing so. Suppose, for example, that I have long been proud of my reckless disregard for the future, and have treated my lack of a pension as a symbol of that devil-may-care attitude. Having been granted a pension, I can of course choose not to draw upon it; but the very fact of my entitlement to draw upon it may be seen by some (and perhaps even by myself) as casting doubt upon the substantial reality of my much-vaunted recklessness. In such circumstances I might well wish to insist upon my right not to be granted a pension that I never sought or consented to. In fact, the *negative* recognition accorded to choice by the granting of an immunity is always of value to us in so far as we wish to control our own lives and the conditions within which they are conducted. A change may in itself be advantageous, but if it occurs without our consent it will (to that extent) encroach upon our desire for autonomous control. Generally, the advantageous aspect of the change will outweigh any encroachment, and the pervasive and unavoidable nature of the limits to our autonomy will render particular encroachments scarcely worthy of note. In such cases, assertion of one's immunity as a 'right' may seem odd or impertinent, but it need not for that reason be incorrect.

In common with many other theorists, L. W. Sumner has argued that individual Hohfeldian elements cannot be regarded as 'rights': rights must be conceived of as complex clusters of Hohfeldian elements. Somewhat more unusually, one of Sumner's suggestions

---

[55] HLA Hart, *Essays on Bentham* (Oxford: Clarendon Press, 1982), 191.

Rights at the Cutting Edge

to this effect consists in the claim that a Hohfeldian power cannot in itself be regarded as a right.[56] A key premise in Sumner's argument, however, is his assertion that the Hohfeldian power to alter some legal relation is compatible with having *no* power *not* to alter it.[57] From this premise, Sumner argues that a power to alter must, at a minimum, be combined with a power not to alter before the power can be regarded as a right. Sumner's basic premise is clearly mistaken. His justification for maintaining it consists in the claim that, from a logical point of view, powers are the second-order counterparts of liberties. A Hohfeldian liberty to do X is simply the absence of a duty not to do X: it is therefore a *unilateral* liberty (a *bilateral* liberty being the conjunction of two unilateral liberties).[58] Similarly, Sumner asserts, a Hohfeldian power must be the unilateral ability to alter a legal relation without the ability *not* to alter that relation: the bilateral ability to alter or not alter would be a conjunction of two Hohfeldian powers.

Sumner's argument seems question-begging. To establish that powers are, from the point of view of logic, the second-order counterpart of liberties, one must establish the symmetry of structure in the two concepts by reference to features that are attributed to those concepts on independent grounds. One cannot ascribe to the notion of a power features that are of dubious coherence or intelligibility by employing the thesis of logical symmetry as a basic assumption. Hohfeld defines a liberty to do X as the absence of a duty not to do X: the character of a liberty as unilateral rather than bilateral follows from that definition. But a power is defined as the ability to alter legal relations: there is nothing in this definition to entail a unilateral character for powers. Indeed, it is doubtful whether the notion of a power to alter without any power not to alter makes any sense. For the law to confer on me a power is for the law to attach importance to my behaviour. This is so even if my behaviour is constrained by legal duty or by material circumstance. If I have no power *not* to alter a legal relation, my behaviour has no effect in bringing about any alteration: in short, if I have no power not to alter, I have no

---

[56] LW Sumner, *The Moral Foundation of Rights* (Oxford: Clarendon Press, 1987), 35–6.
[57] ibid, 29.
[58] The distinction between unilateral and bilateral liberties was made by Hart, *Essays on Bentham* (n 55 above), 166–7.

power to alter. Unlike liberties, therefore, powers are essentially bilateral.

Many of Hohfeld's critics have failed to acknowledge the fact that his analysis is concerned to deny the existence of certain presumed logical entailments between legal propositions: he is not concerned to deny the existence of pragmatic implications resembling those presumed entailments. Take, for example, the Hohfeldian notion of 'liberty' or 'privilege'. As should be clear to any reader of Hohfeld, the existence of a liberty does not entail the presence of a duty on others not to interfere with actions exercising the liberty. The liberty entails the absence of a duty on the holder of the liberty, but not the presence of a duty on anyone else. It is perfectly true that when people assert a 'right' to act in this or that way, they are often concerned to resist some threatened interference from others. This feature of rights has even been invoked in support of the claim that all rights are authorizations to invoke or deploy coercion, in accordance with a Kantian theory of equal freedom.[59] Yet there is no necessity for Hohfeld to deny this feature of our moral and legal discourse if he is to maintain his concept of 'liberty' or 'privilege' as entailing no duties for other persons.

The assertion of a 'right' to speak freely (for example) must, on Hohfeld's analysis, be a liberty, since it relates to the right-holder's own actions (claim-rights relate to the actions of persons other than the right-holder). Being a liberty, the right to speak freely does not in itself entail any duties incumbent upon anyone else. The asserted right may nevertheless pragmatically *imply* the existence of such duties which constrain the ability of others to interfere with the right-holder's free speech, in the sense that the assertion might in some contexts lack a practical point if such duties did not exist. This will not invariably be so: if you complain that I failed in my duty by speaking freely, my assertion of a liberty has a practical point even in the absence of any such implication. But such an implication will frequently be present, and will frequently be justified. As Hart has pointed out,[60] general duties such as the duty not to assault have the effect of providing a 'perimeter of protection' to actions performed in the exercise of Hohfeldian liberties. The existence of such laws is the general background assumed by assertions of liberties, where

---

[59] Hart, 'Are There Any Natural Rights?' (n 35 above).
[60] Hart, *Essays on Bentham* n 58 above), ch 7.

those liberties are asserted with the intention of resisting interference. Hohfeld says nothing which denies the existence of such pragmatic implications, and his analysis provides a most enlightening basis for their explanation.

A failure to appreciate the dependence of such implications upon particular contexts can easily lead theorists astray. Thus it is sometimes argued that individual Hohfeldian elements (such as liberties) cannot be regarded as rights: only a complex assemblage of such elements can constitute a right. Such arguments tend to appeal to semantic intuitions about the proper use of the word 'right'. Our intuitions concerning the appropriateness of an assertion of right, however, are always dependent upon the pragmatic context in which the assertion is made. When presented with an example in which a Hohfeldian liberty (for example) is asserted as 'a right', we may feel the assertion to be inappropriate. This perceived inappropriateness, however, may simply reflect our puzzlement as to the practical *point* of the assertion in the context described. Consider, for instance, the following example offered by Carl Wellman:

A contestant in a foot-race has a legal liberty, and presumably a moral liberty also, to run faster than the other entrants and thus to win the race. But it would be an abuse of language to say that he has a right to win the race because if another crosses the finish line first, the loser cannot complain that his right to win the race has been violated.[61]

Wellman's example will be persuasive only for those who have already decided to reject Hohfeld on other grounds. There is no abuse of language in saying that the contestant had a right to win the foot-race. What *is* true is that the circumstances in which such an assertion will seem appropriate are likely to be quite unusual. Jack's claim that he enjoys a Hohfeldian liberty to win will lack any practical point if it is not made to resist a claim (made by some Jill) that he is under a duty not to win. The invocation of a Hohfeldian liberty will normally have a practical point only when it is made in resistance to such a claim of duty. When given an example in which Jill has made no claim concerning Jack's duties, but Jack has nevertheless claimed a 'right', we naturally assume that Jack's assertion must be intended to ground some prescriptions concerning the conduct of others; since a bare liberty could ground no such prescriptions, we conclude that (if Jack possesses only such a liberty) it

[61] Carl Wellman, *An Approach to Rights* (Dordrecht: Kluwer, 1997), 3.

is inappropriate for him to claim a 'right'. Yet we need only think of a context where Jack is resisting the assertion that he had a duty not to win (let us suppose that he is involved in a contractual dispute with his sponsor) and we see quite clearly that the provision of a pragmatic point for the assertion of a bare liberty dissipates our sense of inappositeness.

MacCormick versus Hohfeld

Neil MacCormick has put forward a critique of the Hohfeldian analysis that goes well beyond simple appeals to semantic intuition. MacCormick is concerned to oppose Hohfeld's commitment to the analysis of legal concepts in terms of jural relations between pairs of individuals. A legal right, in MacCormick's view, is not (or, at least, need not be) correlative to a duty incumbent upon some other individual. Legal rights provide reasons for imposing duties, rather than being the simple correlative of the duty. More precisely, a law conferring a right is 'best understood in terms of a standard intention to confer some form of benefit... upon the members of a class severally rather than collectively'. Such benefits are to be 'secured to individuals in that the law provides normative protection for individuals in their enjoyment of them'. The relevant 'normative protection' may include 'any or all of the various modes identified by Hohfeld and others'. Thus, a right may be protected by duties, disabilities, or liabilities placed upon others, as well as by liberties enjoyed by the right-holder himself.[62]

By way of example, we are introduced to section 5(1) of the Trade Union and Labour Relations Act 1974, from which MacCormick quotes the following passage:

...(E)very worker shall have the right not to be — (a) excluded from membership (b) expelled from membership, of a trade union... by way of arbitrary or unreasonable discrimination.

MacCormick tells us that this provision confers upon the worker protections falling into three different Hohfeldian categories: '(a) people at large are put under a duty not to injure any worker by getting him excluded or expelled from a trade union, (b) every

[62] DN MacCormick, 'Rights in Legislation' in PMS Hacker and J Raz (eds), *Law, Morality and Society* (Oxford: Clarendon Press, 1977). The quotations are from pages 203–5.

worker is in law free to apply for membership of a union of his choice, and (c) any act of purported exclusion of a worker from his union lacks legal effect if it is to be judged to be "by way of arbitrary or unreasonable discrimination".'[63] 'Thus,' MacCormick concludes, 'using the terminology (in my view indispensable) of "rights" the legislature can in short and simple words achieve complex legal protections for the several members of a given class.'[64]

MacCormick's analysis appears to conflict with that of Hohfeld in several respects. In the first place, the analysis claims that a single right can give rise to a variety of different legal protections and to a host of diverse jural relations: this contrasts very obviously with Hohfeld's approach which sees each right as one side of a single bilateral jural relationship. Secondly, the right provides a reason or justification for providing some set of legal protections as may be deemed appropriate in the circumstances, whereas Hohfeld would see rights and legal protections as standing in relationships of mutual entailment. (MacCormick sometimes speaks of the legal protections as 'entailed' by the right, but this cannot represent his considered view, since it would contradict his claim that the right may give rise to a variable set of protections.) Thirdly, legal rights for MacCormick play a fundamental role in the dynamics of legal reasoning, since they provide a justification for the development of appropriate forms of legal protection; Hohfeld, by contrast, neither asserts nor denies the possibility of rights playing such a role in legal thought.

Suppose that a Hohfeldian is presented with the passage that MacCormick quotes from section 5(1). If that passage is taken in isolation, the Hohfeldian judge would have to conclude that it is ambiguous. It may confer claim-rights against union officials, or it may confer claim-rights against all persons; it may be employing the term 'right' in the sense of 'immunity', so that it would be correlative not to a duty on union officials but to a disability; it may (given an appropriate background of legal doctrine and other assumptions) confer a claim-right with regard to exclusions, and an immunity with regard to expulsions; and so on. MacCormick's view, by contrast, seems to be that the provision exhibits no ambiguity at all:

---

[63] ibid, 206. I have discussed MacCormick's other example (s 2 of the Succession (Scotland) Act 1964) in my book *Central Issues in Jurisprudence* (London: Sweet and Maxwell, 1986), 134–5.
[64] ibid, 206.

the judge could infer any or all of these protections from the right, as appropriate. Presumably his idea is that the right introduces a legal reason for creating such forms of protection, but that reason has to be balanced against countervailing considerations, so that the protections that finally result are the outcome of this calculus of conflicting reasons.

If this interpretation of MacCormick is correct, it provides an insidious account of doctrinal reasoning which converts adjudication into an instrumental process of balancing interests. For the 'short and simple words' of the provision do not in fact *entail* any particular set of duties or disabilities: they merely (on this analysis) identify a very important interest, and leave it open to the court to decide how it is to be protected. This does not seem to resemble much of the legal doctrinal argument with which we are familiar. Nor is it an accurate representation of the rights conferred by the Trade Union and Labour Relations Act 1974.

On being presented with the passage from section 5(1) that MacCormick quotes, most lawyers would (I think) *either* regard it as ambiguous, and therefore go on to seek clarification of its meaning from its wider context, *or* they would suspect it of being a merely preliminary statement of aim, and would go on to seek the real substance of the matter elsewhere. Since the distinction between these two approaches would not be evident or important to practical people, the upshot is the same in both cases: they would read on. They would then discover that section 5(1) is clearly not intended to be read in isolation. For example, one 'ambiguity' that might be discerned in section 5(1) concerns the identity of the party against whom the right lies: is it a right holding against trade unions only, or does it hold (as MacCormick informs us) against 'people at large' who may secure the expulsion or exclusion of a worker from a union? A preliminary answer is found in sections 5(3) and 5(4) which make it clear that the statutory remedy lies against the union. It is simply not true that the 'short and simple words' quoted by MacCormick 'achieve complex legal protections': such legal protections as are created by section 5 are created by the section as a whole.

There are many different ways in which a section having the same effects as section 5 could have been drafted. It is precisely because the legal effect of the statute is separable from its style of drafting that it is unwise to build a legal theory upon such styles of drafting;

and it is particularly unwise when the theory appears to have the dramatic implications of MacCormick's account.

Consider once again the three forms of legal protection that (according to MacCormick) are conferred by section 5(1):

> That confers protection of at least... three kinds; it being presumed that membership of a union is beneficial to any worker in normal circumstances (a) people at large are put under a duty not to injure any worker by getting him excluded or expelled from a trade union, (b) every worker is in law free to apply for membership of a union of his choice, and (c) any act of purported expulsion of a worker from his union lacks legal effect if it is judged to be 'by way of arbitrary or unreasonable discrimination'.

But how many of these rights actually were conferred by section 5 (let alone by the sub-section that MacCormick quotes)? Certainly the liberty to apply for membership of a union was not so conferred: that liberty is simply the consequence of there being no duty not to apply for membership, and it pre-existed the Act. Nor is the duty placed on people at large (not to injure workers by getting them excluded or expelled) a consequence of section 5. If there is such a duty, it is presumably a result of the position at common law, whereby securing the expulsion of a member from a union might amount to the tort of inducing a breach of contract.[65] Indeed, section 5(5) of the Act is careful to preserve such rights at common law.

Even if MacCormick were correct to say that section 5(1) had all of those complex consequences in law, it would not have had those consequences simply in virtue of the wording of the sub-section alone. When we take the sub-section in isolation, it is impossible to tell whether it confers a claim-right against union officials who exclude or expel, or a claim-right against any person who brings about an exclusion or expulsion. Likewise, one cannot tell whether the provision imposes upon the union a disability preventing them from expelling members in the prohibited manner, or simply a duty not to expel members. Perhaps labour lawyers in 1974 were able to reach confident conclusions about the legal effect of the provision; but, if that was so, their judgment was guided by a great many considerations other than the wording of this sub-section. The

---

[65] See also the judgment of Lord Denning in *Enderby Town Football Club* v *Football Association* [1971] 1 All ER 215. In that case Lord Denning asserted a judicial power to control the activities of unions on various grounds, which would include protecting the 'right to work' against discriminatory expulsion by a union.

sub-section needed to be read in the context of the section and of the legislative scheme as a whole, and the legislation needed to be applied within the context of a rich and complex body of common law principles. If this is indeed an instance of 'complex legal protections' being achieved by the 'short and simple' terminology of 'rights', the achievement seems to be in large part a function of the doctrinal background against which that short and simple word operated.

Suppose that I am correct thus far. Nevertheless, does not Mac-Cormick still retain a damning point against the Hohfeldian view? For, when the Hohfeldian judge has attached a definite meaning to section 5(1) and decided (for example) that it confers a claim-right against union officials, is he not then prevented from inferring other consequences (in the form of different Hohfeldian relationships) from the same right? Does not MacCormick therefore have a sound objection to Hohfeld's regimentation of rights into distinct categories and atomic relationships, in so far as that regimentation obscures the way in which a single entitlement may provide good reason for the recognition of numerous different forms of protection in law?

There is a short answer to this argument, but before I come to it a brief reminder of a point made earlier is desirable. Remember that we must distinguish superficial issues about forms of drafting from deeper theoretical issues concerning forms of analysis. A draftsman might well find it convenient to draft a section in which a general 'right' is proclaimed at the outset and various forms of 'protection' for that right are established in subsequent provisions. Hohfeld would not deny the fact of such provisions, nor need he deny their desirability (in appropriate cases) on grounds of verbal economy and simplicity. What he would insist upon is that an accurate analytical representation of the *effect* of such enactments should respect and employ the distinctions established by his analysis. Now to the short answer.

The short answer is as follows. Nothing that Hohfeld says involves a denial of the claim that the existence in law of one sort of right may provide a reason for creating a different sort of right. Hohfeld is simply not concerned with relationships of this type. His concern is with relationships of entailment, and he would no doubt point out that (even for MacCormick) these different rights (or forms of protection) do not *entail* each other.

The short answer, however, simply leads to a reformulated objection. Is it not wrong of Hohfeld to concentrate to the exclusion of all else upon relationships of entailment? Does this approach not obscure much that is distinctive and valuable in the discourse of rights and in the character of legal reasoning with rights?

The answer here, if not so short, can at least be equally firm: and it is 'no'. MacCormick's analysis is intended to accommodate the tendency of legal doctrine to develop organically or dynamically, in response to reasons which are in some sense 'internal' to the law.[66] The endeavour to build a theory of this complex phenomenon on the back of an analysis of 'rights' is, however, a mistake. For it is far from clear that the forms of doctrinal argument whereby legal systems develop are best understood in terms of 'rights'. Much of the law develops by the analogical extension and application of concepts such as 'possession', 'consideration', 'remoteness', 'foreseeability', 'intention', 'causation', 'good faith', and so forth. The law is far more of an arcane science than the legal theoretician may suspect or be willing to acknowledge.

Take, for example, the question of whether third parties (that is, parties other than the worker and the union) are under a duty not to take action designed to secure the exclusion or expulsion of a worker from a union. It is far from obvious that this question would be approached by identifying the right conferred by section 5(1), treating that right as a general reason for establishing appropriate forms of legal protection, and then seeing whether there are any countervailing considerations which argue against the establishment of this particular form of protection. On the contrary, it is likely that the court would be much less concerned with the general balancing of interests, and much more immersed in the technicalities of legal doctrine. Having established that no duty is imposed on third parties by the statute, one would then have to consider whether conduct aimed at securing the exclusion or expulsion of a worker might fall within the scope of some existing tort. The factors relevant to that question might be quite unrelated to the scope of the worker's interest supposedly recognised by section 5(1). For example, the tort of inducing a breach of contract could be relevant only if the union's conduct amounted to a breach of contract. This might

---

[66] For a similar attempt, see Joseph Raz, *Ethics in the Public Domain* (Oxford: Clarendon Press, 1994), chs 10 and 11.

well be true of an expulsion from the union, but not of an exclusion (since one who has never been a member of the union has no contract with the union). The court might therefore reach the conclusion that third parties were under certain duties with regard to expulsions but not with regard to exclusions, thereby drawing a distinction unrelated to the interest that (in MacCormick's view) should provide the guiding star for legal development.

This is not, of course, to suggest that the categories of tort law are forever closed: in time specific torts such as inducement of breach of contract might be replaced by a more general tort of interfering with business or employment without lawful excuse. Such developments occur, however, by a process of analogical extension: frequently the recognition of a new basis for liability consists in the retrospective reflection that such a basis provides the best explanation for a series of existing precedents, no one of which was decided as an act of conscious innovation. The realization that some important interest of workers in union membership underlay many of the decisions might well play a part in this process of extension, and might fuel recognition of a more general remedy; but the picture of this process presented within MacCormick's analysis is misleadingly simple.

The complex and arcane character of legal doctrinal argument, and its frequent remoteness from any obvious connection with the 'interests' protected or 'policies' served by the law, has long been a target for the criticism of academic theorists. They have frequently urged upon the courts a more open and explicit concern with the goals and consequences of the law, and have attacked conventional legal arguments as subordinating policy goals to opaque doctrinal distinctions.[67] MacCormick's advocacy of a concept of 'right' that would, as he puts it, draw attention to 'the intended aim and object' of the law shares some of the impetus of these proposals. The danger inherent in all such proposals is equally familiar: that by converting legal doctrinal questions into questions concerning the balancing of interests or the advancement of desirable social goals, they will convert legal argument into an arm of the state's distributive or aggregative agenda, and will in that way erode the integrity of those domains of liberty that are protected by rights.

---

[67] See, for example, the views of Atiyah, discussed in Nigel Simmonds, *The Decline of Juridical Reason* (Manchester: Manchester University Press, 1984), 77–8.

The issues raised here are complex and it might well be considered a mistake to presuppose some response to them in constructing our analysis of rights. Nor is such a conflation of issues in any way necessary. Even if courts do take the existence of one legal right as a reason for conferring other forms of protection upon the interest protected by that right, this need not be in consequence of the logical features of the concept of 'a right'. In some cases, it could be in consequence of specific features of legal doctrine: for example, the tort of inducing a breach of contract may mean that X's contractual rights against Y give rise to certain non-contractual rights against Z. On the most general plane, the creation of new rights in response to existing rights could result from the courts' concern for the justice and internal coherence of the law. To propose an analysis of these features of doctrine as one aspect of an analysis of rights is to invite confusion. When the analysis proposed is the modern type of 'Interest' Theory developed by MacCormick, it is also to invite a collapse of doctrinal argument into the open-ended balancing of interests and pursuit of policy goals.

Liberty in the Jural Realm

We owe to H. L. A. Hart the observation that a Hohfeldian liberty may appropriately be described as 'a right' only in virtue of its connection with the 'perimeter of protection' afforded by the general prohibitions on assault and other gross forms of interference. Thus, Hart pointed out that it would be odd to say 'that a class of helots whom free citizens were allowed to treat as they wished or interfere with at will, yet had rights to do those acts which they were not forbidden by law to do'.[68]

A number of difficulties are posed by Hart's example of the helots. In the first place, we might wonder whether the helots can appropriately be spoken of as standing within jural relationships at all. The applicability of legal concepts seems to presuppose an interest in determining the exact limits and requirements of the law as applied to individual instances. Such an interest might stem from a belief in the general moral duty to obey the law, or from a concern to predict the possibility of official interference with conduct (sanctions). Our reasons for hesitating to apply the concept of

---

[68] Hart, *Essays on Bentham* (n 58 above), 173.

a right to the helots may therefore stem from a belief that they fall outside the scope of any probable interest in the applicability of law.

It is of course possible to imagine circumstances in which there might be a concern to establish the content and applicability of prohibitions relating to the helots: if, for example, we think of each breach of prohibition by a helot as the occasion for the incidence of a duty (to punish) incumbent upon some dutiful official. It is important to note, however, that here the helot's contravention of a prohibition functions precisely as the *occasion* for the performance of someone else's duty: it is analogous to the situation where a fall in temperature activates a duty on the part of some officials to make payments to pensioners. So long as the helots receive no protection whatever from the law, there is unlikely to be any well-grounded interest in applying the law to their conduct as a basis for the guidance of that conduct (as opposed to the guidance of the conduct of others, such as sanction-applying officials). For what reason could one have for guiding one's conduct by the law in a context where even law-abiding conduct is not protected? By avoiding any breaches of duty, a helot might reduce though not eliminate the risk of being subjected to interference by officials; but (since even their lawful conduct is unprotected) their compliance with duty might also, in some cases, *increase* the risk of their being penalized by other citizens (citizens annoyed by the helots compliance with their duty of Sunday morning bell-ringing, for example). Given the absence of any protection for their lawful conduct, a general policy of being guided by the legal rule would probably be inferior to a strategy of guidance by *ad hoc* prediction of the likelihood of interference. If the applicability of legal concepts such as 'right' and 'duty' depends upon an 'internal' point of view that seeks to regulate conduct by reference to the rules, we may be tempted to conclude that such concepts are simply inapplicable to the helots, since the helots themselves would have no such perspective on the rules. It can make sense to talk of the rights and duties of those members of a populace who simply obey rather than accept the laws; but, in the case of the helots, we have people who would not orientate their conduct by law at all, their compliance with law being purely contingent upon the *ad hoc* balancing of different threats. From the viewpoint of others (such as the officials) the helots' conduct would function merely as the *occasion* for the incidence of duty rather than being a focus for rule-based appeals independently of the duties of others. It is in this sense that the helots may be said to stand outside of jural relations entirely.

Hart's example of the helots was aimed at Bentham, who (according to Hart) was inclined to refer to liberties as 'rights' even when they were devoid of any perimeter of protection. We might, however, regard Hart's analysis as suggesting an elucidation of Hohfeld rather than a criticism. For it must be remembered that Hohfeldian liberty exists and has its being within a system of jural relations. It should therefore not be confused with such extra-legal phenomena of liberty as obtain in a state of nature. Hohfeldian liberty is not a residual pocket of dry land left by the incoming tide of legal regulation, for the existence of the general prohibitions on assault and trespass provide a 'perimeter of protection' for liberty that effectively transforms its pre-legal nature into a specifically juridical phenomenon.[69] The inclusion of general prohibitions upon assault and trespass is, perhaps, not a logically necessary feature of legal systems: but it may well be a feature that is grounded in certain *natural* necessities, and that is in that sense non-contingent.[70]

In this way, Hohfeld's analysis can lead us to see the transforming effects of juridical ordering, and to challenge the popular forms of rhetoric that portray 'liberty' within the juridical realm as the mere abstention of the law. Given the existence of a legal system, what the law permits it also enables and empowers, and the collectivity bears responsibility for the consequences of such enabling just as much as for the consequences of prohibition. Indeed, this is only one respect in which Hohfeld's analysis can generate insights of extensive significance. Some of Hohfeld's brief remarks on property, for example, spawned important insights into the coercive aspects of the supposedly 'free' private realm.[71] By contrast with the simple dichotomy between 'freedom' and 'unfreedom' that has characterized so much modern political philosophy, these analyses contribute to the realization that action is located within a complex field of consequences wherein choice is never excluded, but is equally never

---

[69] I have followed the general modern practice of substituting the term 'liberty' for Hohfeld's term 'privilege'. It is worth observing, however, that Hohfeld's terminology does have the significant advantage of marking out the concept as a specifically juridical one, not to be confused with the mere absence of legal regulation.
[70] HLA Hart, *The Concept of Law*, (Oxford: Clarendon Press, 1961), ch 9.
[71] Hohfeld, *Fundamental Legal Conceptions* (n 44 above), 97.

without cost: freedom as the pure absence of constraint is revealed to be a chimera.[72]

Claim-rights and Liberties

Traditional legal scholarship has tended to assume that rights render actions both permissible and inviolable. On this view, if an action is performed within the scope of a right it is clearly not a legal wrong, and is in that sense permissible; but such an action should also be protected from interference, and is in that sense inviolable. To interfere with a permissible action, it is assumed, is to interfere with the rights of another; it is therefore to do wrong, to violate one's duty, to do that which one has no right to do. In this way, the notion of rights as rendering actions both permissible and inviolable divides the juridical universe (at least of private law) into the two categories of actions which exercise rights, and actions which violate rights. This naturally suggests a picture of mutually compatible liberties, with law as the demarcation of the boundary between such liberties, and legal wrong as the violation of a boundary.

This general scheme of assumptions depends upon a concept of legal rights as spheres of permissibility and inviolability: as notional spaces within which one is free to act as one pleases. Such a concept of right appeared to provide an important focal point for the systematization of law, for various prohibitions on action could be interrelated by their varying relationships to notional spheres of entitlement. A further inference was also tempting for traditional legal scholars: that the various spheres of individual entitlement might themselves be systematically interrelated by means of the formal conditions for jointly possible freedoms. Thus, seemingly natural and harmonious assumptions combined to form a scheme of thought that found its most articulate expression in the jurisprudence of Kant. The Kantian conception of justice as a universal law of freedom appeared to be the immanent significance of doctrinal systematicity.

Such a claim may seem absurdly exaggerated when applied to the pragmatic and anti-theoretical common law. Common law judges,

---

[72] A rich and fertile seam of philosophical thought challenges the contrast between freedom and constraint. For two accessible modern examples see: Frithjof Bergmann, *On Being Free* (Indiana: Notre Dame, 1977); Stanley Fish, *Doing What Comes Naturally* (Oxford: Clarendon Press, 1989).

we might say, knew little about Kant and cared less (we will discover in a moment that there were exceptions to this general proposition). But assumptions about the mutual compatibility of freedoms could find expression in doctrinal argument without any need for an underpinning theory: indeed, such assumptions may be especially effective and determinative when they are simply a part of the taken-for-granted common sense of practical men.[73] When we pass to the level of more explicit attempts at doctrinal systematization, the picture changes. For here we should not forget the enormous prestige, even in the common law world, of the German tradition of legal scholarship which had been founded by Savigny and was fundamentally informed by Kantian assumptions. As Mathias Reimann notes:

> The Germans' historical and systematic works had gradually composed a complex and logical legal order which looked to many common-law scholars in their chaotic wilderness like the Garden of Eden. Nothing comparable existed in the common-law world, and for many it seemed obvious that the course of the Germans should be followed.[74]

We can see the assumption of joint permissibility and inviolability at work in the judgment of Lord Lindley in *Quinn v Leathem*,[75] a case discussed by Hohfeld. We can also see here how Hohfeld's analysis exposes gaps in the judge's reasoning which would not otherwise be visible.

Quinn had tried to force Leathem, a butcher, to sack his non-union employees and employ only union members. In pursuit of this objective, Quinn threatened a strike at the shop of one of Leathem's customers unless the customer would stop doing business with Leathem. Leathem sued Quinn. In a passage quoted by Hohfeld, Lord Lindley set out a line of reasoning that may be represented thus:

(i) Leathem had a right to earn his living in his own way;
(ii) this right included the right to deal with other persons who were willing to deal with him;

---

[73] Undefended assumptions about the mutual compatibility of freedoms may, for example, have played an important part in the thinking of prominent liberals such as JS Mill. See Richard Bellamy, *Liberalism and Modern Society* (Cambridge: Polity, 1992), ch 1.

[74] Mathias Reimann, 'The Common Law and German Legal Science' in Robert W Gordon (ed) *The Legacy of Oliver Wendell Holmes, Jr.* (Edinburgh: Edinburgh University Press, 1992), 92.

[75] [1901] AC 495.

(iii) therefore, everyone was under a duty not to prevent the exercise of that right;
(iv) Quinn had violated that duty.

On the assumption that rights entail both permissibility and inviolability, this argument appears to be sound. If Lord Lindley has accurately identified Leathem's rights, it follows that Quinn has failed in his duty.

Hohfeld's analysis of rights, however, has the effect of splitting the notion of permissibility from the notion of inviolability, and the analysis thereby exposes an equivocation in Lord Lindley's argument. In Hohfeldian terms, the 'right' identified at step (i) would be a liberty or privilege. This entails the absence of a duty on Leathem not to earn his living in his own way: in other words, it denotes permissibility. But Leathem's liberty entails no duties for anyone else: one cannot deduce the existence of a duty from the existence of a liberty. Only claim-rights entail duties, and Lord Lindley's argument does nothing to demonstrate the existence of a claim-right in Leathem.

One might, of course, seek to restore the deductive character[76] of Lord Lindley's argument by claiming that the 'right' identified at step (i) is a claim-right, and therefore does entail a duty for some other person. But such an interpretation would face the following two difficulties. In the first place, Hohfeldian claim-rights do not relate to the actions of the right-holder, but to the actions of the duty-bearer. It therefore makes no sense to suggest that Leathem had a claim-right to earn his living in his own way. One would have to reconstrue the content of the right as, for example, a right not to be interfered with in the course of earning his living in his own way. This leads us to the second difficulty, which is that the proposition set out at (i) forms an uncontroversial starting point for legal reasoning *only* if it is construed as asserting a liberty. If it is construed as asserting the existence of a claim-right, it could not have constituted a sound doctrinal basis for the judge's reasoning. This is particularly so once the right is reconstrued along the lines suggested above (to fit the point that claim-rights relate to the actions of others): for such a highly general right not to be interfered with would have sweeping, unforeseeable, and quite possibly unacceptable implications.

---

[76] I am here ignoring more general doubts about the possibility of deductive arguments in normative contexts.

Lord Lindley assumes that a right entails both permissibility and inviolability. Quinn had violated a duty *not* because his conduct fell within the bounds of some already well-defined legal prohibition, but because it interfered with the lawful activities of another: the division between permissible activities and impermissible interferences is the critical distinction at work here. Since the assumptions that inform this argument are those characteristic of a broadly Kantian view of rights, it is therefore interesting to note that Lord Lindley had studied in Bonn and was familiar with the prestigious traditions of German jurisprudence that were so strongly influenced by Kant and the classical Will Theory. As a young barrister, Lord Lindley had translated the general part of Thibaut's *System des Pandekten Rechts*,[77] a work which shared the view of rights characteristic of the classical Will Theory. His translation of Thibaut makes it clear that rights combine the features of permissibility and inviolability (in the sense of protection by a correlative duty):

[E]verything done in exercise of a right is juridically speaking lawful... Every right is as such accompanied by a power of compelling the performance of or forbearance from some positive act.[78]

Lord Lindley's assumed view of rights is undermined by the Hohfeldian analysis. Yet why should we accept the Hohfeldian analysis? As I observed earlier, our formal intuitions about the concept of 'a right' can be regimented in a variety of ways, and the Hohfeldian system is only one such. Each systematic analysis of rights departs at certain points from our ordinary understandings (this being the price of systematization) and one cannot plausibly claim that decisive considerations favour Hohfeld's view as against the alternatives. So why should we not sustain Lord Lindley's argument by rejecting Hohfeld and retaining the joinder of permissibility and inviolability?

---

[77] Nathaniel Lindley, *An Introduction to the Study of Jurisprudence*, (being a translation of the general part of Thibaut's *System Des Pandekten Rechts*) (London: Maxwell, 1855). Pollock dedicated the first edition of his treatise on contract to Lord Lindley, saying that Lindley had taught him 'to turn from the formless confusion of textbooks and the dry bones of students' manuals to the immortal work of Savigny' (quoted in Cheshire, Fifoot, and Furmston, *The Law of Contract*, 13th edn (London: Butterworths, 1996), 18). I am grateful to Gareth Jones for letting me see his essay on Lord Lindley written for the forthcoming *New Dictionary of National Biography*.

[78] Lindley (n 77 above), 52–3.

The answer to this very reasonable question must be as follows. Lord Lindley's argument might be construed in two different ways. He might be read as assuming that permissibility entails inviolability. The starting point of his argument would then be a claim about the permissibility of Leathem's actions, and that premise would lead directly to conclusions about Quinn's duties. We will call this the 'straight entailment' reading.

Alternatively, the argument might be construed as claiming that *rights* entail both permissibility and inviolability, although permissibility does not itself entail inviolability. On this construction, a claim about the permissibility of Leathem's action would lead to a conclusion about Quinn's duty only via an interim judgement concerning Leathem's entitlements. In other words, the argument would begin with a claim about permissibility and, from that premise (in conjunction with certain other premises) would infer that Leathem possessed a right (of the non-Hohfeldian type that entails both permissibility and inviolability); from the claim that Leathem possessed such a right, certain conclusions could be reached about Quinn's duty. We will call this the 'entitlement' reading of the argument.

Hohfeld has demonstrated (if any demonstration were needed) that the permissibility of an action does not entail its inviolability and therefore does not entail any conclusions about the impermissibility of other actions. Such a demonstration is wholly independent of any views that we or Hohfeld may have about the concept of 'a right'. Simple permissibility does not in itself entail inviolability. So, on the simple entailment reading, Lord Lindley's argument fails.

But what of the entitlement reading? If Lord Lindley is correct in his apparent assumption that rights entail both permissibility and inviolability, then he is justified in inferring Quinn's duty from Leathem's right. But is he equally justified in inferring Leathem's right from the permissibility of his actions? For the only uncontroversial premise from which Lord Lindley can proceed is one concerning the permissibility of Leathem's actions; and if 'right' signifies more than a Hohfeldian liberty (if it entails both permissibility and inviolability) then the existence of a right cannot be inferred simply from the existence of a permissibility. The problematic step exposed by Hohfeld's analysis is (on this reading) the step from 'permissibility' to 'right'.

We must conclude, therefore, that one does not evade Hohfeld's exposure of indeterminacies in doctrinal argument simply by clinging to a non-Hohfeldian conception of 'rights'. Such a move does not eliminate the gap in the reasoning, but merely relocates it: instead of having to bridge a gap between the right to act (a Hohfeldian liberty) and the duty not to interfere, we have to bridge a gap between the permissibility of an action and a complex entitlement to perform the action.

Bridging the Gap by Diluting Entitlements

The mere fact that the steps in Lord Lindley's argument are not deductive on their face does not mean that appropriate premises could not be supplied that would render them deductive; but the Hohfeldian analysis would tend to suggest that such premises will not be propositions concerning the content and applicability of existing rights. Rather, relevant premises will have to provide arguments of justice or social policy that give us a reason for creating or conferring new forms of entitlement. In the case of *Quinn v Leathem*, for example, Lord Lindley needed to decide whether Leathem's acknowledged liberty (or 'privilege') should be protected by a claim-right against conduct of the kind in which Quinn had engaged. Hohfeld's point is simply that the claim-right is not entailed by the liberty: but he does not deny that considerations of justice or policy may give us a reason for conferring such a claim-right.

The anti-Hohfeldian may be unimpressed by this analysis, however. For it may be argued that existing features of the law can point to the existence of a (non-Hohfeldian) entitlement which justifies the imposition of a duty upon Quinn. The judgment that Quinn bears a duty, and Leathem a claim-right, may itself be grounded in considerations of existing legal entitlement.

An argument to this effect might begin by proposing a conception of rights wherein a right is not the correlative of an existing duty, but a reason for imposing a duty. The most popular versions of this position identify rights with important individual interests that are sufficiently weighty to provide good reason for the imposition of a duty on some other person, or for the institution of some other normative protection for the interest. The various legal concepts composing Hohfeldian jural relations are treated on this view as instrumentalities which can be deployed to protect true 'rights', the latter lying on the deeper level of justification rather than on the cutting edge of legal remedies.

The next step in the argument would be to identify some important interest corresponding to Leathem's interest in pursuing his living in his own way. Such an interest would have to be sufficiently weighty to provide a reason, in principle and in the abstract, for imposing a duty on others. The interest would be shown to be a legal right by demonstrating that it already provided the justification for a number of existing legal provisions: for example, for the liberties enjoyed by Leathem in pursuing his trade, the powers possessed by him in that regard, and so forth. Having in this way established that the interest amounted to a legally recognised right, one would have a legal reason for imposing an appropriate duty on Quinn.

It is tempting to imagine that such a conception could be employed to bridge the gap in Lord Lindley's argument. The argument reconstructed would now begin (as before) from Leathem's general liberty to pursue his trade. From that starting point, we would move to the identification of an interest in pursuing such trade, and to the observation that that interest is recognised in law to the extent of being protected by various existing rules: Leathem's power to contract; his liberty to operate a butcher's shop in the relevant location without being guilty of a nuisance; and so forth. We now seem to have bridged the gap between 'liberty' and 'entitlement'; it only remains for us to make the next step, from Leathem's 'entitlement' to Quinn's duty.

Unfortunately for the anti-Hohfeldian, this gap is not so easy to bridge. For the view currently being considered proposes that rights are reasons for imposing duties only in general and in the abstract. The existence of such a right possessed by Leathem does not itself entail that a duty should be imposed upon Quinn: only that such a duty should be imposed if there are no weighty competing considerations. Consequently, if we are to pass from the judgment that Leathem has a right to the conclusion that Quinn has a duty, we must pass through a complex process of identifying, evaluating and weighing the many diverse and competing considerations that will inevitably obtain in any concrete situation.

I mentioned earlier the possibility of reading Lord Lindley's judgment in two different ways. It might be read as assuming that permissibility entails inviolability (liberties entail duties); or, alternatively, it might be read as assuming that *entitlements* entail both permissibility and inviolability, although permissibility in itself does not entail inviolability. On the first reading, the argument is exposed as deficient by Hohfeld's analysis, which clearly exposes the gap between permissibility and inviolability. But on the second reading, the argument is equally deficient: the difference is simply that here the gap has been relocated. On the second reading the problematic step has been shifted to Lord Lindley's assumption that an entitlement (entailing permissibility and inviolability) can be inferred from a mere permissibility. Once the Hohfeldian analysis has exposed this gap in rights-based reasoning we may, by devising various alternative conceptions of 'right', shift it around: but we cannot eliminate it. Like an attempt to patch up a gap in the fabric of a spider's web, our efforts to carry out repairs will simply cause the rift to appear in a different location.

We can now see that the currently fashionable Interest Theory of rights[79] is less successful than its widespread popularity might lead us to believe. For, even if we are prepared to accept the rather loose and uncertain way in which legal rights are identified on this theory, we will find that the troubling rift in our rights-based reasoning still persists. Now the rift appears as a gap between the judgment that someone has a right (a weighty interest which, other things being equal, might justify the imposition of a duty) and the conclusion that someone else ought to be placed under a duty. To bridge the gap, in any concrete set of circumstances, we must engage in a complex process of balancing many diverse and conflicting interests. Talk of 'a right' has simply served to identify one of the interests involved in that process.

Somewhat earlier, we considered a Kantian conception of rights that linked the notions of permissibility and inviolability. We saw how Hohfeld's analysis effects a separation of these two facets that the Kantian has joined together. We have now seen how a non-Kantian, but equally non-Hohfeldian, view of rights as weighty interests tries to provide a suitable bridge between permissibility and inviolability: permissibility does not *entail* inviolability, but may possibly constitute legal recognition of the importance of the interest, and the interest may in turn provide a reason for imposing a duty (thus conferring inviolability).

---

[79] By the phrase 'currently fashionable' I mean to distinguish the type of Interest Theory proffered by Raz and MacCormick from the (currently unfashionable, but more defensible) type of Interest Theory developed by Kramer.

One attraction of the Kantian view lies in the strong connection that it asserts between rights and the authorization to use coercion.[80] This grounds the initial connection made by Kant between rights and the value of freedom: since rights are distinctive in their power to authorize coercion, it is appropriate to think of them as based upon a value that is distinctively at stake when coercion is deployed. But the initial connection between rights and coercion reflects our sense that rights are in some sense peremptory: that if I have a *right* that you should perform a certain act, your performance of that act is not a matter for calculation or debate, but may be demanded 'as of right'.

In the currently fashionable Interest Theory of rights, however, the 'peremptory' character of rights is lost. My 'right' to speak freely, for example, is (according to that theory) neither the correlative of anyone else's duty nor coincident with a liberty possessed by myself. The right establishes only that I have an interest in speaking freely which would justify the imposition of a duty on someone else 'other things being equal'. To pass from the judgment that I have a right to the conclusion that someone else has a duty we must enter into a complex calculus in which competing interests are weighed and alternative ways of protecting my interest are considered. The assertion that I have a right is no longer a peremptory demand: it merely draws attention to an interest of which account must be taken.

4 Hohfeld and the Kantians

The Integrity of Rights Revisited

We noted above that the competing values of collective and private project pursuit seek a stable coexistence within the framework of the rule of law. By guaranteeing a realm of private rights that exhibit a degree of integrity from the aggregative and distributive concerns of the public realm, it is hoped that proper recognition and scope can be given to each of the competing values. Yet, as I pointed out, the notion of the rule of law can be interpreted in a diversity of different ways, and these differences to some extent mirror the dichotomies of the rights debate.

[80] Kant, *Metaphysics of Morals* (n 30 above).

Where the Interest Theory relied upon the separation of legislative and adjudicative decisions, the classical Will Theory of rights tended to emphasize the contrast between public and private law. The former was seen as a body of instrumental rules serving collective goals, while the latter was seen as an autonomous body of principles structured and informed by reasoned reflection upon the requirements of jointly possible domains of autonomy. Private law (on this view) demarcates the boundaries between different individual domains, and its content is dictated in large part by the rational requirements of such a demarcation.

Whatever his own understandings and intentions, Hohfeld has been seen as a contributor to, or a forerunner of, the American realist movement. That rich and varied movement had a great diversity of different aspects and concerns,[81] and it would be absurd to seek to reduce it to some single theme. Yet if there is one theme in particular that later jurists have tended to associate with realism, it is the attack upon the idea of law's determinacy: the attack, in short, upon the positivist idea that legislation and adjudication can be sharply or clearly separated. Realists were anxious to point out the huge scope for pliability of interpretation made available by any system of legal rules, and the extensive indeterminacies which permeate every body of legal doctrine. Nor could their analyses be reasonably dismissed as exhibiting an undue concern with the 'problems of the penumbra' at the expense of the core of settled meaning that gives content to every legal provision.[82] For the realists would have been quick to point out that even the 'core of settled meaning' rested upon shared values and shared understandings of the point or purpose of the rule, rather than upon some ordinary acontextual meaning of the words composing the rule: even decisions within the core of settled meaning involve (as Alexy observes) a 'negative value judgement'.[83]

---

[81] Neil Duxbury, *Patterns of American Jurisprudence* (Oxford: Clarendon Press, 1995).
[82] Hart, *The Concept of Law* (n 70 above), ch 7.
[83] Robert Alexy, *A Theory of Legal Argumentation* (Oxford: Clarendon Press, 1989), 8. Hart, at pp 7–8 of his book *Essays in Jurisprudence and Philosophy* (Oxford: Clarendon Press, 1983), retracts his earlier view that the indeterminacy of legal rules is always a linguistic matter: 'In fact, as I came later to see... the question whether a *rule* applies or does not apply to some particular situation of fact is not the same as the question whether according to the settled conventions of language this is determined or left open by the words of that rule. For a legal system often has other resources besides the words used in the formulations of rules which serve to determine

When read against the background of the realist assault upon positivist determinacy in law, Hohfeld's analysis is important for its exposure of social policy judgments within the framework of what might superficially appear to be deductive exercises in rule-application. Lord Lindley cannot validly infer Quinn's duty from Leathem's liberty; therefore Lord Lindley's judgment must contain the suppressed premise that Leathem's liberty *ought* to be protected by a claim-right and correlative duty.

Yet to view Hohfeld's contribution in this light is to underestimate its importance. If we assume that Hohfeld is important for his exposure of indeterminacies in legal reasoning, we might reasonably be led to ask how he has done more than point to a number of isolated errors. Why is it assumed that Hohfeld's discussion of *Quinn v Leathem* and other cases is more than a catalogue of judicial errors or oversights or failures to set out reasoning in full? Why is it assumed that Hohfeld has made some *general* point about legal indeterminacy?

Hohfeld's discussion of *Quinn v Leathem* reveals Lord Lindley's apparent assumption that rights entail both permissibility and inviolability; but this revelation has some *general* importance only if such assumptions can be regarded as pervasive in conventional legal thinking. What reason do we have for believing that Lord Lindley's assumptions are or were widely shared?

So long as we take *positivism* to be the intellectual system that primarily merits our scrutiny, an answer to this question will not be readily available. For there is no particular reason for thinking that assumptions of conjoint permissibility and inviolability (or permissibility and empowerment, etc: depending on which set of Hohfeldian relations we address) will be pervasive within positivist legal thought. Positivism makes no particular claims about the *systematic* character of law's content, and is therefore inherently unlikely to be committed to any such assumptions. If we are to find these views at work in doctrinal thinking, they will be within a system of thought that emphasizes the systematic character of law's content, rather than the positivist character of its sources. In other words, we must shift our attention from positivism to Kantianism.

<small>their content or meaning in particular cases. Thus... the obvious or agreed purpose of a rule... may serve to show that words in the context of a legal rule may have a meaning different from that which they have in other contexts.'</small>

We saw above how nineteenth-century German jurisprudence was fundamentally shaped by a broadly Kantian theory of rights. This theory, as John Lightwood explained, viewed law as 'an invisible line of demarcation between the provinces of different individuals', so that within each such province 'the will of the individual reigns.'[84] Kant's *Metaphysics of Morals* had claimed to trace the 'immutable principles for any giving of positive law' by finding the limits of legitimate coercion in 'the sum of conditions under which the choice of one can be united with the choice of another in accordance with a universal law of freedom'.[85] Accordingly, the notion of an ideal realm of equal freedom was to provide a guiding model for legal scholarship, since law could claim to be fully legitimate only in so far as it expressed and embodied the ideal.

If the systematic analysis and exposition of legal doctrine was to be guided by a theory of this type, diverse and fragmentary legal rights would need to be assembled into domains of liberty within which the individual's will was supreme. To the extent that this was possible, the existence of one specific entitlement would imply the existence of a number of others. An established duty on Y correlative to a (Hohfeldian) claim-right in X might suggest that X also possessed a complex of associated liberties, powers, and immunities. To speak less anachronistically by avoiding Hohfeld's terminology, a right was assumed to amount to a domain of freedom protected by a complex array of permissibilities, powers, and correlative duties: the rationale of such a complex assemblage being the attempt to make the right-holder's will supreme within a certain province of concerns.

Within this type of jurisprudential thought, the theory of rights and the associated Kantian theory of justice formed a system of ideas that mediated the application of concrete legal provisions and lent them greater determinacy than they might otherwise have possessed. Discrete legal rules could not only be interpreted against the background of a broader theory of justice, but could also be fitted into a wider and integrated system within which they might acquire an importance not confined to the strict bounds of their own wording and immediate objectives.

Whether consciously or not, it is this broader system of ideas which informs the judgment of Lord Lindley in *Quinn v Leathem*

---

[84] John Lightwood, *Nature of Positive Law* (n 17 above).
[85] Kant, *Metaphysics of Morals* (n 30 above), 55–6.

and which was to be fundamentally undercut by the Hohfeldian analysis. For, as we have seen, Hohfeld's apparatus of concepts and distinctions makes it transparently clear that connections between permissibility and inviolability, or between permissibility and empowerment, or between empowerment and immunity, are not grounded in the logic of entitlement at all. A substantive political theory such as the Kantian theory of justice may propose that we ought to ascribe complex sets of Hohfeldian advantages to individuals in order to protect the supremacy, within some sphere, of the individual will. Such a substantive proposal, however, must rest upon an appeal to its own merits, and cannot appear to receive support from an inherent logic of entitlement.

Hohfeld versus Steiner

At this point in our reflections, it will be enlightening to examine the Kantian theory of justice developed by Hillel Steiner. For Steiner's theory has undergone at least one metamorphosis, consequent upon his attempt to fit the theory to a Hohfeldian analysis of rights. In an early version, Steiner based his argument four-square upon the assumption that rights render actions both permissible and inviolable. Perceiving that Hohfeld had exposed this assumption as fallacious, Steiner attempts, in his recent book *An Essay on Rights*,[86] to revise the argument in a way that takes account of Hohfeld's insights but nevertheless preserves the substantive conclusions of the theory. We will see that this attempt fails precisely because it fails to acknowledge that the gaps in rights-based reasoning exposed by Hohfeld's analysis cannot be easily bridged: if one is to pass from judgments about permissibility to conclusions about inviolability (for example) one must step outside the channels of rights-based reasoning.

Steiner's version of a Kantian theory of justice is particularly interesting for our purposes because it proceeds from a set of analytical claims about the general nature of rights. In a sense, this is in line with Kant's own procedure, for Kant begins from the basic analytical claim that rights constitute authorizations to employ coercion;[87] he infers from this that rights are based upon the

---

[86] (Oxford: Blackwell, 1994).
[87] Kant, *Metaphysics of Morals* (n 30 above), 57.

value of equal freedom, that they concern only the form of the will (and the relationship between the wills of different individuals) and not its content; etc. Yet Steiner's approach is in some respects more demanding than that of Kant. For Kant's analytical claims about rights do not go beyond a set of very broad intuitions that could be interpreted in a diversity of ways. This results in a theory of equal freedom that has long been accused of being a mere empty formalism without real content. Steiner's theory, by contrast, seeks to ground a relatively determinate set of guidelines for principles of justice; and it proceeds not by loose connections between general intuitions, but by claims about logical possibility and contradiction.

Steiner argues that we should approach the discussion of justice by reflecting upon 'the elementary particles of justice', the elementary particles being 'rights'. By understanding more about the formal characteristics of rights, we can learn about the content of possible principles of justice. The connection is made by means of the notion of 'compossibility'. The logical characteristics of rights determine which *sets* of rights are logically possible (which rights are 'compossible'); and, since principles of justice establish sets of rights, the analysis of rights constrains the content of possible principles of justice. Steiner believes that this search for compossible rights enables us to reject many proposed principles of justice and perhaps to identify one theory of justice as unique in its consistency with the established analytical features of rights.

Steiner's basic thesis is that principles of justice which are capable of generating conflicts between rights lead to logical contradictions; the rights conferred by such principles are not 'compossible', and the principles are therefore unacceptable. Systems of rights can be free from conflict only when it is not possible for the actions authorized by the rights to conflict; and conflict between actions is *impossible* only when those actions share no physical or spatial components. Compossible rights, Steiner concludes, must take the form of entitlements to the exclusive use of objects and spaces: genuine rights, in short, are exclusive property rights.

The key step in this argument (or at least the step upon which I wish to focus) is the claim that conflicts between rights generate logical contradictions. In the context of the present essay there are very good reasons for isolating this claim for special attention. Steiner has had two separate stabs at sustaining the argument, and his shifts in position seem to be responses to a growing appreciation of the importance for his theory of Hohfeld's analysis. By reflecting upon the problems that Hohfeld causes for Steiner's theory we can learn a good deal about the blow that Hohfeldian analysis dealt to forms of legal scholarship that rested upon fundamentally Kantian assumptions about rights. We have seen how legal scholars influenced by Savigny, and even common law judges such as Lord Lindley, tended to assume that the legal order (or at least private law) could be reconstructed as a series of domains of liberty. Each such domain was thought to consist of permissible actions that were also inviolable, in the sense that interference with action within the domain would be a wrongful breach of duty. The conception of justice underpinning these assumptions, and informing doctrinal analyses, was that of a realm of non-conflicting entitlements, where action could be divided into the permissible exercise of entitlements, and the impermissible interference with such exercise. Steiner's theory seeks to sustain a broadly similar picture by arguing that a conception of justice as conferring inviolable, non-conflicting, domains of liberty is the only acceptable one, since all other theories fail the test of compossibility.

Steiner hopes to show that conflicts between rights would involve logical contradictions, and that genuine or valid rights therefore cannot conflict. Consequently, the only logically possible systems of rights are systems which make conflict between rights impossible. While this general argument has remained constant throughout his work, however, he has shifted his position on the precise nature of conflict between rights.

In the earlier version of his argument, Steiner assumed that rights entail both permissibility and inviolability: the possessor of a right may exercise it, and no one else may permissibly interfere with that exercise. Conflict between rights on this model would involve Agent A having a right to perform action X, while Agent B has a right to perform action Y, the two actions (X and Y) not being jointly performable. In such circumstances action X would be *permissible* as an exercise of A's right, but would also be *impermissible* as an interference with the exercise of B's right. It is logically contradictory to assert that an action is both permissible and impermissible;[88] therefore a set of rights that can generate conflict between

---

[88] Setting on one side special contexts where I might be evaluating the permissibility of the action from the viewpoint of different normative systems.

rights leads to logical contradiction; therefore such a set of rights is impossible.

The problem with this early version of the argument was the way in which it ignored Hohfeld's assault upon the assumption of joint permissibility and inviolability as a necessary characteristic of rights. In the hypothetical example where *A* has a right to do *X*, and *B* has a right to do *Y*, Hohfeld would say that the 'rights' in question are liberties,[89] since they relate to the right-holder's own actions (whereas claim-rights relate to the actions of someone else). As liberties, they can certainly conflict in the sense of authorizing actions where the performance of either action will impede or prevent the performance of the other. Nothing in the notion of a liberty, however, guarantees freedom from such interference: for that the exercise of the liberty would have to be protected by some appropriate claim-right. There is no action here which is both permissible and impermissible, and there is therefore no logical contradiction.

In the later version of his argument, presented in his book *An Essay on Rights*, Steiner revises his claims to take more adequate account of Hohfeld's analysis. The objective is the same: to demonstrate that conflicts between rights will lead to logical contradictions, so that systems of rights that do not exclude the possibility of such conflicts can be rejected as logically impossible. The assumption of joint permissibility and inviolability as a characteristic of rights is, however, abandoned.

Hohfeld's analysis makes it clear that a liberty entails nothing about duties incumbent upon other people; but Hohfeld would not seek to deny the point made by Hart to the effect that liberties frequently find a perimeter of protection in claim-rights protecting one from such interferences as assault and trespass. Even though I may possess only a liberty of free-speech (since others are under no duty not to interfere with my speaking freely), I may be effectively protected from interference by the fact that preventing me from speaking would necessitate an assault upon my person or a trespass upon my property, and I *do* possess claim-rights against assault and trespass. Hohfeld would merely seek to point out that the effectiveness of such a perimeter of protection is a purely contingent matter: it is not *entailed* by the concept of a right.[90]

---

[89] Hohfeld, of course, would use the term 'privilege'.

[90] It is worth reiterating a point made earlier. Hohfeld would be profoundly unimpressed by the observation, made repeatedly by his modern critics, to the

Duly armed with Hart's notion of the perimeter of protection which may surround Hohfeldian liberties, Steiner makes a distinction between what he calls 'vested' and 'naked' liberties. The distinction turns upon whether or not it is possible to permissibly interfere with the exercise of the liberty in question. The distinction is, Steiner tells us, one of degree when applied to *types* of action: my liberty to wear a hat may be more or less well protected by my claim-right not to be assaulted, depending on the circumstances. But the distinction is one of *kind* when applied to act-tokens: either it is possible for you, here and now, permissibly to stop me from donning my hat, or it is not. Vested liberties are those liberties which, by virtue of the efficacy in the circumstances of the relevant perimeter of protection, cannot permissibly be interfered with; while naked liberties are, by contrast, exposed to the cold wind of permissible interference.

Steiner now focuses the key steps of his argument upon the concept of a 'naked liberty'. Suppose that the performance of a certain duty (undertaken, for example, by contract) requires me to exercise a naked liberty.[91] Since the liberty is *naked*, my exercise of it may be permissibly obstructed by others. In such a situation, I may be able to perform one duty (the duty undertaken by contract, for example) only by violating another duty (such violation may be necessary if I am to resist the interference with my liberty). Steiner equates this conflict of duties with a conflict of rights, and argues that a compossible system of rights would be one in which such

---

effect that an assertion of a right to perform an action ordinarily suggests the wrongfulness of interference with the action. Certainly it does, and the notion of a 'perimeter of protection' for liberties explains why that might often be the pragmatic implication of such an assertion. But there is a difference between what will, in many contexts, be pragmatically implied and what is logically entailed by the asserted entitlement. The difference is made transparent by those contexts where my assertion of a right to perform an action is simply intended to resist a charge of wrongdoing, but does not assert a claim-right against interference because it is clear that no such claim-right exists (eg 'I have a right to make a profit').

[91] Since duty excludes liberty, this may seem to be an odd way of speaking; but it is simply a way of highlighting the absence of a claim-right not to be interfered with in one's performance of the duty-act. Imposition of a duty to do X deprives me of the liberty not to do X. If, prior to the duty, I enjoyed a bilateral liberty (that is, a liberty either to do X or not to do X), imposition of the duty will leave me with a unilateral liberty to do X. It is in this sense that we can speak of a duty to exercise a bare liberty. Kramer is right to emphasise, however, (as against theorists such as LW Sumner) that imposition of a duty does not itself entail the existence of a liberty to perform the duty-act.

conflicts are impossible. The relevant type of conflict arises when the performance of a duty depends upon a naked liberty. Consequently, a conflict-free system of rights would be one that provides an impenetrable perimeter of protection to liberties. Steiner concludes that only a system of property rights could provide such an impenetrable perimeter of protection for liberty.

There are two problems with this argument. The first, which I have explained elsewhere but will only briefly outline here,[92] concerns Steiner's equation of conflict of duties with logical contradiction. In the earlier version of his argument, where rights were assumed to confer both permissibility and inviolability, conflict of rights did indeed generate logical contradiction, since it led to a situation where an action could be said to be both permissible and impermissible. The proposition that a certain action is impermissible does indeed contradict the proposition that the action is permissible, since an assertion of permissibility seems to be a simple denial of impermissibility, and vice versa. But the later version of the argument leads, not to conjoint permissibility and impermissibility of an individual action, but to a conflict of duties. Here it is far from clear that there is a logical contradiction. '*A* has a duty to do *X*' does not seem to contradict '*A* has a duty to do *Y*', even on the assumption that *X* and *Y* are incompatible. *A* may have a duty both to do *X* and not to do *X*, and the assertion of such conflicting duties is not contradictory. The contradictory of '*A* has a duty to do *X*' is *not* '*A* has a duty not to do *X*' but 'It is not the case that *A* has a duty to do *X*'. Whether *A*'s duty not to do *X* entails the absence of a duty to do *X* is precisely the point at issue, and would require further theoretical argument of a kind that is not provided by Steiner.

The second problem with Steiner's argument concerns his assumption that situations where my performance of a duty is permissibly obstructed involve conflicts of duty. As I have pointed out elsewhere, this is not necessarily so. Once again it is Hohfeld's distinction between claim-rights and liberties that plays the key part in the demonstration. The permissibility of interference with my action does not entail the impermissibility of interfering with the interference. Those who can permissibly interfere with my action possess a liberty to interfere; but the possession of such a liberty

---

[92] Nigel Simmonds, 'The Analytical Foundations of Justice', 54 Cambridge LJ 306 (1995).

does not entail the possession of a claim-right not to be interfered with. Thus, when a lawful demonstration prevents me from performing my duty to deliver certain flowers to a wedding (in Steiner's example), the mere fact of a permissible interference with my performance does not entail a conflict of duty. In thinking that such a conflict of duty is indeed a consequence, Steiner is assuming that I can perform my duty (to deliver the flowers) only by violating some claim-rights of the demonstrators; but the permissibility of their demonstration does not entail the wrongfulness of my interference with their action. Therefore, no conflict of duty need be involved.

Of course, the demonstrators will possess claim-rights against assault and trespass, and so forth, and their liberty will enjoy a perimeter of protection in consequence. Perhaps I can get my delivery of flowers to the wedding only by using tear-gas on the demonstrators, or by ramming them with my delivery van. Conflicts of duty will therefore be a common and frequent consequence of situations where duty-acts may permissibly be interfered with. Steiner's argument, however, seeks to lead us to a theory of justice via a series of claims about compossibility. Alternative schemes of rights are to be eliminated not as counter-intuitive or unattractive, but as self-contradictory. He therefore cannot be justified in treating certain rights (such as the rights which provide a perimeter of protection for liberty) as already in place prior to the commencement of the argument. The existence of such rights cannot be invoked to support an otherwise invalid step in the argument, because all such rights are to be derived from the theory itself.

Many aspects of Steiner's analysis are Kantian in inspiration. This is true of his conception of rights as authorizing coercion, and (in the early version of his theory) as entailing both permissibility and inviolability; it is true of his vision of justice as a realm of jointly possible freedoms; and of his desire to ground his theory in purely *formal* considerations of the nature of liberty and of the will, in abstraction from its content. Ultimately, however, the Kantian resemblances carry with them certain Kantian vulnerabilities. Steiner is in the end vulnerable to precisely the objection that Hegel made against Kant: that he can only derive content from the essentially formal character of his theory by taking for granted many of our concrete juridical institutions and features of our existing moral life.

The Essential Modernity of Hohfeld

The failure of Steiner's argument serves to demonstrate that a conception of justice as a system of non-conflicting domains of liberty cannot be derived from intellectually austere claims about the formal properties of rights. The logic of rights seemed to dictate such a patterning of entitlements only on the assumption that rights entail both permissibility and inviolability. Once that assumption is abandoned in response to Hohfeld's analysis it can be seen that nothing in the logic of rights guarantees their orderly arrangement around a conflict-free system of jointly exercisable liberties.

This is not, of course, to say that such a Kantian theory of justice might not be developed independently of claims about the formal properties of rights. Nor have we said anything to demonstrate that doctrinal scholars might not find it possible to systematize the multiplicity of entitlements in terms of such an ordering of domains of liberty.

This gives rise to the following thought. Perhaps a basic working premise of legal doctrinal scholarship might be the assumption that the law seeks to protect domains of liberty. In this way, the permissibility of an action might raise a presumption that interference with the action is wrong. The perimeter of protection surrounding liberties might be reinforced in appropriate ways when such reinforcement seemed necessary to protect the exercise of liberty against new forms of interference. Perhaps some such presumption underpinned Lord Lindley's judgment in *Quinn v. Leathem*, for example. Rather than assuming (in anti-Hohfeldian fashion) that rights entail both permissibility and inviolability, Lord Lindley may have been acting upon a theory of doctrinal system that invited him to add to the perimeter of protection surrounding Leathem's liberties when those liberties had proved vulnerable to the interferences of Quinn. Such a theory might treat Leathem's existing legal liberties as providing a non-conclusive reason for extending their protection, such reason needing to be balanced against other conflicting considerations. The *justifiability* of such a theory might of course be debatable, although its attractions for an age caught up in libertarian rhetoric should be obvious. What concerns us at present, however, is not its justifiability but its *coherence*.

Is it true that the position is coherent? We are invited to think of Lord Lindley recognizing that the permissibility of Leathem's action does not entail the inviolability of that action, but then going on to consider whether the action's permissibility might not give him good reason to *render* it (in this specific respect) inviolable. In that case, we may ask, why does Lord Lindley's reasoning not begin from Quinn's liberty rather than from Leathem's? For are not Quinn and Leathem symmetrically placed? Each has a project that they wish to pursue: Quinn hopes to eliminate the employment of non-union labour at Leathem's workplace, and to achieve this objective by organizing industrial action at the premises of those who deal with Leathem; while Leathem hopes to continue trading as a butcher with a non-union workforce. What we have here, on the face of it, are two conflicting liberties which must necessarily interfere with each other.

Perhaps, someone might say, the symmetry is broken once we assume that Leathem's liberty to deal with whomever he wished was a permissibility already established in law prior to the decision in *Quinn v Leathem*, whereas the permissibility of Quinn's action in seeking to persuade others to stop dealing with Leathem (by threatening a strike at their premises) was not. At this point it is difficult to avoid being drawn into complex debates concerning the nature of permissions in law. Can we, for example, assume that everything that is not prohibited is permitted? Did the permissibility of Leathem's conduct simply consist in the absence of an appropriate prohibition? If so, were not Quinn's actions also permissible in the same sense, prior to Lord Lindley's decision? Or can we coherently say that on the matter of Quinn's conduct there was a 'gap' in the law, with the conduct being neither prohibited nor permitted? Alternatively, could we say that Leathem's conduct was permitted in a stronger sense than that captured by the mere absence of a prohibition?[93]

A more familiar line of argument would urge that Quinn's conduct is coercive (involving a threatened withdrawal of labour) and therefore constitutes an encroachment upon liberty in a way that Leathem's conduct does not. Certainly the fact that Quinn's coercion was aimed in the first place against third parties, and only indirectly against its real object (Leathem) should not be decisive against this argument. But the matter is considerably complicated by the embeddedness of the parties' actions and projects within a

---

[93] Joseph Raz, *Practical Reason and Norms* (London: Hutchinson, 1975), 85–97.

legal situation that is already structured by the coercive apparatus of legal entitlements. Quinn's threat to organize strikes is after all only a matter of persuading people not to work: we need to invoke the existence of contracts and legal obligations before this begins to look troublingly coercive. Similarly, Leathem's freedom to employ whomever he wishes seems unproblematically independent of any basis in coercion only so long as we ignore his exclusive control over certain physical resources, an exclusivity guaranteed and made realizable by the coercive power of the state.

Arguments such as these would involve us in complexities going far beyond the scope of this essay. Suffice it to say that, even if one can in some way break the apparent symmetry in the positions of Quinn and Leathem, it is unlikely that any such manoeuvre would carry conviction on the fundamental point at issue. Even if we can somehow disentangle the parties' actions from the structuring framework of coercive laws, and uphold a clear distinction between the liberties of Quinn and of Leathem, we will still be forced to confront the fact that the concept of liberty alone, detached from the content of particular liberties, provides us with insufficient guidance.

For example, let us take it as established that Quinn's actions 'interfere' with Leathem in a sense in which Leathem's actions do not 'interfere' with Quinn. It is nevertheless unlikely that Lord Lindley would have felt bound to protect Leathem's liberty of trade against every possible interference. Suppose, for example, that a trade association prohibited members from dealing with Leathem on pain of financial penalty. Would Lord Lindley have protected Leathem from the action of the trade association? In fact the question is probably incapable of an answer until we know something about the objectives being pursued by the trade association: operation of a cartel (for example) or enforcement of trading standards intended to protect the public. It is of course true that such a legal judgment would be mediated and structured by doctrinal categories: it would not be a matter of balancing conflicting liberties at large. For example, the trade association's power to fine members would be based on a contract, and contracts in restraint of trade are void, while contracts to maintain standards of care and hygiene for the public are valid and enforceable. Nevertheless, such doctrines are the accumulated expression of earlier adjudications in which precisely such evaluative issues had to be more directly addressed.

What we have here is a simple illustration of a point that was mentioned earlier: notions of 'equal freedom' are in themselves empty, until given content by a series of judgements about 'the good'. We cannot adjudicate upon the conflict between Leathem and Quinn by appealing to 'the sum of conditions under which the choice of one can be united with the choice of another in accordance with a universal law of freedom'.[94] In every conflict of will upon which we must adjudicate there will be gains and losses of freedom whatever decision we give. These gains and losses cannot be measured and balanced otherwise than by a judgment concerning the *importance* of the freedoms in question. There is no metric for the extent of freedom apart from such questions of importance. Thus, talk of 'maximizing' or 'equalizing' freedom can possess real substance only when some criteria of importance are taken for granted. Such criteria may be of an individualistic or of a communitarian character, but in either case they are likely to embody a conception of excellence that goes beyond the question of the *form* of the will,[95] and enters into an evaluation of its *content*.

Steiner's theory, as we established, needs to assume the existence of certain rights (rights to bodily integrity, for example) before it can treat the existence of naked liberties as creating the potential for conflicts between duties. Within the confines of his argument, Steiner has no warrant for making this assumption. Nevertheless, the mere acceptance of certain moral institutions as an unquestioned background for judgment is one way in which a Kantian theory of equal freedom can appear to take on real content. Of course, such tacit acceptance cannot be made explicit, for it conflicts fundamentally with the Kantian aspiration to find a categorical foundation for justice and to subject all existing institutions to radical critique. But a taken-for-granted background of institutions can nevertheless lend to the Kantian theory of justice an appearance of real content that it does not deserve.

Such a taken-for-granted background probably explains how a Kantian account of justice concerned solely with the *form* of the will could exert such a powerful influence upon the doctrinal systematization of nineteenth-century German jurisprudence. Lukacs' comment (quoted earlier) about the bourgeois belief that the form

---

[94] Kant, *Metaphysics of Morals* (n 30 above), 56.
[95] 'All that is in question is the *form* in the relation of choice' Kant, ibid, 56.

of law could determine its content must therefore be glossed by reference to Marx's observation that bourgeois thought took the structures of civil society as a natural basis, in need of no further grounding.[96] The jurisprudence of equal freedom amounted to a flattering mirror which gave back to the enraptured gaze of the jurist a convincing representation of society's existing features, but under the rubrics of 'equality' and 'freedom'. Ironically, however, the appearance of real substance attaching to the theory was dissolved, along with all other apparent solidities, by the very market society whose liberties the theory sought to protect.

A traditional agricultural society may give rise to relatively few conflicts between rights that are not already regulated by established customary rules, easements, or the like. There will be little scope or necessity for innovative judicial decisions defining the precise boundaries of conflicting liberties. The rise of industry, however, generates a host of new ways in which the actions of one person may impact upon the activities of another; while new forms of corporate capital and labour organization give rise to modes of association and inter-relation that cannot always conveniently be subsumed under traditional legal categories. As greater pressure is put upon the traditional fabric of the law, the sense of stable horizons against which an abstract conception of justice might operate is increasingly rendered problematic. As Marx observed:

All fixed, fast-frozen relations, with their train of ancient and venerable prejudices and opinions, are swept away, all new formed ones become antiquated before they can ossify. All that is solid melts into air, all that is holy is profaned, and man is at last compelled to face with sober senses, his real conditions of life, and his relations with his kind.[97]

When forced repeatedly to confront new ways in which the conduct of one could adversely affect the interests and liberties of others, the courts became increasingly conscious of the fact that remedies for such adverse impact could not and should not invariably be made available. It became obvious that there were numerous situations where one person could harm another and yet no legal remedy should be provided. Indeed, the most obvious form of

---

[96] Marx, 'On the Jewish Question' in *Karl Marx: Early Writings* (London: Penguin, 1975), 234.
[97] Marx and Engels, 'Manifesto of the Communist Party' in Karl Marx, *The Revolutions of 1848*, edited by David Fernbach, (London: Penguin, 1973), 70.

such harm arose directly out of the operation of a fluid and expanding market economy: businesses compete, and it is inherent in such competition that some businesses will drive others to the wall. It became obvious that a multiplicity of entirely permissible actions might nevertheless interfere with other equally permissible actions. Clearly, the new-found prevalence of *damnum absque injuria* could not easily be reconciled with a theory of rights that linked permissibility to inviolability.[98]

The classical Will Theory of rights was not simply or primarily an analytical exposition of the formal features of the concept of 'a right'. It was but one facet of a broader theory of justice and of legitimacy. Proceeding from the claim that rights authorize coercion to the conclusion that rights protect the autonomous will in abstraction from its particular content, the Will Theory purported to trace the limits and conditions of fully legitimate law-making: 'the immutable principles for any giving of positive law'.[99] Within such a theory, the assertion of a right amounted to an assertion of both permissibility and inviolability, for it was the conjunction of permissibility and inviolability that linked rights to the justification of coercion.

We have seen how Hohfeld's analysis breaks the association of permissibility and inviolability as necessary features of the concept of a right, and undercuts theories such as that offered by Hillel Steiner which seek to ground a Kantian theory of justice in the conceptual claims about the logic of rights. Yet we saw also that this demonstration would not prevent someone from employing a Kantian position as a background theory for the systematization of legal doctrine. The fact that the theory could not be derived from the logic of rights would not be fatal to its truth; the absence of a necessary connection between entitlement, permissibility and inviolability would not invalidate moral principles licensing a defeasible inference from one to the other. Such a background theory might mediate between the raw materials of law and the juristic conclusions drawn from those materials, inviting particular forms of systematization and inference, and grounding such forms in a wider theory of justice.

The *value* of such a juristic theory, however, was eroded by the very liberties that the theory sought to exalt. The increasing fluidity

---

[98] See Joseph Singer, 'The Legal Rights Debate in Analytical Jurisprudence from Bentham to Hohfeld', (1982) Wisconsin L Rev 975.
[99] Kant, *Metaphysics of Morals* (n 30 above), 55.

of civil society produced ever new forms of harmful activity that were not regulated by the existing customs and property rights of a traditional agricultural society. At the same time, the emergence of new laws to confront such evolving practices fed an increasing awareness of the alterable character of civil society. Basic social and economic structures were no longer regarded as a natural horizon against the background of which law, politics and adjudication might be conducted. The law came increasingly to be used as an instrument for the restructuring and regulation of these mutable practices.

Perhaps Marx was justified in claiming that bourgeois political thought took the structures of civil society for granted as a natural foundation. We have already seen how formalistic libertarian theories of justice derived much of their content from some such assumed background. Certainly it is the case that an increasing awareness of the alterable character of these structures, and the consequent rise of the notion of 'social justice', seemed to dissolve the discourse of justice and rights in a pliable rhetoric of conflicting claims. Law came increasingly to be used as an instrument for the pursuit of diverse competing or even conflicting social policies.

Various facets of this development contributed to the growing instability of forms of doctrinal thought that had been founded upon the classical Will Theory. The loss of taken-for-granted backgrounds began to expose the hollowness and vacuity of doctrinal rationalizations framed in terms of a theory of equal freedom, while the consequent decline in private law's appearance of intellectual integrity seemed to erase the distinction between private and public law, and to present private law as but another arm of governmental policy. Meanwhile, the great diversity of policies pursued by the law made any possibility of a systematic integration of public and private law seem a mere pipe-dream. In such a context it is in the highest degree unlikely that legal scholars or judges will find it possible to reconstruct the law in terms of a set of liberties constituted by permissible actions and enjoying some degree of inviolability. The guiding image of such doctrinal reconstructions had for a long time been the realm of compossible freedoms described by Kantian jurisprudence, but the emergence of new forms of commercial and industrial activity combined with the new scope and diversity of law-making to render that image implausible. Lawyers were increasingly aware of the pervasive conflicts that existed between individual interests, even when those interests were recognized in law and received some degree of protection. Doctrinal arguments seeking to articulate substantive principles of justice gave way to crude balancing tests, inviting a straightforward comparison of conflicting interests;[100] or the law crystallized into rules that bore only a blunt and oblique relationship to considerations of justice.[101]

Hohfeld's account of rights is very well-suited to this complex and conflict-ridden situation. By breaking the analytical connection between permissibility, inviolability, empowerment, and immunity, Hohfeld demonstrates with great clarity that common associations between these different facets are grounded, not in the formal structure of the concept of a right, but in purely contingent features. The law may or may not protect certain liberties with claim-rights, or combine powers with liberties to exercise them. Some combinations may be frequent, but all are in principle possible. Since the modern law is too complex and fragmentary to admit of being reconstructed in terms of a Kantian (or perhaps any other) theory of justice, so the concepts in which its content is reported must be capable of accommodating that complex and fragmented nature. Associations between permissibility and inviolability that flowed from (and in turn supported) the Kantian Will Theory must be rejected on the analytical plane if the realities of the modern legal order are to be adequately confronted.

Hohfeld's analysis reflects a concentration upon the remedial cutting-edge of the law, and a relative lack of concern with the deeper doctrinal structures that might be invoked to order and rationalize the array of rules and remedies. This admirably suited a situation where there was ample room for scepticism about the very possibility of deep organizing principles. To insist upon preserving a traditional conception of doctrinal legal thought in a context where the necessary internal coherence of the law has been eroded, is to propel doctrinal analysis into abstraction, since coherence must of necessity be sought at increasingly abstract levels if the apparent conflicts at ground level are to be transcended. Ultimately the meretricious expedient of an infinitely pliable notion of 'equality' is likely to come to hand: a development that not only renders the content of law increasingly uncertain, but also contributes to the

[100] Horwitz, *Transformation of American Law* (n 40 above).
[101] Nigel Simmonds 'Bluntness and Bricolage' in Hyman Gross and Ross Harrison (eds), *Jurisprudence: Cambridge Essays* (Oxford: Clarendon Press, 1992).

rise of an empty and pernicious rhetoric in which 'rights' are constantly, and without constraint, asserted in the name of 'equality'. Hohfeld's insistence on a more cool and precise language, in which correlative duties must be assigned, and permissibilities must be distinguished from inviolabilities, seems a voice of sanity and reason in this context.

5 The Interest Theory of Rights

Positivism and Instrumentalism

Having examined the collapse of the classical Will Theory, we are now well placed to examine the Interest Theory of rights. As we have seen, the classical Will Theory depended in a general way upon a Kantian theory of justice as a realm of equal freedom. The theory sought to abstract the form of the will from its content, and thus to achieve an ordering of legal doctrine in terms of the value of liberty alone, without regard to the interests that liberty might serve to promote. The theory collapsed partly as a result of the erosion of taken-for-granted base-lines which could be used to give content to an otherwise empty formalism: the realm of equal juridical freedoms was revealed to be nothing more than a flattering mirror in which society might find its own features reflected. New forms of economic activity combined with new bodies of legislative regulation to expose, across an extensive range, the *conflicts* of interest and liberty which characterize social life.

As we observed earlier in this essay, the classical Will and Interest Theories of rights could be viewed as interpretations of the form of moral association that finds expression in our law. Each theory both embodies an account of the central problematic for liberal political communities, and suggests the basis for a solution. At a certain level of abstraction, the theories conceive of the central problem in the same way: as concerning the relationship between the general choices and standards of the polity, as expressed in law, and the particular projects and concerns of individuals, as protected by rights. The Will Theory, however, sees this as a problem of rendering diverse individual liberties compatible, and of protecting spheres of individual freedom from the distributive and aggregative projects of the state. It seeks a solution in the separation between public and private law, and the attempt to develop principles of private law that reflect the form of mutually compossible wills in abstraction from their content. The Interest Theory, by contrast, rejects the possibility of a formalistic theory of justice that abstracts from questions of substantive interest and value; it accepts the inevitability and pervasiveness of conflicts between interests; and, rather than pinning its hopes upon the organic development of a rationalistic private law, the theory emphasizes the capacity of positive law to choose and to demarcate the boundaries between conflicting interests.

Some immediate problems face this version of the Interest Theory. Consider, for example, Ihering's famous conversion from being a doctrinal scholar in the tradition of Savigny to being an impassioned advocate of legal instrumentalism and opponent of what he now came to think of as pointless doctrinal hair-splitting. The conversion came about, it will be recalled, in consequence of Ihering's realization that legal rights might be thought of as representing 'interests' rather than protected spheres of autonomy or 'will'. This forced Ihering to transfer his focus of inquiry from 'subjective rights' to 'objective right' and ultimately to the notion of positive law as an instrument of purpose.

If, however, all legal questions are to be subordinated to the purposes served by the law, what scope remains for the integrity of private rights? Whether rights are conceived as areas of autonomy or as individual interests, there is a considerable difference between guaranteeing the integrity of such rights, and simply allotting a place to the relevant liberties or interests in a set of collective goals informing all legal interpretations. The Interest Theory of rights has a natural tendency to convert 'rights' into interests even when it does not simply equate rights with interests. If rights are interests protected by law (by, for example, the imposition of duties on others, or the conferment of liberties, powers, or immunities on the right-holder) then their scope and integrity depends upon the forms of legal interpretation that we employ. A 'purposive' mode of interpretation will threaten the integrity of such rights, in so far as an Interest Theorist will view the law's purpose in terms of some aggregative or distributive project.[102] The extent of one's rights will

---

[102] A more modern type of Interest Theory claims to overcome these problems by treating rights in a more 'individuated' manner. But, as we will see later, such theories

be determined by the impact that one's actions have upon the collective goals.

The Interest Theory will find it possible to avoid a collapse into naked instrumentalism, where rights enjoy no genuine integrity, only if a non-purposive mode of interpretation and adjudication can be adopted. To make this possible, legal rules must have a degree of 'semantic autonomy'[103] and it must be possible to identify the relevant right-holders without dependence upon an appeal to purposes supposedly served by the rule. Unfortunately, while depending in this way upon the availability of a positivist theory of law and of legal interpretation, the Interest Theory of rights has found it necesary to violate the requirements of such positivism.

The problem arises as soon as we ask for the criteria by which we infer the existence of certain rights from the given fact of this or that positive legal rule. The Interest Theory claims that positive laws seek to protect interests, by imposing duties or in other ways. Focusing for the moment on duty-imposing laws, we might begin our search by looking for those persons who would be benefited by the performance of the relevant duty. This criterion of simple benefit, however, proves far too inclusive and too arbitrary in its operation. Suppose, for example, that A owes B money, who in turn owes money to C. A's performance of his duty to pay B will indeed benefit C, by providing C's debtor with assets that could be used to pay C's debt. Yet we would be loath to conclude that C has a right against A. On such a criterion of simple benefit, rights would certainly proliferate: each duty might give rise to a host of rights, receding into infinity (for might not C's mother be more likely to receive a generous Christmas present from her son if he is likely to be paid by his debtor?).

To avoid this limitless proliferation of rights, Interest Theorists have tended to go in one of two directions. On the one hand, they have abandoned the positivism required by their theory, and have suggested that rights correspond only to those interests which it was the *purpose* of the duty to protect. By inviting an inquiry into the rule's purpose in order to identify the right conferred by the rule, the theory then falls into the problems of instrumentalism discussed

---

are quite unable to explain the nature of the special overriding weight that they claim to assign to rights.

[103] See Frederick Schauer, *Playing by the Rules* (Oxford: Clarendon Press, 1991).

above. One must now establish the identity and scope of legal rights by reference to the purposes served by the rule.

On the other hand, Interest Theorists may be tempted by the identification of rights with those interests the encroachment upon which would be sufficient[104] to establish a breach of the duty. This preserves the positivism of the theory, but at the price of disconnecting the theory from its wider significance. The classical Interest Theory invites us to imagine a world of conflicting interests in which the law-maker intervenes by introducing positive rules. These rules aim to protect some interests by limiting the pursuit of others. The precise mode of protection afforded is, of course, dependent upon a host of detailed and entirely pragmatic considerations. The content of a duty may therefore have a purely contingent connection with the interests that the duty is intended to protect. Bodily integrity, for example, may be protected by a law against carrying offensive weapons; the integrity of the home may be protected by a prohibition on possession of skeleton keys or jemmies. But it will not be possible to identify these interests in bodily or domestic integrity simply by reference to the conditions necessary or sufficient for a breach of the duty. Under this dispensation, a very large number of rights will fall into the residual category of rights possessed by the state[105] and the theory will be remote from any informative or enlightening clarification of the bases of legitimacy. A theory originally aimed at important intellectual objectives will have been converted into a regimentation of linguistic usage; such regimentation seems to be of doubtful value if disconnected from wider goals.

One final response remains available to the classical Interest Theory. For it might be alleged that the criticisms formulated so far have simply confused two different issues: the interpretation of the requirements of a legal prescription, on the one hand, and judgments concerning the existence and location of rights conferred by such a prescription, on the other. Even if it is true that we can only determine the location of any rights conferred by a law by reference to the purpose of that law, it does not follow that the prescriptive requirements of the law itself must themselves be determined in a purposive manner. Therefore, the Interest Theory does not commit us to a purposive mode of adjudication,

---

[104] See Kramer's essay, above, in this volume. [105] See Kramer, above.

Rights at the Cutting Edge 199

even if the identification of rights itself involves a purposive form of reflection.

On this interpretation of the classical Interest Theory, conflicts between interests are regulated by posited rules, and the judge's primary task must be the interpretation and enforcement of such rules. What part of the adjudicative process is then occupied with the identification of rights? The observation that a law confers this or that right on this or that individual seems, in this theory, to play no part in the forms of adjudicative reasoning. It amounts at best to an interesting footnote addressing a question which can never be raised within the context of the application and enforcement of the law.

In some cases, however, the rules may fail to make it clear who has *locus standi* to complain of a breach of the rules. Perhaps the question of rights will arise in this context, even for a version of classical Interest Theory that rejects a purposive mode of interpretation for the posited rules more generally. Since powers of enforcement are (for the Interest Theory) at best contingently associated with rights, decisions on the question of *locus standi* to complain will not themselves constitute decisions on the location of rights; but, in determining the issue of *locus standi*, the court may well wish to determine the purpose of the law, and to identify the individuals whose interests are protected by the law. Such a determination would (on this account) be a determination of the parties' rights, and would represent an intermediate judgment standing midway between the interpretation of the rules and the decision on *locus standi*. *X*'s possession of a right under a certain law would not entail *X*'s *locus standi* to sue, but would be an important consideration in determining that issue.[106]

Yet nothing is gained by describing this intermediate judgment as one concerning the parties' 'rights': indeed, the very contingency of the association between such considerations and the recognition of *locus standi* militates strongly against any such description. We would normally identify the question of *locus standi* to sue for breach of a rule with the question of whether that rule confers a right. What is gained by treating the concept of a right as referring

---

[106] See, for example, MacCormick's observation that 'to interpret a law as right-conferring is to give a justifying reason why there should be a remedy at private law for its breach'. MacCormick, 'Rights in Legislation' in PMS Hacker and J Raz, *Law, Morality and Society* (Oxford: Clarendon Press, 1977), 207.

to an interest that may or may not (when all things are considered, in the concrete circumstances of the case) justify recognition of *locus standi*? If we believe that the *locus standi* to sue should in general (although not invariably) follow the interests served by the relevant rule, we can say as much in straightforward terms: we do not need to hijack the concept of a right in order to defend such a substantive claim.

In a sense, the classical Interest Theory exhibited little concern to ascribe a significant role to the concept of a right. The main impetus behind the theory was a negative one: to reveal as hollow the pretensions of the classical Will Theory, by exposing the inevitability of conflicts between interests, and the illusory nature of a supposed non-conflictual realm within which free wills might be consistently joined. The classical Will Theory certainly gave a central role to the concept of a right, for it was that concept which (by uniting the features of permissibility and inviolability) provided the central structuring principle of the entire position. It was the object of the Interest Theory, by contrast, to emphasize the centrality of posited rules, and the law's need to confront the complex and conflict-ridden substance of human interests. That some versions of the theory rendered talk of 'rights' more or less superfluous might not have been perceived as a real problem.

Our conclusions might therefore be congenial to some advocates of the Interest Theory. Many others, however, have felt uncomfortable with a position that ascribes such a reduced role to rights, and their response has involved a dramatic departure from the analytical insights of Hohfeld. Directly opposing Hohfeld's fragmentation of legal rights, these theorists have sought to restore the notion of a right to a central place within the development and systematization of legal doctrine.

Peremptory Force and the Modern Interest Theory

The classical Will and Interest Theories of rights were sweeping interpretations of the form of moral association that found expression in law. On the one hand was a basically Kantian view that derived the legitimacy of law from a system of rights grounded in the form of the will in abstraction from its content. On the other hand was a theory that viewed the law as being in the service of certain goods, and that derived the law's legitimacy from the need for positive rules to demarcate the boundaries between conflicting interests.

In the classical debate between the Will and Interest Theories, it was the Kantian Will Theory that tended to emphasize law's systematic character. Rights provided the focal point for the systematic presentation of law in so far as they served to unify many facets of legal regulation that were later to be separated by the Hohfeldian analysis: permissibility, inviolability, empowerment, etc. The systematic character of legal doctrine reflected the law's approximation to the Kantian realm of equal freedom, while the latter served to legitimate the law's coercive demands. Within this scheme of thought, legal concepts took on a reality that was independent of positive enactment: the 'heaven of juristic concepts', pursued with ardour by the followers of Savigny and ridiculed by the later Ihering, was a working out of the detailed implications of principles thought to express the possibility of mutually compatible freedoms.

The emphasis upon the systematic coherence and autonomous character of legal doctrine, which was characteristic of the Will Theory, was abandoned by classical versions of the Interest Theory. The rejection of a belief in the Kantian realm of compossible freedoms, and an emphasis upon the pervasiveness of conflicts of interest, seemed naturally to lead to an emphasis upon the posited character of law. Legal reasoning no longer appeared to be autonomous and distinct from the general calculus of public policy: being concerned with constantly proliferating conflicts of interest, the law came to be thought of as a form of 'social engineering'. The most highly general of doctrinal principles were construed as 'jural postulates' serving only to guide a basically instrumental form of reason.

For those who view this collapse into instrumentalism with dismay, various responses to the problem are possible. One response might consist in the insistence that the identification of rights is an entirely separate task from the interpretation and enforcement of the rules that protect the rights. Another might be to revise the theory by abandoning the claim that rights correspond to the interests that it was the law's purpose to protect: instead, rights would be identified with those interests an encroachment upon which formed a sufficient condition for violation of the correlative duty. The first option threatens to reduce rights to an irrelevant appendage to legal thought, while the second option causes the Interest Theory to forfeit any claim to represent an interpretation of our form of moral association, or of the bases of legitimacy (for example, as we pointed out earlier, the theory will have to ascribe, in an uninformative way, a great many rights to the state); it becomes an exercise in conceptual regimentation which many will feel to be of doubtful value or significance.

The most popular versions of the Interest Theory[107] in recent years, however, have adopted a third strategy. In the first place, this modern version of the Interest Theory offers a challenge to the notion that each right (claim-right) is correlative to a duty. Rather than being regarded as the correlative of duties, it is argued, rights should be regarded as marking the interests which *justify the imposition* of duties:[108] duties are imposed to serve the interests of the right-holder. This first argumentative move abandons any attempt to preserve an austere focus on posited rules in the identification of rights, because it builds into the process of identification an inquiry into the law's justification. Such an abandonment of positivism could threaten to make debate concerning the existence of legal rights unacceptably open-ended; but the theory seeks to constrain the potentially open-ended character of the debate by emphasizing the role of rights in the systematization of law. Legal rights are portrayed as representing interests which ground a diversity of legal impositions and entitlements: my right to free speech, for example, may be the basis of certain duties imposed on X, certain liabilities incumbent upon Y, as well as certain liberties and powers possessed by myself. The fragmentation of legal relations embodied in the Hohfeldian analysis is portrayed as a superficial appearance only: beyond the level of Hohfeldian relations is a deeper level of 'rights' where the coherence of the law is made clear.[109] This deeper level of rights not only overcomes the appearance of fragmentation in the

---

[107] I shall refer to these versions collectively as 'the modern Interest Theory'.

[108] The theory in question need not claim that individual interests of the right-holder provide the ultimate justification for the relevant duties. The interests of persons other than the right-holder (or values other than interests) may provide the justification for the duty; this will be consistent with the existence of the right where the relevant justifying interests or values are best served by serving the right-holder's interests. See Joseph Raz, *Ethics in the Public Domain* (Oxford: Clarendon Press, 1994), ch 2.

[109] It might be suggested that 'local' rather than 'global' coherence would be sufficient (see Raz, *Ethics in the Public Domain* (n 108 above), 298–303). My own suspicion is that convincing grounds for claiming the existence of rights fitting the model proposed by the modern Interest Theory would require far more than 'local'

Rights at the Cutting Edge 203

law, but also guides the further development of legal doctrine. For the law may guide its own development, by providing legal reasons for the creation of new legal duties, liberties, powers, and so forth.

To some extent, therefore, a curious reversal has taken place. The mantle of the classical Will Theory, with its emphasis upon the systematic and integrated nature of legal doctrine, has been assumed by the modern Interest Theory. This manoeuvre, however, is only one of two main strategies that need to be adopted if the theory is to prevent a collapse into naked instrumentalism within which the integrity of rights is eclipsed. The second strategy consists in the claim that rights are individuated interests possessing special force or weight.

In Raz's version of the Interest Theory, rights are said to possess 'peremptory force'. This claim should strike us as surprising, since it appears to conflict with the theory's denial of correlativity between rights and duties. When we speak of rights as possessing peremptory force we would ordinarily mean that my possession of a right is not simply one consideration to be taken into account along with many others: my possession of a right concludes the issue of what is to be done. As Hart points out, 'the word "peremptory" in fact just means cutting off deliberation, debate or argument and the word with this meaning came into the English language from Roman law, where it was used to denote certain procedural steps which if taken precluded or ousted further argument.'[110] The 'peremptory force' of rights is captured by both of the classical theories of rights in their acceptance of correlativity. The existence of my right, on either theory, entails the existence of certain duties. To assert that I have a right holding in relation to some individual is not to draw attention to an important consideration that that individual should take account of: it is to claim that that individual bears a duty to act in some relevant way.

Raz tells us that X can be said to have a right 'if and only if X can have rights, and, other things being equal, an aspect of X's well-being (his interest) is a sufficient reason for holding some other person(s) to be under a duty'.[111] Raz does not hesitate to describe

---

coherence. The narrower one's focus in the search for coherence, the more slender will be one's basis for claiming that an interest is recognized in law as a general right.

[110] Hart, *Essays on Bentham* (Oxford: Clarendon Press, 1982), 253–4.
[111] Joseph Raz, *The Morality of Freedom* (Oxford: Clarendon Press, 1986), 166.

this analysis as ascribing 'peremptory force' to rights.[112] Yet such a description hardly seems appropriate. For, within Raz's theory, the knowledge that I have a right will never have the power to conclude the issue that we would ordinarily associate with peremptory force. Rights ground duties, for Raz, only if the reasons for recognizing such a duty are not outweighed by conflicting considerations: the right is a sufficient reason for holding someone to be under a duty only *other things being equal*. Establishing the existence of a right will, for this theory, be only the first step in a potentially complex course of reasoning that may or may not lead to the conclusion that a certain individual is under a duty. Any particular individual against whom I assert my right can respond by saying that, while the existence of my right is accepted, (a) my right establishes that a duty exists but not that he is himself under a duty; (b) whether he is under a duty depends upon how my interests are to be balanced against many competing considerations; and (c) when so balanced, my interests are outweighed: therefore (d) he is under no duty correlative to my duty. It is in this sense that Razian rights, far from possessing 'peremptory force', are in fact simply markers of important interests that are to be taken into account along with a host of competing considerations.

Raz might respond by saying that it is proper to regard Razian rights as possessing peremptory force in so far as we can infer from the existence of a right the existence of a duty somewhere, incumbent upon someone. The inference is possible because an interest that is *permanently* defeated by competing considerations and therefore *never* grounds a duty cannot be ascribed the status of a genuine right.[113] Hence, if we know that every child has a right to education, we will know that there are duties to provide children with education even though we have no idea who bears the duties.[114] This seems a weak defence, however, in so far as it leaves us with no specific individuals against whom our right will possess peremptory force: against any such individual, the right can be connected with a duty only via a complex process of balancing.

---

[112] eg Joseph Raz, *The Morality of Freedom*, 192. Sometimes the point is formulated in a more guarded way, eg at 249 he writes thus: '[R]ights have a special force which is expressed by the fact that they are grounds of duties, which are peremptory reasons for action.' In this formulation, *duties* possess peremptory force while *rights* possess 'special force' but not peremptory force.

[113] ibid, 184.

[114] ibid, 184–5.

It is with regard to legal rights that we possess our clearest and most emphatic sense of the peremptory force of rights. When I demonstrate to a court of law that I have a right to a sum of money that the defendant contracted to pay, I do not expect the court to tell me that they will take account of my right, along with many other factors, in deciding whether to hold that the defendant is under a duty to pay: I expect my right to be conclusive of the matter. In some circumstances (of national emergency perhaps) both rights and duties may be overridden: but, even allowing for that, I expect my right to be as conclusive of the outcome as a finding of duty would be. I do not expect my right to be only one factor that may or may not result in a finding of duty. Nor could Raz defend his weakening of the notion of peremptory force by pointing to the fact that even duties may be overridden in some circumstances, for the effect of his theory is to loosen the bonds of correlativity linking rights to duties, and this is a quite separate issue from that of the ultimate defeasibility of duties.

Individuated Interests and Boundary Conditions

It is important for Raz to defend the idea that rights possess peremptory force within his theory because it is by reference to that notion of peremptory force that he seeks to explain our sense that rights are not simply to be balanced against other conflicting considerations. In his view, the independence of rights from the general balancing of reasons is not to be explained by the *importance* of rights, since some rights have little importance.[115]

If, however, the rejection of simple correlativity between rights and duties does indeed (as I have suggested above) involve abandoning the notion of rights as possessing peremptory force, an attempt might be made by modern Interest Theorists to explain the special force of rights in other terms. One possibility would be to say that, in according to an interest the status of a right, we judge the interest to be of such importance that it cannot adequately be represented within an aggregative perspective, or as a mere facet of the common good.

Take, for example, my interest in free speech. One way of handling the importance of free speech would be to regard it as a

[115] ibid, 186.

consideration within the community's general pursuit of welfare or well-being. Whatever the weight attached to my interest in free speech, it would have to be balanced against other considerations affecting the lives of other persons, such as the need to secure certain benefits for the community as a whole. A sufficiently large improvement in well-being (perhaps constituted by the conferment of small benefits upon a large number of individuals) would justify encroachments upon my interest in free speech. Here the interest in free speech (whether styled 'a right' or not) is simply being added to an overall conception of the common good.

On a different approach, however, my interest in free speech might be accorded a degree of inviolability against considerations of the common good. Such 'inviolability' could be conceived of in different ways. One might speak of rights as 'absolute', and insist that infringement upon their scope can never be justified. Or one might speak of rights as 'side-constraints' on action, which constrain our ability to pursue desirable goals, and which can be encroached upon only in extreme and catastrophic circumstances. Or one might speak of according 'lexical priority' to rights, with the qualification that such lexical priority is to obtain only in relatively favourable circumstances.

Whatever model for the priority of rights is adopted by a theory, however, certain structural conditions must be satisfied if the theory is to retain its internal coherence and plausibility. If rights are not to be presented as constituting the sum total of moral concern, importance must be attached to considerations of the general welfare or the common good when the strict demands of individual rights have been fully satisfied; and if that is so, some boundary conditions must be set upon the scope and requirements of rights, to mark a watershed between the constraining force of rights (on the one hand) and the realm of more general welfare considerations (on the other).

For example, we know that many of our projects expose others to appreciable risks. When a community decides to construct a tunnel or a railway, or to permit the operation of a chemical factory, there is a risk that people may be killed or injured as a result. Now, let us suppose that people have a right not to be killed, and that this right is 'absolute', or enjoys 'lexical priority' over general welfare considerations. If we must at all costs avoid killing people, it would seem that we cannot engage in such risky projects: all of our decisions must be based on an attempt to minimize risks to life, without regard to other interests and values that might be served by actions involving some small risk to life. Even when we allow for the fact that a theory of this type could permit the balancing of rights one against another,[116] it would remain a deeply unattractive position.

It is for this reason that advocates of such strong, overriding rights find it necessary to put boundary conditions upon the requirements of their favoured rights. Thus the 'right not to be killed' must become the 'right not to be killed intentionally', or 'the right not to be killed negligently', or something of that sort. It is then possible for us to consider the construction of a tunnel or a railway, or the operation of a chemical factory: while these enterprises may result in deaths, the deaths will not necessarily be 'intentional' or 'negligent'.

It should not be assumed that this argument (that overriding rights will require boundary conditions) is dependent upon the acceptance of an aggregative account of the general welfare. Some theorists would endeavour to argue that such aggregative notions of 'general welfare' or 'common good' are mired in unacceptable assumptions of monism or commensurability. If we accept the existence of a plurality of incommensurable values (they suggest) we should reject aggregative notions of the general welfare or the common good in favour of interpretations that treat the common good as itself the maintenance of a framework of enabling entitlements and conditions, rather than the pursuit of collective goals.[117] Even on this interpretation, however, the community will presumably still have economic policies to pursue, roads and hospitals to provide, and decisions to take on what private activities it will permit (for example, can I start up a chemicals factory?). While abandoning aggregative notions, such theorists find it necessary to fill the gap by vaguer notions of practical wisdom: they do not suggest that moral and political judgment is wholly a matter of observance of individual rights.

How does the need to establish boundary conditions upon the overriding force of rights pose a problem for this version of the

---

[116] Too great a proliferation of such rights might result in a situation where the process of balancing rights was identical to a general calculus of welfare or balancing of interests at large: this would render the supposed weightiness or inviolability of rights wholly nugatory.

[117] See John Finnis, *Natural Law and Natural Rights* (Oxford: Clarendon Press, 1980).

Interest Theory? The point is as follows. According to the theory now under consideration, to accord to an interest the status of a 'right' is to treat the interest as capable of justifying the imposition of duties upon others. The right is not a simple reflection of the duty (as it could be within, for example, Kramer's version of Interest Theory) but is the ground for imposition of the duty. The boundary condition upon the scope of a right, however, cannot itself be grounded in an individual interest. I have an interest in being alive, and therefore have an interest in not being killed. But I do not have an interest in not being killed intentionally or negligently which is distinguishable from my interest in not being killed accidentally and non-negligently. Whether I am killed intentionally or unavoidably, I am just as dead.

An advocate of the Interest Theory may well suggest that, in offering this argument, I am guilty of a very simple fallacy. For they might point out that what precisely is required by a right will depend not only upon the scope of the interest underlying the right, but also upon a range of conflicting considerations. Perhaps, therefore, boundary conditions do not need to be grounded directly in the relevant interest: they may rather result from the combined force of the interest together with countervailing considerations.

We must remind ourselves, however, of the special overriding force that the theory currently being considered ascribes to the interests that underlie rights. Because of this overriding force, countervailing considerations of a kind that could limit the force and scope of a right would need to possess a similar weightiness. Countervailing considerations of a less weighty character might help to determine the precise way in which the right was protected (a right should be protected *effectively*, but need not be accorded every *conceivable* form of protection) but the point of what I am calling a 'boundary condition' is to demarcate the boundary between the special force of rights and the ordinary force of prudential or policy considerations. If this boundary was itself to be shaped by the calculus of general (non-weighty) considerations, it would scarcely be serving to constrain the range of relevance and force attached to those considerations.

Is it conceivable that the existence of countervailing *rights* might dictate the existence of a boundary between rights and ordinary (non-weighty) considerations of welfare? While one cannot in principle rule out such an outcome as impossible, it would be so remarkably fortuitous that one would need to see the supporting argument set out in detail before being convinced that it was a real possibility. On the face of it, countervailing rights and weighty interests will not assist in the task of clearing a space for the operation of ordinary, non-weighty, welfare considerations.

Someone might object to this argument by suggesting that boundary conditions *can* be grounded in interests. Thus, it could be argued that my interest in not being killed intentionally (for example) is indeed distinct from my interest in not being killed accidentally. In both cases, it is true that I wind up dead; but, in the former case, I suffer the additional moral injury of being treated as a mere conduit for someone else's plans and projects, a disposable instrumentality to be consumed and discarded according to the requirements of another. In itself, this argument has some merit; but it would result in a fragmentation of interests that is incompatible with the way in which any appealing version of the theory would need to identify legal entitlements.

Recall my earlier observation about the curious reversal of positions that has taken place between the Will and Interest Theories. I suggested there that the Interest Theory seems to have taken over the concern with doctrinal coherence and integration that was once associated with the classical Will Theory. This concern for doctrinal coherence arises partly from the need to constrain the ease with which legal entitlements can plausibly be asserted, and partly from the need to justify postulation of a non-Hohfeldian concept of 'right'.

It is true that we may sometimes be able to establish the existence of a legal right by pointing to a legal provision that expressly confers the right (although, as we saw earlier, MacCormick fails to produce a convincing example of the express conferment of a right that fits the Interest Theory's model). In other cases, a specific legal right may be inferred from the express conferment of some more general legal right. To confine the language of rights to such contexts of express conferment, however, would involve a quite radical revision of legal thinking. Apart from anything else, much of the law (at least in a common law system) is not expressed in a canonical set of words resembling a statute or code. Consequently, judges and doctrinal analysts may vary considerably in the frequency with which they expound the law in terms of 'rights' rather than (say) 'duties' or 'doctrines'. It would be strange indeed to make the number of rights conferred by English law depend upon such variations in expository style.

If legal rights may exist even in situations where posited legal rules have not expressly conferred them, this is presumably because (on the Interest Theory) the relevant interests provide an explanatory ground or justification for the relevant legal duties, powers, immunities, and so forth. Given the ease with which discrete legal provisions may be rationalized in a variety of different ways, however, such ascriptions of rights will only be convincing where they can demonstrate an ability to systematize a plurality of discrete laws, exhibiting them all as serving some single interest or constellation of interests.

Indeed, it is the possibility of discovering interests which so systematize a body of law (thereby revealing in that body of law a coherence which might otherwise have escaped notice) that sustains the postulation of a non-Hohfeldian concept of right by the Interest Theory. As we noted earlier, Hohfeld's intention is to establish certain distinctions within the logic of rights: he is not seeking to deny the existence of pragmatic implications or associations surrounding those logical relations. The simple observation that we can employ a non-Hohfeldian notion of rights provided we are satisfied with something less than strict entailment is, as I indicated earlier, a fatuous one. The argument has merit only if it can point to some intellectual gain that is to be won by the adoption of such a non-Hohfeldian conception. Such a gain might well be a reality if the Interest Theory could discover otherwise overlooked pockets of coherence in the law, where discrete provisions can be assembled around a limited set of interests.

Of course, if the relevant interests are simply factors registering in some overall conception of the collective well-being, the theory will have done nothing to advance the integrity of private rights, but will merely have served to exhibit the systematic properties of legal instrumentalism. Thus, to produce a version of the Interest Theory which offers some intellectual foundation for the integrity of rights, we need a theory that combines two features: on the one hand, it must identify interests of such generality that they serve to systematize and order the law; but, on the other hand, the interests must be distinct from the general welfare schedule and be of overriding importance. To satisfy that latter condition (as I argued earlier) we will need to define boundary conditions for the interests; but

Rights at the Cutting Edge 211

such boundary conditions cannot be grounded in the interests themselves. If the last claim is contested, and it is suggested that boundary conditions *can* be grounded in individual interests, the result will be to fragment rights in a way that prevents them from satisfying the requirements of generality and systematic coherence.

6 The Modern Will Theory

Analysis and Interpretation

We are concerned with the analysis of a concept. Yet what is involved in such an activity? On one model, the analysis of a concept is a matter of unearthing deep criteria that regulate our use of a word: criteria that we ordinarily employ with ease, but cannot articulate. In some contexts, for some concepts, such a model of analysis may perhaps be adequate. Elsewhere, however, it is inapplicable. For it is wrong to assume that some relatively complete set of criteria must invariably underpin our use of a word, if that use is to be meaningful and intelligible. Consider, for example, the following observation of Wittgenstein's:

> We are unable clearly to circumscribe the concepts we use; not because we don't know their real definition, but because there is no real 'definition' to them. To suppose that there *must* be would be like supposing that whenever children play with a ball they play a game according to strict rules.[118]

We might well think of the discourse of rights as a game played without strict rules: some more or less regular forms of practice emerge; innovations are made and are accepted or rejected; diverse versions of the game appear. Seen against this background, the enterprise of conceptual analysis may seem to represent, not the articulation of established criteria, but a lack of trust in the free development of the game. By adopting some meticulous analysis or definition, we seek to render words 'rigid, predictable, and invulnerable to the twists and turns that a word receives both in dialogue and in the history of the language in general'.[119]

---

[118] Ludwig Wittgenstein, *The Blue and Brown Books* (Oxford: Blackwell, 1975), 25.
[119] Joel Weinsheimer, *Gadamer's Hermeneutics* (New Haven: Yale University Press, 1985), 1.

There is ample evidence, within the literature on rights, of a lack of trust in the natural development of patterns of discourse. The very prestige attaching to 'rights' in modern culture guarantees that the word will be invoked more and more widely, leading to 'inflation' of the 'currency' of rights.[120] One cure for inflation is the reintroduction of a gold standard, and such a gold standard for the ascription of rights has been the underlying goal of many of the conceptual analyses that have been proffered. The very problems that generate the desire for such a standard, however, also form an obstacle to its introduction. Extensive invocation of the concept of 'a right' stretches our sense of the concept's contours, making retrenchment seem a more radical departure from ordinary usage. In so far as the aim of the analysis is to render certain claims of right misconceived or illegitimate, the analysis can command assent only to the extent that it can resolve the substantial moral questions at issue. Yet such issues are (to put it mildly) hard to resolve, and too austerely 'analytical' a debate about rights scarcely seems the appropriate medium for their resolution.

Some theorists claim that moral and political values need play no part in informing our conceptual analyses: we can select the analysis that makes the simplest and most enlightening job of systematizing our more 'conceptual' intuitions about rights. On the assumption, however, that no clear criteria are available for simple unearthing or articulation, any systematic presentation of the concept of a right will require certain departures from common usage: our choice between different analyses will be a choice between alternative regimentations of the discourse. How can we make such a choice except by deciding what is important and unimportant? One theory denies that small babies have rights. Another theory would say that the citizens of a state may be richly endowed with rights even though the decision whether to enforce such rights is exclusively in the hands of state authorities. Our choice between such theories is a judgment about the importance of claims of precisely this sort. How are we to judge the importance of such claims otherwise than by reliance upon our moral and political understanding?

The claim that our choice can be based on intellectual values such as clarity and simplicity seems to suggest that the systematization of

---

[120] See, for a fairly typical example, the concerns about the 'inflation' of rights discourse, and consequent devaluation of rights, expressed by LW Sumner, *The Moral Foundation of Rights* (Oxford: Clarendon Press, 1987), 1–15.

our discourse about rights will itself make no substantive difference to our representation of the moral issues: as if the substantive points (whatever they may be) can always be made in other terms, and we are here discussing only the best use of a convenient shorthand. To anyone who is sceptical about the very extensive importance now attached to claims of 'right', the idea that the real issues may always be described in other terms is an attractive and plausible one. Yet, even while emphasizing a concern for clarity above all, analytical theorists are quick to attach substantive significance to denials of rights-claims made by their opponents. Thus, when the Will Theorist denies that babies have rights, his opponents are inclined to find in his claim a moral deficiency, and not simply a terminological inconvenience.[121]

Joseph Raz is therefore right to emphasise the fact that, when we are concerned with concepts which are 'deeply embedded in the philosophical and political traditions of our culture', attempts to elucidate those concepts 'are partisan accounts furthering the cause of certain strands in the common tradition'.[122] Raz's version of the Interest Theory would rule out (or at least severely constrain) any employment of the concept of 'a right' within an anti-perfectionist political theory (since convergence in the identification of rights would depend upon some fairly high degree of agreement in our conceptions of well-being). Such an account of rights could not, with any plausibility, be arrived at as a consequence of a purely clarificatory theory that claims to prescind from substantive moral or political issues. Being so deeply embedded within the moral or political debate, the analysis could only form a part of a much broader political theory focused upon conceptions of well-being: it would clearly be a mistake to seek to arrive at the analysis of rights by any less ambitious route. 'One can derive a concept from a theory but not the other way around.'[123]

In my own view, the modern Will Theory of rights is best defended in political terms. An acceptable account of the nature of rights should reinforce those aspects of the tradition of rights discourse that are most distinctive and important, and should address the dangers that most obviously threaten that tradition

---

[121] Kramer is more circumspect in this regard, finding the denial of children's rights to be 'outlandish' but not 'ghastly'.
[122] Raz, *The Morality of Freedom* (n 111 above), 63.
[123] Raz, ibid, 16.

with over-inflation and vacuity. The modern Will Theory is well suited to these objectives; yet, at the same time, it is a surprisingly modest position. It does not presuppose the truth of any very sweeping and monistic account of justice or liberty, nor is it intended to sustain some such view. Indeed, the modern Will Theory arises precisely from the loss of faith in grand theoretical resolutions to the problem of politics, and its virtues are most easily appreciated from the perspective of a mature acceptance of pluralism and conflict within our political values.

The classical Will Theory combined the ideas of permissibility and inviolability: an area of free choice, and a related duty. The notions of freedom and inviolability were firmly grounded in a perceived connection between the concept of a right and the justification of coercive enforcement. Thus the theory gave expression to certain formal intuitions about the character of rights, such as the notion that rights ground peremptory demands, and the idea that rights give us options which we may exercise or not as we choose. The theory was intended to explicate the analytical structure of legal ideas, but at the same time it linked its analysis to a sweeping attempt at the theoretical resolution of central problems of the liberal legal order. The notion of a right was thought to point to an ideal (and essentially Kantian) conception of justice immanent within legal thinking, and in this way to surmount the question of how the impersonal governance of law might be compatible with the integrity of individual projects.

The classical Interest Theory celebrated the failure of this ambitious project, but the fundamental instrumentalism of that theory caused it to neglect the problems that had generated the Will Theory in the first place. Dominated by the single thought that law is an instrument in the service of welfare-based goals, rather than the working out of an immanent scheme of justice, the classical Interest Theory exhibited little interest in the aspects of rights that had been highlighted by the Will Theory. Rights ceased to be thought of as protected options linked to individual project-pursuit, and became the obverse or rationale of duties imposed by posited rules.

Modern versions of the Interest Theory have departed still further from the intuitions that informed the Will Theory. In treating rights as reasons that will justify the imposition of duties 'other things being equal', the theory abandons the idea of rights as possessing peremptory force. The theory possesses few or no resources for explaining the associations (such as that between *choice* and *peremptory force*) that generated the ambitious visions of the classical Will Theory in the first place. Instead, the authors of this theory point out the congruence of their position with 'changes in the climate of opinion', acknowledging that the theory ascribes to 'right' a much wider sense than might have been considered proper thirty or forty years earlier.[124] Far from serving to arrest the process whereby rights-discourse becomes increasingly vacuous, such theories appear to celebrate and accelerate that development.

Classical Virtues in a Modern Context

Hohfeld's analysis had the effect of exposing a rift between permissibility and inviolability, thereby revealing the shortcomings of the classical Will Theory as a piece of analytical jurisprudence. In this way significant gaps were exposed in apparently seamless passages of legal reasoning; and such exposure in turn lent weight to the accusations of emptiness frequently levelled at the Kantian theory of justice. The core ideas of an area of choice and a related duty, however, could be connected otherwise than by the conjunction of permissibility and inviolability; and in this way they could be detached from the grand but implausible ambitions of the classical Will Theory.

Thus we come to the version of Will Theory developed by H. L. A. Hart. Although quite different from the classical Will Theory, and adroitly avoiding the pitfalls of that approach, Hart's theory nevertheless sought to combine some of the key ideas that had formed the core inspiration for the classical position. Thus Hart's theory builds upon the two notions of an area of choice and a correlative duty, and emphasizes the close connections between rights and coercive enforcement; but it does so in a manner that is less ambitious than the older view, precisely because it avoids the latter's sweeping inferences from the conjunction of choice and coercive constraint. In Hart's theory, the duty is not imposed as a protection for free choice: rather it forms the object of the relevant choice. To possess a right, on this view, is to have control over a duty incumbent upon someone else. The right is not the rationale of

---

[124] Raz, *The Morality of Freedom*, 249.

the duty, nor its justification: it is the power to waive or to demand performance of the duty.

This theory has a number of virtues, but two in particular merit our attention. In the first place, the theory reflects our sense that rights are involved with the choices of the right-holder: rights are things that may be exercised, and right-holders have a choice about *how* they shall be exercised. Secondly, it reflects our sense that rights ground peremptory demands that we may make against others: my rights are not simply good reasons for others to behave in certain ways, but preclude any attempt to make the required conduct contingent upon a calculus of my interests along with other considerations. Nor are my rights the *justification* for duties: when I invoke my right, I do not claim that the imposition of a duty on you is justified (still less that it *would* be justified in the absence of competing considerations). I claim that you *are* under such a duty, and the content of that duty makes my choice decisive for you in some particular respect.

In both of these respects, Hart's Will Theory is a great improvement over the most fashionable[125] contemporary versions of the Interest Theory. Theories of the latter type must of necessity deny the existence of any conceptual connection between rights and choices, and therefore must treat the exercisability of a right as a contingent feature that it may or may not possess. Moreover, while proclaiming the centrality of rights within both politics and legal reasoning, they are forced into an unacknowledged abandonment of the peremptory force of rights, and an inability coherently to explain the special weight which is to be accorded to rights by contrast with general welfare considerations.

Whereas the classical Interest Theory found itself uneasily both relying upon positivism and (in its proposals for the identification of rights) undermining positivism, the modern Will Theory does not in any way depend upon positivism, but it is entirely consistent with such truth. In so far as legal positivism is true, the conditions in which a certain legal duty is performable will be ascertainable by reference to positive sources of law. Where those conditions include an exercise of will by some other person, that person enjoys a right which is correlative to the duty. There is no need, on this theory, to

---

[125] Most of the remarks that follow are inapplicable to Kramer's version of the Interest Theory.

embark upon an inquiry into the justifications for the duty, or the purposes of the rule imposing the duty: the existence and content of legal rights will be ascertainable from the content of rules specifying the content of duties.

The Interest Theory, in both its classical and modern versions, is of course dependent upon our ability to identify *interests*. Our ability to reach convergent conclusions about legal rights is therefore dependent upon our ability to reach convergent conclusions about the scope and existence of interests. For example, suppose that local authorities have a duty to ensure that all children spend each day in school. We can agree in our conclusion that this duty is grounded in the childrens' right to education only if we can agree that children have an interest in being educated. If I think that education is a form of social discipline which is detrimental to the interests of the child, I may conclude that the duty is grounded in the adults' interest in not having their houses burgled while they are out at work. We cannot identify interests without some conception of 'the good', however minimal. Therefore, we cannot identify rights (on the Interest Theory) except against the background of a broad range of agreement on 'the good'. Many political theorists, however, seek a set of political arrangements which are not dependent upon such agreement: they seek to make 'the right prior to the good'.[126] Whatever the strengths or weaknesses of such a view, the Will Theory is neutral between such a view and its critics. If neutrality of this kind is a virtue, the Will Theory has this further advantage over its rivals.

Hohfeldian Complexities

By contrast with the classical Will Theory, the modern Will Theory is compatible with the Hohfeldian analysis of rights, for, although the theory links rights with both choices and duties, it does not claim that permissibilities entail inviolabilities: that is, that liberties entail claim-rights. The relevant choice is a choice concerning the waiver or enforcement of the duty, not a reason for imposing the duty or a liberty that is protected by the duty: in the absence of

---

[126] See, for example, John Rawls, *A Theory of Justice* (Oxford: Clarendon Press, 1972). Kramer's version of the Interest Theory is an exception here, since the evaluative judgments upon which his theory depends are sufficiently weak to be untroubling to theorists such as Rawls.

the duty, the choice would not be unprotected, but would simply lack an object.

Compatibility with the Hohfeldian analysis also serves to distinguish the theory from influential contemporary versions of Interest Theory, which seek to locate rights on the level of justificatory considerations underpinning or grounding Hohfeldian jural relations. Although not technically inconsistent with Hohfeld's analysis, such positions tend to downgrade the importance of the analysis by suggesting that it concerns itself with remedial instrumentalities whereby rights are protected, rather than with the rights themselves. The Hartian theory, by contrast, is not committed to this move, and is thereby able to preserve the straightforward and immediate connections between rights and duties which (as we saw above) are an important foundation for understanding the peremptory character of rights.

In fact, Hart's theory is not only compatible with Hohfeld, but may actually cast an interesting light upon some otherwise problematic features of Hohfeld's analysis. For, although the theory is primarily intended to clarify the nature of Hohfeldian claim-rights (in this respect it resembles Kramer's version of the Interest Theory) it is reasonable for us to ask what claim-rights, liberties, powers, and immunities have in common that leads pre-Hohfeldian analysts to confuse them, and that generates our common tendency to speak of them all as 'rights'. Hart's answer was as follows:

> The unifying element seems to be this: in all four cases the law specifically recognizes the *choice* of an individual either negatively by not impeding or obstructing it (liberty and immunity) or affirmatively by giving legal effect to it (claim and power).[127]

Hart's identification of *choice* as the key idea underpinning the notion of rights was subsequently developed by him in a misconceived and non-Hohfeldian way. For, in *Essays on Bentham*, Hart put forward the claim that the idea of a 'bilateral liberty' was central to claim-rights, liberties and powers (although not to immunities).[128] This thesis confronted him with a series of difficulties which he might well have avoided;[129] most significantly it led him

---

[127] HLA Hart, 'Definition and Theory in Jurisprudence' in *Essays in Jurisprudence and Philosophy* (Oxford: Clarendon Press, 1983), 35n.
[128] ibid, 188.
[129] Discussed in Carl Wellman, *A Theory of Rights* (Totowa, New Jersey: Rowman and Allanheld, 1985), ch 3.

to make the misguided concession that immunities could not be adequately accounted for on the Will Theory.[130] This concession is understandably viewed with satisfaction by Interest Theorists, and even theorists seeking to defend a version of the Will Theory have been thrown off course by Hart's claims. Thus, the attempt to accommodate such examples has led theorists such as Wellman to urge upon us the idea that a right should be conceived of as a complex of Hohfeldian elements, rather than as one or other such element taken discretely.

In fact it is not difficult to demonstrate that Hart's original statement (from 'Definition and Theory in Jurisprudence', quoted above) of the unity underlying Hohfeldian diversity provides a better analysis than does his later 'bilateral liberty' view, enabling him to avoid most of the difficulties in which his argument may subsequently have become ensnared.

The passage from 'Definition and Theory in Jurisprudence' sees an immunity as protecting choice 'negatively by not impeding or obstructing it'. It is not necessary to construe such negative protection in a way that would require the immunity to involve a bilateral liberty possessed by the right-holder. An immunity such as the inability to inherit protects choice *negatively* by ensuring that our proprietary holdings will be altered only by our own choice. Our autonomy is thus protected by rendering us immune to a particular kind of interference (albeit one that we might frequently regard as beneficial). An inability to inherit comprises such an immunity combined with a disability preventing us from waiving the immunity. The disability is clearly not a 'right' on the Hohfeldian analysis, but that does not preclude us from regarding the immunity as a right. A similar analysis might be applied to the constitutional immunities which caused Hart to doubt his version of the Will Theory: to the extent that they are immunities, they protect our autonomy from one type of interference; their non-waivability manifests the fact that the right is conjoined with a disability.[131]

Powers can be said to give effect to choices 'affirmatively' even when those powers are not joined to bilateral liberties. The suggestion that, to count as a 'right', a Hohfeldian power must be conjoined with a bilateral liberty is quite mistaken: the argument simply

---

[130] Hart, *Essays on Bentham* (n 110 above), 190–2.
[131] See Hart, *Essays on Bentham* (n 110 above), 190 *et seq*.

confuses the juridical conception of liberty with the fact of choice. If I am placed under a legal duty, I have to that extent forfeited my (juridical) liberty;[132] but I still retain a choice about whether I will perform my duty or not. The law can, if it so chooses, give legal effect to my choice by recognizing it as the valid exercise of a power. Situations where persons possess legal powers that they are under a duty not to exercise are, in fact, not at all unfamiliar.[133]

Hart was therefore correct in his early analysis of the element of uniformity linking claim-rights, liberties, powers, and immunities. It is a mistake to suggest that each type of right involves a liberty to perform an act, the rights varying only with regard to 'the kind of act or act-in-the-law which there is liberty to do'.[134]

Theorists have pondered upon the question of whether rights can be identified with individual Hohfeldian claim-rights, liberties, powers, and immunities, or whether rights must be conceived of as complex conjunctions of simple Hohfeldian elements. We have already seen that certain modern versions of the Interest Theory argue for the 'complex conjunction' view. Hart's later 'bilateral liberty' version of Will Theory tended to support this stance, by suggesting that every right involves a bilateral liberty combined with a Hohfeldian claim-right or power (immunities, by Hart's concession, not fitting the analysis). By rejecting that later version of the theory in favour of Hart's earlier statement, we have to that extent resisted the 'complex conjunction' view of rights, and defended a more austerely Hohfeldian approach.

There remains, however, one final shot in the locker of the complex conjunction view, and it is a shot aimed directly at Hart's version of the Will Theory (including the early version of that theory). For, since Hart analyses claim-rights as involving or amounting to powers of waiver over correlative duties, he may seem to be faced by two alternatives. He can either *identify* claim-rights with powers of waiver, or he can treat claim-rights as *involving* powers of waiver.

---

[132] Hart seems to make a related mistake when he assumes that a duty entails a unilateral liberty. Duties may generally involve unilateral liberties, but this need not invariably be so, because there is nothing in the logic of rights to exclude the possibility of conflicting duties. Hart, ibid, 173.

[133] For example, in situations where the exceptions to the principle *nemo dat quod non habet* apply, a seller of goods may be committing a tort in selling, and yet the sale will nevertheless pass good title to the purchaser.

[134] Hart, *Essays on Bentham* (n 110 above), 189.

The first option seems to introduce a serious confusion of different levels in the Hohfeldian analysis. Claim-rights, liberties, duties, and no-rights occupy the plane of primary rules which are concerned directly to prescribe conduct. Powers, immunities, disabilities, and liabilities, by contrast exist on the plane of secondary rules, which are concerned not to prescribe conduct so much as to provide facilities for the alteration of prescriptions that obtain at the primary level.[135] By insisting that a claim-right is a species of power, therefore, Hart's theory would seem to confuse the importantly distinct categories of primary and secondary legal relations.

The second option, by contrast, appears to concede ground to the complex conjunction view. On this interpretation, Hart's analysis of rights as powers of waiver or control over correlative duties is best read as treating such rights as complex assemblages of Hohfeldian elements. Thus a Hartian right might be said to be a Hohfeldian 'claim-right' combined with a Hohfeldian 'power' (a power of waiver or enforcement). On this interpretation, Hart would not be guilty of the simple confusion alleged against him by the first objection, but might justly be accused of introducing cumbersome complexities into the analysis of rights without any very adequate reason. Furthermore, his theory would (on this account) be reliant upon the notion of a 'claim-right' (such claim-rights forming but one constituent of fully-fledged Hartian rights) while leaving that notion wholly unexplained and opaque.

Most theorists have assumed that Hart would opt for the second approach. Such an interpretation gains weight from the fact that Hart's later 'bilateral liberty' version of the Will Theory is itself committed to a complex conjunction view of rights. Having rejected Hart's later view as clearly inferior to his earlier statement of the Will Theory, we must now see whether we can defend a version of Will Theory that wholly excludes any element of the complex conjunction view: we must therefore see if the first option (identifying claim-rights with powers of waiver) can be defended.

The charge levelled against the first approach is that it confuses the distinct categories of primary and secondary legal relations. For, if duties are correlative to claim-rights, and claim-rights are powers, then concepts drawn from the primary level of conduct regulation

---

[135] Hart, *The Concept of Law* (Oxford: Clarendon Press, 1961).

are being logically tied to concepts drawn from the secondary level of rule-alteration.

At this point we must recall a point explained earlier in the essay. The notion of 'correlativity' in Hohfeld's analysis could be construed in a number of different ways. In particular, we might take Hohfeld to be proposing general definitions of 'duty', 'immunity', (and so forth) wherein the definition of each term entails its correlative. Alternatively, we might take him to be proposing an analytical representation of a bounded sphere: the sphere of 'jural relations', conceived as applying either to law in general, or perhaps to that part of law that deals with relations between individuals (private law). He would then not be asserting that the correlativities obtain in virtue of the general meaning of the words employed, but in virtue of certain general features of the sphere of relations under consideration.

If Will Theorists wish to rely upon Hohfeld's analysis, they are of necessity committed to the latter interpretation of his work. For Will Theorists assert that claim-rights are correlative to duties, but not all duties are correlative to claim-rights. The correlativity therefore cannot obtain in virtue of the meaning of the words: it is correlativity within a strictly bounded sphere. As we explained earlier, this may seem to be a very significant concession, and a weakness in the Will Theory. What needs to be borne in mind, however, is the fact that the tight and general connections that can be established between power and liability (and between immunity and disability) cannot obtain between duty and claim-right, even for the Interest Theory. Unless one is prepared to drain the notion of 'interest' of all content, treating it as an entirely formal notion that bears the name 'interest' only as an arbitrary label,[136] one must concede that duties without corresponding interests are logically conceivable. One may argue that certain contingent features of the real world dictate that it is impossible for duties to exist wholly disconnected from interests: legal duties are bound up with the interest in securing obedience to law, for example; and perhaps moral duties connect with interests by virtue of some constraint

---

[136] In such a theory, the word 'interest' might well be replaced by 'heffalump' or 'strudge'. Kramer's Interest Theory does not employ the term 'interest' in this empty way, but has real, if minimal, content. To the extent that the notion of interest has real content, however, a connection between duties and interests cannot be deduced from the bare notion of 'duty', but requires certain extraneous assumptions.

on the type of duty that can plausibly be regarded as moral in character. But here the existence of relevant interests is entailed by something other than the bare notion of duty: the involvement of duties with interests is deduced from the notion of law, or morality. Even for the Interest Theorist, therefore, the connection between duty and claim-right, as a jural relation obtaining between two persons, is not a necessary feature of the concept of duty.

Once we see that the connections here cannot, with any plausibility, be construed as strictly logical bilateral bonds, the objection to construing a claim-right as a specific type of power becomes less substantial. If the Hohfeldian jural correlatives were bilateral logical bonds, the appearance of powers at more than one point in the analysis might well introduce a serious confusion. Given, however, that the claim-right/duty relation cannot plausibly be construed in this way, it is less clear that any such confusion would be involved. The position would then be that all powers logically entail liabilities. *Some* powers, being powers of waiver and enforcement over duties, entail duties as well as liabilities.[137] Such powers can be labelled claim-rights. The liabilities that they entail (being powers, they must entail liabilities) include such changes in one's jural relations as: a bailee of goods being placed under a duty to restore the property to the owner, upon the owner making demand for it; a contractual bailee of goods being absolved from the duty to restore goods to the owner on a certain day, by the owner saying that a later delivery will be acceptable.

The Importance of Enforcement

The disparate considerations set out above amount to a substantial if inconclusive case in favour of Hart's (early) version of the Will Theory. Earlier in this essay I pointed out that our more formal or conceptual intuitions about rights can be assembled in different ways, and that arguments in favour of a particular conception of rights can be expected to exhibit no more than a degree of persuasiveness. The primary motivation of the classical Will and Interest

---

[137] To avoid confusion, it is worth pointing out that the entailment of duties by such powers differs from the entailment of liabilities in not being content-independent or formal. In other words, the existence of a correlative liability is entailed by the bare notion of a power; whereas any correlative duty is entailed by the *content* of the power.

Theories did not lie in a desire to systematize and clarify conceptual structures and connections, so much as a desire to ground more sweeping theories of legitimacy. In particular, they sought to explain the relationship between *subjective* and *objective* right; or between the private projects of individuals and the collective project represented by the political community's will and expressed in the community's law. At the heart of the classical theories, therefore, lay a concern for the *integrity* of private rights, in the sense of the possibility of ascertaining the bounds of private rights without direct reliance upon the distributive or aggregative projects of the collectivity. In that sense, the classical theories of rights aspired to be theories of the *Rechtsstaat*.

In consequence of the collapse of the Kantian Will Theory, and the entanglement of the Interest Theory with the problems of legal positivism, such sweeping solutions to the problem now seem implausible and optimistic. Indeed, we may perhaps go further and suggest that the desire to place the notion of rights near the centre of our models of legitimacy and legal argument is itself a factor helping to erode the integrity of rights. For this does indeed seem to be the lesson of experience that is to be learnt from the indeterminacies of the classical Will Theory and the vaporous ambitions of the modern Interest Theory.

Perhaps the integrity of rights is best sustained, not by an abundance of theoretical flag-waving, or by constant mention of rights in our doctrinal arguments, but by the careful combining of various expedients, jointly composing a context of legal and moral assumptions that make such integrity possible. Analytical theories of rights cannot be expected on their own to resolve the problem. Yet it is nevertheless the case that some small part of the case supporting such an analytical theory might be the contribution that the theory makes to an intellectual, moral, and institutional context within which the integrity of rights can best be sustained.

We might therefore reflect upon the broad significance of rights within our rival analytical theories. From this perspective, it can easily be seen that the Hartian Will Theory attaches to rights a significance that sits very comfortably with the concern for integrity, whereas versions of the Interest Theory tend to undercut such concern. For all varieties of the Interest Theory, the right-holder is essentially a bearer of interests rather than a locus of choice or will. Classical versions of the Interest Theory find it necessary to identify legal rights by means of an inquiry into the *purpose* of the relevant duty-imposing rules: in this way they threaten a collapse of rights into the aggregative or distributive projects that compose the legislative project. Alternatively, such theories identify rights by reference to the conditions sufficient to establish a breach of the relevant duty: but (as we saw above) this approach is likely to result in a great many rights being assigned to the state rather than to private citizens. Some contemporary versions of Interest Theory, by contrast, avoid these problems only by treating rights as non-conclusive reasons for the imposition of duties. Such an approach results in the suppression of the peremptory character of rights: rights become weighty considerations which are to be balanced against many other considerations in deciding whether a duty should be recognized; and with the loss of their peremptory character, rights are collapsed into the general range of interests that are considered in the context of the state's distributive and aggregative projects.

The modern Will Theory, by contrast, builds the notion of 'a right' firmly upon the twin ideas of choice and peremptory force. Where rights exist, the enforcement of duties is not a matter for the state in pursuit of collective policies, but a matter for the choice of private individuals. Nor are rights reduced by this theory to the status of weighty considerations in a general weighing and balancing of interests. We might well regard the private enforcement of such peremptory demands as an essential hallmark of the *Rechtsstaat*. All versions of the Interest Theory, by contrast, would be compatible with a state of affairs where all powers of enforcement and waiver are monopolized by the state and its officials. There is surely a good deal of force in the Will Theory's claim that, in such circumstances, citizens would have no rights at all, regardless of how effectively their interests might be catered for in the state's policies and enactments. If we regard the choice of a theory of rights as but one facet of a search for interpretations that sustain the integrity of rights within the rule of law, the Hartian Will Theory has much to recommend it.

MacCormick on Waiver and Alienability

Neil MacCormick has offered what is perhaps the best-known and most influential critique of Hart's version of the Will Theory. It is appropriate to conclude this defence of Hart's position by considering MacCormick's arguments.[138]

MacCormick's general position on rights has already been considered. This consists in his claim that rights should not be identified with individual Hohfeldian advantages, but represent the grounds for imposing duties, liabilities, and so forth, and thus for conferring Hohfeldian claim-rights, liberties, powers, and immunities. Hohfeld's analysis represents (on this account) an analysis of the various instrumentalities whereby rights may be protected, rather than being an analysis of rights themselves. A more adequate account of rights would, in MacCormick's view, bring out the dynamic role played by rights in legal reasoning. My response to this position consisted in a direct challenge to the pertinence and accuracy of MacCormick's observations. Before turning to MacCormick's arguments aimed more specifically against the Will Theory, it is perhaps desirable to recapitulate the main points made earlier:

(1) Nothing in Hohfeld's theory denies that the conferment of one legal advantage may in appropriate circumstances provide good grounds for the conferment of some other advantage: the fact that you are already acknowledged to have a power to do X may sometimes be a good reason for conferring the liberty to exercise that power, or even a claim-right not to be interfered with in the exercise of that power. Hohfeld's analysis simply denies that any such consequences are logically entailed by the concept of a right.

(2) MacCormick's account of rights assumes a particular understanding of the character of legal reasoning. It is far from clear,

---

[138] In what follows I ignore MacCormick's most well-known criticism of the Will Theory: that the theory must deny that children have rights. The argument is not one that has ever impressed me, although some find it compelling. The present essay concerns *legal* rights, and Hart offers a quite persuasive set of reasons for ascribing legal rights to children even when the relevant powers of waiver and enforcement are exercised by adults (see *Essays on Bentham* (n 110 above), 184n). As regards moral rights, there is surely much merit in the claim that our moral concern for very small children is based on a concern for their welfare quite independently of their choices; as they grow older, some of our duties towards them come to be contingent upon their will. Is not this moral difference aptly reflected by the Will Theory of rights? The Interest Theory, by contrast, must provide us with some reason for ascribing rights to babies, rather than simply speaking of the importance of their welfare. The special peremptory force of rights does not provide such a reason: for, as we have seen, versions of the Interest Theory (like MacCormick's) that abandon the strict correlativity of rights and duties also, by that very move, abandon the peremptory force of rights. Rights become reasons for imposing duties, which must be balanced against other conflicting considerations.

Rights at the Cutting Edge 227

however, that his picture of legal reasoning is at all accurate. If a statutory provision were to expressly confer a 'right' without explaining the implications of that right (does it entail a duty, and if so on whom? does it involve a power? an immunity? etc), it would be treated as ambiguous or incomplete, not as identifying an interest which the court may then protect in whatever way it considers appropriate. When courts reason from the certainty of one right to the existence of another, they do not generally employ the balancing process suggested by MacCormick's account of rights, but operate with more technical doctrinal considerations. In any case, it is surely a mistake to render one's conceptual analysis of rights so dependent upon a particular and highly contestable account of legal reasoning.

We are now in a position to turn to those arguments offered by MacCormick which do not contest general notions of correlativity, or the general adequacy of Hohfeld's analysis, but which tackle the central claims of Hart's Will Theory. The first argument offered to that effect proceeds from Hart's openly acknowledged difficulties in accommodating immunities within his analysis. MacCormick notes Hart's concessions on this point and then makes what at first seems to be a point supportive of the Will Theory, suggesting that Hart's concessions were unnecessary:

> There is something, on the face of it, odd about Hart's concession that immunities cannot be properly taken into account within the four corners of the 'Will Theory' as propounded by himself. For it is often the case that A's immunity is waivable by A's choice... That being so, it follows that there is a class of immunities which could comfortably be brought within the Hartian version of the will theory, namely the whole class of those immunities in relation to which the immunity-holder has a power of waiver.[139]

This point, however, quickly leads MacCormick to what he deems to be 'the fundamental implausibility of the "Will Theory".'[140] For we may sometimes protect a right by depriving the right-holder of the power to waive that right:

> But there's the rub, there, for the 'Will Theory', the paradox. For it appears that this legal dispensation, be it ever so advantageous from the point of

---

[139] Neil MacCormick, 'Rights in Legislation' in PMS Hacker and J Raz, *Law, Morality and Society* (Oxford: Clarendon Press, 1977), 195.
[140] ibid.

view of securing liberty, is so forceful as to thrust liberty beyond the realm of 'right' altogether. If there be no power to waive or assert the immunity, the claim, or whatever, upon some matter, upon that matter there is, *by definition*, no right either.[141]

It will be remembered that we saw earlier how Hart's concessions in relation to immunities were quite unnecessary and misconceived. This was *not*, however, on the ground suggested by MacCormick (that an immunity may be combined with a power of waiver): for the fact that an immunity may be combined with some other Hohfeldian advantage clearly contributes nothing whatever to establishing that the immunity in itself is a right. The point was rather that (as Hart's early formulation of the position made clear) an immunity recognizes the right-holder's choice not *positively* by giving effect to it, but *negatively* by ensuring that one's legal position is not affected by anyone else's choice. The power to *waive* an immunity is no part of the immunity itself, and may or may not be found together with an immunity. An immunity that is conjoined with a disability to waive will be permanent and inalienable. Since the immunity is inalienable, it will always continue to exist, and its holder will continue to enjoy the protection that it affords. That protection can without distortion be thought of as a (negative) recognition of the right-holder's will, for it has the effect that, within the range of the immunity (and in relation to the person against whom the immunity holds) the right-holder's legal position cannot be altered at the will of others. So far as MacCormick's argument is aimed at *immunities* therefore, it can be defused by invoking Hart's early formulation of the *negative* respect in which immunities protect the will, rather than his later concessions with regard to immunities.

MacCormick's point can, however, be detached from the context of immunities and offered as a more general argument. Claim-rights, liberties, and powers may all be rendered inalienable, and such inalienability is seen as a strengthening of the right, generally reserved for our most important rights. Yet, says MacCormick, 'the will theory seems to cut off the use of "rights"-language at a predetermined point on the scale of protection which the law may confer upon people's interests.'[142] Workers may be unable to

---

[141] Neil MacCormick 'Rights in Legislation' in PMS Hacker and J Raz, *Law, Morality and Society* (Oxford: Clarendon Press, 1977), 196.
[142] ibid, 197.

contract out of the most important forms of protection conferred upon them by safety legislation: but it seems odd to regard the workers' rights as being extinguished by this additional protection, when we more naturally regard them as thereby strengthened.

To accommodate this more general version of MacCormick's argument we cannot rely upon the distinction between positive and negative recognition of the right-holder's choice. Instead, we must distinguish between the *exercise* of a right, and its alienation or *extinguishment*. The worker is prevented from alienating his right precisely so that he continues to possess and enjoy it. So long as he does continue to possess the right, he has certain options (to sue or not sue) that he would not otherwise possess. Since options of precisely that type are amongst the forms of protection of the will emphasised by Hart's theory, that theory need have no difficulty in treating the worker's remaining options as 'rights'. Nor need the Will Theorist deny that the imposition of such disabilities (inalienabilities) can be seen as a strengthening of the worker's rights: one does indeed strengthen a right when one ensures that the right-holder will continue to possess the options represented by the right no matter what transactions he enters into with regard to the right.

It must be admitted that Hart sets out three distinguishable levels in the control exercised by a right-holder (including the ability to extinguish the right) and describes the conjunction of all three levels of control as the 'fullest measure' of control that may be accorded.[143] Does it not then follow that a reduction in the level of control denotes a reduction in the protection of the right (given that the Will Theory treats control by the will as being the very essence of a right)? And does this not conflict with our sense that rendering a right inalienable may strengthen rather than weaken its protection?

The assumptions underlying this objection are overly simplistic. Where we are confronted by different facets of control, the strength or efficacy of the protection given to the individual will cannot be judged simply by the number of facets present in any particular entitlement. The different dimensions of autonomy represented by the different forms of control cut across each other; just as the worker's autonomy to alienate his rights may cut across his

---

[143] Hart, *Essays on Bentham* (n 110 above), 183–4.

continuing autonomy to choose whether or not to sue his employer. To provide all the different facets of control will not necessarily offer the most effective or extensive protection to the right-holder's will. Much depends upon the circumstances and the nature of the threats to choice in any concrete set of circumstances. Given these complexities, there is no reason to assume that it will be possible to range rights monotonically upon a single scale of strength or weakness; there is still less reason to expect such strength or weakness to be a simple function of the number of different facets of choice associated with the right.

MacCormick and Criminal Law

By distinguishing the power to extinguish or alienate a right from the continued option of enforcing a right, we can render consistent with the Will Theory the example of right-holders who are legally disabled from contracting out of their rights. MacCormick offers a further example, however, which is less easily disposed of. The example concerns the limited scope given to consent as a defence in the criminal law. Consent is a defence to charges of minor assault and, in that sense, we may if we wish say that the potential victim of assault has a power to waive the duty not to assault. Consent is not, however, a defence to charges of more serious assault, and no similar power of waiver exists in relation to such assaults. If one follows the Will Theory in identifying rights with powers of waiver, therefore, one seems forced to conclude that we have a right not to be subjected to minor assaults but no right not to be subjected to major assaults.

To deal with this counter-example to the Will Theory, we must address the general question of rights and the criminal law. In the first place, we must bear in mind that the present essay is concerned with the analysis of *legal* rights, and aims to defend the Will Theory of rights simply and solely in that connection. In relation to criminal law, the Will Theorist will contend that legal rights are not conferred by criminal law. Perhaps we have moral rights not to be murdered or assaulted, and perhaps the criminal law is aimed in part at the protection of such moral rights: but these rights are not conferred by criminal law and are, to that extent, not themselves legal rights. If we were to restrict our discussion to rights *conferred by* criminal law, therefore, the Will Theorist would deny that there is a right not to be assaulted, whether the assault be major or minor.

Some of the rights protected (though not conferred) by criminal law are rights conferred by *private* law: the most obvious example being the rights of property that are protected by the law of theft. There is a private law right not to be assaulted, which is manifested in the availability of civil actions for assault, and which may also receive protection from the criminal law. This right extends to both major and minor assaults. The Will Theorist has no difficulty in accommodating this right. In the first place, consent *is* generally a defence in private law, so the power to waive the duty obtains across the range of gravity of the assault; and, secondly, even if consent were not a defence to serious assaults, the decision whether or not to sue would nevertheless remain with the right-holder.

But what of the *moral* right not to be assaulted? The insistence that we are solely concerned with legal rights, and can therefore afford to ignore this question, may seem unsatisfactory. For it is surely the case that legal and moral rights are more than simple homonyms. An acceptable analysis of legal rights must therefore at least imply appropriate ways of analysing moral rights, even if subtle adjustments are required to render the fit fully adequate; and MacCormick's example seems to suggest that the implications of the Will Theory are, in this context, wholly absurd. It is absurd to suggest that we have a moral right not to be subjected to minor assaults, but no moral right not to be subjected to major assaults; since this seems to be an implication of the Will Theory, that theory must be rejected.

What is the point of talking of moral 'rights', rather than simply speaking more straightforwardly of moral right and wrong? One suggestion is that rights represent the 'personal' aspect of morality: rights are involved when your action is not simply wrong but has *wronged* someone, giving that person the moral authority to complain and perhaps to demand compensation.[144] Let us adopt, for present purposes, this broad notion of a moral right on the grounds that it ascribes a distinctive role within morality to the notion of a right, and it sits comfortably with the Will Theory as an analysis of legal rights. We may then say that there is a moral right not to be

---

[144] See eg, David Lyons, *Rights, Welfare, and Mill's Moral Theory* (Oxford: Clarendon Press, 1994), 4–5.

assaulted, but no moral right in relation to assaults to which we have consented: for we cannot reasonably complain of something to which we consented (setting on one side special circumstances of fraud, ignorance of relevant facts, and so forth). Once the point is formulated in this way, we see that it is not the gravity of the assault that defines the limit of our right, but the fact of our consent. We do indeed have a (moral) right not to be subjected to assaults be they serious or minor, since any such assault will give us the authority to complain and demand redress, and the option of exercising that moral authority.

The limits of our moral rights do not, of course, coincide with the limits upon wrongdoing: that is a consequence of having a non-redundant conception of a moral right. Thus, serious assaults may be wrong even when they *are* consented to: they may exhibit and foster a depraved taste for cruelty, or may impair the community's human resources such as capacity for labour. The criminal prohibition of such consensual assaults might also be justified in other terms, without reliance upon the claim that even consensual assaults are morally wrong. Perhaps (for example) the uncertainties of establishing genuine consent in the relevant contexts are such that blanket prohibition is the best way of protecting the vulnerable from non-consensual assault.

What has now become of MacCormick's problem? Once we distinguish between various sorts of rights (moral rights, rights conferred by private law, and rights allegedly conferred by criminal law) we see that at no point is the Will Theorist committed to saying that we have a right not to be subjected to minor assaults, but no such right in relation to serious assaults. Only a tendency to conflate different varieties of rights (or perhaps a question-begging tendency to assume, in relation to moral rights, the truth of the Interest Theory) can account for the contrary impression.

Working Rights

HILLEL STEINER[1]

> *You shall not crucify mankind upon a cross of gold.*
> William Jennings Bryan, 1896
>
> *Inflation is repudiation.*
> Calvin Coolidge, 1922

It's probably fair to say that the merits of hard currency remain as controversial today as in the period bounded by these two remarks.[2] Inflation, latter-day Bryanites might well urge, is not the only way of repudiating serious obligations; to which current Coolidgeans would doubtless rejoin that a cross of gold is not the only instrument for crucifying mankind.

Much the same has long been true with regard to the currency of *rights*, though it's also true that recent academic opinion seems to be swinging decisively toward the less expansive position. It has now become standard practice for philosophical works on the nature of rights to begin their discussion of that subject by complaining of the vast proliferation of (often opposing) moral and political demands that come wrapped in the garb of rights.[3] Indeed, the phrase 'rights explosion' currently makes regular appearances in most forms of popular journalism.

Wesley Hohfeld himself, writing in that same earlier period, is decidedly closer to the spirit of Coolidge than of Bryan:

Recognizing, as we must, the very broad and indiscriminate use of the term 'right', what clue do we find, in ordinary legal discourse, toward limiting the word in question to a definite and appropriate meaning?[4]

---

[1] I'm greatly indebted to Matthew Kramer, Nigel Simmonds, and Wayne Sumner for probing discussion of several arguments advanced in this essay.

[2] Quoted in Simon James, *A Dictionary of Economic Quotations*, (Beckenham: Croom Helm, 1984), 84, 95.

[3] I'm no exception: see my *An Essay on Rights*, (Oxford: Blackwell, 1994), 55. LW Sumner, *The Moral Foundations of Rights*, (Oxford: Oxford University Press, 1987), 1–8, presents a particularly extensive list of these.

[4] *Fundamental Legal Conceptions*, (ed) WW Cook, (New Haven: Yale University Press, 1966), [hereinafter cited as *FLC*], 38.

Hohfeld would have been singularly unimpressed by suggestions that a certain latitude, in applying the 'rights' label to various social relations, is warranted by the functional contribution it can make to their improvement. He favours hard currency.

The authors of this volume all worship at the temple of Hohfeld and share his attitude. That attitude, however, does not bespeak some sort of conservative motivation—such as may well have animated Coolidge—to insulate a *prevailing* set of social relations against the reforming proposals of its critics. Nor, of course, does it imply a desire to support such proposals. What it signifies, rather, is simply a belief that the idea of 'a right' has a meaning with sufficiently definite logical properties, and sufficient independence of the endlessly varying contents of rights, to deny the label of 'rights' to many social relations—prevailing and proposed—that are currently so described.

But my co-authors and I also disagree with one another.[5] Defending the Will Theory, I find *fewer* relations to be constitutive of rights than does Matthew Kramer's formidable defence of the Interest Theory. Nor, in the end, am I persuaded by Nigel Simmonds' highly illuminating case for confining the *descriptive adequacy* of both the Will Theory and the Interest Theory to social relations found only in certain historically specific types of society, namely 'modern political communities'. What this essay aims to show is: (i) that the Will Theory offers a perfectly general account of what it is to have a right in *any* type of society; (ii) that the account it offers is distinctly more plausible than that afforded by the Interest Theory; and (iii) that one significant reason why it is so is that, in conjunction with Hohfeld's analytical apparatus, it supplies us with a more coherent understanding of what a *set* of rights is—more coherent

---

[5] As this book records a debate, it may assist the reader to know—and I'm profoundly grateful for the fact—that, in preparing this essay, I've had the considerable benefit of being previously supplied with my co-authors' respective contributions. It's in the customary nature of a debate that it has proponents and opponents, and that proponents have both the first and last word. In that regard, I suppose there's a sense in which I'm the proponent in this debate, inasmuch as each of my co-authors takes strong issue with my earlier defence of the Will Theory in *An Essay on Rights* (n 3 above), ch 3: a defence which is amplified in the present essay. I'm sure that I've not answered many of their rebuttals at all adequately. Perhaps this is also an appropriate place to acknowledge the immense benefit I've had from reading Simmonds' earlier and extremely challenging discussion of that book's treatment of the present issue, in 'The Analytical Foundations of Justice', 54 Cambridge LJ (1995), 306–41: a discussion to which I'll be referring at several points below.

than Hohfeld himself sought to elaborate and than can be allowed by Kramer and Simmonds.

1 Preliminary Intuitions about Rights

To gain some insight into what rights are, let's begin by focusing on one quite general way that they characteristically figure in our ordinary thinking. But first a caveat. For it's a regrettable fact that neither ordinary usage nor even the more refined technical usage of lawyers can be regarded as canonical in this respect. That, indeed, is Hohfeld's central point and the unifying theme of his seminal essays. For him, and for much philosophical work on the subject, these usages signally fail to be *univocal* in their treatment of rights.

Non-univocality is hardly a cardinal sin. Our cultural lives would be immensely impoverished were we to be deprived of the inventive elasticities it so liberally underwrites in countless works of art and literature. And even apart from cultural artefacts, a certain amount of non-univocality in the terms through which we simply understand various everyday aspects of the world may be perfectly unobjectionable. For many areas of this understanding, it may not matter much whether our common usage sustains a conception of, say, *choices* as both stimulus-driven events and uncaused ones, of *time* as being such that time-travel is both possible and impossible, of the *biosphere* as both a directly created entity and something evolved from entirely non-biotic factors or, for that matter, of the *earth* as both flat and spherical.

But when it comes to matters of *practical* thinking, non-univocality is often felt to entail unacceptable costs. For practical thinking is concerned with our actions: we engage in it for no other purpose than to discover whether we should, may, or should not bring about certain changes in how the world is. And the inconsistencies inherent in non-univocality can easily deliver mutually contradictory answers to particular such questions. Purporting to supply an answer to a practical question, they rather generously supply us with two of them. But then, and rather ungenerously, they obstruct our efforts to establish which one of these answers is what we know one of them *must* be: namely, false. Now we may not mind whether the terms of our *non*-practical thinking yield contradictory answers to questions of whether it's raining, much less why. But such answers become less engagingly entertaining and more downright irritating when delivered as responses to questions of whether to carry an umbrella.

Because we're not here in the business of creating a new language, ordinary and legal usages must certainly be the courts of *first* appeal whenever we encounter mutually inconsistent uses of the term 'rights'. But because neither of those usages is invariably univocal, they often disqualify themselves from serving as courts of *final* appeal. So, to achieve consistency on such occasions, we have perforce to consult our intuitions and to select that one of the two competing meanings that promises to cause us less intuitive discomfort. This is not an easy selection to make. For it's evidently true that philosophical debates, like the long-standing one between the Will Theory and the Interest Theory, thrive on potent mixtures of pro- and counter-intuitive implications generated by each of the opposing views. Their being thus fuelled obviously sets some implicit limit on the conclusiveness of any particular appeal to our common intuitions in such debates. Unfortunately, that limit is vague: no canonical metric of intuitive discomfort as yet exists. However a few likely dimensions of one do appear to be within our reach. For it seems reasonable to suppose that we can relevantly distinguish different *types* of intuition and discern some ranking of them in terms of their relative forensic strength.[6] A suggestion along these lines will be advanced at the end of this essay.

Returning, then, to how rights figure in our ordinary thinking, it's plain that one of their most familiar roles is that of items invoked in what I'll call *adversarial circumstances*. What are adversarial circumstances? Well, one feature of them is certainly *disagreement*. If all of us always and everywhere agreed on what would be the best thing to do in any particular situation, it looks pretty undeniable that rights would quickly disappear from our language. If you and I and everyone else all agreed on the most appropriate destination for my latest salary increment—whether it be a particular charity or the Inland Revenue or my bank account—any talk

---

[6] Thus Simmonds, 'The Analytical Foundations of Justice', 310, surely errs in claiming that 'it is our *values* that determine the level of "discomfort" experienced in the abandonment of any particular intuition'. For although it's obviously true that our values form one dimension of this metric, they are not the only—nor, as I'll later argue, the most decisive—one.

about who has what rights with respect to that increment would be utterly superfluous.

But disagreement is only a necessary, not a sufficient, condition of adversarial circumstances. The sufficient condition is what I call *deadlock*. Suppose I disagree with the coach of the New York Yankees about the fielding strategy to be pursued when the bases are loaded and there's a fairly mediocre hitter up to bat. This is *not* an adversarial circumstance, though it is one of disagreement. It's not an adversarial one because there's nothing I can actually *do* to stop the coach's strategy from being deployed. It would be different—it *would be* adversarial—if, say, I were the Yankees' second-base man. Then I *could* escalate my disagreement into deadlock by refusing to deploy the coach's strategy and doing something else instead. Broadly speaking, then, deadlock occurs when two disagreeing persons' chosen courses of action *intersect*: that is, when what each proposes to do or have done would preclude the occurrence of what the other proposes. Their two courses of action are jointly unperformable or what I've elsewhere called *incompossible*.[7]

It's in these circumstances that people begin to think about ringing up their solicitors to consult them about their rights. Of course, before they start reaching for their rights, each will presumably try to convince the other that his or her own proposed action is the better of the two. And sometimes, perhaps often, one of these attempts at persuasion will succeed. If it does succeed, *it eliminates the deadlock by eliminating the disagreement*. Presumably, if the coach and the second-base man share the same dominant aim—winning the game—a sufficiently detailed scrutiny of various bits of empirical data will result in one of them changing his mind and backing off.

But what if two adversaries can't eliminate their disagreement? What if, agreeing on all the pertinent facts, they nevertheless don't share that same aim or, even if they do, they don't prioritize it in the same way in relation to their other aims?

It's here, I think, that reflection on who has what rights really comes into its own. For the distinctive function of such thinking is to secure the elimination of deadlocks *without* eliminating the disagreements that generate them. Rights supply adversaries with reasons to back off from interference when they have no other reason

---

[7] cf *An Essay on Rights* (n 3 above), 33–41, 86–101, 190–4.

to allow the performance of the actions they're interfering with. The second-base man need concur with neither the coach's dominant aim nor the fielding strategy motivated by it in order consistently to acknowledge the coach's right that he comply with that strategy.

If this suggestion is correct, if it accurately reflects a salient aspect of how we commonly think about rights, then—abstract and general as it admittedly is—one important inference that we can draw from it is this: the general content of such rights is not determined by any of the aims/priorities motivating the disagreement between the adversarial parties. For, *ex hypothesi*, they've already been down the road of searching for a consensus on these aims or priorities, and have returned empty-handed. Their own objectives don't supply either of them with sufficient reasons to do the requisite backing off. So if appeals to rights are going to do any work in resolving their deadlock, without falsely presupposing the absence of their disagreement, the general content of those rights has to be (in some sense) *independent* of the content of adversaries' competing objectives.

The job of rights, on this view, is to demarcate *domains*—spheres of practical choice within which the choices made by designated individuals (and groups) must not be subjected to interference—and to specify those demarcations without reference to the content of the choices to be made within those spheres. It thus requires no very extended argument to show that rights, so conceived, amount to *normative allocations of freedom*. They reserve parts of the world to their owners' discretion and imply that, within those domains, such changes (or continuities) in the state of the world as those owners wish to occur must not be obstructed by others.[8] Those others bear duties to refrain from such obstruction.

This construal of rights as freedom allocations is sufficient to explain why those duties are uncontroversially seen as *enforceable*.[9] For, putting the matter as broadly as possible, we can say that to prevent someone's chosen disposition of elements within his or her

[8] Which is *not* to imply that such changes as owners wish to make within their domains are therefore permissible on other (non-rights-based) grounds. Our Yankee second-base man's acknowledgement—of the rights-based permissibility of his coach's fielding strategy and of his own duty to comply with it—is perfectly consistent with his adamant insistence on other grounds that it is the wrong thing to do.

[9] Uncontroversially, in both common understanding and at least the present version of the Will Theory–Interest Theory debate; on rights as necessarily enforceable, cf. Kramer, 'Rights Without Trimmings', 9, 64 above, and Simmonds, 'Rights at the Cutting Edge', 223–5 above. This is not to say that such an explanation is *true* of every person who shares that understanding.

domain is to diminish that person's allotted freedom: specifically, it makes that person unfree to secure whatever is aimed at in that disposition.[10] A set of rights-creating rules that lacked provision for the enforcement of those duties—that allowed, much less required, rights violations to stand unreversed—could not then consistently be described as doing what it purports to do: namely, assigning that discretionary domain to that person. 'No right without a remedy', as the legal maxim says.

So much, then, by way of informally tracking one familiar usage of rights to some of its general implications. What we need to do now is to examine the Will Theory itself, in an effort to see how its more articulated structure maps on to—*captures*—that common way of thinking about rights.

2 From Hohfeld to Hart: The Modern Will Theory Explored

Few would deny that the classic statement of the modern Will Theory is to be found in H. L. A. Hart's 1973 essay, 'Bentham on Legal Rights'.[11] In a deservedly famous passage, he identifies the fundamental structural components of the sort of discretionary domain I've just sketched. Since the existence of enforceable duties is an uncontested condition for the existence of rights, Hart suggests that these components are best understood as the several ingredients jointly constituting the *control* that one person can have over the duty of another:

> In the area of conduct covered by that duty the individual who has the right is a small-scale sovereign to whom the duty is owed. The fullest measure of control comprises three distinguishable elements: (i) the right-holder may waive or extinguish the duty or leave it in existence; (ii) after breach or threatened breach of duty he may leave it 'unenforced' or may 'enforce' it by suing for compensation or, in certain cases, for an injunction or mandatory order to restrain the continued or further breach of duty; and (iii) he may waive or extinguish the obligation to pay compensation to which the breach gives rise.[12]

---

[10] For an extended analysis of what it is to make someone *unfree*, see my *An Essay on Rights* (n 3 above), ch 2.
[11] Reprinted in HLA Hart, *Essays on Bentham*, (Oxford: Oxford University Press, 1982).
[12] ibid, 183–4.

These ingredients of control are each Hohfeldian *powers*. And the singular clarifying service rendered by this account is to have, in true Hohfeldian spirit, distilled the few basic forms that all powers assume from their myriad contents in any given set of rules. All powers can be exhaustively classified under one or another of these basic forms.[13]

In the passage just quoted, Hart enumerates these powers in 'either–or' pairs. To further sharpen the analysis of the control they are said to confer, and to illuminate some often overlooked aspects of it that are of the utmost importance, let's set his powers out in a slightly more partitioned list. With respect to the duty owed to a right-holder, he or she confronts the following menu of options:

(1) to waive compliance with the duty (ie extinguish it);
(2) to leave the duty in existence (ie demand compliance with it);
(3) to waive proceeding for the enforcement of the duty (ie for the restraint of, or compensation by, the duty-bearer in the face of threatened or actual breach);
(4) to demand proceeding for the enforcement of the duty;
(5) to waive enforcement;
(6) to demand enforcement.[14]

Now what's immediately apparent is that this partitioned menu is not a perfectly *à la carte* one: not every imaginable combination of options is edible, since some are simply impossible while others are indivisible. And that's because significant negative and positive logical relations obtain between these waiving and demanding powers.

---

[13] Possession of these powers endows their possessor X with a discretionary domain in the following sense. Where Y owes X a duty to do the act A, X has two options: (i) that the change (or continuity) in the state of the world implied by A's occurrence—or, in the event of Y's breach, by the occurrence of Y's compensatory act—is deontically necessary or required; or (ii) that this change (or continuity) is deontically unnecessary or indifferent, ie that both its occurrence and non-occurrence are options for Y and neither is required. What X's discretionary domain does *not* include is the option that this change (or continuity) is deontically impossible or forbidden. This latter option would exist only in the domain of someone to whom Y owed the (conflicting) duty to do not-A. The issue of conflicting duties is discussed below.

[14] I add this sixth power to Hart's listed five for the sake of logical completeness. In non-institutional settings there may be no rules enjoining others to provide proceedings or enforcement services and, hence, the third and fourth powers would be absent while the sixth power would simply be one to *secure* enforcement.

Most obviously, each member of a Hartian waiving and demanding pair represents the *contradiction* of its counterpart. To demand performance of an action (compliance, proceeding, enforcement) is to render it deontically necessary, whereas to waive it renders that performance deontically unnecessary. We can usefully label this particular relation of contradiction as one of *preclusion*.

What is preclusion? Like 'stop–go' signals at railway crossings where one signal's being 'on' implies the other's being 'off', the exercise of one power precludes that of its paired counterpart. Moreover, in precluding its counterpart's exercise, it *extinguishes* that counterpart. Thus waiving compliance with a duty precludes demanding it and thereby extinguishes not only the duty itself but also the power to demand compliance with that duty: there is simply no duty to comply with. Furthermore, one or the other signal *must* be on. For what's true of each Hartian pair, considered in isolation from the others, is that it's impossible for the exercise of both counterpart powers to be forborne: compliance with a duty, or proceeding for its enforcement, or that enforcement itself, cannot be both unwaived and undemanded.

Nor does this exhaust the analytical insights furnished by the concept of preclusion. For the reach of this clarifying instrument extends well beyond the relation between members of the *same* Hartian pair to illuminate relations between members of *different* pairs as well. It does so because a relation of *inclusion* holds between some of these options and others: the exercise of the former implies the exercise, and hence the non-extinguishment, of the latter.

Thus a moment's reflection will indicate that the exercise of any waiving power precludes the exercise of all powers higher-numbered than it. And the exercise of any demanding power, in including that of any lower-numbered one, precludes the exercise of every lower-numbered waiving power. We might quip, not inaccurately, that some of these powers are *more powerful* than others! The exercise of (6) implies the extinguishment of (1) and (3) as well as (5): demanding enforcement of a duty implies the preclusion of both waiving compliance with it and waiving proceedings for its enforcement, as well as precluding the waiver of that enforcement itself. And equally significantly, the exercise of (1) extinguishes not only (2) but also all the rest, since extinguishing a duty evidently leaves those remaining powers with no content whatsoever: there simply is no duty to breach nor, therefore, any basis for proceedings and enforcement.

Hence it appears that the core of full control over a duty consists in possession of (1) and (6), since such possession empowers their possessor to extinguish all the other powers. So an obvious question to ask is whether and how we can identify someone as a right-holder if these powers are *not* held by one and the same person. But since this is a question that lies very much at the heart of the present debate, it's worth postponing consideration of it until we've advanced a bit further on our tour of the Will Theory.

Another and highly significant dimension of the complexity attendant on having control over a duty arises from the fact that, as Hart says, each of these waiving and demanding powers is one which its possessor *may* exercise. A power possessor may (possesses a Hohfeldian *liberty to*) exercise that power.[15] But since this suggestion—that possession of powers implies the possession of corresponding liberties—seems to be controversial,[16] it's worth testing it against the rubric of Hohfeldian analysis.

Suppose that a set of rules imposes a duty on you to forbear from assaulting me, and invests me with the paired powers to waive and

---

[15] cf Georg Henrik von Wright, *Norm and Action*, (London: Routledge & Kegan Paul, 1963), 192–3, on powers as higher-order permissions.

[16] cf. Kramer, 'Rights Without Trimmings', 63 above: 'A liberty to make such a choice [between demanding and waiving compliance with a duty] usually accompanies the power to make the choice, but the latter does not *have* to be combined with the former.' It's unclear to me whether Kramer would wish to maintain this 'no necessary combination' thesis in the face of the fact that the liberty and the power 'to make a choice' are more precisely analysed as *pairs* of liberties and powers. Simmonds, 'The Analytical Foundations of Justice' (n 5 above), 315, similarly advances this thesis, citing the following legal example: 'A non-owner of property, who has possession of that property, has in certain circumstances a power to sell that property and pass good title; yet, in selling it, he will be committing a legal wrong, not exercising a liberty'; cf 'Rights at the Cutting Edge', 220 above. *Can* this be correct as stated? Ownership, as we know, consists of a highly variable collection of Hohfeldian positions—ones which, as in the present example, may not include immunities against others selling one's property in certain exceptional circumstances. Can it none the less make sense to say that the non-owning possessor's normal circumstance duty not (absence of liberty) to sell it still applies in such cases? Simmonds doesn't report the nature of these exceptional circumstances. Do they, for instance, include the owner's having granted that possession? Nor does he report the standard disposition of such cases. But if, say, it involves requiring the seller to compensate the owner, then the indicated analysis would seem to be that the only duty which the former bears is one to provide that compensation and not one to refrain from selling. What additional *work* would a duty specifically not to sell be doing here? Hence it appears that, in those circumstances, sellers are not only empowered but also at liberty to sell. Owner-clients who are assured by their lawyers that they have a claim against possessors selling their property in those circumstances are surely in need of better lawyers.

demand your compliance with that duty. Suppose further however that, contrary to the proffered suggestion, that same set of rules also imposes a duty on *me* to waive your duty of non-assault: that is, it denies me the liberty to exercise my power to demand your compliance with your non-assault duty. One and the same set of rules thus appears to vest me with that power and to *disable* me from exercising it. This is evidently quite contrary to Hohfeld's scheme where a *power* with respect to a certain act—in this case, demanding your compliance—is the precise jural opposite of a *disability* (or 'no-power' as Hohfeld characterises it) with respect to that same act. Since I cannot be said to have *both* of these, any set of rules conferring both of them on me is thus contradictory. So rejection of the suggestion that possession of powers implies the possession of corresponding liberties entails a straightforward contradiction. And one very important implication of that suggestion is thus that my having those liberties indicates the presence of Hohfeldian relations between me and other persons apart from yourself.[17] (They have

---

[17] Simmonds, 'Rights at the Cutting Edge' (n 53 above), appears to concede this latter point. As far as I can see, the only available line of rejoinder against the foregoing proof consists in claiming that it's question-begging to presume that duties with respect to second-order acts entail disabilities. That is, such an objector would have to affirm that, despite being forbidden to exercise a power, one can none the less be said to *possess* it: ie the deontic impossibility of its content does not entail the impossibility of its existence. I find it difficult to know what this could mean, in the sense of what normative difference such existence could conceivably make. After all and as Hohfeld remarks (*FLC*, 50), a jural power is not the same as a physical or mental power (or, as we more commonly say, 'ability'). We know what my teacher was trying to teach me when he would say: 'Yes, Steiner, you *can* leave the room to get a drink of water; but no, you *may* not'. Would we have understood him equally well had he said: 'Yes, Steiner, you *can* sell your jurisprudence textbook; but no, you *may* not'? Hohfeld himself declines to offer an analysis of the concept of 'power', remarking that 'Too close an analysis might seem metaphysical rather than useful' and proceeds to offer a series of examples 'as an approximate explanation, sufficient for all practical purposes' (*FLC*, 50). In the one passage (*FLC*, 58) where he considers whether powers must be accompanied by corresponding liberties, his discussion is inconclusive on this issue: 'If X, a landowner, has contracted with Y that the former will not alienate to Z, the acts of X necessary to exercise the power of alienating to Z are privileged as between X and every party other than Y [ie X *has* the liberty to alienate]; but, obviously, as between X and Y, the former has no privilege of doing the necessary acts [ie X *lacks* the liberty to alienate]; or conversely, he is under a duty to Y not to do what is necessary to exercise the power.' Could Hohfeld have any reason for wanting to claim in this latter case that, despite X's duty to Y, X still *has* a power with respect to Y—and Y the correlative liability—in the matter of alienating to Z? What *work* could this claim do? Perhaps Hohfeld would reply that X's act of alienating to Z would still have the effect of conveying good title to Z—and hence place Y under various non-owners' duties to Z—even if it also rendered X liable to enforcement

'no-rights' to my exercise of those powers.) Some amplification of this contention will appear in the next section's discussion of criminal law duties.

This latter discussion might tempt us to think that if control over a duty confers possession of a right, then that right lies with whoever possesses the powers both to waive and to demand compliance with that duty. Being possessed of the two liberties corresponding to those powers, that person appears to be endowed with just the sort of discretion sketched in the previous section: he or she may choose whether such change (or continuity) in the state of the world, as is implied by compliance with the duty, either must or alternatively need not occur. What more could be wanted by way of control? What else could be required to vest that person with a right?

Unfortunately, quite a lot. For as we have every reason to know, a duty's existence does not imply its fulfilment. That's why the previously sketched discretion also included choices about whether, in the event of non-compliance, enforcement must or alternatively need not occur. Not only the ingredients of control over a duty, but also the undisputed conditions for the very existence of a right, include normative provisions for such enforcement. It may well be, as Hohfeld is sometimes taken to suggest, that the existence of a *claim* is a sufficient condition for the existence of a *right*.[18] But even if this were literally what he means, it tells us little about the conditions for the existence of a claim. And it is common ground between Hohfeld, the Will Theory, and the Interest Theory that these conditions include the existence not merely of a duty but also of powers concerning its enforcement.[19]

In this regard, two quite different issues are in urgent need of being more sharply distinguished than is often the case. We might

proceedings by Y. This reply, however, confronts the same objection that was offered against Simmonds' example in the previous note: namely, that if X's act *can* have that effect, then it's misleading to describe the duty he owes Y as one not to alienate to Z. For that duty amounts to no more than that, in the event of his alienating to Z, X owes some payment to Y.

[18] cf Hohfeld, *FLC*, 36ff, where what he actually suggests is that a claim *is* a right 'in the strictest sense'; compare this with the quotation in the following note.

[19] It's the existence of such powers that enables us to distinguish between what Kramer calls *genuine* claims ('Rights Without Trimmings', 9 above) and merely *nominal* ones (100 above). Thus Hohfeld (*FLC*, 38) endorses the remark of Stayton, J that 'A right has been well defined to be a *well-founded* claim, and a well-founded claim means nothing more or less than a claim recognized or *secured* by law' (emphasis added).

label these as the 'location issue' and the 'existence issue'. Just where—in whom—those enforcement powers must be located, in order for the claim correlative to that duty to be a right, is indeed an issue between the two theories and one which we'll presently consider. But what is *not* at issue between them is that a *Hohfeldian* claim – duty relation cannot exist in logical isolation. It must imply the existence of other Hohfeldian relations—'trimmings'—if it is to count as constituting a right.[20] Again, 'no right without a remedy.'

In whom must this remedy lie? The Will Theory standardly contends that *all* powers pertaining to a duty must lie with the claim-holder, if he or she is to be a right-holder. More precisely, the contention is that a right-holder (or a Hohfeldian claim-holder) just *is* that person in whom all those powers lie. Now *if* having control over a duty is what having a right is all about, then our earlier discussion of *preclusion* supplies ample grounds for that contention. For there we discovered that the six Hartian basic forms of power are powerful not only with respect to whatever Hohfeldian (first- and second-order) relations they govern, but also with respect to *one another*, inasmuch as the exercise of any one of them necessarily extinguishes at least one other of them.

---

[20] Kramer seems to oscillate on this point. On the one hand, he embraces Hohfeld's above noted synonymy suggestion that 'claim' and 'right' are simply identical—this presumably being the motivation of the title 'Rights Without Trimmings'. And on that basis he chides the Will Theory for making a 'departure' from this usage, while claiming that 'the Interest Theory ... is happy to join Hohfeld in using "claim" and "right" interchangeably' and that it therefore 'presents a vocabulary closer to Hohfeld's own roster of terms' than does the Will Theory (64–5 above). On the other hand, he asserts that 'a *genuine* right or claim is enforceable' and insists that the proposition 'that claims must be enforceable [is] a proposition with which any adherent of the Interest Theory would firmly agree' (9, 64 above, emphasis added). It's only fair to remark here that Hohfeld's own habit—of sometimes declaring that a right 'in the strictest sense' is simply the claim correlative to an owed duty—doesn't help to discourage the erroneous view (which he doesn't share) that rights are *atomic* rather than *molecular* in their structure: that they imply the existence of only one Hohfeldian relation (claim–duty) rather than several. Commendably seeking to curb one indiscriminate use of 'rights' (as referring indifferently to claims, liberties, powers, and immunities), the unqualified 'synonymy thesis' inadvertently slips into another: namely, that of treating *all* claims as rights. What needs to be borne in mind however, and what ultimately exculpates Hohfeld himself from any charge of fostering non-univocality here, is the fact that he is speaking exclusively of *legal* rights, ie of claims which he simply (and correctly) presumes to be objects of enforcement powers. On atomic and molecular conceptions of rights, see Sumner, *The Moral Foundations of Rights* (n 3 above), 18ff, and Ingmar Porn, *The Logic of Power*, (Oxford: Blackwell, 1970), 51.

More significantly, we found this powerfulness to be unequally distributed amongst them: the exercise of any waiving power extinguishes all powers higher-numbered than it, and the exercise of any demanding power implies the extinguishment of every lower-numbered waiving power.

This finding severely restricts the range of conceivable answers to the question of where these powers can lie, if their possession is to constitute control over a duty. On one view, it minimally suggests that any great dispersal of them—and less minimally, any dispersal at all—among more than one person, *dilutes* each person's control. But it's more accurate to say that all dispersals can be exhaustively classified as ones that either simply *eliminate* control or entirely *transfer* control from one person to another.

Let's first consider a control-eliminating dispersal. Powers (1) and (6)—the powers to waive compliance and to demand enforcement—are, as we previously saw, the most powerful of the six Hartian powers. The exercise of (1) precludes the exercise of, extinguishes, all the rest. And the exercise of (6) implies the same for all the waiving powers. No great amount of insight is required to see that if each of these two powers is possessed by a different person, then we have a situation which may quite properly be described as the deontic equivalent of 'High Noon'. For each of these power possessors is, in Hohfeldian terms, literally in a position to *disable* the other, thereby rendering an action of the poor bewildered duty-bearer—his or her non-compliance—both permissible and impermissible. My waiving compliance with a duty implies that *no* action can count as a breach of it. Your demanding enforcement contradictorily implies that some action *is* such a breach. And because preclusion holds not only within Hartian pairs but also between them, any such non-pair-wise dispersal of Hartian powers generates similar contradictions, and eliminates control.

On the other hand, pair-wise dispersals transfer control. Control over a duty, *prior* to the occasion of compliance, requires that only one person be in possession of all three pairs of Hartian powers. If he or she exercises (1)—if compliance with the duty is waived—then all of the five other powers are extinguished. If, alternatively, (2) is exercised—if compliance is demanded—that extinguishes (1) and, if compliance occurs, then that extinguishes the remaining four powers by depriving them of their contents: the duty is fulfilled and, so, questions of (proceeding for) its enforcement cannot arise. If, however, the demanded compliance does *not* occur then, *prior* to the outcome of any proceedings, control requires that only one person be in possession of the second and third pairs of Hartian powers. If he or she exercises (3)—if proceedings are waived—then all of the three remaining powers are extinguished, again by being deprived of their contents. If, alternatively, (4) is exercised—if proceedings are demanded—that extinguishes (3) and, if judgment is given in favour of the duty-bearer, then that extinguishes the remaining two powers by similarly depriving them of their contents: there is no grant of enforcement and, so, questions of that enforcement's being demanded or waived cannot arise. And finally, if judgment is given against the duty-bearer then, *prior* to the occasion for securing enforcement, control requires that only one person be in possession of the third pair of Hartian powers since they are mutually preclusive. Hence if the persons successively possessing these sets of Hartian pairs *are not one and the same person*, we are bound to conclude that control over the duty does not disappear but rather successively shifts from one person to the next.

So the indicated inference is simply this. The Will Theory's standard contention—that a right-holder is that person who possesses all powers pertaining to a duty—is more accurately stated as the thesis that a right-holder is that person who possesses all the *unextinguished* powers pertaining to that duty.

To say this, however, is not to deny the possibility of powers being *delegated* by a Will Theory right-holder while none the less remaining such a right-holder. Suppose someone owes me a duty of non-assault. And suppose that, having exercised (2), I've none the less been non-compliantly assaulted. The Will Theory thesis just formulated does not imply that, if I empower you with (4) to demand proceedings for enforcement, my exercise of (3) is thereby precluded. Nor, therefore, does it imply that my possession of (3) and, consequently, my control are relinquished. For my empowerment of you can be subject to conditions which I impose and that specify the circumstances in which that power is not to be exercised by you. These might, for instance, include my assailant's offer of an apology. Only in the absence of those self-chosen circumstances is my (3) extinguished, just as it would be if I had retained (4) myself. And if those circumstances occur, this has the effect of depriving you of that power and restoring it to me.

3 Some Apparent Problems with the Will Theory

The Will Theory is not everyone's cup of tea. Reasons for this vary, but what is more important, the *types* of reason for this vary. Some of these reasons share the property of being *moral* in character. They underwrite objections to the Will Theory to the effect that it leads to two broad kinds of what are said to be morally undesirable conclusions. One is the implied impossibility of certain sorts of (what for lack of a suitably alternative general term, I'll call) *creature* having rights. Such creatures are ones who are undisputedly incapable of exercising powers and, therefore, of possessing them. Hence, according to the Will Theory, they cannot be right-holders. The second kind of morally objectionable conclusion is that the theory rules out the permissibility of certain sorts of *action* which are of substantial moral importance. Both kinds of conclusion often fly in the face of entrenched moral convictions, and therefore, so the objections run, the Will Theory must be erroneous. I'll postpone any assessment of the status of morally-grounded objections for the moment.

The other important type of reason for rejecting the Will Theory might be characterized as *conceptual*.[21] Here the argument is that the conditions it imposes on rights-constituting power locations render the theory logically incapable of explaining how the undisputed existence of some perfectly enforceable duties implies rights at all. Indeed some Will Theorists, including Hart himself, simply accept the force of such objections and accordingly maintain that the validity of the Will Theory is restricted to only a subset of all enforceable duties. The duties which are held to have this limiting effect are usually those to be found in *public* or *criminal law*. And such limitations are equally held to be implicit in various *constitutional immunities*. It's this type of objection that we'll now consider.[22]

One thing that's not much disputed is that the Will Theory is unproblematically applicable to the analysis of duties in *private* or *civil* law. The 'small-scale sovereign', referred to in that previously

---

[21] The appropriate classification of some reasons for rejecting the theory is, admittedly, not always clear-cut. Some moral reasons lend themselves to reinterpretation as conceptual ones.

[22] Those who have read *An Essay on Rights* (n 3 above) will see that much of this part of the discussion draws heavily on one offered there at 64–73.

quoted passage from Hart, clearly represents the position of someone to whom civil-law duties are owed and who is an archetypal Will Theory right-holder. What reasons could there be, then, for claiming that no such positions are occupied in respect of criminal-law duties?

It's worth remarking here that writers on the criminal-law themselves continue to reject this claim, inasmuch as they perceive no great conceptual divide between civil and criminal law. In his classic text on the subject, C. S. Kenny observes:

There is indeed no fundamental or inherent difference between a crime and a tort... In the first stages of national development there is little or no police organization and the sanctions of crime are freely left to the hands of ordinary citizens... Crimes therefore originate in the government policy of the moment.[23]

And G. W. Paton, having suggested that the principal reason for distinguishing between public and private law is to accord due recognition to the 'importance of the peculiar character of the State', comments that:

Nevertheless, this distinction has not always been clearly marked. Until the State itself has developed, public law is a mere embryo. Even in the days of feudalism there is much confusion; for no clear line can be drawn between the public and private capacities of the king. Jurisdiction, office and even kingship are looked upon as property—indeed public law might almost be regarded as 'a mere appendix' to the law of real property so far as the feudal ideal is realized.[24]

Nor has the underlying conceptual structure of the juridical relations involved in criminal offences changed with the passage of time. P. J. Fitzgerald reports that it's still the case that:

in England prosecutions are nearly all in theory private prosecutions. Not only may any private person in general prosecute another, but in most cases the prosecutor, who is normally a police officer, prosecutes by virtue of his right to prosecute as a private citizen.[25]

---

[23] JWC Turner, *Kenny's Outlines of Criminal Law*, 19th edn, (Cambridge: Cambridge University Press, 1966), 1, 2, 4. See also Julius Goebel, *Felony and Misdemeanor: A Study in the History of Criminal Law*, (Philadelphia: University of Pennsylvania Press, 1976), *passim*, and Andrew Ashworth, *Principles of Criminal Law*, (Oxford: Oxford University Press, 1991), 1–2.

[24] GW Paton, *A Text-book of Jurisprudence*, (Oxford: Oxford University Press, 1972), 328.

[25] PJ Fitzgerald, *Criminal Law and Punishment*, (Oxford: Oxford University Press, 1962), 2.

The clear implication of these various remarks is that there's simply no obstacle to extending the application of the Will Theory to criminal-law duties and holding that, whereas civil law confers Will Theory rights on private citizens, criminal law (now) vests them in *state officials*.

Why, then, have some Will Theorists—let alone their critics—been reluctant to make this move? The grounds for that reluctance are, perhaps, sufficiently indicated in the following arguments offered by authors otherwise disposed to accept the validity of that theory. Richard Flathman points out, with regard to a criminal law offence, that:

> Jones can be arrested and punished for reckless driving even if no A [private citizen] is harmed or so much as witnesses Jones' violation. Thus on Hart's theory one must say either that Cs (policemen, judges, etc) have a blanket authorization to exercise the rights of As on their behalf or that the element of 'self-administration' [control] that is usually part of having a right is simply not a necessary part of many of the rights one has as a member of society. It seems preferable to say that Jones has the obligation under the law (as opposed to owing it to other citizens with a correlative right) and that Cs have both authority [powers] *and a duty* to arrest and punish Jones for his violation.[26]

And Thomas Kearns, conceding that the Will Theory seems to have the 'awkward result' of conferring rights on state officials, seeks to finesse this apparently unwanted implication by arguing as follows:

> It might be supposed, for example, that under the criminal law I have a right not to be robbed. But unlike, say, a promisee, I cannot discharge the intruder of his obligation not to rob me (the crime, we say, is against the State)... It might appear, then, that my robber offends only an official's rights, but not mine... Two responses are in order. First, it is by no means clear that I acquire any rights under the criminal law... Second, the enforcement official does not acquire any rights on my account for he is *under an obligation* to take the enforcement action and is, therefore, *unfree under the legal rules* to discharge [waive] or in any other way to alter the obligation or forgive its breach.[27]

---

[26] Richard Flathman, *The Practice of Rights*, (Cambridge: Cambridge University Press, 1976), 237–8 (emphasis added). See also Hart, *Essays on Bentham* (n 11 above), 181–6.

[27] Thomas Kearns, 'Rights, Benefits and Normative Systems', *Archiv fur Rechts- und Sozialphilosophie*, lxi (1975), 478 (emphasis added). See also Alf Ross, *On Law and Justice*, (London: Stevens & Sons, 1958), 163–4 and *Directives and Norms*, (London: Routledge & Kegan Paul, 1968), 128.

Both Flathman and Kearns thus attribute the absence of Will Theory rights in state officials to their lack of discretionary control over criminal-law duties. For such officials, though empowered, also bear duties to demand (proceedings for and) enforcement of criminal-law duties against criminals. They lack civil-law right-holders' powers to waive such actions. If state officials *did* have such waiving powers as well as the demanding ones, they would undeniably be Will Theory right-holders.

What's certainly true is that *private citizens* lack such powers over criminal-law duties. For instance, neither other persons' criminal-law duties not to assault me, nor enforcement of those duties, are waivable by me. My expression of a willingness to be assaulted (with the licensed exceptions of things like boxing matches, medical surgery, etc) is insufficient to preclude my assailant's being charged with a breach of duty. These are cases where 'consent is no defence'. And they are thus contrasted with those of, say, your failing to repay my loan, where my consent to non-repayment *does* supply a defence against any breach-of-duty charge. Plainly then, private citizens have no Will Theory rights in the criminal law. Do state officials? Is it as true of them, as of private citizens, that they lack waiving powers in respect of criminal-law duties?

Evidently *some* state officials do. But if these powers were lacking in *all* state officials, we should be very hard put to explain the occurrence of such standard criminal-law practices as plea-bargaining and the granting of clemency, pardons, reprieves, paroles, and immunities from prosecution. In most modern legal systems, these practices account for the disposition of the vast majority of criminal cases.[28] And what they consist of, *inter alia*, is *subordinate* officials having their duties to exercise powers (4) or (6) waived by their *superiors*. It is of course true that, in so waiving, superior officials also impose duties on their subordinates to exercise (3) or (5)—that is, they deprive them of (4) or (6).

The withdrawal of these powers is certainly sufficient grounds for denying that Will Theory rights correlative to criminal-law duties

---

[28] cf Ashworth, *Principles of Criminal Law* (n 23 above), ch 1, and Jeremy Waldron, *The Law*, (London: Routledge, 1990), ch 9. A colourful depiction of these practices at work is provided in Tom Wolfe's novel, *The Bonfire of the Vanities*, (London: Jonathan Cape, 1988). See also Michael Zander, 'How Bargains are Struck', *The Guardian*, 21 Nov 1979, and Alan Wertheimer, 'Freedom, Morality, Plea-Bargaining and the Supreme Court', *Philosophy & Public Affairs*, 8 (1979), 203–34.

are vested in *those* subordinate officials: they lack the requisite control over those duties. But it's not sufficient grounds for denying that such rights vest in their superiors.

Superior officials are related to their subordinates as principals to agents.[29] That relation is one of *delegation*, described previously. In the standard nominal treatment of criminal-law offences, superiors delegate the exercise of (4) and (6) to their subordinates. They thereby mandate them to prosecute and punish offenders. But that mandate is a conditional one. And in many cases, and for a variety of reasons, superior officials withhold (4) or (6) and instead assign and mandate their subordinates' exercise of (3) or (5). That is, in the manner of typical civil-law right-holders, such superiors have either proceedings for breach of a criminal-law duty or its enforcement waived. For what the plea-bargaining or immunity-granting official is doing, in waiving proceedings for the breach of one duty and demanding enforcement of another—breaches whose respective victims may well be different persons—is clearly acting *as if* both of the breached criminal-law duties were ones owed to his or her superior, and certainly not to the victim(s) of those breaches.

Isn't this sufficient to prove that *superior* state officials are indeed vested with Will Theory rights correlative to criminal-law duties? Almost but not quite. For it could none the less be objected that, even if they do possess waiving powers (3) and (5), they still lack (1). That is, although superior officials are empowered to forgive non-compliance with such duties *ex post*, they still lack the power to waive compliance with them *ex ante*. Their being able to waive (proceeding for) enforcement against a robber does not itself imply their being able to waive his or her duty not to rob.

What sorts of argument are needed to prove that such state officials lack (1)? To be disempowered in this way, they must lack the liberty (ie have duties not) to exercise (1). Such a duty constitutes a Hohfeldian disability. For superior state officials to have this disability, they must lack the power to waive a person's duty not to commit a robbery.

Now there are many legal systems where superior state officials clearly do have this power. Having it, they're at liberty to exempt persons from compliance with an otherwise general criminal-law duty such as that not to rob or, in James Bond's case, to kill: they

[29] cf Hohfeld, *FLC*, 53ff.

can confer privileges and immunities upon themselves and others. No doubt this power is exercised sparingly, and for sound reasons. But that is beside the point. In such legal systems, we're bound to conclude, these officials lack any such disability and they therefore possess (1).

However, it's also true that some legal systems are ones where these superior officials lack this power. They lack it by virtue of certain disabling *constitutional* provisions. And indeed, this type of consideration is seen by Hart and others as imposing another limitation on the scope of the Will Theory of rights.[30]

Does it? Hohfeld tells us that disabilities correlatively entail immunities. To claim that no state official can waive compliance with a criminal-law duty is to claim that any such official is encumbered with a disability which is unwaivable by the holder of the correlative immunity. For brevity's sake, let's refer to any such immunity—any immunity whose correlative disability cannot be waived by that immunity's holder—as an *unwaivable immunity*. Can there *be* unwaivable immunities?

Like private citizens, subordinate state officials are standardly disabled from waiving compliance with criminal-law duties. Thus Yellow, a subordinate state official, bears a disability to waive a person's duty not to rob. Yellow's superior, let's call her Black, therefore holds an immunity against Yellow's doing so. Can Black waive her own immunity? What would be implied in denying her the power to do so? For Black's immunity to be an unwaivable one, she, in turn, would have to be encumbered with a disability: namely, the disability to waive Yellow's disability. But if Black does bear such a disability then some still more superior official, call him Green, must hold an immunity correlative to Black's disability.[31]

We could, I suppose, continue indefinitely adding such epicycles to this line of reasoning by imagining that Green's immunity too is unwaivable and identifying yet another even more superior official,

---

[30] cf Hart, *Essays on Bentham* (n 11 above), 188–93. For example, the Fourteenth Amendment to the American Constitution disables state legislatures from denying equal protection of the laws to any citizen.

[31] cf DN MacCormick, 'Rights in Legislation', in PMS Hacker & Joseph Raz (eds), *Law, Morality and Society*, (Oxford: Oxford University Press, 1977), 195–6, for an acknowledgement that immunities which are unwaivable thereby entail the presence of disabilities in the immunity holders themselves. Whereas a waivable immunity implies a single Hohfeldian relation between two persons, an unwaivable immunity-implies a pair of such relations between three persons.

Orange, who in turn holds the immunity correlative to Green's thereby entailed disability. And so on. Let's not do that. For the sufficiently unmistakable point here is that wherever we decide to stop this otherwise infinite regress, it can be stopped only by an immunity which *is* waivable. Unwaivable immunities (eventually!) entail waivable ones. So, yes, there can be unwaivable immunities. But what there can't be are unwaivable immunities without there also being a waivable one. And the waiving of that one renders waivable whatever (otherwise unwaivable) immunity entails it.[32]

What this demonstrates is that state officials' disabilities cannot be absolute ones. An official has a disability only so long as a superior refrains from waiving it. And even if a constitution disables some superior official from waiving it, Hohfeldian logic dictates that

[32] Simmonds, 'The Analytical Foundations of Justice' (n 5 above), 317–320, challenges this case for finding waiving powers over criminal-law duties in state officials. He correctly distinguishes two components in that argument: (i) the empirical one, that the actual existence of plea-bargaining, immunity-granting, etc, practices is inexplicable in the absence of such powers; and (ii) the logical one, that if they are absent, then Hohfeldian analysis generates the aforesaid infinite regress. Ignoring the first of these, he focuses on the second, conceding that an infinite regress is indeed thereby generated but also contending that it can be of a 'spiral' form rather than the above indicated 'linear' or hierarchical one. With respect to a citizen's criminal-law duty, instead of the series of successively higher-order disabilities and unwaivable immunities running Yellow–Black–Green–Orange–etc, Simmonds proposes that it can run Citizen–Yellow–Citizen–Yellow–etc. One unquestionably correct argument adduced for this possibility is that Hohfeldian analysis (unlike the Interest Theory) does not imply that holding an immunity is necessarily or even generally *beneficial for its holder*; (cf Simmonds, 'Rights at the Cutting Edge', 153ff above). It's quite *conceivable* that the holder of the immunity against Yellow's waiving Citizen's duty not to rob is indeed Citizen him- or herself, who is thereby entitled to have Yellow's grant of such permission nullified. Thus the spiral regress consists in that immunity's being unwaivable, which entails that Yellow holds an immunity against Citizen's waiving Yellow's disability to waive Citizen's duty not to rob. And Yellow holds a further immunity against Citizen's waiving Yellow's disability to waive Citizen's disability ... and so forth. Three responses are in order. First, Simmonds is quite correct to suggest that this spiral infinite regress, if it existed, would deny waiving powers and, hence, Will Theory rights to any state official. Second however, it seems evident that *any* form of infinite regress, in thus precluding closure or what Simmonds calls a 'stable resolution', cannot be part of anything describable as a normative (much less legal) system: there are *necessarily* insufficient persons and/or time to sustain it. And if the spiral regress is stopped, ie by a waivable immunity, then that *does* vest a Will Theory right in either Citizen or Yellow, depending on who holds that immunity. (Recall that the basic point at issue here is not *who* can have Will Theory rights in the criminal law but rather *whether* there can be any.) Finally, there's something particularly odd about the spiral form of infinite regress. For its structure is essentially identical with that of a game whose rules include a stipulation that, at the end of any round, either player is entitled to demand a further round. Indeed, it may be doubted that this is a game at all.

there must be some still more superior official in a position to release him or her from that disability. Hence that still more superior official controls (1) and is not disempowered from either conferring it on or withholding it from a subordinate. In most cases, of course, private citizens can be presumed to be *third-party beneficiaries* of this more superior official's withholding, from subordinates, the power to waive compliance with such criminal-law duties as those not to rob.[33]

So the inference to be drawn is *not* that Will Theory rights are absent from criminal and constitutional law. On the contrary, they are very much present in it and are to be found fairly high up in the hierarchy of state officials. Just how high up will depend on whether the legal system contains a constitution and, if so, what its particular provisions are. Hence the general point stands: namely, that no conceptual distinction exists—with respect to the presence or absence of Will Theory rights—between the relationship of superior to subordinate state officials and, say, the relationship of superior to subordinate officers in a private corporation. Both relationships are instances of delegation. The latter uncontestedly offers no resistance to the ascription of (civil law) rights. Nor therefore can the former, as regards ascriptions of (criminal law) rights.[34]

What, then, of the *moral* objections to the Will Theory? These, as I previously remarked, tend to be of two kinds: that the theory wrongly withholds right-holder status from certain creatures and that it withholds permissibility from highly desirable actions.

Let's consider the latter objections first. Although these come in many different variations, they all seem to have the same general form: that Will Theory rights can be such as to afford protection to morally inferior conduct while denying it to, and even prohibiting, morally superior conduct.[35] A clarification is immediately called for here. For such objections entirely lose their point if the rights

---

[33] On the significance, for the present debate, of the general position of third-party beneficiaries, see section 5 below.

[34] Anticipations of this general argument are to be found in: TE Holland, *The Elements of Jurisprudence*, 10th edn, (Oxford: Oxford University Press, 1906), 125–7; John Chipman Gray, *The Nature and Sources of the Law*, (New York: Macmillan, 1921), 19–20, 79–83; Glanville Williams, *Salmond on Jurisprudence*, 11th edn, (London: Sweet & Maxwell, 1957), 264–5.

[35] cf. Kramer, 'Rights Without Trimmings', 72–3 above, where he endorses MacCormick's charge that the Will Theory underwrites the implausible view that protecting our truly vital interests may not be required by rights while protecting inconsequential interests may. And this implausibility is only augmented by the

referred to are *legal* ones. Legal rights, as construed by either the Will Theory or the Interest Theory, are obviously capable of forbidding morally superior actions and licensing inferior ones. Legislators are typically not leading candidates for canonization. And moral criticism of legal rules, along with the rights they generate, is pretty much a fixed feature of the human condition and one which seems unlikely to be dispelled by changes in the way that rights are theoretically construed. Hence where this kind of moral objection gets a grip and presses on the Will Theory is when the rights it targets are themselves *moral* ones, as modelled by that theory. How is it, then, that the theory is exposed to such objections?

Installing persons as 'small-scale sovereigns' and endowing them with the corresponding discretionary domains, the Will Theory apparently thereby commits itself to sustaining the deontic necessity—obligatoriness—of whatever actions constitute compliance with the duties owed to those sovereigns. Since there's no *a priori* reason why those actions need be the morally best ones available in some situations, and since some of the other available actions may be both morally better than the former and not conjunctively performable with them, the aforesaid commitment can imply the deontic impossibility—forbiddenness—of what is morally best. And what adds injury to insult is that the theory arms those sovereigns with powers of enforcement to deal with persons who breach the correlative duties requiring their performance of these morally inferior actions. There you are, toiling selflessly away at doing the right thing; and in comes a small-scale sovereign (with the moral-rights police in tow), branding you a wrongdoer.

Three rejoinders, of successively increasing strength, are warranted. The weakest is that although Will Theory rights *can* indeed generate such normative conclusions, this fact affords no defence to those sovereigns against the charge of having exercised their rights wrongly on such occasions.[36] Will Theory rights do assign to their holders entitlements against certain interferences with their freedom. But their having these entitlements forms no logical obstacle

theory's thereby implied capacity to sustain that requirement even *at the expense of* protection for those vital interests.

[36] cf Ronald Dworkin, *Taking Rights Seriously*, (London: Duckworth, 1977), 188–9; Joseph Raz, *The Authority of Law*, (Oxford: Oxford University Press, 1979), 266ff; Jeremy Waldron, 'A Right to Do Wrong', *Ethics*, 92 (1981), 21–39. Interest Theory rights can be exposed to the same charge.

to moral censure for some of the ways they choose to employ that freedom.[37]

Secondly, although Will Theory rights can generate such normative conclusions and their holders can deservedly incur such charges, they *need not* do so. For these sovereigns, being fully equipped with waiving powers, are necessarily well placed—and better placed than Interest Theory right-holders who can lack such equipment—to extinguish duties to perform morally inferior actions, thereby clearing the path for the performance of their morally superior alternatives.[38] My being vested with a Will Theory right against your use of my belongings does not preclude your acquisition of the liberty to use my lifeboat as an indispensable means to rescue a drowning swimmer. And if I'm a half-way decent fellow, you will acquire it.

But the strongest rejoinder is this. Although the Will Theory is indeed consistent with the denial to you of that liberty, the theory *itself* is insufficient to imply the moral impermissibility of your using the lifeboat, that is, even if I refuse to waive your duty not to use it. And this, for a very significant reason. The claim that my refusal to waive renders your use morally impermissible is not one sustained by the Will Theory *per se*, but rather by the quite distinct premise that rights are morally *peremptory*: that is, by a substantive moral premise which assigns the status of 'trumps' to rights, in their relation to other moral values. The peremptoriness of rights, the priority of compliance with *correlative* moral duties over compliance with other kinds of moral duty, is itself the deliverance of an injunction which lies entirely outside the precincts of the Will Theory and is completely independent of it. Indeed, such peremptoriness is assumed by many advocates of the Interest Theory.[39] Hence persons who believe that my refusal to loan you the lifeboat *does* render your use of it morally impermissible must be persons who endorse that injunction. And they should therefore, so to speak, accept responsibility for doing so and not lay its normative

---

[37] Nor does the truth of the Will Theory presuppose, as some have suggested, the truth of some form of moral relativism—though it's also not inconsistent with that truth.

[38] Indeed, since it appears not to be a requirement of the Interest Theory that *anyone* be possessed of such waiving powers, its implication seems to be that, in their absence, that optimal path must remain obstructed.

[39] Though it's also true, as Simmonds shows in 'Rights at the Cutting Edge', *passim*, that cogent arguments can be mounted against their entitlement to do so.

consequences at the door of the Will Theory (nor that of the Interest Theory either).

Moreover the very conception of how mutually alternative actions are assessable as morally better or worse is often confused in the hands of such objectors. We can all agree that it's obviously better for you to perform the lifeboat rescue than not. And this, in the simple situation described, is sufficient to imply that it's morally best for me to waive your duty and thereby loan you the lifeboat. But these facts are still insufficient to imply that the morally worst alternative is for me to deny you the use of the lifeboat and thereby prevent the rescue. For since rights are involved here, there are three—not two—mutually exclusive and jointly exhaustive morally relevant alternatives present: (a) my loaning you the lifeboat and your thereby effecting the rescue; (b) my denying you the lifeboat and thereby preventing the rescue; and (c) my denying you the lifeboat, but your none-the-less taking it and effecting the rescue.

Now if rights are peremptory, a different moral ranking must be placed on the two inferior alternatives than would otherwise be the case. Both those who accept and those who reject the peremptoriness of rights can agree that (a) is best and that (b) and (c) are worse. Where they must differ is with regard to whether (b) is worse than (c) or vice versa. Acceptors of peremptoriness must assess (c) as the worst alternative, while its rejectors must assign this status to (b). This is because acceptors, though unquestionably committed to the moral worth of rescuing persons from danger—and hence, to the optimality of (a)—are also committed to according higher priority to respecting rights than rejectors do. For acceptors of peremptoriness, any action that fails to leave rights intact, however morally worthy its other consequences may be, simply cannot count as a morally better alternative.[40] The contention that it can entails the rejection not of the Will Theory, but of peremptoriness and, perhaps, of the moral worth of rights themselves.

There are, to be sure, strong conceptual grounds for accepting rights as peremptory and I'll review some of them toward the end of the next section. For the moment, my point is simply that an action's being *rights-impermissible* is not conclusive of its moral impermissibility, much less of the Will Theory's moral inadequacy.

[40] cf my 'Duty-Free Zones', *Aristotelian Society Proceedings*, xcvi (1996), 231–44.

Rights do not, and arguably cannot, exhaust the moral universe.[41] And nothing in the Will Theory's construal of rights prevents you from saying, with perfect consistency, *both* that my refusal to loan you the lifeboat is indeed within my rights *and* that so much the worse for my rights: you are duty-bound to take the lifeboat and effect the rescue.

The other, not unrelated but perhaps more common, kind of moral objection to the Will Theory is that it wrongly withholds right-holder status from certain sorts of creature.[42] More common because, unlike the previous objection, no amount of analytical scrutiny will find (any version of) the Interest Theory equally exposed to it. In *any* world, there are going to be far fewer Will Theory right-holders than Interest Theory right-holders. For the set of creatures who are capable of exercising powers can never amount to more than a very small subset of the creatures who have interests, however interests are construed. Hence foetuses, minors, the comatose, the mentally disabled, and also (as I've argued elsewhere)[43] the dead and members of future generations—to say nothing of members of virtually all other known species—must all lack Will Theory rights. How morally damaging is this fact?

Very damaging, if we take the sort of Bryanite soft-currency view mentioned at the outset of this essay. For there can be little doubt that we do have significant moral duties, both individually and collectively, to protect the interests of these *unempowerable* creatures as well as those of their empowerable counterparts. And hence, especially in our current cultural climate, a theory that denies us the latitude to regard that protection as owed to them as a matter of their rights, appears to place itself well beyond the pale of moral acceptability. Insistence on a gold standard for membership in the set of right-holders seems to threaten a moral prospect at least as bad as the crucifixion of mankind.

What is the Will Theorist to say, in the face of this damning indictment? I presume that the main path of rejoinder must lie in

---

[41] Though Kramer, 'Rights Without Trimmings', 25–6 above, advances the unusual view that other kinds of morally valuable act, such as beneficent and (possibly) brave ones, can equally be construed as contents of correlative duties owed to others as a matter of their rights.

[42] Sometimes the objection is formulated quasi-conceptually as one to the *implausibility* of such withholding. But the intuitions typically appealed to, by arguments brought in support of it in this form, are of an unmistakably moral character.

[43] cf *An Essay on Rights* (n 3 above), ch 7(C).

the usual direction: namely, seeking an alternative culprit who can be held responsible for this daunting prospect. Fortunately, we don't have to search all that far to find a likely villain. For our current cultural climate is replete with shady-looking characters who are more than sufficient to fill the bill. One of these might appear to be the proposition which we've just previously encountered: the claim that rights are morally peremptory. Isn't it precisely this claim—or, at least, the belief that it's one which is widely endorsed—that largely explains the motivation of those many different campaigning groups who urge the correlation of our duties to protect unempowerable creatures' interests with rights vested in those creatures themselves?

I think the correct response to this question is of the 'Yes, but...' variety. Evidently, seeking to enshrine such protection as a matter of rights does strongly indicate a presumption of their widely endorsed peremptoriness. But why the anxiety to secure such peremptory status in the first place? Only two answers seem possible, and they are far from being mutually exclusive. One is that our total inventory of moral duties is overloaded, greater than we can bear. And hence, we have to ensure that the more important of these— many of which are certainly ones to protect the unempowerable— are given appropriate priority.

This answer is, however, inconclusive. For while the assignment of rankings to various kinds of moral duty does indeed imply that some of them are morally peremptory, what it doesn't imply is that they need to be accorded the *enforceability* which—according to both the Will and Interest Theories—inherently accompanies duties correlative to rights. So the other possible answer, which thus turns out to be also necessary, is that persons' chosen conduct may deviate from that required by these rankings and may often be lamentably uninformed by any duties at all.

It seems clear that our current cultural climate is amply beset by both these sorts of deficiency: conduct reflecting either wrongly prioritized duties or utter neglect of them. Nor is it always an easy matter to tell the two apart. What is clear, however, is that the blame for our being confronted with the aforesaid dismal moral prospect should be borne by that climate—by those whose conduct betrays these deficiencies—and not by the Will Theory.

To this, however, the theory's critics have a ready reply. For they can say that, even if it's true that the main culprit here is our cultural climate, the Will Theory lends itself to aiding and abetting this climate's advance along that morally deplorable trajectory. By construing rights as discretionary domains and confining their possession to only the empowerable, the theory licenses those right-holders whose conduct displays those deficiencies to neglect the interests of the unempowerable. And it protects their choices to do so. Is it not patently better, the theory's critics urge, to adopt a conception of rights that allows unempowerable creatures to hold rights and then to place the powers accompanying the correlative duties in the hands of those best qualified to protect those creatures' interests?

Will Theorists have, I think, only one line of rejoinder open to them here. But it's a decisive one and is, perhaps, best put in the form of a question: What scintilla of a practical or analytical difference can it make if we construe the rights correlative to those protection duties as ones held *by those power-possessors* rather than ones held by unempowerable creatures? As far as I can see, none. And if those power-possessors are indeed the holders of those rights, then, as we saw in the previous discussion of criminal law, the rights they hold are none other than Will Theory rights.[44]

The lesson, plain enough I suppose, is this. Rather than excoriating the Will Theory, those concerned for the interests of the unempowerable should be a little less discreet in acknowledging the truism that the powers associated with duties to protect those interests can and must lie only with the empowerable. And they should draw the consequent conclusion, namely, that their labours would be better employed in the twin tasks of identifying who should be empowered to control those duties and of changing our cultural climate. It certainly can't be said that either of these tasks is easily accomplished. But what can be said, with equal certainty, is that rejection of the Will Theory impedes—rather than expedites— their accomplishment, since it obscures our view of how and where arrangements for that protection are effectively to be sought. Presumably, multiplying right-holders at the cost of analytical

[44] That is, they also hold *waiving* powers over those protection duties. For if they don't, then they must be the disabled subordinates—delegates or agents—of others who do, and who are therefore the (Will Theory) right-holders here. And, by definition, such others cannot be among the unempowerable. Nor will it do to say that, by locating the rights in the unempowerables themselves, the discretion of those who hold those powers can be construed as constrained by a duty of *trust*. For we have then to ask the Hohfeldian question of where the powers controlling *that* duty are located. Trust adds epicycles; it doesn't dispense with Will Theory rights.

perspicacity would be no more acceptable to Hohfeld than multiplying rights was.⁴⁵

4 From Hart to Kant: The Classical Will Theory (Partly) Redeemed

Will Theory right-holders are small-scale sovereigns. Their realms amount to what I've called 'discretionary domains'. We can usefully think of every particular owed duty as constituting a mini- or subdomain for the person to whom it's owed. And we can thus construe that person's entire domain as composed of the entire set of duties owed by others to him or her, *minus* the duties he or she owes to others.

Those sets of duties are, typically, mixtures of both negative (forbearance) and positive (performance) ones. A domain's owner, in being the controller of those duties, is thereby endowed with a portion of *action-space*. He or she alone is entitled to decide whether certain changes (in how that portion of the world is) should, need not, or must not be brought about. Some of these changes are ones resultant from the owner's own unimpeded actions, while others are ones effected by the conduct of other persons. And where the conduct of those others has proved non-compliant with that owner's decisions, he or she alone is entitled to decide whether they should or need not effect alternative remedial changes. In short, and since performances and forbearances are inter-definable, owners decide what conduct must or need not occur within their domains. The total set of domains is, as Simmonds puts it, 'a realm of nonconflicting entitlements, where action [can] be divided into the permissible exercise of entitlements and the impermissible interference with such exercise'.⁴⁶ And the normative system constituting this realm is thereby one assigning portions of freedom to each domain-owner.

---

⁴⁵ Thus Kramer, 'Rights Without Trimmings', 76ff above, quite justifiably condemns the use of 'a fundamentally political basis for one's choice of a deontic vocabulary', but quite unjustifiably indicts Will Theorists—rather than their critics—for so doing; see the discussion of 'evaluative stance' in section 5 below.

⁴⁶ Simmonds, 'Rights at the Cutting Edge', 182 above. Impermissible interferences are thus of two broad types: (i) X's self-chosen non-performance of X's duty to Y to do A; (ii) Z's self-chosen performance of B which prevents X's performance of X's duty to Y to do A. In the latter case, X's remedial claim against Z includes redress for whatever remedial duty X owes to Y.

An obvious worry, then, is the possibility that these domains may *intersect*: that one person's domain may contain elements which are also elements of another's domain. Of course, this needn't be a worry in cases where the action required of a duty-bearer in respect of the former's domain is identical with that required of the same person in respect of the latter's. In this happy circumstance, that duty-bearer can, so to speak, kill two birds with one stone: discharge both duties with one action. It may, however, be more of a worry if the two duties each require *different* actions of that duty-bearer and those two actions, though separately performable, are *jointly unperformable*. Even here, all is not (necessarily) lost. For it's quite possible that the two domain-owners are of one mind on the matter of which of these two owed actions is to be preferred. They need not be adversaries. In which case, one of them will exercise the appropriate waiver and extinguish one of the conflicting duties. And even where such consensus is absent, it's still not necessarily the case that all is lost. For then, although the duty-bearer is perforce bound to breach one of these duties in discharging the other, he or she may be perfectly able to remedy that breach through provision of redress. All these contingent possibilities—identical compliances, right-holders' consensus, capacity to redress—and perhaps others as well, can serve to diminish the actual impact of the otherwise very serious problem posed by the idea of intersecting domains or jointly unperformable duties. So why worry?

The answer to this question obviously lies in the sentence preceding it. Solutions to conflicts of duty, and hence of rights, may be able to be generated from *within* the set of Hohfeldian relations structuring a set of domains but, equally, they may not. Let's call any that can be so generated *internal solutions*. The availability of internal solutions is entirely dependent on the content of owed duties, on right-holders' wishes, on the extent of duty-breachers' resources and on other such contingencies. Hence that availability falls some way short of being a guaranteed certainty. And in cases where an internal solution is not available, only an external one will do the job.

What is an *external solution*? Such solutions consist in postulating sets of Hohfeldian relations *additional* to the ones implied by that set of domains. More precisely, they postulate a third party who is outside the set of domain-owners and who is possessed of powers to *alter* the Hohfeldian positions of any domain-owners whose rights are in conflict. In *An Essay on Rights* I christened this person 'Adjudicator'.

Adjudicator's problem—but not only Adjudicator's problem—is that of resolving conflicts where no internal solution is available. Hart has aptly labelled this problem as 'the Nightmare' and offered the following sketch of its legal form:

> The Nightmare is this. Litigants in law cases consider themselves entitled to have from judges an application of the existing law to their disputes, not to have the law made for them... The Nightmare is that this image of the judge, distinguishing him from the legislator, is an illusion... that judges make the law which they apply to litigants and are not impartial, objective declarers of existing law... [but rather exercise] what Holmes called the 'sovereign prerogative of choice'.[47]

It's thus only slightly hyperbolic to say that, in so far as the resolution supplied by Adjudicator is *not* one inferable exclusively and uniquely from the Hohfeldian relations constituting the set of domains in question, Adjudicator's sovereignty displaces that of (at least one of) those domains' owners. For that resolution modifies or extinguishes at least one of the two conflicting owed duties through the exercise of a waiving power held by Adjudicator.[48] It's Adjudicator's decision, rather than domain-owners' positions—*might* rather than *rights*, so to speak—that normatively determines who gets to do what.

---

[47] Hart, *Essays in Jurisprudence and Philosophy*, (Oxford: Oxford University Press, 1985), 126, 127, 134. The passage comes from his essay 'The Nightmare and the Noble Dream', where the nightmare is associated with some of the doctrines of Legal Realism while the noble dream refers to those of the classical Will Theory. Needless to say, conflicts of duties correlative to *moral* (rather than legal) rights pose even more nightmarish problems, since obvious candidates for a moral Adjudicator are pretty thin on the ground.

[48] cf Carlos E Alchourron and Eugenio Bulygin, 'The Expressive Conception of Norms', in Risto Hilpinen (ed), *New Studies in Deontic Logic*, (Dordrecht: D Reidel, 1981), 115–16: 'If by "normative system" we understand an ordered set of norm-contents, then every modification of the ordering relations modifies *eo ipso* the system itself... [T]here is a widespread idea that derogation (that removes altogether certain norm-contents) is a much more fundamental operation than simple ordering, and that therefore the judge, though he can impose a new ordering or modify the existing one, cannot derogate legislated norm-contents for the same reasons that he cannot promulgate new norms ... But this idea is wrong ... The much debated problem whether judges 'create' law or only apply it, can be settled in favor of the first thesis, at least in the sense that they modify the legal system by imposing orderings on its elements when they have to resolve contradictions, disregarding some of the norm-contents (which amounts to derogating them).'

The essence of the classical version of the Will Theory is a noble attempt to *dispense with external solutions*. It does not, of course, aspire to dispense with Adjudicator. Classical Will Theorists were not, typically, anarchists. Nor were they invariably concerned to deny that state officials, too, can be right-holders. Rather, their aim was to reveal the necessary structural features of any set of rights in which Adjudicator's powers could coherently be confined to purely procedural ones: ones for ascertaining empirical facts which, when taken solely in conjunction with an *already specified* set of domain-constituting relations, would yield fully inferable solutions to all conflicts.[49]

We can speculate about the sorts of motivation that drove these enquiries. Were they noetic ones of achieving intellectual economy and coherence? Or political ones of restraining tyranny and its concomitantly inflated realm of criminal or public law? Or socio-economic ones of making the world safe for capitalism and commercial society? I'll have a bit more to say in this regard when we come to consider whether the Will Theory is, inherently, an historically and culturally situated construct and, hence, one of correspondingly restricted validity. For the moment, the point to be made is simply that the project engaging these classical Will Theorists can be characterized, in a more recent phrase, as one to exhibit the conditions of *rights-compossibility*: conditions under which all apparent conflicts of duty are, upon examination, found to be unreal.[50] To this ambitious end, they and their followers erected marvellously elaborate doctrinal edifices of legal analysis, the general tenor of which is brilliantly conveyed in much of Simmonds' work, including his present essay.

Unfortunately, their remarkable efforts were seriously flawed, and in at least two significant respects. They failed clearly to distinguish the purely conceptual from the substantively moral premises underpinning their intellectual constructs, mistakenly presuming the latter to be simply absent. And they failed to achieve a discriminating Hohfeldian understanding of the fundamental elements of jural

---

[49] Adjudicator's powers would also extend to securing the enforcement of those solutions.

[50] The notion of 'compossibility' is itself due to Leibniz; cf *An Essay on Rights* (n 3 above), 2. It denotes the idea of *joint possibility*: some things (objects, events, concepts) which are each independently possible—which are not self-contradictory, like 'round squares'—may not be jointly possible, ie elements of one and the same possible world.

relations. For what they took to be the pure Kantian formalism informing their analyses was shown to be *tainted*—as indeed it was in the case of Kant himself—by logically independent moral assumptions. And their insufficiently differentiated conception of rights—particularly in respect of claims and liberties—led them into grievous mistakes and inconsistencies in their analytical dissection of particular legal provisions. I'll presently try to isolate the nature and source of that taint in their self-avowed formalism. But first, let's examine the significance of their failure to anticipate Hohfeld.

Simmonds ably demonstrates just how disastrous that failure was for their project. Hohfeld is persuasively cast as a clear-sighted analytical fox whose penetrating forays into the various reasonings of these lumbering doctrinal hedgehogs—and especially those of their judicial followers—wrought irreparable havoc with their heroic attempts to bring forth a cosmos from a chaos. For

[i]f the systematic analysis and exposition of legal doctrine was to be guided by a theory of this type, diverse and fragmentary legal rights would need to be assembled into domains of liberty within which the individual's will was supreme. To the extent that this was possible, the existence of one specific entitlement would imply the existence of a number of others.... [A] right was assumed to amount to a domain of freedom protected by a complex array of permissibilities, powers, and correlative duties: the rationale of such a complex assemblage being the attempt to make the right-holder's will supreme within a certain province of concern.[51]

Since the basic building blocks of the classical Will Theory's great doctrinal edifices were crudely undifferentiated conceptions of rights, those edifices were perfect sitting targets for the fragmentation of legal relations implicit in Hohfeld's analysis, which

had the effect of shattering the law's appearance of system and integration by fragmenting into a diversity of different jural relations the 'rights' which might otherwise have been proffered as focal points for the systematic reconstruction and presentation of the law.[52]

Under the impact of having their pervasive fault-lines thus exposed, the great edifices simply buckled and collapsed. The 'Noble Dream' they embodied lay, apparently, in ruins.

[51] Simmonds, 'Rights at the Cutting Edge', 179 above.
[52] Simmonds, 'Rights at the Cutting Edge', 146 above; see especially his probing discussion of *Quinn v Leathem*, at 169ff above (with which I entirely agree), as well as numerous other passages in his essay.

Interestingly, in a series of passages immediately following the one just quoted, Simmonds offers some reasons for thinking that 'this radical achievement... may have been quite contrary to Hohfeld's own intentions'. For despite his seemingly Legal Realist (ie fox-like) concentration on the cutting edge of law—treating legal rights 'as operating on the level of specific legal remedies, acts, and causes of action'—his conception of jural relations as ones obtaining between pairs of individuals, with its focus on disputes between them, suggests that 'Hohfeld may have been following an older tradition of formalistic legal scholarship'. This *adversarial* focus

might well be seen as a consequence of the formalistic Kantian view that a right is an authorization to use coercion, and that the system of rights demarcates the legitimate bounds between potentially conflicting wills.

If so, Simmonds goes on to comment, 'the result is richly ironic: for it is precisely the centrality given by Hohfeld to the bilateral character of jural relations that leads to his dramatic (and perhaps unintentional) destruction of the Kantian notion of a right'.[53]

I doubt whether the suggested basis for this irony is indeed present. For I think that the unquestionable clarity which Hohfeld's schema brings to our understanding of rights simply has no subversive bearing at all on the possibility of identifying the conditions for rights-compossibility—the underlying project of the classical Will Theory. (I'm driven parenthetically to add that persons who have never thought of themselves as anything other than analytical foxes, myself included, might take some comfort from Simmonds' conjecture that the destruction of that project may have been no part of Hohfeld's intention either!) The purifying impact of Hohfeldian analysis, in this regard, is more appropriately seen as working to supply that project with sounder basic building blocks which have been purged of, *inter alia*, the distinctly *moral* assumptions that the classical theorists, Kant included, additionally wove into their intellectual constructs. Purged of these assumptions, and duly informed by the analytical refinements which the Hohfeldian schema imposes, the project of identifying the conditions for rights-compossibility—of abolishing the need for external solutions to conflicts of duty—remains a live option.

---

[53] Simmonds, 'Rights at the Cutting Edge', 146–8 above. On legal formalism, see Ernest Weinrib, *The Idea of Private Law*, (Cambridge, Mass: Harvard University Press, 1995), 22–55.

The structure of that compossibility basically derives from two kinds of consideration: (i) the conditions required for two or more actions to be jointly performable,[54] and (ii) the normative modal relations exhibited by standard deontic logic.[55] In section 2 above, we saw that having the control over a duty, that Hart says a Will Theory right confers on a person, places that right-holder in a variety of distinct Hohfeldian relations with *others*, as well as with the duty-bearer him- or herself. For in addition to having a claim and a full complement of powers with respect to that duty-bearer, that person is also thereby possessed of certain liberties and immunities with respect to others that he or she would *not* possess as merely the delegated agent of a right-holder.[56] All the relevant conduct of whoever is implicated by his or her occupation of these numerous positions, is waivable or demandable solely at that person's discretion. The salient previously-noted consequence of these positions, and particularly of their thereby-entailed waivable duties

---

[54] An analysis of these conditions is offered in *An Essay on Rights* (n 3 above), ch 2; for a further defence of them, see my 'Freedom, Rights and Equality', *International Journal of Philosophical Studies*, 6 (1998), 128–37.

[55] In particular, that obligatory actions form a subset of permissible actions; cf GE Hughes and MJ Cresswell, *An Introduction to Modal Logic*, (London: Methuen, 1972), 301: '"Whatever is obligatory is permissible" remains a sound principle'; similarly AN Prior, *Formal Logic*, (Oxford: Oxford University Press, 1962), 220ff, and his essay on 'Deontic Logic' in *The Encyclopedia of Philosophy*, (ed) Paul Edwards, (New York: Macmillan, 1967), vol 4, 509–13. This principle is evidently entailed by a basic axiom of deontic logic, sometimes called the 'principle of permission', which states that 'for any act p, either p or $not\text{-}p$ is permissible' or, more simply, 'nothing is both obligatory and forbidden (impermissible)'. Thus, since nothing impermissible is obligatory, if p is obligatory, then p is not impermissible, ie p is permissible. Contrast Simmonds, 'Rights at the Cutting Edge', 184, n 91 above: 'The imposition of a duty does not itself entail the existence of a liberty to perform the duty-act'; also Kramer, 'Rights Without Trimmings', 18 above: 'Sumner errs when he proclaims that "an act is permitted if it is required" and that a...duty to undertake something must entail a liberty to undertake it'. The hypothetical example Kramer offers in support of this contention is one in which a person undertakes a (private- or civil-law) contractual duty to forbear what he has a public- or criminal-law duty to perform, ie a *lack* of liberty to forbear. Kramer's view is that there's no contradiction here. I discuss contradictory duties below. But it's worth pointing out here that the view, that both of these duties can be valid, implies precisely what the 'consent is no defence' maxim effects to deny: namely that private or civil contracts are not constrained or overridden by public- or criminal-law duties. Were this view actually true, we might expect to see more suits, for breaches of contract to commit murder, than we normally do.

[56] As I tried to show in the section 2 discussion of powers as entailing corresponding liberties, and the section 3 discussion of subordinate state officials' positions with respect to criminal-law duties.

and disabilities in others, is the creation of a normatively protected domain of freedom for that person: a domain within which the actions which he or she chooses to occur are both permissible and impermissibly obstructable by others.

In *An Essay on Rights*, I develop an account of the dense and far-flung web of Hohfeldian relations implied by the presence of such rights in two (or more) persons. Alas, even that lengthy account affords no more than a fragmentary and bird's-eye view of the detail implicit in the complex networks thus involved. But its core can be more readily formulated. For it essentially consists in a sequence of arguments to show that *any one person's duty, correlatively entailing a right in another—if it's to be, non-contingently, jointly performable with all other actions permitted or required by a set of such duties—must (non-correlatively) entail the presence of duties in everyone else.*[57]

That's more than a bit of a mouthful. Put more digestibly, the idea is that every right is something closely resembling what's usually described as a right *in rem*: a claim against everyone. It's not strictly identical to a right *in rem*, because all the duties entailed by a right *in rem* are identical to one another and correlative to it—that is, are owed directly to the right-holder by everyone. My thought is that, if a duty owed directly to a right-holder is one which is impermissibly obstructable by anyone—is, so to speak, guaranteed performability—this must be because all of them owe duties of non-interference with it to that duty's bearer or to someone else.[58] Hence that duty, or the right correlatively entailed by it, further entails those other duties. And each of them, in turn, must entail further (and likewise globally distributed) duties of non-interference, so that they too are guaranteed performability. And so forth. The concept that literally and non-metaphorically

---

[57] Why include, among the actions that must be jointly performable with dutiful ones, those actions that are permitted but not required? Simply because such actions can be ones that prevent obligatory ones from occurring: they can render impossible—and hence non-obligatory (on the principle that 'ought implies can')—the performance of actions required to discharge first-order duties or ones to remedy their breach. Accordingly, a set of rules that both *requires* the doing of *A*, and *allows* the doing of *B* which renders *A*'s being done impossible, is a set of rules that contradictorily entails both the impermissibility and the permissibility of *A*'s not being done.

[58] Epicycles, of course, can always be added. Thus all other persons' duties not to interfere in certain ways with the taxi-driving duty you owe me, to take me to the airport, may be ones owed not to you but, instead, to the taxi company which owns the car.

captures this structure, of serially entailed sets of duties and correlating rights, is that of *property rights*. Conceiving persons' respective domains as sets of discretely partitioned property rights gives us sets of duties which are guaranteed joint performability. And it also helpfully prevents that series from regressing to infinity!

This is not to say that the ordinary denomination of the contents of an owed duty—the description of the action discharging it—must include reference to property rights. That would be incredibly cumbersome and, in most instances, entirely superfluous. What it suggests, rather, is that in the event of apparently conflicting duties, reference to underlying property rights will suffice to indicate— without appeal to external normative considerations adduced by Adjudicator—which duty is not a valid one.[59] Where such reference is inconclusive, there's good reason to suspect that property rights are not discretely partitioned. And where they're *not*—where, so to speak, something lies in two men's land and, hence, in no man's land—the person in control can be none other than Adjudicator him- or herself.

Now as far as I can see, there's nothing in this sort of complex construction that Hohfeld would take exception to. Unless he were to disagree with several of the key arguments developed from Hartian premises in section 2 above, it's pretty hard to imagine where he would want to get off the train that runs from there to here. No doubt his own propensity for acutely close dissection of particular cases' juridical details would have induced a commendable caution in contemplating the purchase of the broad-brush picture I've just painted. The devil, we can all agree, is indeed in the detail. And my picture signally fails to enumerate, at his preferred level of fine-grained analysis, all the numerous sets of relations that only one right—let alone several—is sufficient to imply. Nor, on the other hand, does it possess the fully, if also unsoundly, articulated systemic charms of a classical Will Theory edifice. Yet it seems fair to suppose that Kant would have recognized and concurred with a good deal of what's going on here.[60] And if Simmonds' conjecture is correct, so might Hohfeld.

---

[59] Adjudicator may have to supply considerations which Hart oftened labelled as *penumbral*, such as whether a skate-board is a vehicle. But such considerations, though they generate normative consequences, do so only in conjunction with already given norms and are not themselves presumed to be normative.

[60] Thus Kant: 'In geometry, there are two uses of the term "right". On the one hand, we may speak of a right [straight] line ... or on the other hand, we may speak of

Space simply doesn't permit the reproduction here of the full set of arguments advanced in support of that picture, deplorably incomplete as they no doubt are.[61] So instead, and relying primarily on Simmonds' present exposition of some of them, I'll focus on one issue which seems to me to lie at the heart of many of the well-aimed objections which both he and Kramer level at those arguments. I can't pretend that all his other objections turn on this issue, but which ones do is reasonably apparent. At any rate, he seems to agree that much of the case, against the plausibility of at least *some* version of compossibility, avowedly does. That issue, simply put, is whether conflicting duties (and hence, rights) entail a *contradiction*.[62]

Now one not unrespectable response to that question might be another one: *Who cares?* Anyone can see that duty-conflicts are a bad thing and best avoided. And if they do happen, it's obviously better if one of the duties involved can be shown not to be a valid duty after all. I'm not a Hohfeld scholar, so I have no idea what his own attitude to duty-conflicts actually was. But I can't imagine that he would have been especially fond of them. And more than that, I think that, like most people, he would have regarded normative systems that generate duty-conflicts as being, in some (not uncontroversial) sense, deficient. Contradictions, it's generally agreed, are fatal for any set of propositions. But duty-conflicts are bad enough. So who cares if the latter also entail the former?

But perhaps I presume too much here. For perhaps Hohfeld would agree with many of those who have reflected deeply and

---

a right angle ... The unique feature of a right line is that only one such line can be drawn between two points; similarly, where two lines intersect or join each other, there can be only one right angle. The perpendicular forming the right angle may not incline more to one side than to the other, and it divides the space on both sides equally. This bears an analogy to jurisprudence, which wants to know exactly (with mathematical precision) what the property of everyone is'; *The Metaphysical Elements of Justice,* translated by John Ladd, (Indianapolis: Bobbs-Merrill, 1965), 38–9.

[61] Interested readers will, I fear, need to consult at least chs 2, 3, and probably also 6, of *An Essay on Rights,* to collect the full set of supporting arguments.

[62] Thus Simmonds, 'Rights at the Cutting Edge', 181 above says: 'The key step in [Steiner's] argument ... is the claim that conflicts between rights generate logical contradictions'. Simmonds interprets this claim to be one covering both inter-duty conflicts and conflicts between duties and liberties. Of course, and as Hohfeld insists, liberties are not rights and conflicts between liberties pose no problems of contradiction. Where *An Essay on Rights* is insufficiently clear is in distinguishing the sort of contradiction involved in a duty–liberty conflict (see n 57 above) from that which is present in an inter-duty conflict and which I now address.

rigorously on this problem, and would instead counsel resignation to the non-univocality of any conceivable normative system. Duty-conflicts, they might and do say, are not only endemic in the human condition but also a *logically* ineliminable feature of it. The fact that, despite their considerable differences, Aquinas, Kant, Bentham, and most deontic logicians have all thought otherwise, so it has been argued, only shows the limits of their own philosophies.

Appropriately enough, I suppose, I find myself somewhat torn between these two views, whose significance obviously extends well beyond the confines of legal philosophy and far into the realms of moral epistemology and philosophical logic. The literature supporting and attacking each of those views is already vast, rapidly proliferating and, in many instances, of greater formal technicality than I'm simply competent to assess.[63] So it would be laughably naïve to suppose that anything said in the present debate could be conclusive of the profound underlying issue involved. Yet that issue must somehow be addressed here. And the most appropriate way of doing so, it seems to me, is to examine the basis of Simmonds' own argument for believing that duty-conflicts don't entail contradictions.

A *personal* duty-conflict arises when the action rendered obligatory by one duty is forbidden by another duty. In these circumstances, the bearer of those two duties cannot avoid breaching one of them. Since an action's being forbidden entails its being impermissible, and since an action's being obligatory entails its being

---

[63] What amounts to no more than a woefully incomplete sample of the relevant leading work here includes the following items, listed in no particular order: Georg Henrik von Wright, *Norm and Action* (n 15 above), and *An Essay in Deontic Logic and the General Theory of Action*, (Amsterdam: North-Holland, 1972); Risto Hilpinen (ed), *Deontic Logic: Introductory and Systematic Readings*, (Dordrecht: D Reidel, 1971), and *New Studies in Deontic Logic* (n 48 above); Porn, *The Logic of Power* (n 20 above); Nicholas Rescher (ed), *The Logic of Decision and Action*, (Pittsburgh: University of Pittsburgh Press, 1967); Stephan Korner (ed) *Practical Reason*, (Oxford: Blackwell, 1974); Joseph Raz, *Practical Reason and Norms*, (Princeton: Princeton University Press, 1990), and (ed) *Practical Reasoning*, (Oxford: Oxford University Press, 1978); Robert Nozick, 'Moral Complications and Moral Structures', *Natural Law Forum*, 13 (1968), 1–50; Isaac Levi, *Hard Choices*, (Cambridge: Cambridge University Press, 1986); Christopher Gowans (ed), *Moral Dilemmas*, (New York: Oxford University Press, 1987); Walter Sinnott-Armstrong, *Moral Dilemmas*, (Oxford: Blackwell, 1988); Michael Stocker, *Plural and Conflicting Values*, (Oxford: Oxford University Press, 1990); HE Mason (ed), *Moral Dilemmas and Moral Theory*, (New York: Oxford University Press, 1996); Harry Gensler, *Formal Ethics*, (London: Routledge, 1996).

permissible,[64] and since it's contradictory to say that one and the same action is both permissible and impermissible, such a conflict is presumed to entail a contradiction. In Hohfeldian terms, the bearer of these two duties both has and lacks a liberty to comply with each of them.

Simmonds disputes this, claiming that 'it is far from clear that there is a logical contradiction':

> A may have a duty both to do X and not do X, and the assertion of such conflicting duties is not contradictory. The contradiction of 'A has a duty to do X' is *not* 'A has a duty not to do X' but 'It is not the case that A has a duty to do X'. Whether A's duty not to do X entails the absence of a duty to do X is precisely the point at issue, and would require further theoretical argument of a kind that is not provided by Steiner.[65]

One thing that Simmonds is quite correct in suggesting here is that *An Essay on Rights* provides no argument directly showing that a contradiction is indeed present.[66] Let's now remedy that omission.

What's certainly true is that 'It is not the case that A has a duty to do X' doesn't entail 'A has a duty not to do X'. For the former is perfectly consistent, whereas the latter is not, with the claim that 'A (also) has no duty not to do X' (ie that A's doing X is indifferent). What they both *do* entail, however, is that 'A's not doing X is *permissible*'. Whereas what 'A has a duty to do X' entails is that 'A's not doing X is *impermissible*'. And this is a plain contradiction.

It's then a relatively simple matter to extend this reasoning to *interpersonal* cases where the two duties which conflict are each borne by a *different* person. For as I argued above, a well-partitioned set of domains is such that everyone bears duties of non-interference with the performance of everyone else's duties. Consequently, any such interpersonal duty-conflict entails that each of those duty-bearers is also the subject of a *personal* duty-conflict. And these, as we've just seen, entail contradictions.

Perhaps, though, and in the light of what was previously said concerning significant philosophical dispute about duty-conflicts

---

[64] See n 55 above.
[65] Simmonds, 'Rights at the Cutting Edge', 185 above; cf Kramer, 'Rights Without Trimmings', 18–9 above.
[66] It does, however—in ch 4 on 'Moral Reasoning', especially at 111–25—offer an extended account of (i) the conditions necessary for a moral code to satisfy the standard rational choice theory axiom of *completeness*, and (ii) the reasons why moral codes that generate duty-conflicts are ones that fail to satisfy those conditions.

entailing contradictions, we should give some consideration to Simmonds' elaboration of his reasons for denying that there is indeed a contradiction here. For these, he refers us to his earlier article where he appeals to an argument famously developed by Bernard Williams to sustain the possibility of irresolvable moral dilemmas.[67] Williams' argument is thus one for the possible unavailability of *internal solutions*. The thrust of that argument is that many duty-conflicts are such that, no matter which duty we ultimately breach, we have good reasons to believe it to be of equal validity to the one we discharge. The principal evidence adduced for the presence of such reasons consists in the facts (a) that we experience feelings of regret for that breach—feelings which, Williams strongly argues, are not irrational—and (b) that we feel it appropriate to compensate those who may have been harmed by that breach.

Obviously, I cannot hope to do justice to this argument here nor, therefore, to the significance of Simmonds' reliance upon it. Nor, of course, should I do them an injustice. So perhaps all that can sensibly be done is simply to note that Williams' argument, from what have come to be called *moral residues,* has itself proved to be a major player in the aforementioned philosophical dispute and has been seriously challenged, as well as defended, in much of the literature I previously listed. Beyond that, it's neither unfair nor irrelevant to note that the view that there can be conflicts between equally valid duties—that a set of norms need not be univocal—evidently places severe restrictions on the analytic powers of deontic logic.[68] And if Kramer's characterization of Hohfeld's formalistic concerns is correct, which I believe it is, he might not have found this prospect altogether pleasing.

We're left with one outstanding issue to be discussed in the present section. This concerns the contingent *moral assumptions* woven into the fabric of the classical Will Theory's self-avowed

---

[67] cf Simmonds, 'The Analytical Foundations of Justice' (n 5 above), 336. Williams' argument is presented in 'Ethical Consistency', reprinted in his *Problems of the Self*, (Cambridge: Cambridge University Press, 1973).

[68] Thus Hilpenen, *Deontic Logic: Introductory and Systematic Readings* (n 63 above), 16, says: 'The principles of deontic logic determine conditions of consistency for normative systems. By a "normative system" we understand here simply any set of deontic sentences closed under deduction. When is a set of deontic sentences consistent? It seems natural to require that at least the following "minimal condition" should be satisfied: ... [that] all obligations in this set can be simultaneously fulfilled, and that [an act] is permitted only if it can be realized without violating any of one's obligations.'

Kantian conceptual formalism. It is these, I suggest, that form the basis of the belief that the Will Theory, *per se*, is of historically or culturally restricted validity and is able to model or analyse jural relations only in certain types of society which Simmonds characterizes as 'modern political communities'.

Now it's worth pointing out that we've already had some evidence that this belief is mistaken. This emerged in our earlier discussion of criminal law where Kenny and Paton testified that, 'in the first stages of national development' and 'even in the days of feudalism', there is no great conceptual divide between public and private law and 'indeed public law might almost be regarded as "a mere appendix" to the law of real property'. That is to say, law in these distinctly un-modern communities sustained what are recognizably Will Theory rights.[69]

How then did Hegel, Marx, Schopenhauer, Ihering and innumerable others come to think otherwise? Why did they claim that Kantian legal philosophy is an empty formalism devoid of any analytical power unless and until substantive moral (or ideological) premises are woven into it? That such premises *were* woven into it, in the construction of the great doctrinal edifices of classical Will Theory, is convincingly demonstrated in Simmonds' essay. So why did Savigny and his followers believe this not to be the case?

To find the underlying answers to these questions, we're probably well advised to go directly to the work of the *master weaver* himself: namely, *Kant*. And the problem here arises, as Hohfeld might characteristically predict, from a failure to make a significant distinction. In this case, it's Kant's failure clearly to differentiate his conception of *rights* from his conception of *justice*. More specifically, he fails to distinguish between a set of rights as a set of domains of personal freedom, and a set of *just* rights as a set of domains of *equal* personal freedom. Jural relations in, say, feudal societies satisfy the former description but not the latter.

In general, the view that such pre-modern societies exhibited simply *no* such domains[70]—as opposed to (highly) unequal ones—is yet another of those many Enlightenment prejudices that still resonate in us today, and it's one that cannot survive Hohfeldian analysis. Moreover it's a prejudice that plainly lends crucial support

---

[69] The same may also be inferable from Simmonds' discussion of jural relations in a society containing a class of helots; cf 'Rights at the Cutting Edge', 165–7 above.

[70] Republican Rome was sometimes deemed an exception.

to the potent belief that, in the presence of *any* set of such domains, all right-holders are *ipso facto* equally free. It's precisely this belief, as we know, that drove Marx and so many subsequent others to distraction. And thus it's plausible to imagine that it was this belief that led them to propose various (unsound) distinctions between *formal* or abstract rights and freedom on the one hand, and *real* rights and freedom on the other.

As one might expect of Kant, there are some very good reasons for his failure to make that critical distinction. I'll discuss these presently. In order to do that, we need first to take a look at some aspects of Kant's characterization of 'a right'. These, I noted above, are correctly reported by Simmonds as including 'an authorization to use coercion, and [hence] the system of rights demarcates the legitimate bounds between potentially conflicting wills'. Now one thing that's noteworthy about this formulation, and vividly illustrates the absence of that aforesaid distinction, is the fact that it's impossible to locate any passage in Kant's text where either this formulation or any of its cognates appears *without* being conjoined to the phrase 'in accordance with a universal law'. The latter, of course, alerts us to the presence of a Kantian moral criterion.

The nearest we get to a focus on the purely conceptual features of 'a right' seems to me to come in the following:

> The concept of Right, insofar as it is related to an obligation corresponding to it (i.e. the moral concept of Right), has to do, *first*, only with the external and indeed practical relation of one person to another, insofar as their actions, as facts, can have (direct or indirect) influence on each other. But, *second*, it does not signify the relation of one's choice to the mere wish (hence also to the mere need) of the other, as in actions of beneficence or callousness, but only a relation to the other's *choice*. *Third*, in this reciprocal relation of choice no account at all is taken of the *matter* of choice, that is, of the end each has in mind with the object he wants... All that is in question is the *form* in the relation of choice on the part of both, insofar as choice is regarded merely as *free*, and whether the action of one can be united with the freedom of the other in accordance with a universal law. Right is therefore the sum of the conditions under which the choice of one can be united with the choice of another in accordance with a universal law of freedom.[71]

[71] Kant, *The Metaphysics of Morals*, translated by Mary Gregor, (Cambridge: Cambridge University Press, 1991), 56. Neither of the two recent English translators of Kant's text has failed to remark on the considerable difficulty posed there, as in other German legal writings, by the non-univocality of the term *recht*. Distinctions

Kant's own purpose, in this far from pellucid passage, is less to identify conceptual features of rights than to differentiate two types of moral duty: correlative and non-correlative. The former, in bearing on only the form of the relationship between persons' wills, differ from the latter which concern the content of person's wills—their 'maxims', ends, or intentions in acting—and which are thus matters of virtue. Correlative duties, by contrast, govern the interpersonal distribution of what Kant calls *external freedom*. And what they do is normatively to constrain their bearers' actions (whatever the ends motivating those actions) to ones consistent with a particular distribution of that freedom. Actions that encroach on other persons' rightful shares of external freedom violate their moral rights.

The rule ostensibly determining each person's rightful share of external freedom is Kant's *Universal Principle of Justice* (or *Right*) (UPJ):

Any action is *right [just]* if it can coexist with everyone's freedom in accordance with a universal law, or if on its maxim the freedom of choice of each can coexist with everyone's freedom in accordance with a universal law.[72]

But 'determining' is far too strong, since this principle is in need of at least some interpretation if it's to serve as a test of an action's justness.

We begin to edge a bit closer to this in the succeeding passages where Kant forges the standard Will Theory link between being a right-holder and possessing powers of enforcement, that is, an authorization to use reciprocal coercion. Coercion, *per se*, is a hindrance to a person's freedom. But *reciprocal* coercion, in counteracting such a hindrance, is consistent with that freedom. This much is a conceptual truth. If you coerce me, you disrupt the prevailing distribution of freedom. And if I then reciprocate your coercion, I in some sense restore that distribution.

---

between its noun and adjectival meanings, between 'objective' and 'subjective' right, and between law in general and right principles of law (or simply 'justice'), are not invariably captured by such devices as the use of upper-case lettering (Recht) and pluralisation. Cf John Ladd's introduction, *The Metaphysical Elements of Justice* (n 60 above), pp. xvii–xviii; similarly, Mary Gregor's note on the text, pp. x–xii, where she adds that 'Kant is to some extent forging his own vocabulary'. In Ladd's translation (34), the word 'justice' is substituted for each use of 'right' in the above quoted passage.

[72] Kant, *The Metaphysical Elements of Justice* (n 60 above), 35.

Obviously, however, this still affords no clear justice-test of my action. For although it indicates that reciprocal coercion is an entailed aspect of rights, it tells us nothing about whether that disrupted and thereby restored distribution of freedom is itself one 'in accordance with a universal law', ie is just. This is what prompts the Hegelian charge of 'empty formalism'. For if it's not a just distribution in the first place, then my reciprocation may well be unjust. As in epicyclical *vendettas*, its being reciprocal of your coercion is necessary but insufficient to make it just. What would make it sufficient?

Kant is evidently presupposing a *distributive baseline* here: a set of rights or domains of freedom that operates as the criterion for distinguishing those coercions which are reciprocal from their counterparts which aren't. When we're faced with a continuous series of exchanged coercions, this set tells us who started it. That this set is one assigning everyone freedom in accordance with a universal law goes, however, only a minimal distance toward specifying that baseline. Some further mileage is supplied by Kant's explication of his otherwise virtually tautologous claim that the right to freedom is the only original or innate right that persons hold. It is said to entail

innate *equality*, that is, independence from being bound by others to more than one can in turn bind them; hence a man's quality of being *his own master*.[73]

This right to freedom thus vests everyone with what is now often called the right of *self-ownership*. It's this right that finds expression in various more familiar types of negative right often enshrined in constitutional bills of rights. And it's this right that is exercised in the creation of all contractually derived rights which, in Kant's legal philosophy, include virtually all other valid rights.

Virtually all, because that original or innate right to freedom can be shown to vest each person with another right which is also logically required for generating a set of discretionary domains but which is, at most, only implicitly found in Kant's text. For as we know from Locke and more recently from Nozick, neither the negative rights implied by self-ownership nor the contractual rights derived from its exercise are, in themselves, normatively sufficient to

---

[73] Kant, *The Metaphysics of Morals* (n 71 above), 63.

yield rights to any *extrapersonal things* whatsoever: they cannot generate a demarcated division of action-space.[74] In Kant, this additionally-required right is one that can be inferred from his concept of an 'original community of land (*communio fundi originaria*)' which he describes as an *a priori* idea of practical reason. The details of his often tortuous discussion here, of how persons (and thence nations) can initially acquire several titles to portions of what amount to the fundamental elements of action-space, need not concern us. Nor, it has to be said, does Kant himself draw the requisite conclusions about the underlying personal entitlements thereby presupposed. Instead, he's content to construe those several titles as somehow being the products of ahistorical contractual undertakings given by something denoted as humanity's General Will.[75] The upshot is that, for him and for his classical Will Theory followers, the right of self-ownership and its derivatives appear to exhaust the contents of the aforesaid distributive baseline. And it's in their so doing that they expose themselves to the (misleading) charge of sustaining only a formal, and not a real, equality of rights and freedom.

Be that as it may, once we have a distributive baseline, we're equipped to apply the requisite distinction between reciprocal and non-reciprocal coercions to actual cases. And that being so, the charge that Kant's theory is an *empty* formalism is quite misplaced. Simmonds cites Schopenhauer's claim that the theory tries

> to allow the concept of right to exist by itself pure and *a priori*. ... With Kant, therefore, the concept of law or right hovers between heaven and earth, and has no ground on which it can set its foot.[76]

---

[74] cf n 60 above.

[75] cf Kant, *The Metaphysics of Morals* (n 71 above), 71–4; see my 'Kant, Property and the General Will', in Robert Wokler (ed), *The Enlightenment and Modernity*, (London: Macmillan, forthcoming). In *An Essay on Rights*, chs 3(D), 6(C,D), 7, 8, I offer an account of the other kind of right thereby entailed. And I try to show that the combination of these entitlements with everyone's right of self-ownership is sufficient to generate a quite determinate conception of distributive justice, without recourse to any additional moral principles. Briefly described, that conception is one embracing the conjunction of a *laissez-faire* order with egalitarian (global) redistribution of all land/natural resource values. One possible instantiation of the sort of globally equal entitlement sustained by the latter is what's currently called an *unconditional basic income*—though probably an *unconditional basic initial endowment*, being less paternalistic, would be a more Kantian or liberal instantiation of it. For an extended account of one justice-based argument for unconditional basic income, see Philippe Van Parijs, *Real Freedom for All*, (Oxford: Oxford University Press, 1995).

[76] Simmonds, 'Rights at the Cutting Edge', 136 above.

This is mistaken. And the clearest indication of its being mistaken is the fact that the jural relations of feudal and other pre-modern societies clearly exhibit Will Theory rights. What they *don't* exhibit are universally distributed rights of self-ownership. For it's centrally distinctive of them that not all persons are, in Kant's phrase, *their own masters*. The thing that each such person lacks is precisely 'independence from being bound by others to more than [he or she] can in turn bind them'.

Yet despite Kant's account of just rights being thus non-empty, he and those who followed him also believed it to be necessarily true. That is, the claim that the very concept of a right implies that rights possess the aforesaid content and distribution is one of those propositions which Kant deemed to be *synthetic a priori* truths. Why did he think this? The explanation is worth exploring, not least because it also sheds some light on the grounds for the significant and previously discussed view that rights are *peremptory*.

This perceived necessary truth is essentially imputable to the presumed status of one of Kant's formulations of the Categorical Imperative. Its second major formulation (CI_2) famously states:

Act so that you treat humanity, whether in your own person or in that of another, always as an end and never as a means only.[77]

Kant scholars have plausibly viewed UPJ as grounded in CI_2.[78] Certainly there's a strong connection, perhaps even extensional equivalence, between these two injunctions.[79] The latter is generally interpreted as requiring everyone to respect the agency of others by performing no action that subordinates their sets of purposes to his or her own. Warner Wick argues that:

to treat someone as a mere means is to regard his purposes as if they did not count—as if he were just an object that entered one's calculations as an instrument to be used or an obstacle to be pushed aside.[80]

---

[77] Kant, *Foundations of the Metaphysics of Morals*, translated by Lewis White Beck, (Indianapolis: Bobbs-Merrill, 1959), 47.

[78] cf Mary Gregor, *Laws of Freedom*, (Oxford: Blackwell, 1963), 39ff; Bruce Aune, *Kant's Theory of Morals*, (Princeton: Princeton University Press, 1979), 137.

[79] For an argument supporting something like their extensional equivalence, see my 'Persons of Lesser Value: Moral Argument and the "Final Solution"', *Journal of Applied Philosophy*, 12 (1995), 129–141, esp 138–9.

[80] Kant, *The Metaphysical Principles of Virtue*, (Indianapolis: Bobbs-Merrill, 1964), Wick's introduction, p. xix.

Since one's freedom is a necessary condition of one's pursuing any purposes at all, actions that diminish one's freedom to less than that enjoyed by their perpetrators are pretty strong candidates for being described as actions subordinating one's purposes to theirs. Justice or equal freedom is thus a necessary condition, perhaps also sufficient, for the non-subordination of anyone's set of purposes to those of others. So given this close affinity between UPJ and CI_2, as well as the criterial role played by the Categorical Imperative in the general Kantian account of moral permissibility, it might seem quite correct to claim that an action's injustice is a sufficient condition of its moral impermissibility. And this claim entails that rights and their correlative duties are morally peremptory with respect to all other moral duties.

But that claim is incorrect. The view that it *is* correct is based on the belief that CI_2 is an implication of, or equivalent to, the first formulation of the Categorical Imperative (CI_1) which even more famously states:

Act only according to that maxim by which you can at the same time will that it should become a universal law.[81]

CI_1 *is* criterial for moral permissibility. It expresses the formal condition of universalizability and declares that an action's moral permissibility depends on one's willingness to accept that anyone may pursue maxims (intentions, purposes) of the sort informing that action. So CI_1-permissibility and moral permissibility are identical. CI_1 is, so to speak, the definition of a morally permissible act and, as such, expresses a necessary truth.

Now the test of whether CI_2 is implied by or equivalent to CI_1, and shares its necessary truth, consists in seeing if there are actions that conform to one of them but violate the other. And very clearly, there are. If I force you to work for a deserving charity or steal your money on its behalf or, indeed, paternalistically force you to do something that's in your own best interest, I may be perfectly happy to universalize my benevolent intention in so doing. But that willingness in no way implies that my action does *not* reduce your freedom and

---

[81] Kant, *Foundations of the Metaphysics of Morals* (n 77 above), 39. Onora O'Neill, *Constructions of Reason*, (Cambridge: Cambridge University Press, 1989, ch 7, esp 141–4, offers a close discussion of the equivalence claim, noting that Kant himself sees such equivalence as residing in the fact that CI_1 gives the 'form', and CI_2 the 'matter', of maxims of duty.

subordinate your purposes to mine.[82] Conversely, I may malevolently refuse to stake you in a poker game. But the fact that I'm unwilling to universalize this intention to inconvenience you—I might stake others or wish them to stake me—in no way implies that I reduce your freedom or subordinate your purposes to mine.

The reason why an action can conform to one of the Categorical Imperative's formulations and not the other isn't hard to find. CI_1-conformity depends on that intensionally-described action's relation to our substantive moral rules ('universal laws'). But its conformity to CI_2 and to Kant's UPJ doesn't require us to refer that action or its intention to those rules. CI_2 simply *is* such a rule and one that directly prohibits any action in which other persons figure purely instrumentally, whatever our intention in performing that action may be. And the same is true of UPJ:

> For anyone can still be free, even though I am quite indifferent to his freedom or even though I might in my heart wish to infringe on his freedom, as long as I do not through an external action violate his freedom.[83]

The straightforward interpretation of this, as Jeffrie Murphy observes, is that:

> Kant is not telling us merely to plan to leave others' freedom secure; he is telling us to leave it secure *in fact*. Whether or not an act of mine would be compatible with a like liberty for others is something capable of an objective determination and is not a function solely of my intentions.[84]

Since actions can be morally permissible but unjust, or morally impermissible but just, it's simply untrue that an action's being a right-violation is a sufficient condition of its moral impermissibility. If it *were* such a sufficient condition then rights would necessarily be peremptory, since performance of any other moral duty would thereby be enforceably forbidden in all cases where it entailed the breach of a correlative duty.

Accordingly the view that rights *are* peremptory—that their violation is a sufficient condition of moral impermissibility—and that they may thus be enforced even against otherwise morally dutiful actions, itself presupposes a *moral commitment* to UPJ

---

[82] That this is true even of my paternalistic forcings is due to the fact that they imply *my* gainsaying *your* lower prioritization of your interests.

[83] Kant, *The Metaphysical Elements of Justice* (n 60 above), 35.

[84] Jeffrie Murphy, *Kant: The Philosophy of Right*, (London: Macmillan, 1970), 104.

and/or CI_2 themselves. Whereas CI_1 expresses a necessary truth about moral permissibility in general, UPJ expresses a necessary truth only about the content and distribution of *intrinsically valued* moral rights. It expresses no necessary truth about the moral impermissibility of actions violating moral rights as such. And, indeed, there's no conceptual reason why there can't be moral theories that at once embrace CI_1 and eschew anything resembling CI_2 and UPJ: that is, theories which either deny the existence of moral rights altogether or treat their contents as entirely (instrumentally) contingent upon the demands of other moral values.[85]

The classical Will Theory, then, stands only partly redeemed. Its conception of sets of rights, as sets of compossible discretionary domains, proves entirely consistent with Hohfeldian analysis and is arguably its natural extension, albeit one unsoundly articulated by Savigny and his non-Hohfeldian followers. But the classical Will Theorists were plainly mistaken in their belief that these articulations, in being informed by Kantian formalism, thereby reflect only necessary truths and are devoid of contingent moral assumptions.

Unlike the Will Theory *per se*, the classical Will Theory is indeed an historically or culturally situated account of rights, and for two reasons. First, and Kant notwithstanding, justice is simply not a conceptually necessary part of morality nor of legality. And lest we overlook that fact, we have the moral and legal codes of pre-modern societies, *inter multa alia*, to remind us of it. Second, Kant's account of justice, in treating self-ownership as the *sole* constituent of its required distributive baseline, thereby underwrites a form of commercial society that is unconstrained by the universal distributive entitlements implicit, but unexplored, in his discussion of original rights to extra-personal things. Regardless of what the classical Will Theorists may have thought, the jural relations of a *laissez-faire* order cannot be the whole story of Kant*ian* justice.

5 Some Real Problems with the Interest Theory

There are several versions of the Interest Theory. The proponents of some of them will be able to take little comfort from numerous

---

[85] See, for example, RM Hare, *Moral Thinking*, (Oxford: Oxford University Press, 1981).

arguments advanced in Matthew Kramer's essay above, where much of his critical fire is directed at those versions themselves. I agree with many of those criticisms and find that even those which are unconvincing clearly demand a response. Fortunately, it's no part of my brief here to defend Interest Theorists against one another's attacks: limitations of both space and supererogatory inclination suffice to preclude that. Instead, I'll focus on what I see as problems remaining for the Interest Theory in general, as well as problems for Kramer's particular version of it. Several of these were indicated in passing during the course of my previous discussion of the Will Theory's alleged defects. That said, five (somewhat interrelated) problems seem to warrant more extended exploration.

A difficulty with which the Interest Theory has been perennially taxed is that posed by the position of *third-party beneficiaries* of contracts. Here I should immediately acknowledge that Kramer is absolutely correct in his demonstration that much of the criticism (including my own) previously levelled at the theory in this connection is simply question-begging and implicitly appeals to Will Theory assumptions.[86] Nevertheless, I think the Interest Theory remains vulnerable on this topic. What's the problem here?

Suppose you and I conclude a contract which imposes a duty on you to make a payment to my brother: he is the third-party beneficiary of our agreement. According to the Will Theory, I am the only right-holder involved in this arrangement. I can demand your compliance or, alternatively, waive it and thereby extinguish your duty. (I may also be construable as benefiting from your compliance, but that, for the Will Theory, is simply irrelevant.) According to the Interest Theory, however, not only am I definitely a beneficiary[87] but also my brother, as another beneficiary, is also a rightholder in respect of your duty. True, he has no control over that duty. But that is irrelevant in determining his right-holder status, so far as the Interest Theory is concerned.

One apparent difficulty raised by this view is the danger of a proliferation of right-holders. For if my brother proposes to use that payment to purchase something, then it looks like his vendor is a *fourth-party* beneficiary of my contract with you. And if that vendor will, in turn, pay to someone else the funds paid to her by

---

[86] cf Kramer, 'Rights Without Trimmings', 66–8 above.

[87] By virtue of the theory's ascription to me of an important interest in having my discretionary choices implemented.

my brother, then our contract seems to sustain the possibility of perhaps an indefinitely long series of beneficiaries, all of whom must therefore be deemed Interest Theory right-holders in respect of the contractual payment duty you owe me. My right against you appears, on this view, to spawn a vast number of additional Hohfeldian relations ('trimmings'?) in the form of countless others' rights against you and your correlatively entailed duties to them.

Recognizing the grave implausibility of this implication, Kramer seeks to avert it by limiting the range of relevant beneficiaries. To do this, he resourcefully invokes an eligibility test devised by Bentham.[88] Bentham suggests that a person is properly included in the set of a duty's beneficiaries only if the breach of that duty would be a *sufficient* condition of that person's interests being damaged. This test obviously does supply the requisite surgical remedy by cutting my brother's vendor (and her successive beneficiaries) out of that set. Your failure to honour your contract with me is not a sufficient condition of my brother's vendor having her interests damaged.

Two responses are in order. The first simply asks why we should accept Bentham's test for being a relevant beneficiary. Kramer is right to suggest that it will do that rescue job. But he offers no independently motivated defence of it and would, I'm sure, be the first to agree that the fact that it rescues the Interest Theory from an implausibility can hardly count as such a defence. Moreover, it's not clear to me that it *can* be independently motivated. If I supply you with the security codes for a bank vault, I supply a necessary but insufficient condition of your robbing that vault. Our ordinary understanding of 'interests', it seems to me, is such that my action would none the less count as detrimental to whatever interests persons have in that vault's not being robbed. And if that's so, your failure to pay my brother *does* count as detrimental to the interests of his vendor, whatever Bentham may say to the contrary.

But second, and even if we accept Bentham's test, there's a serious cart-before-horse problem in the above line of reasoning. For it's customarily the case that contractual duties can be *waived* at the sole choice of whichever of the two contracting parties is not the duty-bearer: in the present example, myself.[89] Now why should we

---

[88] Kramer, 'Rights Without Trimmings', 81ff above.
[89] In jurisdictions (eg Scotland) where they sometimes cannot be waived by that contractor, that waiving power is to be found in someone else who, accordingly, is the Will Theory right-holder involved; cf *An Essay on Rights* (n 3 above), 63–4.

suppose that my decision to waive your payment duty to my brother *ipso facto* signifies that his interest in your compliance with that duty has diminished or even ceased to exist altogether? For this is precisely what the Interest Theory requires us to suppose. That theory, to be non-trivially different from the Will Theory, must rely on a conception of persons' interests that allows us to identify them independently of the choices which persons make. This is an important point, to which I'll return in discussing several other problems below. For the moment all that needs to be said is that, whatever that conception of interests is, it will not sustain the view that whether one is a beneficiary of a duty—and hence an Interest Theory right-holder to whom it's owed—can *vary* simply and solely with others' choices about whether compliance with that duty is required. Yet just such variability seems to be entailed by the Interest Theory's ascription of rights to third-party beneficiaries since, at least in legal contexts, my waiver of your contractual duty to me leaves you owing no enforceable duty to my brother or anyone else. The Interest Theory is ill-equipped to explain this undisputed fact.

Another problem with the Interest Theory is its sponsorship of *paternalism*. But I hasten to add that this complaint is not what it appears, on its face, to be: solely a moral one. Why not? Noting a standard difference between criminal and civil law claims—that is, that the former are unwaivable ('inalienable') by ordinary citizens whereas the latter are not—Kramer endorses MacCormick's remarks that:

> extremely important interests such as one's interest in remaining alive are typically protected by inalienable claims, whereas a variety of less important interests such as retaining one's possession of certain books are typically protected by alienable claims... According to the Will Theory, then, only the latter set of claims will count as rights. Yet we thus are forced to conclude that—according to the Will Theory—the firmest protections of our truly vital interests do not amount to rights, whereas the less formidable protections of relatively inconsequential interests do amount to rights.[90]

To see why this argument is truly misleading, let's consider just *whom* such unwaivable claims formidably protect their holders *against*.

---

[90] Kramer, 'Rights Without Trimmings', 73 above. Recall that I previously argued, contrary to some Will Theorists, that criminal-law duties *do* entail rights—in superior state officials.

Clearly, if the claim against your murdering me were a Will Theory right held by me, that would afford some protection to my extremely important interest in not being murdered by you. Is that protection actually *strengthened* by stripping me of the waiving and demanding powers over your duty not to murder me, and thus converting that right into an Interest Theory one? It's hard to see how. For the only warranted inference about what's thereby happening is that control over whatever protection is afforded by that claim is merely being shifted from me to whoever now possesses those powers. There's simply no implication whatsoever that this protection is thereby strengthened.

What is admittedly true is that, under this new dispensation, my interest in not being murdered by you is now also protected *against me*. As a Will Theory right-holder, I was at least nominally exposed to some danger from myself because I was empowered to waive your duty not to murder me. Now I'm not. So Interest Theory rights afford stronger protection to persons' interests only in the sense that they protect those persons against themselves. Now I don't want to suggest that persons' interests can never be in need of some form of protection against themselves.[91] But the view that those very persons can be the holders of enforceable rights to it, with the consequence that even some of their own conduct may thereby be punishable, places considerable strain on our ordinary understanding of rights as well as on the Hohfeldian conception of jural relations as ones obtaining between *pairs* of persons. The pair of persons involved in my having an Interest Theory duty not to attempt suicide look to be rather metaphysically elusive characters.[92]

But even if we could make sense of the idea that my interests can need protecting against me *as a matter of my rights*—protection which only Interest Theory rights can deliver—this still wouldn't imply that such rights afford stronger protection of those interests than do Will Theory rights. Being disempowered, I may be better protected against myself but, at the same time, worse protected against others. For whether that protection is strengthened or

---

[91] Though it's also true that persons who are *persistently* in need of such protection tend to be regarded less as ones who *should be* disempowered and more as ones who simply *are* unempowerable. Just how large the set of such persons is will vary directly with, *inter alia*, how 'thick' our conception of vital interests is.

[92] Attempted suicide was a criminal offence in England until 1961.

weakened, by stripping me of the powers to control the correlative duties involved, is entirely dependent on the inclinations of those who thereby come into possession of those powers. If they're more solicitous for my interests than I am, those interests are better protected. If not, not. Hence there's simply no warrant for the MacCormick-Kramer suggestion that interests protected by claims which their holders can't alienate *ipso facto* enjoy more formidable protection than is afforded by claims which they can alienate.

Which brings us to a third, and not unrelated, problem besetting the Interest Theory. This concerns a difficulty that theory encounters in adhering to what Kramer describes as Hohfeld's *Correlativity Axiom*: roughly, that the content of any one jural position is strictly identical to the content of another jural position, each of which is occupied by a different specifically assignable party. Other Interest Theorists have found this axiom too demanding and have attacked Hohfeld for insisting upon it. In a probing series of counter-arguments, Kramer defends the axiom against those attacks.[93] Yet in so doing, he recognizes that the Interest Theory may thereby be rendered incapable of identifying the assignable holders of rights correlative to many familiar sorts of enforceable duty.

Most notable among these duties are the so-called public duties such as the duty to pay taxes or the duty to engage in military service when required.[94]

Recall that the Will Theory solution that was offered for this problem, in my previous discussion of criminal-law duties, is one which adheres to the Correlativity Axiom and which suggests that the rights correlative to such duties are to be found in the state officials who control them.[95] Kramer, however, dismisses this solution as a 'misunderstanding [of] the nature of such duties' and proposes an alternative one that requires us to accept the notion of *irreducibly collective rights*.

Acknowledging that this notion clearly cuts against the grain of Hohfeld's own reductionist thinking—which insistently analysed

---

[93] Kramer, 'Rights Without Trimmings', 24–49 above.

[94] Kramer, 'Rights Without Trimmings', 58 above. Kramer might well wish to include the aforementioned duty not to attempt suicide in this category.

[95] This solution is one which some Will Theorists, such as Flathman and Kearns, reject. As I indicated earlier, they prefer instead to deny the existence of *any* rights correlative to such duties. Thus they join Kramer's Interest Theory opponents inasmuch as they implicitly deny—or, at least, restrict the scope of—the Correlativity Axiom.

any collectivity's (eg corporation's) jural position as a set of individuals' positions—Kramer argues at some length in defence of non-reducibility and for its compatibility with the broader Hohfeldian analytical framework. Moreover he suggests that the importance of this move should not be underestimated. For:

Unless we recognize the reality of collective entitlements, we shall have to conclude that numerous duties are uncorrelated with any [Interest Theory] rights... [However] once we have grasped that a collectivity's legal positions are quite as real as an individual's legal positions, we can submit that any public duty is owed to a collectivity (the state, the nation, the community) which holds the correlative right.[96]

Having recognized the reality of such entitlements, there's obviously no problem in then identifying just such a collectivity as the otherwise elusive beneficiary of—and hence, assignable holder of Interest Theory rights correlatively entailed by—taxpayers' and military conscripts' duties.

My response to this move is *not* to challenge the notion of irreducibly collective entitlements, challengeable though it indeed is.[97] Rather, what we need to ask is whether such a move can be non-question-beggingly distinguished from the aforementioned Will Theory proposal, which Kramer regards as a misunderstanding and which locates the rights correlative to those public duties in individual state officials. (He himself, after all, includes the state as one possible collective right-holder.)

Readers may well recognize the bearing of this question as having more than a passing resemblance to that of one which was posed earlier, in connection with the Interest Theory contention that the *unempowerable* can be said to be right-holders. Near the end of section 3 above, I asked:

What scintilla of a practical or analytical difference can it make if we construe the rights correlative to those protection duties [ie duties to protect the interests of unempowerable creatures] as ones held *by those powerpossessors* rather than ones held by unempowerable creatures [ie as Will Theory rights]?

In the present context, we need only substitute 'individual state officials' for 'those power possessors', and 'collectivities' for 'unempowerable creatures', to get the same answer: namely, *none*.

[96] Kramer, 'Rights Without Trimmings', 58, 59 above.
[97] cf Porn, *The Logic of Power* (n 20 above), 78–9.

It obviously won't do to protest that rights correlative to tax-paying and conscription duties can't be located in state officials *because* the interests which are served by compliance with those duties are not theirs. For such an objection would indeed be question-begging as a defence of the Interest Theory. Moreover, in many past and present political systems, it would also be simply false. And, as Kramer himself has suggested, we certainly don't want a conceptual model of rights that is of politically restricted validity. So we're forced to conclude that the 'irreducible collectivity solution' to the Interest Theory's difficulty with Hohfeld's Correlativity Axiom lacks the generality it needs to have if that theory is to be capable of analysing the jural relations pertaining to any enforceable duty.

Yet another problem besetting the theory lies in the uncontested fact that it sponsors *duty-conflicts*. I've already discussed duty-conflicts at some length and noted that there are very strong—albeit not universally accepted—reasons for regarding them as entailing contradictions. What *is* universally accepted is that contradictions are fairly fatal for any theory. But since Kramer is among those who don't accept that duty-conflicts entail contradictions, and since the issue is one that takes us too far beyond the confines of this book, I'll not pursue it any further here. What may be worth some discussion are the implications of the fact that Interest Theory rights are likely candidates for generating duty-conflicts.

That they are such candidates is widely conceded and does not, perhaps, require a great deal in the way of supporting philosophical argument. We pretty much know, from everyday experience, that the very range of creatures constituting the set of Interest Theory right-holders is so vast that—however their vital interests may be construed—these are bound to conflict. Indeed, this looks to be undeniably true even if we arbitrarily confine our attention to the small subset of those creatures who are empowerable. To say this is not to counsel futility. There are undoubtedly many things we can do, and many things which our *non-correlative* moral duties oblige us to do, to protect those vital interests and to sacrifice at least our less vital interests in so doing. And persons who refuse to do so are richly deserving of moral censure.

But that, of course, is beside the point. The point is—as we already know from equilibrium theory in economics—that even when we *do* devise a set of enforceable duties that strike what is deemed to be a socially optimal balance between all these conflicting interests, that balance is at best a precarious one, needing constant adjustment in the face of changes in the myriad interest-affecting variables that inhabit our world. The serious difficulties this poses for Interest Theory rights are well delineated in Simmonds' essay and many of his other writings, so I'll content myself with merely sketching their broad outline.

What they basically amount to is that, in legal contexts, the theory constitutes a recipe for the chronic application of *external solutions*.[98] Duty-conflicts become opportune occasions for socially optimal adjustment of—trade-offs between—the contents of opposing litigants' ostensible rights in the light of judicial interpretations of legislative intent. Moreover, the intentions which judges select for interpretation are not confined solely to those motivating the enactment of the particular duties in conflict, for interest-affecting circumstances may have changed in the interval since then. Hence the set of candidates counting as relevantly interpretable intentions extends beyond these to include more recent indications of what legislators believe the socially optimal balance between conflicting interests to be. In short, individuals' duties and their correlative rights are thereby instrumentalized in the service of public policy-objectives. Thus Simmonds argues that, unlike the endogenous compossibility of individuals' rights that might be sustainable by the Will Theory,

> the Interest Theory ... rejects the possibility of a formalistic theory of justice that abstracts from questions of substantive interest and value; it accepts the inevitability and pervasiveness of conflicts between interests; and ... emphasizes the capacity of positive law to choose and to demarcate the boundaries between conflicting interests. ... If, however, all legal questions are to be subordinated to the purposes served by the law, what scope remains for the integrity of private rights? ... [T]here is a considerable difference between guaranteeing the integrity of such rights, and simply allotting a place to the relevant liberties or interests in a set of collective goals informing all legal interpretations.[99]

Of course, Kramer's previously discussed suggestion, that *collectivities* can have entitlements which are irreducible to individual rights,

---

[98] As I indicated previously, it's not entirely clear what an external solution would *be* in moral contexts. So it's not surprising that those moral theories in which such socially optimal balances are assigned high or exclusive priority characteristically construe the existence of the *state* as non-contingently imperative.

[99] Simmonds, 'Rights at the Cutting Edge', 196 above.

might provide the Interest Theory with a nominal escape from some aspects of the conceptual problem here. For it could allow the theory to avoid the conclusion that what we have here is Hart's 'Nightmare' with judges simply exercising their own 'sovereign prerogatives of choice'. Instead, these constant judicial adjustments of individuals' rights and duties can be alternatively construed as so many exercises of the sovereign collectivity's unchanging right to protection of its vital interests. And to the extent that judicial interpretation can indeed be read as treating those interests as decisive, the duty-conflict resolutions thereby generated can be regarded as *internal solutions*.

But this means of escaping the Nightmare is not entirely cost-free. For it commits its users to one or another of two claims, each of which gravely impairs its efficacy as a defence of the Interest Theory. How so? The two claims involved express opposing views about the identity of the collectivity whose interests are thereby subserved. On the one hand, it might simply be the collectivity formed by those legislative and judicial officials themselves. But if it were *that* collectivity then, as we just saw in discussing the problem of the Correlativity Axiom, there would be no grounds for denying that the rights involved here are Will Theory rather than Interest Theory ones. For since the holders of those rights would thereby be identical with those empowered to control the correlative duties, the fact that the content of those duties is interest-protection would be entirely irrelevant. On the other hand, if the presumed collectivity is *not* those officials—if, say, it's 'the public'—then the theory is back in the clutches of Simmonds' objection. For it must construe not only those officials but also all private individuals as successively delegated agents of that collectivity, and ones whose several right–duty relations with one another are merely the current and modifiable reflexes of the public's overriding right to have its interests protected in ever-changing circumstances. And this, as Simmonds argues, is considerably at variance with the common view that a person's rights furnish him or her with determinate and peremptory claims against the demands of others. So Kramer's unquestionably correct reminder—'That a right is justified instrumentally does not make it any less a right in its functioning'[100]—though not irrelevant in this regard, cannot be said fully to finesse the indicated predica-

---

[100] Kramer, 'Rights Without Trimmings', 89 above.

ment, since the holders of the instrumental rights involved here are non-identical with the ostensible holder of the right they subserve.

The last problem besetting the Interest Theory concerns what Kramer refers to as its *evaluative stance*, otherwise describable as its unavoidable embrace of a conception of 'the good'. His trenchant engagement with this issue evidences a clear-sighted appreciation of its profound significance and, accordingly, he deploys what amounts to a three-pronged defensive strategy: (i) to acknowledge that this evaluative stance is undesirable in any account of the meaning of a concept; (ii) to reassure us that its presence in the Interest Theory is unobtrusively 'thin'; and (iii) to argue vigorously that the Will Theory suffers from the same defect. What I'll try to show is that only (i) survives scrutiny.

Let's begin with the acknowledgement. In this regard, Kramer frankly states:

Notwithstanding that this essay aspires to present a version of the Interest Theory without political trimmings, it cannot completely eschew evaluative assumptions. ... [I]f we could locate each right by simply finding out who holds the power to enforce or waive the duty that is correlative with the right, we could avoid the fuzziness introduced by any reliance on evaluative presuppositions. ... A purely descriptive account of the formal aspects of rights would be highly desirable indeed, and so the Will Theory's ability to yield such an account would tell strongly in favour of that theory and against the Interest Theory.[101]

The reasons for thinking that the Will Theory *does* yield such a desirable account are, by now, familiar enough and indicated in this quotation itself. For its criteria for identifying and locating rights have entirely to do with the occupation of Hohfeldian second-order positions which, as Kramer notes, are objects of purely descriptive judgement:

[T]he distinctive functions of the second-order positions are defined in purely descriptive terms. Those distinctive functions consist in abilities, inabilities, susceptibilities, and insusceptibilities, all of which are detectable without any reliance on further evaluative notions. ... [A]n ascription of a second-order entitlement to X does not necessarily mean that X's interests are generally served by his being endowed with such an entitlement. ... [M]any second-order entitlements can be disadvantageous to their holders

---

[101] Kramer, 'Rights Without Trimmings', 91, 98 above. It should be added that, as far as I'm aware, this acknowledgement applies equally to all other versions of the Interest Theory.

not only in some specific applications but also in general. . . . [I]n inquiring whether someone holds a power of waiver and enforcement, we do not have to rely perforce on any evaluative assumptions.[102]

Things are obviously quite different if we go searching for rights by instead looking for the beneficiaries of enforceable duties. For, to do that, we have to be equipped with some prior notion of what counts as a *benefit*. And

[a]fter all, decisions about what counts as a benefit and what counts as a detriment must stem from assumptions concerning what is generally good for human beings... [and] a reliance on such presuppositions is a shortcoming—because it lessens the analytical rigour of one's overall account of rights.[103]

Severely damaging as these facts might appear to be for the Interest Theory, Kramer believes that they are not. For, fortunately, its undivorceable evaluative stance is

'thin' in the sense that its assumptions are largely uncontroversial and indeed commonplace... [D]ependence on evaluative presuppositions is not a cause for great distress. All or most of the requisite presuppositions can be pitched at a high level of abstraction and can therefore remain gratifyingly uncontroversial.[104]

Just how *thin* can this stance be? For as in most weight-loss programmes, how thin you can get depends a lot on how much you want to be able to do when you've got there. In the present context, it very much depends on how much analytical or explanatory power the Interest Theory is to possess.

The basic problem here is one of cultural relativity. This becomes particularly evident when we reflect on certain kinds of public or criminal law duties. Many such duties are thought to confer indisputable benefits on each ordinary citizen, so the theory has no problem in seeing those persons as the ones vested with its rights. Duties to forbear from acts of murder, assault, and robbery are placed in this class, and the evaluations which put them there are taken to be uncontroversially thin. On the other hand, the beneficiaries of duties to forbear from sexual activity with another consenting adult of the same gender or a different race, to wear a veil in

---

[102] Kramer, 'Rights Without Trimmings', 92, 93, 98 above.
[103] Kramer, 'Rights Without Trimmings', 92, 101 above.
[104] Kramer, 'Rights Without Trimmings', 91, 101 above.

public places or to refrain from attempting suicide, are less easily located. And even if, as Kramer might propose, such duties are best understood as benefiting a collectivity ('the public') rather than assignable individuals, this makes it no easier to see how the evaluations underlying their construal as beneficial can be described as 'thin'.

Of course, reasons can be and have been given for the existence of such duties: presumably few enforceable duties have ever been enacted frivolously. No doubt those sets of reasons can include some evaluative claims which are sufficiently abstract to be uncontroversial and which, in conjunction with other premises, form logically coherent grounds for concluding that what those duties deliver is indeed a benefit. But this fact is not what usually counts as evidence of the thinness of all the evaluations needed to generate that conclusion. In many societies, past and present, the justifications demonstrating the beneficial qualities of some enforceable duties incorporate highly controversial metaphysical and theological premises. And if their entailed evaluations do *not* thereby count as *thick*, then it's difficult to know what would.

Accordingly the Interest Theory is confronted with a serious dilemma, each horn of which implies a severe restriction of its analytical and explanatory scope. Either it must deny that such enforceable duties correlate to rights, because they confer no plausible benefits: in which case, it forgoes analysis of the jural relations in which those duties are embedded. Or it must embrace the thicker evaluations that underly those duties. But the problem with that move, and the reason why philosophers are generally reluctant to make it, is that such duties may well conflict with those generated by thinner evaluations. For there are no *a priori* grounds—and not many empirical ones either—to suppose that all thin benefits form a neat subset of all thick ones. If persons' rewards are believed to come in the next life or in some succession of lives after the present one, or if their culture embodies exotic conceptions of personal well-being and responsibility, then what counts as beneficial or detrimental for them will not necessarily include the duty precipitates of what we regard as thin evaluations. An Interest Theory that embraces thick evaluations may therefore be unable to analyse many jural relations in societies (like our own) which are largely uninformed by such beliefs. The theory, we might say, is hard to sustain through thick and thin.

Is the Will Theory bound to be caught in a similar trap? Kramer emphatically contends that it is:

> Any theory of rights, be it a version of the Interest Theory or a version of the Will Theory, must adopt at least a thin evaluative stance... [T]he Will Theory cannot eschew evaluative assumptions while retaining a minimal degree of plausibility as a theory of rights. ... [I]f the Will Theorists want to present their doctrine as a minimally credible account of rights, they will not be able to keep themselves aloof from a thin evaluative stance. ... Neither account of rights can transcend the need for a set of basic presuppositions that distinguish what is generally desirable from what is generally undesirable for normal human beings.[105]

There are essentially two arguments advanced in support of this contention and neither of them, I think, proves convincing.

One of these consists in the extended deployment of an imaginary example in which (it's parenthetically worth noting) the main actors are persons who bear little resemblance to 'normal human beings'. These are state officials who, while imposing a duty on persons to inform the regime of their parents' seditious utterances, also empower those parents to *waive* that duty. Kramer's correct inference here is that, if the Will Theory is to retain its detachment from any evaluative stance, it will have to conclude that those parents are thereby the holders of a *right to be informed on* (since they control the duty involved). And such a right certainly strikes us as being highly counter-intuitive.[106]

All this is undeniably true. No doubt persons with utterly eccentric motivations will continue to create highly counter-intuitive rights and duties long after they've had the enlightening experience of reading this book. The point about Kramer's example, however, is that its chief accomplishment is to score an *own goal*. For it's quite unclear how the *Interest Theory* can offer any analysis at all of the jural relations involved in this case. *Whom* can it identify as the beneficiaries of this arrangement?

Apparently perceiving this problem, Kramer at one point floats the suggestion that the regime might believe 'that its citizens should not be informed upon and punished unless they recognize that they ought to be.'[107] But this solution only undermines, rather than

---

[105] Kramer, 'Rights Without Trimmings', 91, 98, 99, 101 above.
[106] Cf. Kramer, 'Rights Without Trimmings', 91ff above.
[107] Kramer, 'Rights Without Trimmings', 98 above.

advances, his contention against the Will Theory's plausibility. For then, the regime's arrangement *is* one conferring a benefit on those citizens. And that being so, the Will Theory is not beset by the aforesaid counter-intuitiveness in identifying them as the rightholders here.

Kramer's other argument, for holding the Will Theory to be equally tarred with an evaluative stance, is one which takes us back to an issue discussed in section 2 of this essay. Any non-evaluative Will Theory, which finds rights only where there are enforceable duties, is said to be burdened with the 'bizarre implication' that it is debarred

> from acknowledging the existence of any *nominal* claims, which would correlate with *nominal* duties. ... Thus, for instance, if Y's duty to reimburse Z for some goods or services is unenforceable. ... then Z has no claim at all against Y, not even a *nominal* claim. Ergo, Y's *nominal* duty to reimburse Z for the goods or services is not owed to Z! Nor, indeed, is the *nominal* duty owed to anyone else; after all, nobody has a power to enforce it, and thus nobody has a claim that correlates with it.[108]

The short reply here is simply that neither the Will Theory nor, for that matter, the Interest Theory is a theory about *nominal* claims and duties at all. Adherents of either theory are, as such, logically at liberty to acknowledge or deny the existence of any such *non-jural* relations.

For as was noted in section 2, it's common ground between the two theories, and Hohfeld as well (except in his more declamatory moments), that the duties involved in jural relations are *all* enforceable ones.[109] The theories do divide on the question of whether the claims correlative to those enforceable duties must be located in the possessors of the enforcement powers. But they do not differ over the matter of whether those powers must exist for those duties to exist. And this leaves it equally open to both of them to recognize the possibility of persons owing non-enforceable moral duties (of the sort instanced in Kramer's example) to others. Neither the Will Theory nor the Interest Theory precludes the existence of moral duties that run beyond the writ of rights. And it would be a sad day for them if they did. So I'm bound to infer that there's simply no case for construing the Will Theory as

---

[108] Kramer, 'Rights Without Trimmings', 100–1 above (emphasis added).
[109] cf nn 18–20 above.

wedded to any evaluative stance—any conception of 'the good'—thin or otherwise.

What, then, should we conclude about the comparative merits of the Will and Interest Theories? Perhaps the least contentious claim here would be that theories of rights don't come cheap. Buying either one of them involves paying some price in the currency of counter-intuitiveness. Nor, I should add, has this centuries-long debate about the nature of rights ever revealed any distinct third theory that even approaches their levels of generality, let alone promises to undercut their prices. So if a purchase has to be made, it looks as though the only way of doing it at all rationally is to note the cost of each of those counter-intuitions and plump for the less expensive package.

Unfortunately, as was suggested near the outset of this essay, those counter-intuitions don't come with their prices stamped on their foreheads. And that being so, it seems to me that the only way of estimating their respective costs is to classify them and then see whether there are good reasons for treating certain *types* of counter-intuition as more affordable than others. Perhaps the most efficient way of embarking on this exercise is briefly to review the perceived problems besetting each of the two theories.

In the case of the Will Theory, these amounted to three. There was, first, a problem of restricted analytical scope arising from its alleged inability to find claims correlative to criminal and public law duties.[110] Second, in construing rights as discretionary domains, it was said implausibly to license the prioritization of morally indifferent or impermissible actions over morally desirable ones. And finally, in denying rights to the unempowerable, it was said to leave their interests seriously unprotectable, which, again, is morally implausible.

The Interest Theory was seen to suffer from five shortcomings. One is the restricted analytical scope problem implicit in its treatment of contractual third-party beneficiaries. Another is that posed by paternalism, which I also interpreted as an analytical scope problem in so far as there are no reasons to believe that unwaivable claims are generally more beneficial for those who are disabled from waiving them than they would be in the absence of those disabilities.

---

[110] And waivable immunities correlative to constitutional disabilities.

The third problem, surrounding the Correlativity Axiom, is again one of analytical scope. Here we saw that, on one reading of it, the Interest Theory is simply incapable of finding rights correlative to certain public-law duties. Alternatively, and with the aid of Kramer's irreducibly collective positions, it can find them, but only either (i) by assimilating the rights involved to Will Theory ones, or (ii) by restricting their presence to certain kinds of political system. Fourth, there is the rule-of-law problem implicit in the Interest Theory's unavoidable reliance on discretionary judicial interpretation. This is, perhaps, ultimately best viewed as a moral problem though, as I tried to show, it also cuts against the grain of a widely-shared understanding of what having a right is supposed to mean. And finally, the theory's undivorceable evaluative stance was seen to entail yet another aspect of restricted analytical scope.

Now it's evidently true that the fact that we have here a 5–3 score in favour of the Will Theory cannot, in itself, be conclusive of the issue of which theory carries a heavier load of counter-intuitions. Nor do my section 3 arguments against the three objections to the Will Theory suffice to settle the matter. This is because, although I believe the first and third of these objections to have been fully met, there may be something more to be said for the second, in the light of the subsequent evaluative stance discussion. For if we accept the not implausible view that rights are indeed morally peremptory, then the Will Theory's discretionary domains must more readily license morally sub-optimal conduct than the Interest Theory's rights. Why is this so?

Interest Theory rights, being irremovably anchored in an evaluative stance, are thereby such that duties correlative to them must generally be presumed to deliver some amount of moral good. *How much* good they deliver will of course depend on what their content is, how thick their generating evaluations are, and whether occurrent circumstances present morally better alternatives to compliance with them. None the less, *some* moral good is thereby guaranteed delivery. The same simply cannot be said of duties correlative to Will Theory rights, since they embody no evaluative stance and therefore indiscriminately reflect or protect choices which may be good, bad, or entirely indifferent.

Hence a more considered view of the score is that the Will Theory carries one moral counter-intuition against it, whereas the Interest Theory, in addition to carrying a moral counter-intuition, is also encumbered with four counter-intuitions all pertaining to its explanatory adequacy. Even this number-counting, however, is simply too crude to be decisive since we still don't know the weights of these various counter-intuitions. I suggest that, to get nearer to them, we need to consider the comparative demerits of moral implausibility and explanatory inadequacy in a theory. And not unpredictably, I contend that the latter is the more serious type of shortcoming.

My underlying thought here is simply that we have to know *what* something is before we can know *that* it's good (or bad). In the present context, we have to know what rights are in order to know whether a right is beneficial to its holder. (Parenthetically, this seems to have been Hohfeld's thought too.) There's no doubt that we tend to think of our rights as beneficial to us. That belief is, indeed, the very well-spring of whatever intuitive strength the Interest Theory enjoys. But the Will Theory can fully account for this belief. For since all rights are waivable,[111] we virtually never have occasion to confront rights which their holders regard as non-beneficial. Trivially, the only rights we hang on to—the only correlative duties that we demand compliance with rather than extinguish—are those that we're actually interested in, precisely because they promise to be beneficial to the objects of our concerns. But since we also benefit from many of other persons' actions which are uncontroversially *not* ones owed to us—your subscribing to a journal helps to keep it financially viable and available to me—the mere fact of an action's being thus beneficial affords not even a necessary condition of what its being owed as a matter of right actually *means*.

We can and do distinguish the meaning of words from their evaluative import. This is, admittedly, not always easy and evidence of its difficulty isn't all that hard to devise. An unqualified claim that 'cruelty is good', for instance, is so jarring to our normal ways of thinking that we're tempted to believe that those who would utter it sincerely are not wicked but rather merely deficient in their understanding of English. Often, of course, we should yield to this temptation: English is not a universal language and its vocabulary is unlikely to have been fully mastered even by those for whom it's their native tongue. But in cases where there's no independent

---

[111] As was argued in section 3, where unwaivable rights were shown to be incoherent by virtue of their entailing an infinite regress.

evidence of such linguistic incompetence, yielding to that temptation may be an extravagantly generous move. Where there's no reason to think that those speakers have simply failed to grasp the meaning of 'cruelty', 'good', and, for that matter, 'is', horror seems the far more likely reaction than perplexity. And if that's true, then it suggests that our criteria for identifying acts as ones of cruelty are independent of—do not include—our criteria for identifying the goodness or badness of actions.[112] Correspondingly, our criteria for identifying rights are independent of our criteria for determining whether they're beneficial. So the fact that the Interest Theory is logically committed to denying this is, as Kramer himself suggested, a fact which tells strongly against it.

The Will Theory, in affirming that independence, is better placed to tell us *how things actually are* in a set of jural relations. And that, I would think, ought to tell strongly in its favour even with persons whose demands for theoretical adequacy include ones for high levels of moral plausibility. For they, at least as much as anyone else, need to know how rights *work*, in order to know how they can be used to produce morally better results. After all, there's little chance of putting things right if our vocabulary disables us from recognizing when they're wrong.

---

[112] Against this, Simmonds, 'The Analytical Foundations of Justice' (n 5 above), 312–3, presses Bernard Williams' view 'that this type of argument could be used to advocate "value-free" definitions of "thick" ethical concepts such as cruelty, treachery, and loyalty. Such a proposal, if widely accepted, would have a dramatic effect upon the character of our moral life, massively reducing the shared fabric of understandings which sustains morality as a *social* phenomenon rather than a purely individualistic matter of personal commitment'; cf Williams, *Ethics and the Limits of Philosophy*, (London: Fontana Press, 1985), 129–55. Evidently, and like the earlier issue of whether duty-conflicts entail contradictions, this one can hardly be resolved here. Nevertheless several responses seem warranted. One is the familiar complaint that disallowing value-free definitions of such concepts would implausibly immunize societies against moral criticism of any of the thick-concept-based practices they endorse. Secondly, the claim that what sustains morality as a social phenomenon is a shared fabric of understandings, rather than a shared commitment to the same values, is precisely what's at issue here and is therefore not appropriately invoked as a reason against value-free definitions. Finally, the suggestion that widespread rejection of that claim would dramatically affect the character of our moral life—which I read as a suggestion that it would undermine it—seems to presuppose precisely what it needs to deny: namely, that it's individuals' beliefs about what others' evaluations are that sustain their own evaluative views. For if my holding the moral belief that cruelty is bad is sustained by my empirical belief that others believe cruelty to be bad, my acceptance of the fact that (on the value-free proposal) there's no logical necessity for them to believe that, is simply irrelevant to whether I continue to hold my moral belief.

Index

abortion 2
abstraction 120–2, 194–5
Alchourron, Carlos 264 n48
Alexy, Robert 177
Anderson, Alan 8 n1, 19 n7, 92 n34
animal rights 2, 31, 78, 259–62
Aquinas, Saint Thomas 272
Arnold, Thurman 117
Ashworth, Andrew 249 n23, 251 n28
Aune, Bruce 270 n78
authorization, legal 63

Bellamy, Richard 169 n73
Benditt, Theodore 12 n3, 13 n4, 16–17 n6, 25 n11, 45 n18, 66 n25, 70, n27
Bentham, Jeremy 139 n37, 167, 272
  and identification of right-holders 81–2, 285
Bergmann, Frithjof 168 n72
Bronaugh, Richard 104 n38
Bryan, William Jennings 233
Buckley, R. A. 34 n14
Bulygin, Eugenio 264 n48

Campbell, A. H. 50 n21, 102 n36
Categorical Imperative 280–3
charitableness, duty of 25 n11
children's rights 31, 37–8, 69–70, 78, 226 n138, 259–62
collective entitlements 49–60, 78–9, 288–90, 292–3, 299
collective project pursuit 124–6, 144–5
competence, legal 63–4
compossibility of rights 181–6, 265–74
conceptual analyses, political underpinnings of 212–14
concrete rights 42–4
conflicts between duties 9, 17–19, 263–9, 271–4, 290–2
contradictions between legal positions 8 n1, 12–13, 181–6
contrary rights 19–20
Coolidge, Calvin 233, 234
Correlativity Axiom 24–49, 222–3

and collective entitlements 58–60, 288–90
Cresswell, M. J. 268 n55
criminal law
  duties imposed by 58, 59, 142, 294–5
  rights conferred by 70–2, 78, 230–2, 248–55

Davies, Howard 25 n11, 45 n18
dead people, rights of 31–2, 259
Detmold, Michael 37 n16
Dias, R. W. M. 13 n4, 25 n11, 50 n21, 66 n25, 79 n30, 92 n34, 102 n36, 106 n41
disabilities 21
duties 9
  conflicts between 17–19, 263–9, 271–4, 290–2
duty-focused justifications 35–41, 59–60
Duxbury, Neil 177 n81
Dworkin, Ronald 16 n6, 36–37, 45 n18, 86 n32, 125 n16, 256 n36
dynamic aspect of rights 41–4, 114

Eleftheriadis, Pavlos 9 n2, 17 n6
empirical arguments against Hohfeld 22–35
enforceability 9, 33–4, 62–3, 238–47
entitlements 9–22
  homologies between 21–2
  logical structure of 22 n8
  specifiedness of 45–8
  unwaivability of 250–5, 286–8
equality 122–3, 194–5
equivocality of meaning 235–6
euthanasia 2
evaluative assumptions 3, 4, 60
  in the Interest Theory 91–101, 217, 293–5, 299–301
  in the Will Theory 98–101, 296–8
explicability, distinguished from reducibility 51–7

Feinberg, Joel 17 n6, 19 n7, 20, 25 n11, 45 n19, 66 n25
feudalism 122–3, 133

304 Index

Finnis, John 12 n3, 16 n6, 61 n23, 66 n25, 207 n117
Fish, Stanley 168 n72
Fitch, Frederic 13 n4, 19 n7
Fitzgerald, P. J. 249
Flathman, Richard 12 n3, 13 n4, 25 n11, 70 n27, 91 n33, 105–6, 107, 250–1, 288 n95
  on third-party-beneficiary contracts 66 n25
Freeden, Michael 12 n3
Fuller, Lon 18 n7, 72

general rights 42–4, 47–8
Gensler, Harry 272 n63
Glock, Hans-Johan 118 n4
Goebel, Julius 249 n23
Gowans, Christopher 272 n63
Gray, John Chipman 255 n34
Gregor, Mary 280 n78

Habermas, Jürgen 137 n34, 142
Halpin, Andrew 8 n1, 13 n4
Hare, R. M. 12 n3, 283 n85
Harris, J. W. 13 n4, 23 n9, 25 n11, 102–3
Harrison, Jonathan 12 n3
Hart, H. L. A. 12 n3, 85 n31, 109 n42, 155 n58, 156, 177 nn82 & 83, 250 n26, 270 n59
  on adjudication 264
  on children's rights 69–70
  on Correlativity Axiom 25 n11, 26–7
  on criminal-law rights 72 n28
  on enforcement and waiver 62–3
  on Hohfeld 50 n21
  on identification of right-holders 81–2
  on immunities 106 n41, 154
  on liberties 165–7, 183
  on peremptoriness 203
  on third-party-beneficiary contracts 66 n25
  on Will Theory 115, 137 n35, 215–25, 227–30, 239–47, 248, 253
Hegel, G. W. F. 130, 136, 275
helots, legal status of 165–7
Heuston, R. F. V. 34 n14
Hilpinen, Risto 272 n63, 274 n68
Hobbesian state of nature 12, 15, 109
Hohfeld, Wesley 2–3, 7–22, 44, 146–76, 210, 233–5, 288
  and bilaterality of legal relations 147–9, 151–2
  and collective entitlements 49–57, 288–9
  commentators' misunderstandings of 101–11
  and conflicting duties 271–2, 274
  and Interest/Will debate 61, 64–6
  and Kantianism 178–95, 265–6, 267
  and Legal Realism 177–8
  MacCormick's differences with 226–7
  and private law 142–4
  and *Quinn v. Leathem* 169–75, 178–80
  and stipulative approach to jurisprudence 22–35
  and Will Theory 217–23, 270–1
Holdcroft, David 25 n11, 45 n18
Holland, T. E. 255 n34
homologies between entitlements 21–2
Horwitz, Morton 141 n40, 194 n100
Hudson, Stephen 12 n3
Hughes, G. E. 268 n55
Husak, Douglas 12 n3

Ihering, Rudolf von 140–1, 196, 201, 275
immunities 21, 106–7, 153–4
  and the Will Theory 219, 228
inalienability of entitlements 227–32
instrumental rights 88–91
intentions in interpretation 85–8
interests, distinguished from entitlements 44
Interest Theory of rights 1–2, 46 n20
  classical version of 138–41, 214
  comparison with Will Theory 298–301
  criticisms of 195–211, 283–95
  defense of 78–101
  exposition of 61–6
  moral/political nature of controversy with Will Theory 117–22
  Raz's and MacCormick's version of 149–52, 202–11
  and third-party-beneficiary contracts 79–83, 284–6
interpretation 84–91
inviolability 205–11
  distinguished from permissibility 168–76, 178–87, 192

Jacobson, Arthur 8 n1, 25 n11
Jaconelli, Joseph 50 n21, 93 n35
jural logic, contrasted with modal logic 19
justice, Kant's conception of 275–83

Index

Kamba, Walter, 105
Kanger, Helle 13 n4
Kanger, Stig 13 n4
Kant, Immanuel 119–20, 186, 270 n60, 272
  on law, 135–7, 168–9, 171, 179
  on rights 176, 275–83
Kantian jurisprudence 123–7, 132–4, 168–9, 171, 178–87, 190–5, 214, 215, 274–83
  and systematic coherence of law 201
  and Will Theory, 113–14, 135–8, 265–7
Kearns, Thomas 250–1, 288 n95
Kennedy, Duncan 17 n6
Kenny, C. S. 249
Körner, Stephan 272 n63
Kriegel, Blandine 132 n26

labour-relations statute, 23–4, 158–65
Larmore, Charles 120 n9
legal positivism 139–40, 144–5
Legal Realism 177–8
Levi, Isaac 272 n63
liabilities 20–1, 107–8
liberties 10–19
  accompanied by rights 11–12, 156–7, 167–8, 183–6
  and powers 242–4
Lightwood, John 126 n17, 179
Lindley, Lord 169–75, 178–80, 182, 187–90
Llewellyn, Karl 9 n2, 103 n37
Locke, John 278
Lukàcs, Georg 123, 190
Lyons, David 66 n25, 85 n31, 91 n33, 93 n35, 106–7, 110–11, 153, 231 n144

MacCormick, Neil 5, 66 n25, 75 n29, 91 n33, 175 n79, 199 n106, 209, 253 n31, 255 n35
  on advantageousness of rights 93
  anti-Hohfeldian stance of 61, 149–51, 158–65
  and children's rights 70 n27
  on Correlativity Axiom 25–9, 37–8
  on duty-focused and right-focused theories 37–8
  on labour-relations statute 23–4, 158–65
  and the specification of entitlements 45–8
  and unwaivable rights 72–3
  on the Will Theory 225–32, 286–8

MacIntyre, Alasdair 119, 120 n9
Marmor, Andrei 19 n7, 25 n11, 37 n16, 42 n17, 70 n27
Marshall, Geoffrey, 50 n21, 70 n27, 72 n28, 108–10
Martin, Rex 14 n5, 45 n18, 108
Marx, Karl 115–16, 122, 124, 127–8, 129–33, 191, 193
  on Kant 275, 276
Mason, H. E. 272 n63
Michelman, Frank 17 n6
Miller, David 25 n11, 66 n25
minimum-wage laws 70, 78, 94–5
modal logic, contrasted with jural logic 19
morality, contrasted with legality 8–9
Mullock, Philip 8 n1, 19 n7
Murphy, Jeffrie 282

Nietzsche, Friedrich 130
nominal duties 33–4, 100–1, 297
nominal entitlements 8–9
non-entailment
  between liberties and rights 14–15
  between rights and liberties 14–17
  between duties and liberties 17–19
no-rights 10
Nozick, Robert 272 n63, 278

Oakeshott, Michael 119 n5
Offe, Claus 124 n14
O'Neill, Onora 281 n81

Paton, G. W. 249
Paul 57 n22
Penner, J. E. 28 n13, 45 n18
peremptoriness of rights 203–5, 214–16, 257–60, 280–3
permissibility, distinguished from inviolability 168–76, 178–87, 192
Perry, Thomas 12 n3, 13 n4, 50 n21
Pörn, Ingmar 245 n20, 272 n63, 289 n97
Posner, Richard 45 n18
Pound, Roscoe 141 n40, 150 n52
powers 20–1, 102–6, 154–5, 219–20
  of enforcement/waiver 240–2, 244–7
  and liberties 242–4
Prior, A. N. 268 n55
private law 141–4
private project pursuit 124–6
private rights, integrity of 196–205
public duties 58–60, 78–9, 83–4, 288–90
public/private divide 113–14

Index

Quine, W. V. O. 118 n4
Quinn v. Leathem 169–75, 178–80, 187–90

Radin, Max 10 n2, 50 n21, 109 n42
Rawls, John 91 n33, 217 n126
Raz, Joseph 5, 19 n7, 85 n31, 91 n33, 93 n35, 175 n79, 188 n93, 256 n36, 272 n63
  anti-Hohfeldian stance of 10 n2, 61, 149–51
  on collective entitlements 50 n21
  on conceptual analysis 213
  on Correlativity Axiom 25 n11
  and dynamic aspect of rights 41–4, 163 n66
  on the Interest Theory 202–5
  on legal powers 104–5
  on specification of entitlements 45–8
Reimann, Mathias 169
Rescher, Nicholas 272 n63
right-focused justifications 35–41, 59–60
right-holders, identification of 67, 80–101, 197–200, 285–6
rights 9–20, 236–9
  as accompaniments of liberties 11–12, 156–7, 167–8, 183–6
  compossibility of 181–6, 265–74
  contrarieties between 19–20
  as domains of choice 238–9, 240 n13, 262–83
  enforceability of 238–47
  generality of 42–4
  held against the world 10 n2, 151–2
  integrity of 223–5
  inviolability of 205–11
  peremptoriness of 176, 203–5, 214–15, 216, 257–9, 260, 280–3
  and unwaivability 70–5, 78
Ross, Alf 12 n3, 66 n25, 70 n27, 75 n29, 91 n33, 106 n40, 107–8, 250 n27
Ross, W. D. 46 n20

Savigny, Friedrich 131–4, 142, 147, 169, 196, 275
Schauer, Frederick 197 n103
Schopenhauer, Arthur 136, 275, 279
second-order legal relations 20
  distinctiveness of 92–3
  self-ownership 278–80
Singer, Joseph 16–17, 192 n98
Sinnott-Armstrong, Walter 272 n63
Stein, Peter 132 n27
Stocker, Michael 272 n63
Stone, Roy 8 n1
Sumner, L. W. 22 n8, 75 n29, 91 n33, 212 n120, 245 n20
  on collective entitlements 50 n21
  on conflicting duties 18
  on duty-focused and right-focused theories 37 n16
  on legal powers 103, 154–6

Tapper, C. F. H. 103–4
third-party-beneficiary contracts 34, 66–8, 79–83, 284–6
Turner, J. W. C. 249 n23

Unger, Roberto 128 n21
Universal Principle of Justice 277–83
unwaivable rights 70–5, 78, 250–5, 286–8
utilitarianism 77

Waldron, Jeremy 5, 17 n6, 91 n33, 93 n35, 123 n12, 251 n28, 256 n36
  on collective entitlements 50 n21
  and conflation of rights and interests 45 n18
  on Correlativity Axiom 25 n11, 26
  on duty-focused and right-focused theories 36 n15, 38
  on dynamic aspect of rights 42 n17, 43
  on political basis of Will Theory 75 n29
Warren, E. H. 56–7
wealth-maximization 77
Weinrib, Ernest 267 n53
Weinsheimer, Joel 211 n119
Wellman, Carl 152 n53, 157, 218 n129, 219
Wellman, Christopher 10 n2, 17 n6
Wertheimer, Alan 251 n28
White, Alan 17 n6, 72 n28, 91 n33
  on Correlativity Axiom 25, 29–34
  on third-party-beneficiary contracts 66 n25
Whitman, James 132 n26
Wick, Warner 280
Wieacker, Franz 138 n36
Williams, Bernard 274, 301 n112
Williams, Glanville 13 n4, 14, 16, 18 n7, 255 n34
Will Theory 2, 61–6
  and children's rights 69–70, 226 n138, 259–62

classical version of 127, 134–8, 214, 265–7, 274–83
comparison with Interest Theory 298–301
criticism of 66–78
and evaluative assumptions 98–101
Hartian version of 215–25, 227–30, 239–83
and Hohfeld 217–23
and inalienable entitlements 227–32
MacCormick's critique of 225–32
moral objections to 255–62
political basis of 75–8, 137–8, 213–15, 223–5
and private law 141–4
and public/private distinction 248–55
and systematic coherence of law 201

Wittgenstein, Ludwig 211
Wolfe, Tom 251 n28
Wright, Georg Henrik von 242 n15, 272 n63

Zander, Michael 251 n28